NEWMAN AND HISTORY

By the Same Author

Newman and his Contemporaries
Newman and his Family
Culture and Abortion
Adventures in the Book Pages: Essays and Reviews

NEWMAN
AND
HISTORY

Edward Short

GRACEWING

First published in England in 2017
by
Gracewing
2 Southern Avenue
Leominster
Herefordshire HR6 0QF
United Kingdom
www.gracewing.co.uk

All rights reserved.
No part of this publication may be reproduced, stored in a retrieval system, or transmitted in any form or by any means, electronic, mechanical, photocopying, recording or otherwise, without the written permission of the publisher.

The right of Edward Martin Octavius Short to be identified as the author of this work has been asserted in accordance with the Copyright, Designs and Patents Act 1988.

© 2017 Edward Martin Octavius Short

ISBN 978 085244 919 6

The publishers have no responsibility for the persistence or accuracy of URLs for websites referred to in this publication, and do not guarantee that any content on such websites is, or will remain, accurate or appropriate.

Typeset by Word and Page, Chester, UK
Cover design by Bernardita Peña Hurtado

CONTENTS

Foreword by Prof. J. J. Scarisbrick	vii
Preface	ix
Acknowledgements	xi
Abbreviations	xiii
1. Newman, Gibbon and God's Particular Providence	1
2. Newman, Superstition and the Whig Historians	81
3. Travesties of Newman	117
4. Newman and the Liberals	133
5. Signs of Contradiction, Signs of Hope	203
6. Port Middlebay: Tractarians Abroad	221
7. Newman, C. S. Lewis and the Reality of Conversion	229
8. Newman Distilled	257
9. Newman and the Law	265
10. Newman in his Letters	285
11. Hagiography, History and John Henry Newman	297
Epilogue	327
Index	331

Whatever else is right, the theory that Newman went over to Rome to find peace and an end of argument, is quite unquestionably wrong.

G. K. Chesterton, *The Victorian Age in Literature* (1903)

Were Christianity a mere work of man, it, too, might turn out something different from what it has hitherto been considered; its history might require re-writing, as the history of Rome, or of the earth's strata, or of languages, or of chemical action. A Catholic neither deprecates nor fears such enquiry, though he abhors the spirit in which it is too often conducted. He is willing that infidelity should do its work against the Church, knowing that she will be found just where she was, when the assault is over. It is nothing to him, though her enemies put themselves to the trouble of denying everything that has hitherto been taught, and begin with constructing her history all over again, for he is quite sure that they will end at length with a compulsory admission of what at first they so wantonly discarded.

John Henry Newman,
Lectures on Certain Difficulties Felt by Anglicans in Submitting to the Catholic Church (1850)

The world is a rough antagonist of spiritual truth: sometimes with mailed hand, sometimes with pertinacious logic, sometimes with a storm of irresistible facts, it presses on against you. What it says is true perhaps as far as it goes, but it is not the whole truth, or the most important truth. These more important truths, which the natural heart admits in their substance, though it cannot maintain, — the being of a God, the certainty of future retribution, the claims of the moral law, the reality of sin, the hope of supernatural help, — of these the Church is in matter of fact the undaunted and the only defender.

John Henry Newman, *The Idea of a University* (1873)

How shall we persuade ourselves of the great truth that, in spite of outward appearances, human society, as we find it, is but part of an invisible world, and is really divided into two companies, the sons of God, and the children of the wicked one, that some souls are ministered unto by angels, and others led captive by devils.

John Henry Newman,
"The Individuality of the Soul" (1836),
in *Parochial and Plain Sermons*

What will it avail us then, to have devised some subtle argument, or to have led some brilliant attack, or to have mapped out the field of history, or to have numbered and sorted the weapons of controversy, and to have the homage of friends and the respect of the world for our success — what will it avail to have had a position, to have followed out a work, to have re-animated an idea, to have made a cause triumph, if after all, we have not the light to guide us from this world to the next?

John Henry Newman,
"Illuminating Grace" (1849),
in *Discourses to Mixed Congregations*

FOREWORD

Why does Blessed John Henry Cardinal Newman so fascinate us that there is now more written about him than perhaps even Shakespeare or any British monarch? Because he was so saintly and engaging a human being; because his "defection" to Rome from the Tractarian party that he had done so much to create inflicted a blow from which the Anglican Church has never really recovered—and still rankles deeply in some quarters; because his arrival in the English Catholic community of his day had very varied and salutary repercussions; because he was immensely learned and a gifted wordsmith; because he possessed prodigious physical, mental and spiritual energy; because his extant letters and diaries fill thirty-two volumes; because he founded two Oratories and a university and wrote at least three books—the *Grammar of Assent*, the *Apologia pro Vita Sua* and *An Essay on the Development of Christian Doctrine*—that alone would have assured him a distinguished place amongst the best English authors; because he was much else besides—tireless preacher, prolific and elegant essayist, poet and no mean violinist. There seemed to be no limit to his gifts.

We are powerfully reminded of all that in this book, the third that its author has written about John Henry and his achievements. It is a wonderfully varied and erudite collection of essays which is not so much to be read straight through from cover to cover as "cherry-picked" to suit mood and occasion. Thus, the first chapter, on how and why Newman laid into Edward Gibbon's bitterly anti-Catholic, tendentious masterpiece, and how the great and the good reacted to the assault, could be exactly right for a lengthy rail or air journey. And given its rich complexity, it could serve the return trip, too.

Another essay, entitled "Newman and the Liberals," complements this first chapter nicely—for Newman saw clearly that the sneering anti-Catholicism of Edward Gibbon was a hallmark of the greatest evil facing Christian society. Born of the Enlightenment, it had produced the unspeakable horrors of the French Revolution and now threatened to de-Christianise Christendom. Call it what you like - rationalism, secularism, Whiggery—it was the work of the Evil One, an implacable enemy of religion. It edited sin, Hell and the Devil out of the Gospel. Newman fought it from his earliest Evangelical days. He watched it emasculate Anglicanism and the rest of non-Catholic Christianity. Eventually he came to see that only the Catholic Church could resist it (even if some Continental Catholics and, for a while, even a pope—Pio Nono—flirted with it dangerously). It was Liberalism. And in this chapter we not only follow Newman's utterly consistent combat against it but the unblushing attempts of some current-day liberal pundits to argue that Newman was really fighting not against Liberalism but Evangelicalism and, in effect, deceiving himself.

After such demanding, indeed, profound chapters, the reader can relax with an intriguing chapter comparing and contrasting the conversions of Newman and C. S. Lewis, as well as a discerning review of a "portrait" of Newman derived from his letters.

If both these studies would make good bedtime reads, two others certainly would not. The first is a review of a recent collection of essays on Newman, all but one of which is hostile, not to say malicious, regurgitating as it does many of the accusations made against the convert in his own lifetime. For example, that he had never ceased to be an Evangelical and that his Catholic conversion was self-deceptive. They get short shrift here. And then there is an essay entitled "Newman and the Law," which ends with a vivid account of a disgraceful miscarriage of justice, thanks to the gross anti-Catholic bigotry of the presiding judge. (Newman was found guilty of libel for what he had written about an ex-Dominican scoundrel called Giovanni Giacinto Achilli.) Although this story has a happy ending—the Catholic community rallying round to pay Newman's £100 fine—it would surely inflict angry insomnia on any Catholic reader today if read before bedtime.

There is much else in this learned book: memorable things that Newman said about how careful we should be when we talk of "superstition"; how profoundly important martyrs and hagiography have been to the Church's life and always will be, and how what Newman called "God's particular Providence" plays out in history.

Finally, perhaps we can usefully remind ourselves that, when we speak of Newman and history, by "history" we can mean three rather different things: empirical history, in this case the history of the Church (in which Newman was deeply versed); or we can mean sacred history, the story of God's providential dealings with mankind, from the Creation to the present; and closely allied to this, we can think of Christian history as Newman so memorably taught us to do, that is, the story of a living community, guided by the Holy Spirit, coming to ever deeper and richer understanding of itself and its teaching, changing in order to be more completely itself, uncovering, discovering, making explicit what had not hitherto been articulated—often amidst and thanks to fierce controversy. All of this, of course, was the antithesis of Protestantism, which taught that the truth was given, fixed, sealed (and therefore dead); that it had no history; that theology was akin to archaeology; that authentic theology consisted in cutting away medieval and later accretions to discover the authentic original. Hence Newman's oft-quoted but still devastating verdict: "to be deep in history is to cease to be a Protestant."

All of these themes, too, are illumined in this book. *Tolle et lege.*

J. J. Scarisbrick

PREFACE

In *Newman and History*, I endeavor to show how the historian in Newman was essential not only to the convert in him but to the good shepherd as well. History, as I am sure my readers agree, is a noble art, and when it is taken up by someone of Newman's genius, it is a wonder to behold. Newman was a good historian because he had, to an extraordinary degree, an uncanny understanding of his own place in history, whence that history had come, and whither it was tending. And he presents his interpretation of events not so much in formal, full-dress "histories" as in his occasional writings, his sermons, his extended essays, his autobiographical writings, and his letters, which give his readings of history an immediacy and *éclat* not always present in more conventional histories. In this sense, Newman is a good example of how the best history can sometimes be written by those who do not call themselves historians, and one of the reasons why I wrote *Newman and History* was simply to share with my readers his brilliant historical insights, many of which can help us to make sense of our own increasingly tragic history. For example, in Newman's various animadversions on his own nineteenth-century history, we can see England emerging from under the shadow of the French Revolution only to acquiesce, decade after decade, in what he called the "great *apostasia*," though in his lifelong campaign against liberalism we can also see that the history he did so much to prophesy and elucidate is still unfolding.

The passage in which Newman's memorably apt phrase first appeared — the speech he gave when he was given his red hat by Leo XIII in 1879 — is worth quoting at length, showing as it does how well he understood the gathering calamity of unbelief, which was not altogether self-evident to many of his contemporaries.

> Hitherto the civil Power has been Christian. Even in countries separated from the Church, as in my own, the *dictum* was in force, when I was young, that: "Christianity was the law of the land." Now, everywhere that goodly framework of society, which is the creation of Christianity, is throwing off Christianity. The *dictum* to which I have referred, with a hundred others which followed upon it, is gone, or is going everywhere; and, by the end of the century, unless the Almighty interferes, it will be *forgotten*. Hitherto, it has been considered that religion alone, with its supernatural sanctions, was strong enough to secure submission of the masses of our population to law and order; now the Philosophers and Politicians are bent on satisfying this problem without the aid of Christianity. Instead of

the Church's authority and teaching, they would substitute first of all a universal and a thoroughly secular education, calculated to bring home to every individual that to be orderly, industrious, and sober, is his personal interest. Then, for great working principles to take the place of religion, for the use of the masses thus carefully educated, it provides—the broad fundamental ethical truths, of justice, benevolence, veracity, and the like; proved experience; and those natural laws which exist and act spontaneously in society, and in social matters, whether physical or psychological; for instance, in government, trade, finance, sanitary experiments, and the intercourse of nations. As to Religion, it is a private luxury, which a man may have if he will; but which of course he must pay for, and which he must not obtrude upon others, or indulge in to their annoyance. The general character of this great *apostasia* is one and the same everywhere.[1]

If we look at the good historians of Newman's time, we can see much to admire. Lingard, Cobbett, Carlyle, Macaulay, Froude, Stubbs, and Acton were all marvelous historians in their way. Yet none of them understood what the rise of apostasy portended for the "goodly framework of society" with anything like Newman's perspicuity. A good deal of what I have to say in this book about Newman the historian must be seen in light of his understanding of the full meaning of this "great *apostasia*."

Edward Short
24 June 2017
Feast of the Nativity of St. John the Baptist
Astoria, New York

---

[1] *Addresses to Cardinal Newman with his Replies*, ed. William Neville (London: Longman, Green & Co., 1905), 65–7.

ACKNOWLEDGEMENTS

In making my acknowledgements to those from whom I received vital help in the writing of this book, I have many debts of gratitude to pay. Once again, I am deeply grateful to Mr. Tom Longford of Gracewing for his good counsel and generous support. We in America have many fine things but we do not have gentlemen publishers who treat unworldly, obscure authors to lunch at the Carlton Club. I am also profoundly grateful to Sister Mary Joseph, O.S.B., Librarian of the Venerable English College in Rome, who prepared (with saintly patience) what must often have seemed an unfinishable manuscript for the typesetter. I am equally grateful for the scholarly advice and friendship of Father Dermot Fenlon, Father Ian Ker, Father Carleton Jones, O.P., and Dr. Paul Shrimpton, all of whom have helped me, in varying degrees, to understand the fascinating figure at the heart of my book. Without their help and encouragement, in one way or another, many of the pieces in *Newman and History* might not have seen the light of day. Despite their encouragement, I must hasten to say, all errors in what follows, all solecisms and all stupidities, are mine and mine alone.

Then, too, I am warmly grateful to Prof. J. J. Scarisbrick. There is so much to admire about the learned author of the definitive life of King Henry VIII—his faith, his wit, his bonhomie, his dedication to English cricket, his dedication to the unborn and to the LIFE charity he founded to protect the unborn. Now to all of these admirable qualities I must add (with more than a little compunction) his willingness to help a necessitous friend puff a rather ramshackle book.

From my publisher Gracewing in faraway Herefordshire, I should like to express my deep thanks to Mrs. Monica Mainwaring and Miss Bernardita Peña Hurtado. Monica gamely finds ways to interest reviewers in my books—never an easy task—and Bernardita has graciously assisted me with the design of my cover. I am also grateful to Mrs. Rebecca Federman, Research Coordinator at the New York Public Library for her generous and persevering assistance.

My acknowledgements would be incomplete if I were not to extend abundant thanks to Dr. Clive Tolley for the exacting care he took in helping me to prepare my text for the printer.

I should also like to thank these other generous souls for giving me more indirect help and encouragement: Mr. Robert Trexler, Dr. Humfrey Butters, Prof. John Batchelor, Prof. Richard Greene, Prof. Dwight Lindley, Dr. Andrew Nash, Mr. Timothy Matthews, Mr. John Smeaton, Mr. Paul

Beston, Dr. Carl Olson, Robert Crotty, Esq., Neil Merkl, Esq., Lord Conrad Black, Mrs. Caroline Nogier, Prof. James McGlone, Mrs. Virginia McGlone, Mrs. Kathleen Toth, Dr. Robert Christie, Miss Margaret Fernandez, Mrs. Helen Varsam, Mrs. Stephanie Saris, Prof. David Deavel, Father Aquinas Guilbeau, O.P., Father Charles Shonk, O.P., Prof. Jo Anne Sylva, Mr. Philip Georgini, Mrs. Lucy Zepeda, Mrs. Kaitlin Walker, Prof. John Orens, Mrs. Constance C. Short and Mr. Daniel Joyce.

I must also thank two museums for helping me with my front and back cover illustrations. The front cover shows the *carte de visite* of Cardinal Newman by Herbert Rose Barraud (*circa* 1888) and is reproduced by kind permission of the National Portrait Gallery, London; and the back cover shows Giovanni Bellini's painting of the Mother and Child (late 1480s) and is reproduced by kind permission of the Metropolitan Museum of Art, New York City.

Lastly, I am thankful to my darling wife Karina. To be married to so sweet, so gentle, so sensible a lady is a blessing beyond words. Without her faithful forbearance, I should never have been able to begin or finish *Newman and History*. I am also grateful to my bright and beautiful daughter Sophia. Children, as Newman understood so deeply, are heralds of eternity; and now that so many of those whom I wished to please when I began this book are gone into the world of light I prize those heralds more than ever.

ABBREVIATIONS OF WORKS BY JOHN HENRY NEWMAN

Apologia	*Apologia pro Vita Sua*, ed. Martin J. Svaglic (Oxford, 1967)
Difficulties Felt by Anglicans	*Lectures on Certain Difficulties Felt by Anglicans in Submitting to the Catholic Church* (London: Burns & Lambert, 1850)
Discourses to Mixed Congregations	*Discourses Addressed to Mixed Congregations* (London: Longman, Brown, Green & Longman, 1849)
Discussions on Various Subjects	*Discussions and Arguments on Various Subjects* (London: Basil Montague Pickering, 1872)
Essay on Development	*An Essay on the Development of Christian Doctrine* (London: James Toovey, 1846; references in the current book are to the revised edition: London: Basil Montagu Pickering, 1878)
Essays Critical and Historical	*Essays Critical and Historical*, 2 vols (London: Longman, Green & Co., 1907)
Grammar of Assent	*An Essay in Aid of a Grammar of Assent*, ed. I. T. Ker (Oxford: Clarendon Press, 1985)
Idea of a University	*The Idea of a University*, ed. I. T. Ker (Oxford: Oxford University Press, 1976)
LD	*The Letters and Diaries of John Henry Newman*, ed. Charles Stephen Dessain *et al.*, 32 volumes (London: Thomas Nelson and Oxford: Oxford University Press, 1961–2008). Angle brackets in the text of the letters indicate where Newman made interlinear corrections and additions to the text of his letters.
PPS	*Parochial and Plain Sermons* (London: Longman, Green & Co., 1891)
Present Position of Catholics	*Lectures on the Present Position of Catholics in England* (London: Burns & Lambert, 1851)
Sermons on Subjects of the Day	*Sermons Bearing on the Subjects of the Day* (London: J. G. F. and J. Rivington, 1869)
Sermons on Various Occasions	*Sermons Preached on Various Occasions* (London: Burns and Lambert, 1857)

University Sermons	*Fifteen Sermons Preached before the University of Oxford*, ed. James David Earnest and Gerard Tracey (Oxford: Oxford University Press, 2006)
Via Media	*The Via Media of the Anglican Church: Illustrated in Lectures, Letters and Tracts Written between 1830 and 1841*, 2 vols (London: Pickering & Co., 1877)

For my newborn son,
Edward John Joseph Sebastian Short

1

Newman, Gibbon and God's Particular Providence

The theologian may indulge the pleasing task of describing Religion as she descended from Heaven, arrayed in her native purity. A more melancholy duty is imposed on the historian. He must discover the inevitable mixture of error and corruption, which she contracted in a long residence upon earth, among a weak and degenerate race of beings.

Edward Gibbon, *The Decline and Fall of the Roman Empire* (1776)

During its time of exile here the heavenly city makes use of earthly peace; it also maintains and seeks to promote agreement between the wills of men in all matters relating to man's mortal nature, so far as that can be done without violation of piety and religion. But it relates this earthly peace to heavenly peace, for that is peace in the fullest sense, that is, the only thing which the rational creation ... should think of or speak of as peace, consisting as it does in the perfectly ordered and perfectly harmonious society of those who enjoy God and one another in God. When we arrive there life will no longer be mortal life but life complete and real, and the body will no longer be an animal body whose corruptibility weighs down the soul but a spiritual body free of all want ... The heavenly city possesses this peace even while it lives in exile and by faith. It lives a life of righteousness based on this faith when it refers every good action it performs, whether towards God or neighbor (for the life of the city is certainly a social one) to the acquisition of this heavenly peace.

St. Augustine, *The City of God* (AD 426)

I ADORE Thee, my God, as having laid down the ends and the means of all things which Thou hast created. Thou hast created everything for some end of its own, and Thou dost direct it to that end. The end, which Thou didst in the beginning appoint for man, is Thy worship and service, and his own happiness in paying it; a blessed eternity of soul and body with Thee for ever. Thou hast provided for this, and that in the case of every man. As Thy hand and eye are upon the brute creation, so are they upon us. Thou sustainest everything in life and action for its own end. Not a reptile, not an insect, but Thou seest and makest to live, while its time lasts. Not a sinner, not an idolater, not a blasphemer, not an atheist lives, but by Thee, and in order that he may repent. Thou art careful and tender to each of the beings that Thou hast created, as if it were the only one in the whole world. For Thou canst see every one of them at once, and Thou lovest every one in this mortal life, and pursuest every one by itself, with all the fulness of Thy attributes, as if Thou wast waiting on it and ministering to it for its own sake.

John Henry Newman,
"The Providence of God,"
in *Meditations and Devotions* (1907)

Newman, Gibbon and God's Particular Providence

I

WHENEVER WE THINK OF JOHN HENRY NEWMAN and his contemporaries—on so many of whom he had so indelible an influence—we must always be struck by how many were drawn to him by some particular Providence. As he pointed out in the *Apologia*, "it was not I who sought friends, but friends who sought me. Never man had kinder or more indulgent friends than I have had ... I expressed my own feeling as to the mode in which I gained them ... in the course of a copy of verses. Speaking of my blessings, I said, 'Blessings of friends, which to my door, *unasked, unhoped,* have come." They have come, they have gone; they came to my great joy, they went to my great grief. He who gave, took away.'"[1] At the Solemn Requiem for Newman at the Oratory in South Kensington on 20 August 1890, Cardinal Manning nicely summed up the cynosure of this particular Providence: "beyond the power of all books has been the example of his humble and unworldly life; always the same, in union with God, and in manifold charity to all who sought him. He was the centre of innumerable souls, drawn to him as Teacher, Guide, and Comforter through long years, and especially in the more than forty years of his Catholic life. To them he was a spring of light and strength from a supernatural source."[2]

One of these "innumerable souls" was Charles Stanton Devas (1848–1906), who would teach political economy in Manning's short-lived Catholic University College in Kensington and at the Royal University in Dublin. At Eton, Devas's Housemaster Oscar Browning advised him to read Gibbon's *Decline and Fall of the Roman Empire* and reading it proved a most unexpected Providence; indeed, it would have baffled Gibbon himself. Hitherto, Devas had been an unremarkable scholar. It is true that he might have been "a

---

[1] *Apologia*, 27.
[2] Manning, quoted in Edward Sheridan Purcell, *The Life of Cardinal Manning* (London: Macmillan & Co., 1896), II, 752.

singularly charming boy, sweet and lovable, of very high character"; but he was "lethargic and without interest." His only "desire seemed to be to lead a happy, thoughtless life, to go to a comfortable college at Oxford, and to enjoy his not inconsiderable means. He had no ambition and no care for the studies of the school." After dipping into Gibbon, however, all of this changed. "The effect of this study upon him was very remarkable," Browning recalled.

> His ambition began to develop. He determined to go to Balliol, instead of the college which he had previously selected, and worked hard to prepare for the entrance examination. He had little or no capacity for languages, at least for the ancient languages, but he overcame his dislike to them, and taught his mother the Greek characters that she might assist him in his lessons. He went up for Balliol and was successful. He had now finished his course of history, and how was he to spend his time before he went to the University? I suggested Political Economy, and the study of Adam Smith in preference to Mill. When he had mastered *The Wealth of Nations*, I asked my friend Henry Sidgwick to examine him, and he reported that he was a thorough master of Economic Science, so far as it could be learnt from Adam Smith. Sidgwick could not understand why I had advised him to read Adam Smith and not Mill, which was very characteristic of Sidgwick. At this time he was captain of my house, performing his duties admirably. He was to leave Eton at the end of July, and a few days before he left he came and said that he had a most important communication to make to me, that he was a Roman Catholic, and wished to be admitted to that Church. I asked him how he had been converted, and he replied that he had been converted by no man and by no book, but that the serious study of history had convinced him that Roman Catholicism was the only true religion. I should imagine that this was the first time that any one was made a Roman Catholic by the study of Gibbon. He said that I was the first person to whom he had communicated his intention, but that he wished to obtain his parents' permission on the next day, and to be admitted on the day following, which was Sunday. I said that I had so deep a respect for his mind and character that I could not but feel that he had done what was right. My only fear was lest he might be disappointed … He said that he was sure that that would not be the case. The event proved that he was right, and he lived and died a distinguished and honoured member of the Roman Catholic Church. At Balliol he had a successful career. I have been told that Jowett, after hearing his first essay at Balliol, said to him, "Are you a Quaker?" which did not show any great amount of insight.[3]

3 Oscar Browning, *Memories of Sixty Years at Eton, Cambridge, and Elsewhere* (London: John Lane, 1910), 124–6.

In 1867, Devas went up to Balliol College and took a First in Law and Modern History. Three of his six sons joined religious orders, one of his daughters became a nun, and the eldest of his grandchildren was none other than Charles Stephen Dessain, who would join the Birmingham Oratory and found the magnificent edition of Newman's *Letters and Diaries* (1961–). As an economist, Devas pointedly rejected socialism, seeing it as antagonistic to the interests of the family. Moreover, according to Peter Doyle in the *Oxford Dictionary of National Biography*, Devas was no "dreamy-eyed medievalist"; in fact, he "welcomed modern industrialized society." For him, "the challenge was to structure it so as to benefit all its citizens." In all events, "Socialism was not the answer: its view of humanity was fundamentally unhistorical, its programmes would be unworkable, and, above all, there was total incompatibility between it and the family. The family was the basic unit of society, with rights and duties anterior to those of the state, to be protected at all costs."[4] Of course, the pope who canonized Newman, Leo XIII, made no bones of his own view of the sacrament of marriage *vis-à-vis* the civil authority. "Marriage has God for its Author," the great friend of St. Thomas reminded the world in his encyclical *On Christian Marriage* (1880); "and was from the very beginning a kind of foreshadowing of the Incarnation of His Son; and therefore there abides in it a something holy and religious; not extraneous, but innate; not derived from men, but implanted by nature. Innocent III, therefore, and Honorius III, our predecessors, affirmed not falsely nor rashly that a sacrament of marriage existed ever amongst the faithful and unbelievers. We call to witness the monuments of antiquity, as also the manners and customs of those people who, being the most civilized, had the greatest knowledge of law and equity. In the minds of all of them it was a fixed and foregone conclusion that, when marriage was thought of, it was thought of as conjoined with religion and holiness."[5] In the antinomian forces now attempting to separate the Church from the moral law, with regard to marriage and so many other matters, Newman would have seen a melancholy continuation of the liberalism that he spent so much of his life combatting.

It was fitting, in light of his own defense of marriage, that Devas should have been so keen an admirer of Newman. In the preface to *The Key to the World's Progress* (1906), a defense of his Catholic faith, he spoke of his "guide and teacher the Great Master of the nineteenth century John Henry Newman, who, looking before and after, foresaw the intellectual problems of the future, and whose work, though part was concerned with the transient controversies and peculiar opinions of his own time, was

---

4 Peter Doyle, "Devas, Charles Stanton (1848–1906)," in *Oxford Dictionary of National Biography* (Oxford: Oxford University Press, 2004).
5 Leo XIII, "On Christian Marriage" (Rome: Vatican, 1880), 32–3.

mainly concerned with the lasting needs and chronic infirmities of our nature." He also referred to Newman as one who "even now is not yet understood, and for many years in time past was covered by a cloud of misunderstanding, the inevitable penalty of intellectual pre-eminence."[6] Certainly, one of the things about Newman that many admirers of his do not understand is what a fine sense of history he had. Like Devas, Newman was converted by the study of history, though in his case it was the study of the early Fathers of the Church, not Edward Gibbon, who helped him to see that the Catholic Church was "the one true fold of the Redeemer."[7] Still, he was a close reader of Gibbon; indeed, Newman called him not only the Church's "relentless and scoffing foe"[8] but a great English author, who, if "a proud and rebellious creature of God," was still "gifted with incomparable gifts."[9] Despite his lifelong reading and rereading of Gibbon, it was only in the tenth chapter of *An Essay in Aid of a Grammar of Assent* (1870) that Newman had occasion to take the formidable historian to task for his account of the rise of Christianity. In this essay, I shall revisit that chapter and some other writings of Newman to share with readers what strike me as instructive differences between Newman and Gibbon, which nicely highlight Newman's trenchant sense of history. Specifically, I shall show how Newman countered Gibbon's account of the rise of Christianity by insisting on the role that God's particular Providence plays in that rise and I shall also show how, for Newman, Gibbon's rationalist history adumbrates the liberalism that he spent so much of his long life opposing. Indeed, in many critical ways, Gibbon helped to refine Newman's understanding of the errors of liberalism, which had their roots in the rationalist zeal of the Enlightenment. But before I proceed, I should say a few words about Gibbon's life.

II

Edward Gibbon (1737–94), the son of a country gentleman, was born in Putney, the only child to survive of his six siblings. He was largely neglected by his mother, Judith, who died in 1747, when Gibbon was only ten. After his mother's death, his father devoted what time he could spare from the neglect of his estate to gambling, though his dissipations fell short of entirely depleting Gibbon's patrimony. The future historian was educated at Westminster School and Magdalen College, where he indulged his great

---

6 Charles Stanton Devas, *The Key to the World's Progress* (London: Longman, Green & Co., 1912), v.
7 Newman to Henry Wilberforce (7 October 1845), in *LD*, XI, 3.
8 *The Idea of a University*, 181.
9 Ibid., 255.

love of reading. In his autobiography he is critical of Magdalen, deploring what he characterized as its lazy and bibulous fellows. He was particularly critical of the religious instruction he received at Oxford. "It might at least be expected that an ecclesiastical school should inculcate the orthodox principles of religion," he remarks in his autobiography. "But our venerable mother had contrived to unite the opposite extremes of bigotry and indifference. An heretic or unbeliever was a monster in her eyes; but she was always, or often, or sometimes, remiss in the spiritual education of her own children," —a charge with which Newman would not have disagreed when he was an Oxford don in the 1820s and 1830s. Nevertheless, it was at Oxford that Gibbon converted, fleetingly, to Roman Catholicism. In his autobiography, he speaks with a certain bemused incredulity of falling under the sway of "popish books." As he recalled: "The blind activity of idleness urged me to advance without armour into the dangerous mazes of controversy, and at the age of sixteen I bewildered myself in the errours of the Church of Rome."[10] Curiously enough, the Catholic author who seems to have persuaded Gibbon to secede from the Church of England was Robert Persons (1546–1610), the Jesuit charged with establishing the Jesuit mission in Elizabethan England, about whom the historian of the English Jesuits, Bernard Basset remarks: "Whereas [Edmund] Campion drew large crowds with his charm, learning, and reputation, Persons was a born leader, with courage, an eye for detail, and an astonishing capacity for making personal friends."[11] When Gibbon's family learned of their son's defection, they were astounded. "My father was neither a bigot nor a philosopher," Gibbon wrote, "but his affection deplored the loss of an only son; and his good sense was astonished at my strange departure from the religion of my country."[12] Losing no time, Gibbon's father removed his errant son from Oxford and packed him off to Lausanne, where a Reformed Calvinist pastor, Daniel Pavillard returned him to the Protestant fold after a solid regimen of Protestant indoctrination.[13] By the age of seventeen, Gibbon relates, "The various articles of the Roman creed disappeared like a dream; and after a full conviction, on Christmas Day

---

10 *The Memoirs of Edward Gibbon and a Selection of his Letters with Occasional Notes and Narrative by Lord Sheffield*, ed. Henry Morley (London: George Routledge and Sons, 1891), 74.

11 Bernard Basset, S.J., *The English Jesuits: From Campion to Martindale* (London: Burns & Oates, 1967), 46. Apropos Persons, Basset also writes, "Whether or not he was intolerant, pigheaded, interfering, by sheer determination, in adverse conditions, he created a remarkable system for the education of future priests. Those who dislike the Catholic Church, or the Counter-Reformation must also dislike Robert Persons, but there is now no need to be unfair about him."*Ibid.*, 94.

12 *Memoirs of Edward Gibbon*, 75–6.

13 *Ibid.*

1754, I received the sacrament of the Church of Lausanne. It was here that I suspended my religious inquiries."¹⁴ Like the controversialist William Chillingworth (1602–44), another impulsive young man who would abjure his conversion to popery, Gibbon "returned home, resumed his studies, unraveled his mistakes, and delivered his mind from the yoke of authority and superstition."¹⁵ The historian's one romantic foray occurred when he fell in love with Susanne Curchod, a poor minister's daughter. However, when Gibbon's father forbade the marriage, the young scholar accepted the paternal interdict with comical promptitude: "I sighed as a lover; I obeyed as a son." (Curchod would later go on to marry Jacques Necker [1732–1804], Louis XVI's financial minister and give birth to the future Mme. de Staël [1766–1817], whose brilliant *salons* dazzled Parisian literary and political society before and after the French Revolution.) In Lausanne, Gibbon made friends with Jacques-Georges Deyverdun, a tutor and litterateur, with whom he would have a long relationship, remarking after his friend's death in 1788: "I thought I was prepared but this blow has overwhelmed me. After thirty-three years—Adieu."¹⁶ Thanks to his friend's will, however, Gibbon confessed to a grief bordering on cupidity: "few men of letters, perhaps, in Europe, are so desirably lodged as myself. But I feel, and with the decline of years, I shall more painfully feel, that I am alone in Paradise."¹⁷ In England, from 1759 to 1762, Gibbon served as captain in the South Hampshire militia and in 1779 he was given a post with the Board of Trade, where he paid close attention to Lord North's ingenious, if doomed conduct of the American Revolutionary War.¹⁸ Both experiences were helpful to the historian of *The Decline and Fall of the Roman Empire* (1776–88), which he resolved upon after toying with the idea of undertaking a history of the Liberty of the Swiss. Fortunately, the archival materials for that project were, as the historian confessed later, "fast locked up in the obscurity of a barbarous old German language," in which he was not proficient. It was in Rome in 1864, while standing in front of the ruins of the Capitol, "while the barefooted friars were singing vespers in the temple of Jupiter," that Gibbon conceived the idea of writing his great

---

14 *Ibid.*, 88.

15 *Ibid.*, 78.

16 *The Letters of Edward Gibbon*, ed. J. E. Norton (London: Cassell, 1956), III, 156.

17 Gibbon, quoted in Patricia Craddock, *Edward Gibbon: Luminous Historian, 1772–1794* (Baltimore: The Johns Hopkins University Press, 1989), 282.

18 "Edward Gibbon dedicated the fourth and final volume of *The Decline and Fall of the Roman Empire* (1787) to Lord North, writing of 'the lively vigour of his mind, and the felicity of his incomparable temper.'" Andrew Jackson O'Shaughnessy, *The Men who Lost America: British Leadership, the American Revolution, and the Fate of the Empire* (New Haven: Yale University Press, 2013), 49.

history, which took him over twenty years to complete.[19] (King George III's brother, William Henry, Duke of Gloucester, allegedly met one of the volumes of Gibbon's history with the immortal words: "Another damned, thick, square book! Always scribble, scribble, scribble! Eh, Mr. Gibbon?"[20]) The scale of Gibbon's history is enormous, spanning from the second century AD to the fall of Constantinople in 1453. When its first volume appeared, it met with universal success: "My book was on every table, and almost on every toilette," Gibbon recalled.[21] The history made Gibbon famous and, by all accounts, he enjoyed fame, until he had had enough, and returned to Lausanne. The historian's contemporaries left vivid recollections of the learned exile. James Boswell (1740–93) clearly did not see the point of the man, confiding to his journal that 'Gibbon is an ugly, affected, disgusting fellow, and poisons our literary club to me.' (Gibbon became a member of Johnson's famous literary Club in 1774.) Edmond Malone (1741–1812), the Irish Shakespeare scholar, found him "uncommonly agreeable. He had an immense fund of anecdote and ... erudition ... and such a facility of elegance of talk that I had always great pleasure in listening to him."[22] The historian John Bagnell Bury (1861–1927), who edited the *Decline and Fall*, remarked that the historian "was exceedingly vain, sensitive, and ready to take offence. Austere moralists will perhaps discover an index of deplorable vanity in his scrupulous attention to the adornment of his person ... In a letter to his friend Holroyd (Lord Sheffield) he describes himself as 'writing at Boodle's in a fine velvet coat with ruffles ...' His attire on another occasion was criticized by an observer as 'a little overcharged perhaps ...' He was always anxious to make a good impression; he was worldly and suave, inclined to be all things to all men."[23] Yet Bury also saw in Gibbon "the singular happy union of the historian and the man of letters ... perhaps the clearest example that brilliance of style and accuracy of statement are perfectly compatible in an historian."[24] In retirement in Lausanne, the historian whom Bury ranked with Tacitus and Thucydides lived quietly and simply, playing shilling whist, and putting on an occasional ball. A good deal of Gibbon's last years were spent conferring with his long-term friend and confidante, Lord Sheffield, who compiled his posthumous

---

19 *Memoirs of Edward Gibbon*, 151.
20 See David Morrice Low, *Edward Gibbon* (New York: Random House, 1937), 315.
21 *Memoirs of Edward Gibbon*, 168.
22 Boswell and Malone, quoted in *The Samuel Johnson Encyclopedia*, ed. Pat Rogers (London: Greenwood Press, 1996), 160.
23 *Autobiography of Edward Gibbon*, ed. J. B. Bury (Oxford: Oxford University Press, 1907), vii–viii.
24 J. B. Bury, Introduction to Edward Gibbon, *The History of the Decline and Fall of the Roman Empire*, ed. John Bagnell Bury (London: Macmillan, 1909–14), I, vii.

autobiography, which includes the wonderful passage in which Gibbon recalls the day on which he downed tools on the *Decline and Fall*:

> It was on the day, or rather the night, of the 27th of June, 1787, between the hours of eleven and twelve, that I wrote the last lines of the last page in a summer-house in my garden. After laying down my pen I took several turns in a *berceau*, or covered walk of Acacias, which commands a prospect of the country, the lake, and the mountains. The air was temperate, the sky was serene, the silver orb of the moon was reflected from the waters, and all Nature was silent. I will not dissemble the first emotions of joy on the recovery of my freedom, and perhaps the establishment of my fame. But my pride was soon humbled, and a sober melancholy was spread over my mind by the idea that I had taken my everlasting leave of an old and agreeable companion, and that, whatsoever might be the future fate of my history, the life of the historian must be short and precarious.[25]

Gibbon died in London at the age of 56 in 1794 on 16 January, the feast of St. Fursey, the seventh-century Irish monk, of whose visionary sanctity the Venerable Bede was a great admirer.[26]

After his death, Gibbon's magnificent library (comprising 1,412 volumes) was bought by William Beckford (1759–1844), the eccentric art collector, who gave memorable expression to that loathing of authors common among book collectors: "The time is not far distant, Mr. Gibbon," Beckford wrote in one of the volumes of the *Decline and Fall*, "when your most ludicrous self-complacency ... your affected moral purity ... your heartless scepticism ... your tumid diction, your monotonous jingle of periods will be still more exposed and scouted than they have been. Once fairly knocked off ... your lofty, bedizened stilts, you will be reduced to your just level and true standards."[27]

---

25 *Memoirs of Edward Gibbon*, 188. Cf. "Last Thursday, the 28th at 7 o'clock in the evening, I wrote the last lines of the poor old *Newcomes* with a very sad heart ... That finis at the end of a book is a solemn word. One need not be Mr. Gibbon of Lausanne to write it." William Makepeace Thackeray to Kate Perry (2 July 1855), in *The Letters and Private Papers of William Makepeace Thackeray*, ed. Gordon N. Ray (Cambridge, Mass.: Harvard University Press, 1946), III, 459.

26 See Bede, *History of the English Church and People*, trans. Leo Sherley-Price (London: Folio Society, 2010), 133–6.

27 Lewis Melville, *The Life and Letters of William Beckford of Fonthill* (New York: Duffield & Co., 1910), 272–3. The architect and collector Sir John Soane (1753–1837) was more partial to Gibbon. "Soane's ... preferred reading was solidly that of the Enlightenment and he remained unreceptive to James Peacock's advice to study Macknight's *Truth of the Gospel History* and 'burn Voltaire, Hume, Gibbon and the rest of the infidel rout.'" Gillian Darley, *John Soane: An Accidental Romantic* (New Haven: Yale University

Newman, Gibbon and God's Particular Providence

If Beckford had an unremittingly low opinion of Gibbon, this was never the case with Newman, who might have found fault with the historian but was always ready to concede his considerable talents. In *The Idea of a University* (1873), he speaks of the writer in Gibbon in only the most exalted company. "How real a creation, how *sui generis*, is the style of Shakespeare, or of the Protestant Bible and Prayer Book, or of Swift, or of Pope, or of Gibbon, or of Johnson!," he exclaims.

> Even were the subject-matter without meaning, though in truth the style cannot really be abstracted from the sense, still the style would, on that supposition, remain as perfect and original a work as Euclid's elements or a symphony of Beethoven. And, like music, it has seized upon the public mind; and the literature of England is no longer a mere letter, printed in books, and shut up in libraries, but it is a living voice, which has gone forth in its expressions and its sentiments into the world of men, which daily thrills upon our ears and syllables our thoughts, which speaks to us through our correspondents, and dictates when we put pen to paper. Whether we will or no, the phraseology and diction of Shakespeare, of the Protestant formularies, of Milton, of Pope, of Johnson's Tabletalk, and of Walter Scott, have become a portion of the vernacular tongue, the household words, of which perhaps we little guess the origin, and the very idioms of our familiar conversation.[28]

Something of Newman's own even-handed approach to history can be seen in his summing up of the character of Julian the Apostate (*c.* 331–63), in which he nicely assesses Gibbon's handling of the recusant pagan. Here, the discriminating literary critic in Newman gives a good example of the gifted writer in Gibbon without glossing over the "godless intellectualism" that so much of his famous style extols:

> He, in whom every Catholic sees the shadow of the future Anti-Christ, was all but the pattern-man of philosophical virtue. Weak points in his character he had, it is true, even in a merely poetical standard; but, take him all in all, and I cannot but recognize in him a specious beauty and nobleness of moral deportment, which combines in it the rude greatness of Fabricius or Regulus with the accomplishments of Pliny or Antoninus. His simplicity of manners, his frugality, his austerity of life, his singular disdain of sensual pleasure, his military heroism, his application to business, his literary diligence, his modesty, his clemency, his accomplishments, as I view them, go to make him one of the most eminent specimens of pagan virtue which the world has

Press, 1999), 159. See also Geoffrey Keynes, "A Gibbonian Adventure," in *The Gates of Memory* (Oxford: Oxford University Press, 1981), 246–51.
28 *The Idea of a University*, 258.

ever seen. Yet how shallow, how meagre, nay, how unamiable is that virtue after all, when brought upon its critical trial by his sudden summons into the presence of his Judge! His last hours form a *unique* passage in history, both as illustrating the helplessness of philosophy under the stern realities of our being, and as being reported to us on the evidence of an eye-witness. "Friends and fellow-soldiers," he said, to use the words of a writer, well fitted, both from his literary tastes and from his hatred of Christianity, to be his panegyrist, "the seasonable period of my departure is now arrived, and I discharge, with the cheerfulness of a ready debtor, the demands of nature ... I die without remorse, as I have lived without guilt. I am pleased to reflect on the innocence of my private life; and I can affirm with confidence that the supreme authority, that emanation of the divine Power, has been preserved in my hands pure and immaculate ... I now offer my tribute of gratitude to the Eternal Being, who has not suffered me to perish by the cruelty of a tyrant, by the secret dagger of conspiracy, or by the slow tortures of lingering disease. He has given me, in the midst of an honourable career, a splendid and glorious departure from this world, and I hold it equally absurd, equally base, to solicit, or to decline, the stroke of fate ... He reproved the immoderate grief of the spectators, and conjured them not to disgrace, by unmanly tears, the fate of a prince who in a few moments would be united with Heaven and with the stars. The spectators were silent; and Julian entered into a metaphysical argument with the philosophers Priscus and Maximus on the nature of the soul. The efforts which he made of mind as well as body, most probably hastened his death. His wound began to bleed with great violence; his respiration was embarrassed by the swelling of the veins; he called for a draught of cold water, and as soon as he had drank it expired without pain, about the hour of midnight." Such, Gentlemen, is the final exhibition of the Religion of Reason: in the insensibility of conscience, in the ignorance of the very idea of sin, in the contemplation of his own moral consistency, in the simple absence of fear, in the cloudless self-confidence, in the serene self-possession, in the cold self-satisfaction, we recognize the mere Philosopher.[29]

Seeing this, one wonders whether Evelyn Waugh was reading Newman before he wrote that brilliant passage in *Helena* (1950) where he has the Christian apologist Lactantius (240–320),[30] "the greatest living prose stylist" say to Helena, the mother of the Emperor Constantine:

---

29 *Ibid.*, 167–9. Newman quotes Gibbon's account of the death of Julian in ch. XXIV of *Decline and Fall*, II, 543–4.

30 Lucius Caecillius Firmanus Lactantius was an advisor to the Emperor Constantine and "one of the most popular of the Latin Church Fathers, whose *Divinae institutiones* ('Divine Precepts'), a classically styled philosophical refutation of early-fourth-century

> Suppose in the years to come, when the Church's troubles seem to be over, there should come an apostate of my own trade, a false historian, with the mind of Cicero or Tacitus and the soul of an animal ... A man like that might make it his business to write down the martyrs and excuse the persecutors. He might be refuted again and again but what he wrote would remain in people's minds ... That is what style does—it has the Egyptian secret of the embalmers. It is not to be despised.[31]

Criticism of Gibbon's bad faith can also be seen in Joseph Milner (1744–97), the Evangelical divine, whose five-volume *History of the Church of Christ* (1794–1809) introduced Newman to the Fathers:

> Either Mr. Gibbon believes the Bible to be God's word or he does not ... Under none of these suppositions can his conduct be justified. As to the first case, words are superfluous: the second would ask a more manly and more open way of opposition; even the impious honesty of Lord Bolingbroke, horrible as it is, is less offensive to a lover of plain dealing than the sly, insinuating, artful mode of Mr. Gibbon ... For one thing is clear, amidst all the mazes of his pen ... he cordially hates Christianity.[32]

---

anti-Christian tracts, was the first systematic Latin account of the Christian attitude toward life. Lactantius was referred to as the 'Christian Cicero' by Renaissance humanists." See *Encyclopedia Britannica*.

31 Evelyn Waugh, *Helena* (Harmondsworth: Penguin Books, 1963), 80. One reader who would have agreed with Waugh about the captivating brilliance of Gibbon's style was Winston Churchill, who recalled in his autobiography: "Someone had told me that my father had read Gibbon with delight; that he knew whole pages of it by heart, and that it had greatly affected his style of speech and writing. So without more ado I set out upon the eight volumes of Dean Milman's edition of *Gibbon's Decline and Fall of the Roman Empire*. I was immediately dominated both by the story and the style. All through the long glistening middle hours of the Indian day, from when we quitted stables till the evening shadows proclaimed the hour of polo, I devoured Gibbon." Winston Churchill, *My Early Life: A Roving Commission* (London: Thornton Butterworth, 1930), 110.

32 Joseph Milner, *Gibbon's Account of Christianity Considered* (York: A. Ward, 1781), 2–4, quoted in J. G. A. Pocock, *Barbarism and Religion* (Cambridge: Cambridge University Press, 2010), V, 357–8. Pocock's response to Milner has something of his master's rhetorical agility: "The problem becomes that of history. In the course of his narrative, Gibbon encountered something of which any statement must be a statement about belief, and what is unforgivable is that he makes no such statement. We may wish to say that he did not hate Christianity so much as he was untouched by it; but we have to do with Christians for whom you could not reject God's infinitely demanding love without hating it." Elsewhere, Pocock laments the fact that "Gibbon had to contend with a clerical culture for whom the meaning of history might be found in prophecy." *Ibid.*, 358 and 359. However, the question that Pocock sidesteps is whether Gibbon refused to acknowledge his infidelity because he knew it would damage his reputation. On this score, Roy Porter is wise to quote from one of Lord Chesterfield's letters to his son:

As an evangelical Christian, Milner could be expected to find fault with Gibbon, but even Lord Brougham (1778–1868), the great champion of the "march of mind" and admirer of Voltaire, took exception to Gibbon's handling of his Christian subject. "The greatest charge against Gibbon's historical character remains," Brougham contended in his *Men of Letters of the Time of George III* (1855): "he wrote under the influence of a deeply rooted prejudice, and a prejudice upon the most important of all subjects—the religion of his age and nation." More specifically, what Brougham found objectionable was the historian's elaborate, teasing irony, the fact that

> there runs a vein of sneering and unfair insinuation always against Christians and their faith ... through almost every part of the work in which any opportunity is afforded by the subject ... [,] any opportunity of gratifying a disposition eminently uncharitable, wholly unfair, and tinged with prejudices quite unworthy of a philosopher, and altogether alien to the character of an historian. Nor is the charge lessened, but rather aggravated, by the pretence constantly kept up of his being a believer, when any reader of the most ordinary sagacity at once discovers that he is an unrelenting enemy of the Christian name. Nothing can be more discreditable to the individual, nothing, above all, more unworthy the historian, than this subterfuge, resorted to for the purpose of escaping popular odium. All men of right feelings must allow that they would far more have respected an open adversary, who comes forward to the assault with a manly avowal of his disbelief, than they can a concealed but bitter enemy who assumes the garb of an ally, in order to screen himself and injure more effectually the cause he affects to defend.[33]

Another critic of Gibbon's historical method was Newman's good Tractarian friend, Dean Church (1815–90), who wrote in *The Gifts of Civilization* (1881) apropos the historian's treatment of Byzantium: "He has brought out with incomparable force all that was vicious, all that was weak, in Eastern Christendom ... In telling [the history of Byzantium], his immense and usually exact knowledge gave him every advantage in supporting what I must call the prejudiced conclusions of a singularly cold heart; while his wit, his shrewdness, and his pitiless sarcasm gave an edge to his learning, and a force which learning has not always had in shaping the opinions

---

"Depend upon this truth, that every man is the worse looked upon & less trusted, for being thought to have no religion, in spite of all the pompous & specious epithets he may assume, of esprit in fort, free thinker or moral philosopher; a wise atheist (if such a thing there is) would, for his own interest, & character, pretend to some religion." Lord Chesterfield, quoted in Roy Porter, *England in the Eighteenth Century* (London: Penguin Books, 1990), 159.

33 *The Works of Henry Lord Brougham, Men of Letters of the Time of George III* (London and Glasgow: Richard Griffin & Co., 1855), II, 425–6.

of the unlearned. The spell of Gibbon's genius is not easy to break."[34] The sprightly historian John Julius Norwich would echo Church's exasperation, noting that "The long campaign of denigration" with regard to Byzantium was "given its initial impetus by Edward Gibbon, who, like all classically educated Englishmen and Englishwomen of his day, saw Byzantium as the betrayal of all that was best in ancient Greece and Rome."[35] As for Newman, as much as he would have agreed with Waugh about how Gibbon's style had rendered the falsehoods of the *Decline and Fall* well-nigh inexpellable, he also saw in Gibbon's ecclesiastical history a revelatory tale about the limits of Protestant England's appetite for true history.

> Whatever be historical Christianity, it is not Protestantism. If ever there were a safe truth, it is this. And Protestantism has ever felt it so. I do not mean that every Protestant writer has felt it; for it was the fashion at first, at least as a rhetorical argument against Rome, to appeal to past ages, or to some of them; but Protestantism, as a whole, feels it, and has felt it. This is shown in the determination of dispensing with historical Christianity altogether, and of forming a Christianity from the Bible alone; men never would have put it aside, unless they had despaired of it. It is shown by the long neglect of ecclesiastical history in England, which prevails even in the English Church. Our popular religion scarcely recognizes the fact of the twelve long ages which lie between the Councils of Nicaea and Trent, except as affording one or two passages to illustrate its wild interpretations of certain prophesies of St. Paul and St. John. It is melancholy to say it, but the chief, perhaps the only English writer who has any claim to be considered an ecclesiastical historian, is the unbeliever Gibbon. To be deep in history is to cease to be a Protestant.[36]

III

Gibbon presents the rise of Christianity against what he regards as the golden age of Antonine Rome, when, as he says, "The policy of the emperors and the senate, as far as it concerned religion was happily seconded by the reflections of the enlightened, and by the habits of the superstitious, part of their subjects. The various modes of worship which prevailed in the Roman world were all considered by the people as equally true; by the philosopher as equally false; and by the magistrate as equally useful. And thus toleration produced not only mutual indulgence, but even religious

---

34 Richard William Church, *The Gifts of Civilization* (London: Macmillan & Co., 1891), 191.

35 John Julius Norwich, *Byzantium: The Early Centuries* (London: The Folio Society, 2003), xxi.

36 Newman, *Essay on Development*, 7–8.

concord."[37] The upshot of his history, therefore, has a certain bold simplicity: it results in "the triumph of barbarism and religion"[38] because, as Gibbon saw it, following Voltaire, tolerant, civilized Rome fell and intolerant, barbarous Christianity rose.[39] As Gibbon told his friend Lord Sheffield, after the completion of his prodigious labors, "The primitive church, which I have treated with some freedom, was itself, at that time, an innovation, and I was attached to the old pagan institution."[40] Christian apologists might favor the bold convert Constantine, the man who responded so gratefully to his providential *labarum*,[41] but Gibbon never stopped lamenting the lost cause of Julian the Apostate. The historian Algernon Cecil makes an incisive point about Gibbon's lament for the older civilization: "A world, highly organised and intellectually brilliant as our own, had fallen, not suddenly by some strange chance, but slowly and after a prolonged trial of strength before the attacks of barbarous hordes. That was, as it seemed to Gibbon, the greatest tragedy of which history has to tell. The barbarians alone could not have done it. For so unnatural an event there must have been an unnatural reason. That reason he found in Christianity, with its doctrines of a supernatural life and miraculous intervention."[42]

Since Gibbon worked squarely in the Enlightenment tradition, it might be helpful to say a few words about that tradition and to see how Gibbon

---

37 Gibbon, *Decline and Fall*, I, 31.

38 Ibid., VII, 321.

39 Gibbon pinched his famous phrase from Voltaire, who complained that "Two scourges ruined this great colossus [Rome]: the barbarians and rows over religion" ("Deux fléaux détruisirent enfin ce grand colosse, les barbares et les disputes de religion"), Voltaire, *Essai sur les mœurs et l'ésprit des nations* (II), in *Œuvres complètes de Voltaire*, XXII (Oxford: Voltaire Foundation, 2009), 212. See also Pierre Force, "'The Exasperating Predecessor': Pocock on Gibbon and Voltaire," *Journal of the History of Ideas*, 77, no. 1 (January 2016), 129–45.

40 *Memoirs of Edward Gibbon*, 227.

41 Evelyn Waugh is amusing on the topic of the *labarum*, the standard with which Constantine defeated Maxentius at the Battle of the Milvian Bridge (312): "Msgr. Knox writes in an easy, conversational style but it is the conversation of pre-1914 Oxford when it was bad form to be pompous or overbearing or abstruse, but when a great deal of common ground was taken for granted … and it is on this common fund of knowledge that Msgr. Knox invariably draws when he seeks an apt illustration to his argument. Take, for example, this fine passage from *God and the Atom*, a book explicitly designed for the 'plain man': 'At the moment of victory a sign appeared in heaven; not the comforting Labarum of the Milvian Bridge, but the bright, evil cloud of Hiroshima. In this sign we were to conquer.' How many members of the House of Commons today, how many editors or air marshals, know what the Labarum was?" Evelyn Waugh, "Msgr. Ronald Knox" (1948), in *The Essays, Articles and Reviews of Evelyn Waugh*, ed. Donat Gallagher (London: Methuen, 1984), 351.

42 Algernon Cecil, *Six Oxford Thinkers* (London: John Murray, 1909), 23–4.

adhered to it. Gibbon was influenced not only by writers of the French Enlightenment, such as Voltaire, D'Alembert, Diderot, Rousseau, Condorcet and Montesquieu, but those of the Scottish Enlightenment as well, including Hume, Adam Smith, Ferguson and Robertson. After the religious wars and the advances in the natural sciences in the seventeenth century, as well as the philosophical speculations of Descartes, there arose in Europe in the eighteenth century a consensus amongst intellectuals that radical reform was in order; society and its institutions needed remaking; reason, not prescription should order these reforms; and rationalism should supplant faith, especially the Faith of the Roman Catholic Church, which the innovators of the Enlightenment regarded with plenary hostility. Accordingly, the influential, indeed prize-winning, historian Peter Gay (1923–2015) saw the Enlightenment as "the rise of modern paganism" and gave passionate expression to what he saw as its animating principles:

> There were many philosophes in the eighteenth century, but there was only one Enlightenment. A loose, informal, wholly unorganized coalition of cultural critics, religious skeptics, and political reformers from Edinburgh to Naples, Paris to Berlin, Boston to Philadelphia, the philosophes made up a clamorous chorus ... The men of the Enlightenment united on a vastly ambitious program, a program of secularism, humanity, cosmopolitanism, and freedom, above all, freedom in its many forms—freedom from arbitrary power, freedom of speech, freedom of trade, freedom to realize one's talents, freedom of aesthetic response, freedom, in a word, of moral man to make his own way in the world. In 1784, when the Enlightenment had done most of its work, Kant defined it as man's emergence from his self-imposed tutelage, and offered as its motto, *Sapere aude*—"Dare to know": take the risk of discovery, exercise the right of unfettered criticism, accept the loneliness of autonomy.[43]

Elaborating on Gay's identification of the core elements of the Enlightenment, the historian of ideas J. G. A Pocock explains that "In Voltaire and Hume, as well as in Gibbon, we find an avowed preference for Greco-Roman polytheism as permitting philosophy to develop independently of the gods, whereas the assertion—whether Platonic or Semitic—of a single

---

43 Peter Gay, *The Enlightenment: An Interpretation: The Rise of Modern Paganism* (New York: Alfred A. Knopf, 1966), 1. Gay's account of the "freedom" to which the Enlightenment aspired should be contrasted with the Church's view of the matter, which the brilliant spiritual director Jacques Philippe captures with characteristic succinctness: "At the center of the Gospel stand the Beatitudes. The first one sums up all the others: 'Blessed are the poor in spirit, for theirs is the Kingdom of Heaven.' ... Spiritual poverty, utter dependence on God and his mercy, is the condition for interior freedom." Jacques Philippe, *Interior Freedom*, trans. Helena Scott (New York: Scepter, 2002), 132.

godhead condemned it to the embrace of theology."⁴⁴ The Enlightenment, according to the historian R. G. Collingwood, "in its narrower sense, as an essentially polemical and negative movement, a crusade against religion, never rose higher than its source, and Voltaire remained its best and most characteristic expression." For Collingwood, the Enlightenment was "based on the idea that human life is and has always been in the main a blind, irrational business," though one still "capable of being converted into something rational." How? One could delve backwards into the past and make some rational order of what were otherwise irrational forces or, alternatively, undertake "a forward-looking or more practical and political development, forecasting and endeavoring to bring about a millennium in which the rule of reason shall have been established ... Gibbon, a typical Enlightenment historian, agreed with all of this to the extent of conceiving history as anything but an exhibition of human wisdom." Thus, Gibbon "finds the motive force of history in human irrationality itself, and his narrative displays what he calls the triumph of barbarism and religion."⁴⁵

The incoherence of the Enlightenment view of the human person and human development, let alone history, speaks for itself. If the proponents of the Enlightenment found "the motive force of history" in "human irrationality," Newman found it in the Incarnation, what St. Athanasius called "the effulgence and wisdom of the Father."⁴⁶ Newman's view of the licentious misuse of reason, a misuse which continues to animate admirers of the Enlightenment in our own day, was at the core of his lifelong fight against liberalism. "Liberty of thought is in itself a good," he wrote, "but it gives an opening to false liberty ... Liberalism then [to which the Enlightenment gave rise] is the mistake of subjecting to human judgment those revealed doctrines which are in their nature beyond and independent of it, and of claiming to determine on intrinsic grounds the truth and value of propositions which rest for their reception simply on the external authority of the Divine Word."⁴⁷ Yet Pocock is right: a good deal of Gibbon's own affinity

---

44 J. G. A. Pocock, *Virtue, Commerce and History* (Cambridge: Cambridge University Press, 1985), 144.

45 R. G. Collingwood, *The Idea of History*, revised edn (Oxford: Oxford University Press, 1993), 78–9.

46 St. Athanasius, "Against the Arians III," 29–34, quoted in *Documents in Early Christian Thought*, ed. Maurice Wiles and Mark Santer (Cambridge: Cambridge University Press, 1975), 52. Cf. "Looked at in the light of this world our Savior's passion appears to us enshrouded in gloom, but how radiant it must be when seen from on high, as the culminating point of history, that point to which everything in the Old Testament led up and from which everything in the New descends!" Reginald Garrigou-Lagrange, *Providence: God's Loving Care for Men and the Need for Confidence in Almighty God* (Rockford, Illinois: TAN Books, 1998), 139.

47 *Apologia*, 255–6.

for the "modern paganism" of the Enlightenment came of his respect for Roman civilization, which can be seen in a famous paragraph of his history:

> If a man were called to fix the period in the history of the world during which the condition of the human race was most happy and prosperous, he would, without hesitation, name that which elapsed from the death of Domitian to the accession of Commodus [i.e., 96–180]. The vast extent of the Roman empire was governed by absolute power, under the guidance of virtue and wisdom. The armies were restrained by the firm but gentle hand of four successive emperors, whose characters and authority commanded involuntary respect. The forms of the civil administration were carefully preserved by Nerva, Trajan, Hadrian, and the Antonines, who delighted in the image of liberty, and were pleased with considering themselves as the accountable ministers of the laws.[48]

However peace and prosperity might compel the historian's admiration, the most appealing feature of this golden age for Gibbon was that "The superstition of the people was not embittered by any mixture of theological rancor; nor was it confused by the chain of any speculative system. The devout polytheist, though fondly attached to his national rites, admitted with implicit faith the different religions of the earth."[49] The golden age, in other words, was one in which religion was relative, unbinding, and the reverse of intolerant, though Gibbon always shows the limits of his own tolerance whenever he makes reference to the Church, as here, when he deprecates her miraculous character:

> The duty of an historian does not call upon him to interpose his private judgment in this nice and important controversy; but he ought not to dissemble the difficulty of adopting such a theory as may reconcile the interest of religion with that of reason, of making a proper application of that theory, and of defining with precision the limits of that happy period, exempt from error and from deceit, to which we might be disposed to extend the gift of supernatural powers.

For the skeptical Gibbon,

---

48 *Decline and Fall*, 1, 85–6. The historian Adrian Goldsworthy agrees with Gibbon about the relative stability of Antonine Rome: "It was not an unreasonable conclusion at the time of his writing ... The Roman emperors he mentions were probably amongst the most decent and capable men to hold the supreme office. They were all mature men when they came to power, worked hard at the job and eventually died natural deaths"—a rarity for most emperors of the late empire. Adrian Goldsworthy, *How Rome Fell: Death of a Superpower* (New Haven: Yale University Press, 2009), 50.

49 *Decline and Fall*, II, 32.

> From the first of the fathers to the last of the popes, a succession of bishops, of saints, of martyrs, and of miracles is continued without interruption, and the progress of superstition was so gradual and almost imperceptible that we know not in what particular link we should break the chain of tradition.[50]

Here one can see that fair-minded objectivity was never a forte of the Enlightenment historian; he could only show contempt for matters he had chosen in advance to regard as contemptible. Apropos miracles, for example, he sums up the view he takes of Christianity throughout his history: "Credulity performed the office of faith; fanaticism was permitted to assume the language of inspiration, and the effects of accident or contrivance were ascribed to supernatural causes."[51] Then, again, when scoundrels found their way into the papacy, Gibbon could scarcely contain his glee. John XXIII (1410–15) is a good case in point. After a career of unparalleled profligacy, the Neapolitan antipope, Baldassare Cossa was arraigned before the Council of Constance in May of 1415 and made to ratify his own deposition. Indeed, he has never since been granted a place on the canonical list of popes. (Cardinal Angelo Roncalli was apparently unconcerned about Cossa's notorieity and adopted the name of John XXIII in honor of his father.) In all events, the historian's summation of the first John XXIII's end is vintage Gibbon: "The most scandalous charges were suppressed: the Vicar of Christ on earth was only accused of piracy, murder, rape, sodomy and incest."[52] If contempt for Catholicism lay at the heart of Enlightenment thought, no one proved a more consistent and, indeed, effective proponent of it than Edward Gibbon.

How did history come to play so influential a role in Enlightenment thought? Joseph Ratzinger answers some of that large question in his *Introduction to Christianity* (1968), in which he sees rationalist history as part and parcel of the "revaluation of all things" that commenced with the Enlightenment and "made subsequent history really a 'new' age as compared with the old one." Specifically, he cites the Italian philosopher, Giambattista Vico (1668–1744), who broke with the mediaeval Schoolmen in seeing truth, not in what God has made (*vera est ens*), but as something that we have made for ourselves (*vera quia factum*). For Ratzinger, "This means that the old equation of truth and being was replaced by the new one of truth and factuality." By the eighteenth century, "History, previously despised and regarded as unscientific, now remained, alongside mathematics, the only true science left." And Ratzinger proceeds to show how it was the new scientific approach to history that repudiated the mediaeval

---

50 Ibid., II, 30.
51 Ibid., II, 31.
52 Ibid., VII, 300.

understanding of man and his development, an approach in which Gibbon's anti-Christian history had played an inaugural part.

> That which alone had hitherto seemed worthy of the free mind, thinking about the meaning of being, now seemed an idle and aimless enterprise offering no hope of attaining genuine knowledge. Thus mathematics and history now became the dominant disciplines; indeed, history devoured, so to speak, the whole world of learning and transformed it all fundamentally. Through Hegel, and in a different way through Comte, philosophy became a historical question, in which being itself is to be understood as a historical process. With F. C. Baur, theology turned into history, and its path became that of rigorous historical research, which asks what happened in the past and thereby hopes to reach the bottom of the matter. With Marx, economics was given a historical slant. Indeed, even the natural sciences were affected by this general tendency toward history: with Darwin, the classification of living beings was understood as a history of life; the constancy of what stays as it was created was replaced by a line of descent in which all things came from one another and could be traced back to one another. Thus the world finally appeared no longer as the firm housing of being but as a process whose continual expansion is the movement of being itself. This meant that henceforth the world was only knowable insofar as it was something made by man. In the last analysis man was no longer in a position to look beyond himself except on the level of the fact, where he had to recognize himself as the chance product of age-old developments. This now produced a very curious situation. At the very moment when radical anthropocentrism set in and man could know only his own work, he had to learn to accept himself as merely a chance occurrence, just another "fact." Here, too, the heaven from which he seemed to come was torn down, so to speak, and he was left with just the earth and its facts in his hands—the earth in which he now sought with the spade to decipher the laborious history of his development.[53]

Newman's critique of Gibbon can be seen as a critique of the ahistorical anthropocentrism at the core of the historian's view of Christianity. He opens his appraisal of Gibbon's account of the rise of Christianity by putting that rise in some historical context: "According to our Lord's announcements before the event, Christianity was to prevail and to become a great empire, and to fill the earth; but it was to accomplish this destiny, not as other victorious powers had done, and as the Jews expected, by force of arms or by other means of this world, but by the novel expedient of sanctity

---

53 Joseph Cardinal Ratzinger, *Introduction to Christianity*, revised edn (San Francisco: Ignatius Press, 2004), 58–63.

and suffering. If some aspiring party of this day, the great Orleans family, or a branch of the Hohenzollern, wishing to found a kingdom, were to profess, as their only weapon, the practice of virtue, they would not startle us more than it startled a Jew eighteen hundred years ago, to be told that his glorious Messiah was not to fight, like Joshua or David, but simply to preach. It is indeed a thought so strange, both in its prediction and in its fulfilment, as urgently to suggest to us that some Divine Power went with him who conceived and proclaimed it."[54]

Thirty-five years before the publication of *Grammar of Assent*, in his sermon "The Kingdom of the Saints" (1835), Newman had emphasized the sheer marvel of the rise of Christianity, which the rationalist in Gibbon sedulously downplayed. For Newman, taking in this wonder, in all of its unlikelihood, is crucial to understanding the history that Gibbon and the Enlightenment so entirely misunderstood.

> In the midst of a great Empire, such as the world had never seen, powerful and crafty beyond all former empires, more extensive, and better organized, suddenly a new Kingdom arose. Suddenly in every part of this well-cemented Empire, in the East and West, North and South, as if by some general understanding, yet without any sufficient system of correspondence or centre of influence, ten thousand orderly societies, professing one and the same doctrine, and disciplined upon the same polity, sprang up as from the earth. It seemed as though the fountains of the great deep were broken up, and some new forms of creation were thrown forward from below, the manifold ridges of some "great Mountain," crossing, splitting, disarranging the existing system of things, levelling the hills, filling up the valleys, — irresistible as being sudden, unforeseen, and unprovided for, — till it "filled the whole earth." [Isa. 41:15, 16] This was indeed a "new thing"; and independent of all reference to prophecy, is unprecedented in the history of the world before or since, and calculated to excite the deepest interest and amazement in any really philosophical mind. Throughout the kingdoms and provinces of Rome, while all things looked as usual, the sun rising and setting, the seasons continuing, men's passions swaying them as from the beginning, their thoughts set on their worldly business, on their gain or their pleasures, on their ambitious prospects and quarrels, warrior measuring his strength with warrior, politicians plotting, and kings banqueting, suddenly this portent came as a snare upon the whole earth. Suddenly, men found themselves encompassed with foes, as a camp surprised by night. And the nature of this hostile host was still more strange (if possible) than the coming of it. It was not a foreigner who invaded them, not a

---

54 *Grammar of Assent*, 293–4.

barbarian from the north, nor a rising of slaves, nor an armament of pirates, but the enemy rose up from among themselves. The first-born in every house, "from the first-born of Pharaoh on the throne, to the first-born of the captive in the dungeon," unaccountably found himself enlisted in the ranks of this new power, and estranged from his natural friends. Their brother, the son of their mother, the wife of their bosom, the friend that was as their own soul, these were the sworn soldiers of the "mighty army," that covered the face of the whole earth.

Newman also stressed that "when [Roman authorities] began to interrogate this enemy of Roman greatness, they found no vague profession among them, no varying account of themselves, no irregular and uncertain plan of action or conduct. They were all members of strictly and similarly organized societies." Such unanimity, by any chalk, was extraordinary, though it was a unanimity for which the would-be philosophical historian in Gibbon had no explanation. Newman accounts for this unprecedented unanimity by pointing to the authority of Heaven, not something that either the French or the Scottish Enlightenment was inclined to credit.

> These small kingdoms were indefinitely multiplied, each of them the fellow of the other. Wherever the Roman Emperor travelled, there he found these seeming rivals of his power, the Bishops of the Church.[55] Further, they one and all refused to obey his orders, and the prescriptive laws of Rome, so far as religion was concerned. The authority of the Pagan Religion, which in the minds of Romans was identified with the history of their greatness, was plainly set at nought by these upstart monarchies. At the same time they professed and observed a singular patience and subjection to the civil powers. They did not stir hand or foot in self-defence; they submitted to die, nay, accounted death the greatest privilege that could be inflicted on them. And further, they avowed one and all the same doctrine clearly and boldly; and they professed to receive it from one and the same source. They traced it up through the continuous line of their Bishops to certain twelve or fourteen Jews, who professed to have received it from Heaven ... And lastly, in spite of persecution from without, and occasional dissensions from within, they so prospered, that within three centuries from their first appearance in the Empire, they forced its sovereigns to become members of their confederation; nay, nor ended there, but as the civil power declined in strength, they became its patrons instead of its

---

55 Cf. "the episcopal cause was indebted for its rapid progress to the labours of many active prelates, who, like Cyprian of Carthage, could reconcile the arts of the most ambitious statesman with the Christian virtues which seem adapted to the character of a saint and martyr." *Decline and Fall*, II, 47.

victims, mediated between it and its barbarian enemies, and after burying it in peace when its hour came, took its place, won over the invaders, subdued their kings, and at length ruled as supreme; ruled, united under one head, in the very scenes of their former suffering, in the territory of the Empire, with Rome itself, the seat of the Imperial government, as a centre. I am not entering into the question of doctrine, any more than of prophecy. I am not inquiring how far this victorious Kingdom was by this time perverted from its original character; but only directing attention to the historical phenomenon. How strange then is the course of the Dispensation![56]

Having established this Dispensation's ungainsayable strangeness, Newman asked whether the rise of Christianity is "a history that admits of being resolved, by any philosophical ingenuity, into the ordinary operation of moral, social, or political causes," since "various writers" had "attempted to assign human causes in explanation of the phenomenon," including Gibbon, who pointed to five human causes for its rise: "the zeal of Christians, inherited from the Jews, their doctrine of a future state, their claim to miraculous power, their virtues, and their ecclesiastical organization." Newman then asks whether Gibbon has any proof that these five causes alone or combined led to the rise of Christianity. And here we see the rigor with which Newman entered into the historical challenges that any respectable historian must resolve in adducing his evidence:

> He thinks these five causes, when combined, will fairly account for the event; but he has not thought of accounting for their combination. If they are ever so available for his purpose, still that availableness arises out of their coincidence, and out of what does that coincidence arise? Until this is explained, nothing is explained, and the question had better have been let alone. These presumed causes are quite distinct from each other, and, I say, the wonder is, what made them come together. How came a multitude of Gentiles to be influenced with Jewish zeal? How came zealots to submit to a strict, ecclesiastical *régime*? What connexion has a secular *régime* with the immortality of the soul? Why should immortality, a philosophical doctrine, lead to belief in miracles, which is a superstition of the vulgar? What tendency had miracles and magic to make men austerely virtuous? Lastly, what power was there in a code of virtue, as calm and enlightened as that of Antoninus, to generate a zeal as fierce as that of Maccabæus? Wonderful events before now have apparently been nothing but coincidences, certainly; but they do not become less wonderful by cataloguing their constituent causes, unless we also show how these came to be constituent. However, this by the way; the real question is this, — are these historical char-

---

56 "The Kingdom of the Saints" (1) (1835), Sermon 20, in *PPS*, II, 236–9.

acteristics of Christianity, also in matter of fact, historical causes of Christianity? Has Gibbon given proof that they are? Has he brought evidence of their operation, or does he simply conjecture in his private judgment that they operated? Whether they were adapted to accomplish a certain work, is a matter of opinion; whether they did accomplish it is a question of fact. He ought to adduce instances of their efficiency before he has a right to say that they are efficient. And the second question is, what is this effect, of which they are to be considered as causes? It is no other than this, the conversion of bodies of men to the Christian faith. Let us keep this in view. We have to determine whether these five characteristics of Christianity were efficient causes of bodies of men becoming Christians.[57]

One by one, Newman proceeds to show how none of Gibbon's five causes, alone or in combination, sufficiently accounts for the rise of Christianity. "They might have operated now and then; Simon Magus came to Christianity in order to learn the craft of miracles, and Peregrinus from love of influence and power; but Christianity made its way, not by individual, but by broad, wholesale conversions, and the question is, how they originated?"[58]

In addressing Gibbon's causes in his *History of English Thought in the Eighteenth Century* (1876), the Victorian rationalist Leslie Stephen might seem to have agreed with Newman:

> How … did the Jews and Christians come to be zealous? Had not their zeal a supernatural source? Why did the Jewish religion throw off its narrowness? Why did the doctrine of a future life simultaneously reveal its power over the minds of so many races? What caused the miraculous stories, common enough in all rude ages, to become such effective engines for conversion? To what did Christianity owe its moral power, and whence came the cohesive power of the organisation? To these and similar questions Gibbon either gives no reply, or contents himself with hinting an indirect answer. Christianity, on his showing, sprang up like a mushroom. No particular reason can be given for it, any more than for any passing fashion of thought. Such a theory is at least reconcilable to a belief in its supernatural origin. Gibbon, indeed, is as incapable of understanding the spiritual significance of the phenomenon as of assigning a cause for it. From his pages little can be learnt as to the true significance of the greatest religious convulsion that has transformed the world's history.[59]

---

57 *Grammar of Assent*, 294–5.
58 Ibid., 297.
59 Leslie Stephen, *History of English Thought in the Eighteenth Century* (London: Smith Elder, 1876), I, 449.

Yet Stephen no sooner concedes the fundamental flaw in Gibbon's causes than he turns round and praises the historian for stripping away the "vague halo of assumption which gave a totally unreal character to all discussions about the origins of Christianity." For Stephen, "it is true, not merely that Gibbon struck a heavy blow at Christianity, but that he struck by far the heaviest blow which it had yet received from any single hand. What he did was to bring the genuine spirit of historical enquiry for the first time face to face with the facts. Little as he may have appreciated the deeper significance of the process whose external symptoms he describes, his method must provide the primary data from which a reasonable judgment must be formed. He did not explain the phenomenon, but he reduced it within the sphere of the explicable."[60] However unpersuasive, this at least shows the logic on which rationalists rely when they argue that the best way to confute Christianity is to treat its spiritual substance, as opposed to its appearances as unreal. The historian Roy Porter pursues a variation of this logic when he attempts to defend Gibbon by arguing that the historian of the *Decline and Fall* "parades these causes before the reader with some detachment, not to say cynicism. He is of course concerned to establish neither the theological truth of Christianity's claims nor even the sincerity of its believers, but the impact achieved by its *appearances* ... Gibbon showed no sympathy for the Church's aspirations, and shed no tears over its martyrs. This does not, however, vitiate his understanding or interpretation of the human causes of the rise of Christianity."[61]

Newman roundly rejects this logic: such *appearances*, or "externals," as he calls them, could never adequately account for the rise of Christianity. The human causes of the rise of Christianity cannot be separated from its divine causes. After all, the divine causes of the Faith were what drew converts to the Church. They were also what inspired martyrs to lay down their lives for the Faith. The historian Arnaldo Momigliano (1908–87) may have been right when he said that "We owe it to Gibbon that the problem of the relations between Christianity and the political and social developments of Europe has come to stay in European historiography," but this is largely the result of Gibbon refusing to pay attention to Christianity on its own terms.[62] In this, he was not unlike Voltaire, who memorably expressed his impatience with historical evidence he preferred to ignore by exclaiming, "*Malheur aux détails! c'est une vermine qui tue les grands ouvrages!*"[63] In taking

---

60 Ibid., I, 450.

61 Roy Porter, *Gibbon: Making History* (New York: St. Martin's Press, 1988), 122–3.

62 Arnaldo Momigliano, "Gibbon's Contribution to Historical Method," *Historia: Zeitschrift für alte Geschichte*, 2, no. 4 (1954), 461.

63 Voltaire to A. M. L'Abbé Du Bos (30 October 1738), *Oeuvres complètes de Voltaire* (Paris: Garnier Frères, 1880), vol. XXV, 30.

issue with Gibbon's causes, Newman was insisting that the historian in Gibbon exhibit not only more sympathy with his subject but more humility before the evidence of his subject, which is never merely "human" in the sense in which Porter uses that word:[64]

> It is very remarkable that it should not have occurred to a man of Gibbon's sagacity to inquire, what account the Christians themselves gave of the matter. Would it not have been worth while for him to have let conjecture alone, and to have looked for facts instead? Why did he not try the hypothesis of faith, hope, and charity?[65] Did he never hear of repentance towards God, and faith in Christ? Did he not recollect the many words of Apostles, Bishops, Apologists, Martyrs, all forming one testimony? No; such thoughts are close upon him, and close upon the truth; but he cannot sympathize with them, he cannot believe in them, he cannot even enter into them, *because* he needs the due formation for such an exercise of mind.[66]

That Newman should insist on this "due formation for such an exercise of mind" is important because it was the lack of such formation that hampered so many of his contemporaries—especially those of a rationalist bent—from entering into the true character of the rise or, indeed, any other aspect of Christianity. Elsewhere, in the *Grammar of Assent*, Newman writes that "we need the interposition of a Power, greater than human teaching and human argument, to make our beliefs true and our minds one."[67] A good example of the wild errors into which Gibbon was led by not having any proper formation in the study of Christianity as a religion can be seen in his claim that "the *real* difference between … [John Calvin

---

64 Cf. "after all, a good historian should start by appreciating the past. It is true that Gibbon, the greatest of our historians, had nothing but contempt for his chosen subject; this merely shows that genius can disregard all the rules. In lesser men Whig rationalism produces what has been called the 'linotype school of history;' in which everyone behaves according to rule, the mysteries of human behavior vanish and everything moves relentlessly towards infinite improvement—or to infinite disaster." A. J. P. Taylor, "Tory History" (1950), in *From Napoleon to the Second International: Essays on Nineteenth-Century Europe*, ed. Chris Wrigley (London: Allen Lane: The Penguin Press, 1993), 45.

65 Jacques Philippe nicely describes how the theological virtues animate the lives of Christians: "True freedom, the sovereign liberty of Christians, resides in the possibility of believing, hoping, and loving in all circumstances, thanks to the assistance of the Holy Spirit who 'helps us in our weakness.' Nobody can ever prevent us. 'For I am sure that neither death, nor life, not angels, nor principalities, not things present, not things to come, nor powers, nor height, nor depth, nor anything else' in all creation, will be able to separate us from the love of God in Christ Jesus our Lord.'" Philippe, *Interior Freedom*, 24.

66 *Grammar of Assent*, 297.

67 Ibid., 242.

and St. Augustine] is invisible even to a theological microscope."[68] Yet it has to be remembered that Gibbon was hostile to theology *per se*. One of the reason why he respected Islam was precisely because it was non-theological, an aspect about the historian's point of view that Thomas Carlyle found congenial. The historian of the French Revolution, as Prof. David R. Sorensen points out, "valued the contrast that the author of *The Decline and Fall* established between seventh-century Christianity, fractured by increasingly arcane and mystical theological disputes, and Islam, strengthened by a resolutely nonmiraculous faith in one God and His apostle Mahomet. Gibbon reinforced Carlyle's conviction that theology had little to do with religion, a conviction that had been buttressed by the latter's distaste for the controversies of the Oxford Movement."[69]

Like Carlyle, most historians favorable to Gibbon's Enlightenment history might naturally regard the "due formation" on which Newman insists as favoring precisely those attitudes partial to Christianity that Gibbon wrote his own secular, philosophical history to baffle. Yet Newman shows that the presumed dichotomy between faithful Christian history, on the one hand, and philosophical history, on the other, is false. As he pointed out in the first of his Oxford University Sermons, "The Philosophical Temper, First Enjoined by the Gospel" (1826):

> Although ... Christianity seems to have been the first to give to the world the pattern of the true spirit of philosophical investigation, yet, as the principles of science are, in process of time, more fully developed, and become more independent of the religious system, there is much danger lest the philosophical school should be found to separate from the Christian Church, and at length disown the parent to whom it has been so greatly indebted. And this evil has in a measure befallen us.[70]

In 1874, Newman wrote a correspondent to express his exasperation with the intellectual arrogance of scientists when it came to religion:

> Doubtless theologians before now meddled with science — and now

---

68 *Decline and Fall*, III, 431.

69 David R. Sorenson, "In Defense of 'Religiosity': Carlyle, Mahomet, and the Force of Faith," in *On Heroes, Hero-Worship, and the Heroic in History: Thomas Carlyle*, ed. David R. Sorensen and Brent E. Kinser (New Haven: Yale University Press, 2013), 213. In "The Hero as Poet" (1841), Carlyle, always susceptible to what V. S. Pritchett once referred to as "the mutinies of the observant mind," came round to the view that Mahomet was not so much the founder of a religion preferable to the dogmatic Christianity of the Tractarians as "a wild Arab lion of the desert," whose Koran was "a stupid piece of prolix absurdity." *Ibid.*, 101–2.

70 Newman,: "The Philosophical Temper, First Enjoined by the Gospel" (1826), Sermon 1, in *University Sermons*, 23.

scientific men are paying them off by meddling with theology. With you, I see nothing in the theory of evolution inconsistent with an Almighty Creator and Protector—but these men assume, assume with an abundance of scorn ... and superciliousness, that religion and science are on this point contradictory, and on this audacious assumption they proceed dogmatically to conclude that there is no truth in religion. It is dreadful to think of the number of souls who will suffer while the epidemic lasts—but Truth is too powerful not in the end to get the upperhand.[71]

Gibbon, for his part, can never speak of the intellectual character of the Church without disparaging it. Here, for instance, he speaks of the Christians of the Early Church: "Their credulity debased and vitiated the faculties of the mind; they corrupted the evidence of history; and superstition gradually extinguished the hostile light of philosophy and science."[72] This was the same Church that produced Origen (c. 185–c. 254) and Tertullian (c. 160–c. 220), St. Irenaeus (c. 130–c. 200) and St. Clement of Alexandria (c. 150–c. 215), St. Athanasius (c. 297–373) and St. Gregory of Nazianzus (330–90), St John Chrysostom (c. 347–407) and St. Basil the Great (c. 329–79), St. Cyril of Jerusalem (c. 315–86) and St. Gregory of Nyssa (331–95), St. Augustine (354–430) and St. Leo the Great (c. 390–461). Only the light of philosophy and science obscured by the Enlightenment could approve so gross a misjudgment.

One of the more clear-sighted critics of Gibbon's pretensions to a genuinely philosophical understanding of history was Samuel Taylor Coleridge (1772–1834):

> Gibbon's style is detestable, but his style is not the worst thing about him. His history has proved an effectual bar to all real familiarity with the temper and habits of imperial Rome. Few persons read the original authorities, even those which are classical; and certainly no distinct knowledge of the actual state of the empire can be obtained from Gibbon's rhetorical sketches. He takes notice of nothing but what may produce an effect; he skips on from eminence to eminence, without ever taking you through the valleys between: in fact, his work is little else but a disguised collection of all the splendid anecdotes which he could find in any book concerning any persons or nations from the Antonines to the capture of Constantinople. When I read a chapter in Gibbon I seem to be looking through a luminous haze or fog :—figures come and go, I know not how or why, all larger than life, or distorted or discoloured;

---

71 Newman to David Brown (4 April 1874), in *LD*, XXVII, 44.
72 *Decline and Fall*, IV, 80. Cf. "Gibbon learnt from Bayle to blend malice with erudition." Momigliano, "Gibbon's Contribution to Historical Method," 452.

nothing is real, vivid, true; all is scenical, and as it were, exhibited by candlelight. And then to call it a History of the Decline and Fall of the Roman Empire! Was there ever a greater misnomer? I protest I do not remember a single philosophical attempt made throughout the work to fathom the ultimate causes of the decline or fall of that empire. How miserably deficient is the narrative of the important reign of Justinian! And that poor scepticism, which Gibbon mistook for Socratic philosophy, has led him to misstate and mistake the character and influence of Christianity in a way which even an avowed infidel or atheist would not and could not have done. Gibbon was a man of immense reading; but he had no philosophy.[73]

This is in line with what Newman has to say about what he sees as the adverse effects of Gibbon's subjectivism. "[W]e often hear of the exploits of some great lawyer, judge or advocate" Newman writes in the *Grammar of Assent*, "who is able in perplexed cases, when common minds see nothing but a hopeless heap of facts, foreign or contrary to each other, to detect the principle which rightly interprets the riddle, and, to the admiration of all hearers, converts a chaos into an orderly and luminous whole." For Newman, this is "originality in thinking ... the discovery of an aspect of a subject-matter, simpler, it may be, and more intelligible than any hitherto taken." Yet, at the same, time, he cautioned his readers: "such aspects are often unreal, as being mere exhibitions of ingenuity, not of true originality of mind." And Newman saw this especially "in what are called philosophical views of history ... I do not call Gibbon merely ingenious; still his account of the rise of Christianity is the mere subjective view of one who could not enter into its depth and power."[74] Newman crisply defined his own philosophy of history in a letter to T. W. Allies (1813–1903), the convert and church historian: "My notion of the Philosophy of History is the science of which historical facts are the basis, or the laws on which it pleases Almighty Providence to conduct the political and social world."[75]

---

73 *Coleridge's Literary Criticism*, ed. J. W. Mackail (Oxford: Oxford University Press, 1908), 163–4.
74 *Grammar of Assent*, 240.
75 Newman to T. W. Allies (3 September 1854), in LD, XVI, 244. Speaking of the trials he suffered after he converted to Catholicism and had to give up his rectorship at Launton, Allies wrote in his autobiography: "The convert in the first three centuries often met at once the Roman axe, or the torturing hook or scourge, and was released after a glorious conflict; but here the trial, if not so sharp, was far more prolonged. An indeterminate space of time, dark and unredeemed by hope, opened its illimitable lowering desert before us. The first taste of it was utter uncertainty what to do, with the necessity of doing at once. It was certain that my successor at Launton would only be too anxious to get rid of such an ill-omened guest as soon as possible, and the moment my rights as landlord terminated, no quarter was to be expected. Furniture

Facts, in other words, can never be treated as though they exist in isolation from the laws of Almighty Providence.

A good example of the sort of philosophical history that Newman has in mind here can be seen in a passage from Ronald Knox's "The Church and the World," a pastoral sermon which he gave in a series of sermons on "The Mystery of the Kingdom" (1952):

> Not all the sophistries of Gibbon and his followers can blind the eye of the historian to the brute fact that the advent of Christianity is an epoch in the story of our planet ... Not all at once, not with violence and the sword, like the creed of the false prophet, but silently and secretly like the leaven, in a manner foreshadowed by the life-history of its own Founder, when he came to earth.
>
>> He comes, but not in regal splendour dressed,
>> The jewelled diadem, the Tyrian vest;
>> Not like a Prince, all-glorious from afar,
>> Of hosts the captain, and the Lord of War—
>
> a little Baby in a manger, a hunted criminal, a malefactor weighted with the instrument of his own punishment—so our Lord looked to the world, not otherwise did his Church look—does his Church look, to the scornful eye of the politicians that reject it. Christianity was the religion of slaves; it has abolished slavery. It was thrown to the lions in the amphitheatre; it has abolished the amphitheatre. Absolute monarchy, like a flustered giant, laboured to crush it; it has outlived absolute monarchy. Silently, through the centuries, the supernatural miracle has worked, like nature's miracle of fermentation. And while she has spread her influence outwards, the Church has also drawn to herself, by the hidden spell of that heavenly seed once planted in the soil of our dead nature, the souls of such as would be saved.[76]

When it comes to the demands of proper philosophical history, Pocock admits in the concluding volume of *Barbarism and Religion* (2015), his six-volume contextual study of *The Decline and Fall of the Roman Empire* that Gibbon had his hands full trying to master the elements of historical Christianity. For Pocock, "the importance of Chapter 15 lies in Gibbon's acceptance, as

---

and books must be put somewhere, yet it was impossible to fix where we could best go. The harassing perplexity of this situation, the sense of being ruined, of having no field for future exertion, cannot be expressed in words ... In those days ... I was supported continually by Father Newman's advice. He was my polar star, which never set." Thomas William Allies, *A Life's Decision* (London: Burns & Oates, 1894), 292–3. In 1853, Allies became secretary of the Catholic Poor School Committee, a post he held until 1890, after raising £50,000 for Catholic schools.

76 Ronald Knox, *Pastoral and Occasional Sermons* (San Francisco: Ignatius, 2002), 116.

central to the narrative of Decline and Fall, of a species of historiography new to his text ... the language of Christian historiography." And here Pocock concedes that this historiography "possessed its own vocabulary and literature, a class and profession of skilled exegetes and a long history of controversy and debate." It was Gibbon's charge to set himself "to learn to write in it." The problem was that "He found it of course deeply uncongenial—many of its premises seemed to him unreasonable and even absurd—but he had to admit it to his history ... merely to dismiss and deride it would not be sufficient." The question is whether Gibbon did truly admit it to his history—"admit" it, that is to say, in any fair, informed, critical sense. Pocock, the honest chronicler, fairly concedes that Gibbon did not admit this historiography into his history in any proper sense. Why? "He had to treat it as history, taking it seriously until it called for an act of faith he was never going to perform." In other words, Gibbon may dutifully revisit such theological disputes as the Arian controversy but he can only see "unreasonable and even absurd" premises in them.⁷⁷ And, in fact, the pivotal importance of the Arian controversy, which determined whether Christians would accept or reject a rationalist reading of the *fidei depositum* was entirely lost on the scoffing historian, though this is as it should be for Pocock because what makes Gibbon such an exemplary historian is that "he can be seen explaining why any act of faith in an absolute God, especially when supported by philosophy, is necessarily intolerant."⁷⁸ Hence, Gibbon's

---

77 The Arian controversy arose in the fourth century in Alexandria when Arius (*c.* 250–*c.* 336) denied the divinity of Jesus Christ. Opposition to the heresy was led by St. Athanasius (*c.* 920–1003). At the Council of Nicaea (325), the Church reaffirmed the coeternity and coequality of the Father and the Son, using the celebrated word "homoousios" to express this consubstantiality. Thus, the controversy technically pivoted on the meaning of two Greek words: *homoiousios* (ὁμοιούσιος), meaning "of a similar substance," and *homoousios* (ὁμοούσιος), meaning "of the same substance." It was ironic that Gibbon should have mocked what he considered nothing more than "furious contests" over "the difference of a single diphthong" because, at its root, the Arian heresy was an insistence on the same rationalist understanding of the Christian Faith on which Gibbon and the Enlightenment insisted. In other words, they were Arians themselves. *Decline and Fall*, II, 373. Hilaire Belloc is good on the remarkable persistence of heresy. "It is often said that all heresies die. This may be true in the very long run but it is not necessarily true within any given period of time. It is not even true that the vital principle of a heresy necessarily loses strength with time. The fate of the various heresies has been most various; and the greatest of them, Mohammedanism, is not only still vigorous but is more vigorous over the districts which it originally occupied than is its Christian rival, and much more vigorous and much more co-extensive with its own society than is the Catholic Church with our Western civilization which is the product of Catholicism." Hilaire Belloc, *The Great Heresies* (London: The Catholic Book Club, 1938), 57.

78 Pocock, *Barbarism and Religion*, VI, 2. What is striking about Pocock's analysis here is its reliance on what has become the thoroughly discredited concept of "tolerance."

brilliant commentator is no more ready to admit Christian historiography into his own history in any fair, substantive way than Gibbon himself.

As Pocock's commentary shows, perhaps the fairest way to demonstrate the manifold errors that result when historians follow Gibbon in failing to acquire the "due formation" that Newman recommends as necessary to arriving at any proper critical understanding of the character of Christian history is to see what they say themselves about Gibbon's achievement as it relates to his depiction of Christianity. According to the classicist Betty Radice (1912–85), who edited Gibbon's autobiography for Penguin, the historian "never attacked primitive and uncorrupted Christian teaching nor spoke disparagingly of Jesus." He did, however, follow the dictates of multiculturalism sufficiently to deny Christianity "any position of superiority over other forms of religion." After all, Gibbon was keenly interested in "Roman paganism," as well as "the cults of the primitive Germans, Islam ... [and] Zoroastrianism." Still, being "a deist and a sceptic," he held that "religious truth" was not only "unobtainable" but "relatively unimportant." For the philosophical historian, "The Christian Church must be judged by its works and the good or harm it had done to mankind." Moreover, like Montesquieu, he "treated all religions as social phenomena, which ought to express the spirit and aims of society." It is true that he was "fascinated by heresies and the minutiae of theological arguments," but he "deplored the 'deluded enthusiasts'" who "fought over them" — and this would naturally include those who fought over the Arian heresy.[79] Gibbon's interest in the intricacies of religion never blinded him to its dangers.

> With his humanist belief that society should aim at rational freedom and happiness for its members, inevitably he saw Christianity as neither rational, free nor happy; preaching and allegory led to a withdrawal from rational thinking; celibacy and monastic seclusion were "painful to the individual and useless to mankind"; the Christian emphasis on sin and retribution and on preparation for the life to come robbed men of their human right to enjoy life here and now. Consequently, Gibbon devoted the main part of six of his chapters to an attack on the emperor Constantine for establishing Christianity as the official religion of the empire, and Julian the Apostate was one of his heroes for his attempt to restore the old pagan worship.[80]

No one privy to the way dissent is now universally treated in the liberal academy can creditably dispute this. The intolerance of the wars of religion might have been insufferable, but the "tolerance" of the Enlightenment hardly improved matters, especially since it has given rise, in our own day, to the intolerance of political correctness.

79 Betty Radice, "Introduction," in Edward Gibbon, *The History of the Decline and Fall of the Roman Empire* (London: Folio Society, 1983), I, 18–19.

80 *Ibid.*, I, 19. In converting to Christianity in 312 after the Battle of the Milvian

Here, we can see how Gibbon's admirers willy-nilly prove the historian's distortion of Christianity by exposing how he flouts the sort of "due formation" recommended by Newman. Yet Radice's inability to see the Church as anything other than a No Popery caricature is not unusual among current commentators. This is made comically clear by Charlotte Roberts, Lecturer in English at University College, London, who states in her summary of Gibbon's treatment of the rise of Christianity in Chapters XV and XVI:

> The power exercised by the Catholic Church, Gibbon implies, is a direct consequence of imperial power because it is a direct imitation of it. The oppression, sway, and subjugation exercised by the Church testify to the corrupt and greedy usurpation, by first and second century ecclesiastics of immediately visible temporal power. A causal narrative of this sort is only reinforced by conflations of time and space; the pope is the new emperor; Christian Europe a reinterpretation of the imperial territories; St. Peter's Basilica the equivalent of a Roman temple; the papal residence the modern counterpart of Nero's palace; and Catholic dominion equivalent to Nero's cruelties. The transformation from ancient Roman to modern Catholic rule is not signaled by any great shift in historical circumstances but is heralded by tiny manipulations of vocabulary.[81]

The historian Christopher Dawson bears Newman out on the indis-

---

Bridge, Constantine made the Roman state tolerant of the Christian religion; he did not make it the "official religion" of the empire; the Emperor Theodosius founded the Christian state in 380 after converting to Nicene Christianity and outlawing Arianism and other heresies. Gibbon had good things to say about Theodosius, perhaps because the emperor was a student of history: "The serious or lively tone of his conversation was adapted to the age, the rank, or the character of his subjects whom he admitted into his society; and the affability of his manners displayed the image of his mind. Theodosius respected the simplicity of the good and virtuous: every art, every talent, of an useful or even of an innocent nature, was rewarded by his judicious liberality; and, except the heretics, whom he persecuted with implacable hatred, the diffusive circle of his benevolence was circumscribed only by the limits of the human race. The government of a mighty empire may assuredly suffice to occupy the time and the abilities of a mortal; yet the diligent prince, without aspiring to the unsuitable reputation of profound learning, always reserved some moments of his leisure for the instructive amusement of reading. History, which enlarged his experience, was his favourite study. The annals of Rome, in the long period of eleven hundred years, presented him with a various and splendid picture of human life; and it has been particularly observed that, whenever he perused the cruel acts of Cinna, of Marius, or of Sylla, he warmly expressed his generous detestation of those enemies of humanity and freedom." Gibbon, however, does not extenuate the savagery that Theodosius unleashed at Thessalonica (390). See *Decline and Fall*, III, ch. XXVII.

81 Charlotte Roberts, *Edward Gibbon and the Shape of History* (Oxford: Oxford University Press, 2014), 75–6.

pensability of "due formation" in rather less grotesque terms when he says of Gibbon and his editor, J. B. Bury that they were both "freethinkers with a strong bias against Christianity"[82] and this necessarily limited their understanding of their chosen period, "the collapse of the old Empire in the third century AD to the breakup of the reconstituted Eastern Empire in the seventh century under the stress of the Mohammedan invasions," which "is the period of the Christian Empire, the Empire of Constantine and Justinian, the age of the Fathers and of the great Councils."[83] Of course, Gibbon and Bury wrote from "a purely secularist standpoint." And this was fundamentally problematic because, as Dawson persuasively argues, "To neglect or despise the religious achievement of the age is as fatal to any true understanding of it as a complete disregard of the economic factor would be in the case of nineteenth century Europe. For the real interest and importance of that age are essentially religious. It marks the failure of the greatest experiment in secular civilization that the world had ever seen, and the return of society to spiritual principles. It was at once an age of material loss and of spiritual recovery, when amidst the ruins of a bankrupt order men strove slowly and painfully to rebuild the house of life on eternal foundations."[84] For Dawson, Gibbon "had no understanding of specifically religious values. They were for him an unknown dimension. That is his real difficulty in dealing with Christianity: not the scientific incredibility of miracles, or the metaphysical absurdity of dogmas, but the fundamental concepts of religious faith and divine revelation—in short, the idea of what Christianity was about."[85] To substantiate his point, Dawson compares Gibbon to his greatest source, the Port-Royal priest and historian, Louis-Sébastien Le Nain de Tillemont (1637–98), whom the Enlightenment historian affectionately referred to as "the patient and sure-footed mule of the Alps [who] may be trusted in the most slippery paths."[86]

---

82 Christopher Dawson, "St. Augustine and his Age" (1933), in *Enquiries into Religion and Culture*, ed. Robert Royal (Washington: Catholic University Press of America, 2009), 165. As a young man, Dawson, like Newman, gloried in Gibbon; his sister, in her biography of the historian, relates how her brother was actually inspired by Gibbon to become an historian himself; it was only as he aged, and his thinking matured, that he came to qualify his admiration for the Enlightenment historian. See Christina Scott, *A Historian and his World: A Life of Christopher Dawson* (London: Routledge, 1991).

83 Dawson, *Enquiries into Religion and Culture*, 165.

84 Ibid. 165–6.

85 Christopher Dawson, "Edward Gibbon and the Fall of Rome" (1934), in *The Dynamics of World History*, ed. John Mulloy (New York: Sheed & Ward, 1956), 333.

86 *Decline and Fall*, III, ch. XXV, n. 122. Newman was a great admirer of Tillemont as well, telling a correspondent in 1868 that of Christian "authors for history, chronology, and geography ... the best I know is Tillemont ... he religiously gives his authorities for every half sentence of his elaborate work." Newman to Mrs. Hill Buckle (27 October

Tillemont has not a spark of Gibbon's literary genius. He is dry and laborious and narrow-minded, bound by all the prejudices of the most rigid orthodoxy. But he has a profound veneration for the past and his only ambition is to be the faithful interpreter of its spirit. Even his prejudices are the prejudices of the age of which he writes and of themselves do something to recreate the atmosphere of a vanished civilization. And so one feels that he succeeds in the essential task of history—in the understanding of the past, while Gibbon only succeeds in explaining it away. To Gibbon, the story of the Christian Empire and the civilization to which it gave birth is nothing but the history of an illusion. The world had conceived emptiness and brought forth wind. There was nothing left to write about but the battles of kites and crows and the aimless procession of phantom emperors. There remained only the shadow of the great name of Rome like the shadow of a great rock in an empty land.[87]

Moreover, Dawson is right to see Gibbon, *malgré lui*, as only the most celebrated of those "Protestant historians of the past," who "should have had little sympathy for this period." And the reason is simple: "To them it was an age of superstition and ignorance, when all the things that they most disapproved of in Catholicism were most evident—image worship and the veneration of relics, the growth of the Papacy and the power of the clergy, the cult of the saints and the pilgrimages to holy places."[88]

One Whig historian—indeed, the very best Whig historian—put his prejudices aside sufficiently to see that Gibbon had not been able to put his own aside. "It must be acknowledged," Thomas Babington Macaulay (1800–59) wrote, "that [Gibbon] is grossly partial to the pagan persecutors, and quite offensively so. His opinion of the Christian fathers is very little removed from ours; but his excuses for the tyranny of their persecutors gives to his book the character of an anti-Christian diatribe. He writes like a man who had received some personal injury from Christianity, and wished

1868), in *LD*, XXXII, 290.

87 Dawson, *The Dynamics of World History*, 341. Gibbon's respect for Tillemont can be contrasted with his obsessional contempt for Caesar (later Cardinal) Baronius (1538–1607), the Roman Oratorian and pupil of St. Philip Neri, whose *Annales Ecclesiastici* (1588–1607) refuted the Protestant *Magdeburg Centuries* by contending that the Church of Rome and the Church of the first century were one and the same. In chapter XXIV of the *Decline and Fall*, Gibbon refers gratefully to the Abbe de la Bléterie, who "handsomely exposes the brutal bigotry of Baronius." *Decline and Fall*, II, 556. Owen Chadwick speculates that the obsessional nature of this contempt might have arisen from Gibbon's need "to reassure himself about a youthful past [i.e., his youthful conversion to Catholicism] which so long ago he thought himself to have exorcised." Owen Chadwick, "Gibbon and the Church Historians," *Daedalus*, 105, no. 3 (Summer 1976), 122.

88 Christopher Dawson, *The Formation of Christendom* (San Francisco: St. Ignatius Press, 2008), 183.

to be revenged on it, and all its professors."[89] Nevertheless, Lytton Strachey (1880–1932) defended the skeptical historian on the grounds that since all historians must address the problem of exclusion—how much, and what to exclude in their histories—Gibbon was entirely within his rights to give short shrift to Christianity. "Gibbon's style is probably the most exclusive in literature," Strachey contended. "By its very nature it bars out a great multitude of human energies. It makes sympathy impossible, it takes no cognizance of passion, it turns its back upon religion with a withering smile. But that was just what was wanted. Classic beauty came instead. By the penetrating influence of style—automatically, inevitably—lucidity, balance, and precision were everywhere introduced: and the miracle of order was established over the chaos of a thousand years."[90]

This "miracle of order" hardly impressed the historian Hilaire Belloc (1870–1953), who, like Macaulay, could not gloss over the problems that ensue when an historian lacks sympathy with his subject.[91] In a letter to the classicist and critic J. S. Phillimore (1873–1926), Belloc wrote:

> The real point is that Gibbon from beginning to end is an anti-Catholic pamphlet, extremely well-written and, as a presentation of historical development, grossly unhistorical. He is as unhistorical as would be a Frenchman describing the English squires as though they were a bureaucracy, or an Englishman describing the French Parliament as a democratic institution... When people are absolutely wrong as to the nature of a thing they are describing, accuracy of citation (in which Gibbon is usually sound) is worthless. When to ignorance of the nature of a thing one adds irritation with all its expressions one becomes a hopeless historian of it. The period Gibbon chose has for its nature the triumph of the Catholic Church, and through it the transformation of Europe, and Gibbon didn't know the nature of what happened and

---

89 Thomas Babington Macaulay, *The History of England in the Eighteenth Century*, ed. Peter Rowland (London: Folio Society, 1980), 131–2.

90 Lytton Strachey, *Portraits in Miniature* (London: Chatto & Windus, 1931), 163–4.

91 Belloc may have been critical of the historian in Gibbon but he was unqualifyingly laudatory when it came to the writer in him: "I have not read all the books in the English language, but of such as I have read, Gibbon's *Decline and Fall of the Roman Empire* is far and away the most readable. I speak not only for myself, but I believe for hundreds of others, over a period which will soon cover a century and a half, when I say that you can pick him up at any moment, open him where you will, read him for ten minutes or half an hour or half a day and lay him down delighted. I verily believe there is not a dull line in the enormous work. Certainly there is not a dull page. For wit, for concision, for exactitude of expression, for *meat* (the right word), I know not his equal." Hilaire Belloc, *A Conversation with an Angel and Other Essays* (London: Jonathan Cape, 1928), 130–1. For Belloc's biographer, Robert Speaight, "It would be scarcely an exaggeration to say that, outside Homer, Gibbon was Belloc's favourite writer." Robert Speaight, *The Life of Hilaire Belloc* (London: Hollis & Carter, 1957), 403.

at the same time was irritated by its manifestation ... Gibbon was the disciple of Voltaire. You can take one page of Gibbon after another and show how he rests his feelings upon secondary authorities, who are nearly always the French rationalists of the eighteenth century.[92]

With regard to the sneering tone that Gibbon takes towards Christians and their Christian faith, the historian G. M. Young would corroborate Belloc's point:

> a historian must have an extraordinarily fine feeling for the mind of a past age before he can say with any assurance what the men of that age were likely to think or do, or what relation their reports will bear to the facts. The psychology of the eighteen century was narrow, and the French had made of it, as they made of everything, a weapon of offence against established institutions. England, with its revolutions over, its Church under control, and its Nonconformists busy making money, could afford to be large-minded. Gibbon was an Englishman, and his sense of the significance of the past is as profound and pervasive as Burke's. But of all Englishmen he is the most French. Both Burke and Johnson ... have a reserve of ease and tolerance which is lacking in the detachment of Gibbon. There is something alien in his composition, a certain knowingness, quite unlike the dogmatism of Macaulay, equally unlike the searching judgement of Tacitus, but very like that self-centered malice which to an Englishman is often the most conspicuous, and always the least agreeable, element in French literature, French manners and French diplomacy. It is the vital principle of French rationalism.[93]

Newman spent a fair amount of his long life showing up the arrogance and hollowness of rationalism. Wilfrid Ward puts this campaign in its proper historical context, a context which has everything to do with Gibbon's assault on Christianity in his highly influential history:

> Many of the ideas which the [Oxford] movement embodied had found first expression in the writings of Keble, the author of "The

---

92 Belloc to J. S. Phillimore (5 May 1917), *Letters from Hilaire Belloc*, ed. Robert Speaight (New York: The Macmillan Company 1958), 79–80.

93 G. M. Young, *Gibbon* (London: Peter Davies Limited, 1932), 74–5 Cf. Mrs. Thrale: "I have been reading Gibbons Memoirs ... There is a passage ... quoting Bishop Porteus who says Gibbons Style is obscure & affected—so it does appear to be sure enough in his *History*—but in his Letters *Not at all*. It is completely *French*; and I do believe that one Reason Gibbon had for preferring Franny Lausanne (as he called Switzerland) to *la Grand Bretagne* by way of Residence, was that her Language was more easy & familiar to him. In his Letters from the Continent a hundred periods prove to me that he commonly *thought* in French." *Thraliana: The Diary of Mrs. Hester Lynch Thrale (1776–1809)*, ed. Katherine C. Balderston (Oxford: Clarendon Press, 1951), II, 1082–3.

Christian Year." The impulse to take action had largely proceeded from the adventurous spirit of Hurrell Froude. But in Newman's own mind the movement had relation to a deeper problem than the ecclesiastical questions which exercised his two friends. His intellect was more speculative than Froude's, his thought more systematic than Keble's. In much that he wrote he was taking part in that inquiry into the foundations of all belief which the negative thinkers of the eighteenth century had made so necessary—Hume and Gibbon in England, the Encyclopedists in France. It has been truly said that the Oriel Noetic school was in some sense an outcome of the French Revolution. Both his share in their speculations and his subsequent reaction had set Newman thinking, and while Coleridge was preaching a philosophy of conservatism against Benthamism and radicalism, Newman found in the Catholic tradition latent in Anglicanism a more practical antidote to a rationalism which must issue in religious negation. It was in this deeper view of the bearing of the Anglican controversy that his standpoint differed from that of most of his colleagues.[94] From beginning to end the Catholic movement was in his eyes the only effective check on the advancing tide of unbelief. "He anticipates," testifies Mr. Aubrey de Vere some years later, 'an unprecedented outburst of infidelity all over the world, and to withstand it he deems his especial vocation.'"[95]

In *Tract 73*, which he would later entitle "On the Introduction of Rationalistic Principles into Revealed Religion," Newman nicely identified many of the intellectual misuses to which Gibbon put reason in his treatment of Christianity. He argued that

> Rationalism is a certain abuse of Reason; that is, a use of it for purposes for which it never was intended, and is unfitted. To rationalize in matters of Revelation is to make our reason the standard and measure of the doctrines revealed; to stipulate that those doctrines should be such as to carry with them their own justification; to reject them, if they come in collision with our existing opinions or habits of thought, or are with difficulty harmonized with our existing stock of knowledge. And thus a rationalistic spirit is the antagonist of Faith; for Faith is, in its very nature, the acceptance of what our reason cannot reach, simply and absolutely upon testimony.

---

94 This tersely refutes Frederick Meyrick's thesis that the Oxford Movement was simply a rehash of what the eighteenth-century High Church sought to accomplish, a thesis to which Peter Nockles helped himself without acknowledgment in his ahistorical *The Oxford Movement in Context* (1994).

95 Wilfrid Ward, *The Life of John Henry Cardinal Newman* (London: Longman, Green & Co., 1912), 57.

In making this distinction, however, Newman was not minimizing the role that right reason must play in the exercise of faith: he was ensuring that right reason maintain its acuity by maintaining its proper boundaries. For Newman,

> As regards Revealed Truth, it is not Rationalism to set about to ascertain, by the exercise of reason, what things are attainable by reason, and what are not; nor, in the absence of an express Revelation, to inquire into the truths of Religion, as they come to us by nature; nor to determine what proofs are necessary for the acceptance of a Revelation, if it be given; nor to reject a Revelation on the plea of insufficient proof; nor, after recognizing it as divine, to investigate the meaning of its declarations, and to interpret its language; nor to use its doctrines, as far as they can be fairly used, in inquiring into its divinity; nor to compare and connect them with our previous knowledge, with a view of making them parts of a whole; nor to bring them into dependence on each other, to trace their mutual relations, and to pursue them to their legitimate issues. This is not Rationalism; but it is Rationalism to accept the Revelation, and then to explain it away; to speak of it as the Word of God, and to treat it as the word of man; to refuse to let it speak for itself; to claim to be told the *why* and the *how* of God's dealings with us, as therein described, and to assign to Him a motive and a scope of our own; to stumble at the partial knowledge which He may give us of them; to put aside what is obscure, as if it had not been said at all; to accept one half of what has been told us, and not the other half; to assume that the contents of Revelation are also its proof; to frame some gratuitous hypothesis about them, and then to garble, gloss, and colour them, to trim, clip, pare away, and twist them, in order to bring them into conformity with the idea to which we have subjected them.[96]

Here, the precision of Newman's thinking is at its best, justly balancing two distinct types of reasoning that rationalists inveterately muddle and distort.[97]

No one understood these supple confusions better than St Augustine (354–430), who not only shared Gibbon's delight in rhetoric but lived

---

96 *Essays Critical and Historical*, I, 31–2.

97 In his brilliant study of Newman's lifelong fight against the rationalism of liberalism, Robert Pattison amusingly presents Newman's case for the empirical evidence of the Catholic faith as though the convert were a barrister making it in a court of law. "Newman's clients were God and the Church, whom liberalism had arraigned for fraud and deceit. The prosecution was led by Hoadly, Hume, Gibbon, Hampden, Mill—the whole bar of liberalism. How, Newman asked the jury, was the case to be decided?" The passage is unfortunately too long to quote but the upshot is that "On the very grounds of common sense to which the liberals would have recourse, the jury must deliver a verdict in favor of God and dogma." Robert Pattison, *The Great Dissent: John Henry Newman and the Liberal Heresy* (Oxford: Oxford University Press, 1991), 167–8.

through the fall of the Roman Empire after Alaric and his Vandals sacked Rome in 410.[98] In *The City of God* (427), the Bishop of Hippo anticipated the rationalist mischief of Gibbon and his French friends with what might seem uncanny prescience, though such mischief was a staple of the decaying empire—an empire whose worldly ambitions, even in its palmiest days, could never satisfy the unworldly longings of its far-flung subjects. "The unbelievers demand a rational proof from us when we proclaim the miracles of God in the past and his marvelous works that are still to come," the indomitable old bishop declared, "which we cannot present to the experience of the unbelievers. And since we cannot supply the rational proof of these matters (for they are beyond the powers of the human mind), the unbelievers assume that our statements are false, whereas they themselves ought to supply a rational explanation of all those amazing phenomena which we observe ... And if they see that this is beyond man's capacity they should admit that the fact that a rational explanation cannot be given for something does not mean that it could not have happened in the past, or that it could not happen in the future."[99] In light of these distinctions, we can begin to see how St. Augustine's *The City of God* exposes the radical defects of Gibbon's *Decline and Fall*. No anatomy of the rise of Christianity can be true that regards the faithful's appreciation of the influence of the invisible on the visible as *ipso facto* irrational. Christopher Dawson certainly recognized this when he observed of St. Augustine's heavenly city:

> Certainly the Church is not the eternal City of God but it is its organ and representative in the world. It is the point at which the transcendent spiritual order inserts itself into the sensible world, the one bridge by which the creature can pass from Time to Eternity. St. Augustine's point of view is, in fact, precisely the same as that which Newman so often expresses ... Like Augustine, Newman emphasizes the spiritual and eternal character of the City of God and regards the visible Church as its earthly manifestation. "The unseen world through God's secret power and mercy encroaches upon this; and the Church that is seen is just that portion of it by which it encroaches, it is like the islands in the sea, which are in truth but the tops of the everlasting hills, high and vast and deeply rooted, which a deluge covers."[100]

---

98 "At the hour of midnight the Salarian gate was silently opened, and the inhabitants were awakened by the tremendous sound of the Gothic trumpet. Eleven hundred and sixty-three years after the foundation of Rome, the Imperial city, which had subdued and civilised so considerable a part of mankind, was delivered to the licentious fury of the tribes of Germany and Scythia." *Decline and Fall*, III, 339.

99 St. Augustine, *The City of God*, trans. Henry Bettenson (London: Penguin Books, 2003), book XXI, ch. 5, 971.

100 Christopher Dawson, "St. Augustine and the City of God" (1930), in *The*

What is striking about Dawson's recommendation of Newman's insights into the role that the City of God plays in the fallen world is that it shows how, Newman, like St. Augustine, was, in some important respects, a true philosophical historian, certainly in the sense that, while he might not have had the learning of the seventeenth- and eighteenth-century *érudits*, he certainly had deep, imaginative insights into the underlying dynamics of history, which always distinguish the work of good philosophical historians. In his paper on Gibbon, Momigliano shows how the English historian sought to combine the strengths of the *érudits*, antiquarians like Tillemont and Leclerc, with those of the philosophical historians, less learned but often bolder thinkers like Voltaire and Montesquieu. Yet Momigliano also shows that if Gibbon successfully put himself to school to the erudition of Tillemont and the other antiquarians on whom he depended for the facts of his history, he fared less successfully when he relied on Voltaire and Montesquieu for his understanding of Christianity or the nature of Rome's imperial decline. "I have stressed the fact that Gibbon's novelty is to be found in the reconciliation of two historical methods rather than in a new interpretation of a historical period," Momigliano writes.

> But I have no doubt about the importance of the support Gibbon gave to Voltaire's thesis about the causes of the decline of Rome. This thesis is inevitably disappointing to us. The very attitude of the free-thinkers of the eighteenth century made it difficult for them to see how Christianity had worked on the world. They did not dislike Christianity because they liked Paganism, though they sometimes affected to do so. They saw in history the struggle between a few wise men, the predecessors of themselves, against the violence, the superstition and the stupidity of the majority. From their point of view, Christianity did not introduce into history anything which was really new and which therefore would explain something otherwise destined to remain unexplained. They did not only fail to appreciate the new constructive elements which Christianity introduced into moral life. They failed to understand the common people of the pagan world. They identified Paganism with a few enlightened philosophers, and not surprisingly found them to their taste. Then they came to dislike the Byzantine Empire because it was theocratic, and the Western Middle Ages because their culture was dominated by monks and priests.[101]

Throughout his various writings on the rise of Christianity, it is obvious that Newman never set out to exhibit anything even remotely like the

---

Dynamics of World History, 321. The sermon from which Dawson quotes is Newman's "The Communion of Saints" (1837), Sermon 11, in *PPS*, VI, 201.
101 Momigliano, "Gibbon's Contribution to Historical Method," 461.

scale of erudition that Gibbon exhibits in the *Decline and Fall of the Roman Empire*, but he did understand the philosophical, indeed religious, import of the history of the period far better than the Enlightenment historian.

IV

In the *Grammar of Assent,* Newman argues that the only way to make sense of the rise of Christianity is to consult the accounts of those who made the new faith their own, even unto death, and it is his ability to drive home the testimony of martyrdom that distinguishes him from the glib, sardonic Gibbon.[102] "Hagiography" is a word that Newman's latest detractors use with vulgar recklessness, but here one can see that for the historian in Newman there could be no history of Christianity without a fundamental understanding of the force of hagiography, in its primary, altogether honorable sense.

> Epipodius, a youth of gentle nurture, when struck by the Prefect on the mouth, while blood flowed from it, cried out, "I confess that Jesus Christ is God, together with the Father, and the Holy Ghost." Symphorian of Autun, also a youth, and of noble birth, when told to adore an idol, answered, "Give me leave and I will hammer it to pieces." When Leonidas, the father of the young Origen, was in prison for his faith, the boy, then seventeen, burned to share his martyrdom, and his mother had to hide his clothes to prevent him from executing his purpose. Afterwards he attended the confessors in prison, stood by them at the tribunal, and gave them the kiss of peace when they were led out to suffer, and this, in spite of being several times apprehended and put upon the rack. Also in Alexandria, the beautiful slave, Potamiæna, when about to be stripped in order to be thrown into the cauldron of hot pitch, said to the Prefect, "I pray you rather let me be dipped down slowly into it with my clothes on, and you shall see with what patience I am gifted by Him of whom you are ignorant, Jesus Christ." When the populace in the same city had beaten out the aged Apollonia's teeth and lit a fire to burn her, unless she would blaspheme, she leaped into the fire herself, and so gained her crown. When Sixtus, Bishop of Rome, was led to martyrdom, his deacon, Laurence, followed him weeping and complaining, "O my father, whither goest thou without thy son?" And when his own turn came, three

---

102 Cf. "When we read the narrative of a cocksure historian, we tend to forget that the historian can never speak with first-hand authority: he can only piece together the accounts of others." A. J. P. Taylor, "Tory History" (1950), *From Napoleon to the Second International: Essays on Nineteenth-Century Europe,* ed. Chris Wrigley (London: Allen Lane: The Penguin Press, 1993), 45–6.

days afterwards, and he was put upon the gridiron, after a while he said to the Prefect, "Turn me; this side is done." Whence came this tremendous spirit, scaring, nay, offending, the fastidious criticism of our delicate days? Does Gibbon think to sound the depths of the eternal ocean with the tape and measuring-rod of his merely literary philosophy?[103]

If the weight that Newman gives to the evidence of martyrdom puts him at odds with the rationalist history that grew up under the auspices of the Enlightenment, Pocock acknowledges the force of Newman's Catholic view of history by showing how Gibbon—in many respects the Enlightenment historian *par excellence*—deliberately set out to undermine it. In *Barbarism and Religion*, his exhaustive study of Gibbon and the intellectual roots of *The Decline and Fall of the Roman Empire*, Pocock observes how, before the Enlightenment, the history of Christianity "could be written as a branch of sacred history, the church militant as the church triumphant; or it could be written as a history of human actions and passions, and for the great Christian historians the secret lay in the interplay between the two modes of the church's existence." Pocock is fair-minded enough to concede that "Since these corresponded with the two natures of Christ, the writing of history had Christological and theological connotations." Indeed, Pocock insists, we "should recall Cardinal Newman's dictum that to write a civil history of the church necessarily had Socinian consequences, since it entailed a diminution of Christ's divine as opposed to his human nature."[104] He then proceeds to show how Enlightenment history chose as its very *raison d'être* the overturning of Christian truth.

> Since [Christ] had been born in the days of Caesar Augustus and had suffered under Pontius Pilate, his mission on earth, and that of the church after him, had conducted in confrontation with the tremendous edifice of the jurisdiction of the Roman empire, and the history of the Church was seen to consist very largely of the

---

103 *Grammar of Assent*, 310.

104 Speaking of Henry Hart Milman's *History of Christianity to the Abolition of Paganism in the Roman Empire* (1840), Newman wrote: "For the fact is undeniable, little as Mr. Milman may be aware of it, that this external contemplation of Christianity necessarily leads a man to write as a Socinian or Unitarian *would* write, whether he will or not. Mr. Milman has not been able to avoid this dreadful disadvantage, and thus, however heartily he may hate the opinions of such men himself, he has unintentionally both given scandal to his brethren and cause of triumph to the enemy. A very few words will account for this. The great doctrines which the Socinian denies are our Lord's divinity and atonement; now these are not external facts;—what he confesses are His humanity and crucifixion; these *are* external facts. Mr. Milman then is bound by his theory to dwell on the latter, to slur over the former." Newman, "Milman's View of Christianity" (1841), in *Essays Critical and Historical*, II, 202.

erection of another system of jurisdiction whose authority was that of the Spirit. When this in turn came to be challenged, it was sometimes in the name of the civil authority as party to the jurisdiction, sometimes in the name of the Spirit held to act independently of all jurisdiction whatsoever. Each of these claims entailed a certain writing of history sacred, ecclesiastical and civil; but what we have to do with under the name of Enlightenment is an attempt to make civil society paramount, irrespective of the theological consequences and at any cost to history sacred and ecclesiastical.[105]

Of course, Newman entirely rejects this Socinian school of history, not out of any sectarian special pleading but simply because it is false, indeed, ahistorical. Apropos the reality of the Resurrection and what it means for human history, he shares with his readers a dimension of that history that they will look for in vain in Gibbon and his rationalist descendants.[106]

> Corruption had no power over that Sacred Body, the fruit of a miraculous conception. The bonds of death were broken as "green withes," witnessing by their feebleness that He was the Son of God. Such is the connexion between Christ's birth and resurrection ... He who had deigned to be born of a woman, and to hang upon the cross, had subtle virtue in Him, like a spirit, to pass through the closed doors to His assembled followers; while, by condescending to the trial of their senses, He showed that it was no mere spirit, but He Himself, as before, with wounded hands and pierced side, who spoke to them. He manifested Himself to them, in this His exalted state, that they might be His witnesses to the people; witnesses of those separate truths which man's reason cannot combine, that He had a real human body, that it was partaker in the properties of His Soul, and that it was inhabited by the Eternal Word ... Thus manifested as perfect God and perfect man, in the fulness of His sovereignty, and the immortality of His holiness, He ascended up on high to take possession of His kingdom ... Yet we must not suppose, that in leaving us He closed the gracious economy of His Incarnation, and withdrew the ministration of His incorruptible Manhood from His work of loving mercy towards us. "The Holy One of God" was ordained, not only to die for us, but also to be

---

105 Pocock, *Barbarism and Religion*, II, 11–12.
106 While it is true that Newman deplored Gibbon's irreligious treatment of the rise of Christianity, he would not have disputed the historian Peter Green's point that "the Voltairean revolution" in history "had much on its side." For Green, as for Gibbon, "it had broken out of the strait-jacket of political and military narrative to analyze such basic elements of civilization as law, religion, education and commerce—an enormous methodological advance on the essentially static concepts of antiquity." Peter Green, *Essays in Antiquity* (London: John Murray, 1960), 60–1. What Newman did dispute about this revolution was its claims to historical rigor.

"the beginning" of a new "creation" unto holiness, in our sinful race; to refashion soul and body after His own likeness, that they might be "raised up together, and sit together in heavenly places in Christ Jesus."[107]

These are the truths that the martyrs lay down their lives to attest. And for Newman it follows that

> nothing can harm those who bear Christ within them. Trial or temptation, time of tribulation, time of wealth, pain, bereavement, anxiety, sorrow, the insults of the enemy, the loss of worldly goods, nothing can "separate us from the love of God, which is in Christ Jesus our Lord." [Rom. 8:39] This the Apostle told us long since; but we, in this age of the world, over and above his word, have the experience of many centuries for our comfort. We have his own history to show us how Christ within us is stronger than the world around us, and will prevail. We have the history of all his fellow-sufferers, of all the Confessors and Martyrs of early times and since, to show us that Christ's arm "is not shortened, that it cannot save;" that faith and love have a real abiding-place on earth.[108]

And so, again, to validate his claim with respect to the true history of the rise of Christianity, Newman adduces the evidence of the martyrs:

> When the persecution raged in Asia, a vast multitude of Christians presented themselves before the Proconsul, challenging him to proceed against them. "Poor wretches!" half in contempt and half in affright, he answered, "if you must die, cannot you find ropes or precipices for the purpose?" At Utica, a hundred and fifty Christians of both sexes and all ages were martyrs in one company. They are said to have been told to burn incense to an idol, or they should be thrown into a pit of burning lime; they without hesitation leapt into it. In Egypt a hundred and twenty confessors, after having sustained the loss of eyes or of feet, endured to linger out their lives in the mines of Palestine and Cilicia. In the last persecution, according to the testimony of the grave Eusebius, a contemporary, the slaughter of men, women, and children, went on by twenties, sixties, hundreds, till the instruments of execution were worn out, and the executioners could kill no more. Yet he tells us, as an eye-witness, that, as soon as any Christians were condemned, others ran from all parts, and surrounded the tribunals, confessing the faith, and joyfully receiving their condemnation, and singing songs of thanksgiving and triumph to the last.[109]

---

107 Newman, "Christ, A Quickening Spirit" (1831), Sermon 13, in *PPS*, II, 143–4.
108 *Ibid.*, 149–50.
109 *Grammar of Assent*, 311.

Newman's authority for many of these martyrdoms is the evidence offered by the eyewitness historian Eusebius (*c.* 264–340), which Gibbon regards as inadmissible on the grounds that the "gravest of the ecclesiastical historians," as he calls him, only cited evidence favorable to the Christians.

> It would have been an easy task, from the history of Eusebius … and from the most ancient acts, to collect a long series of horrid and disgustful pictures, and to fill many pages with racks and scourges, with iron hooks, and red-hot beds, and with all the variety of tortures which fire and steel, savage beasts and more savage executioners, could inflict on the human body. These melancholy scenes might be enlivened by the crowd of visions and miracles destined either to delay the death, to celebrate the triumph, or to discover the relics of those canonized saints who suffered for the name of Christ. But I cannot determine what I ought to transcribe, till I am satisfied how much I ought to believe. The gravest of the ecclesiastical historians, Eusebius himself, indirectly confesses that he has related whatever might redound to the glory, and that he has suppressed all that could tend to the disgrace, of religion.[110]

In fact, Eusebius openly admits that he chose not to cite the evidence of those who failed to witness to the Faith; he does not claim that there was no evidence of Christians failing to witness to the Faith. After all, he was writing for fellow Christians and to have included accounts of Christians failing to witness to the Faith would have been demoralizing. Such omissions, however, do not nullify his accounts of the martyrdoms of those who did witness to the Faith. Newman, therefore, is justified in following Eusebius in regarding what the historian called the "hallowed ordeals of the martyrs of God's Word" as the decisive factor in the rise of Christianity.[111]

According to Eusebius, before Constantine converted in the fourth century and made the Roman Empire tolerant of Christianity, "It was the one object in life of the enemies of true religion to gain credit for having finished the job. But no such methods could enable them to dispose of the holy martyrs." During the Great Persecution of Diocletian of 303–5, when, as Eusebius states, "an imperial decree was published everywhere, ordering the churches to be razed to the ground and the Scriptures destroyed by fire, and giving notice that those in places of honour would lose their places, and domestic staff, if they continued to profess Christianity, the eyewitness historian pointedly concedes that not all Christians stood firm. The fearful trials of persecution caused some to make "shipwreck of their

---

110 *Decline and Fall*, II, 144.
111 Eusebius, *The History of the Church from Christ to Constantine*, trans. G. A. Wiliamson, revised and edited with an introduction by Andrew Louth (Harmondsworth: Penguin Books, 1989), 235.

salvation."[112] Yet many did stand firm, and it is of these that Eusebius speaks most movingly in his history. "What could I say that would do full justice to them? I could tell of thousands who showed magnificent enthusiasm for the worship of the God of the universe, not only from the beginning of the general persecution, but much earlier when peace was still secure ... a great many soldiers of Christ's Kingdom without hesitation or question chose to confess Him rather than cling to the outward glory and prosperity they enjoyed."[113]

Then, again, to substantiate not only the force of martyrdom but the divine aspects behind the rise of Christianity, Newman cites Origen (c. 185–254):

> In all Greece and in all barbarous races within our world, there are tens of thousands who have left their national laws and customary gods for the law of Moses and the word of Jesus Christ; though to adhere to that law is to incur the hatred of idolaters, and the risk of death besides to have embraced that word. And considering how, in so few years, in spite of the attacks made on us, to the loss of life or property, and with no great store of teachers, the preaching of that word has found its way into every part of the world, so that Greek and barbarians, wise and unwise, adhere to the religion of Jesus, doubtless it is a work greater than any work of man.[114]

Newman's appreciation of the crucial role that martyrdom played in the rise of Christianity is also borne out by later historians. In 1942, Christopher Dawson invoked these martyrs to encourage his readers to continue to withstand the totalitarian evil of the Nazis:

> As the first epoch in the history of freedom is marked by the rise of the free Greek cities and their struggle with Persia, the second is marked by the rise of the Christian Church and its struggle with the

---

112 *Ibid.*, 235.
113 *Ibid.*, 236.
114 Origen, quoted in *Grammar of Assent*, 305–6. Cf. "If passing from unbelief to faith means that we have *passed from death to life*, we should not be surprised to find that *the world hates us*. Anyone who has not *passed from death to life* is incapable of loving those who have departed from death's dark dwelling place to enter a dwelling *made of living stones* and filled with the light of life. Jesus *laid down his life for us*; so we too should lay down our lives, I will not say for him, but for ourselves and also, surely, for those who will be helped by the example of our martyrdom. Now is the time for Christians to rejoice, since Scripture says that *we should rejoice in our sufferings, knowing that suffering trains us to endure with patience, patient endurance makes us pleasing to God, and being pleasing to God gives us ground for a hope that will not be disappointed. Only let the love of God be poured forth in our hearts through the Holy Spirit* [Romans 5:5]." Origen, *Exhortation to Martyrdom* (AD 235). Origen wrote his *Exhortation* during the persecution of Maximianus (235–8).

Roman Empire which had lost the ideals of citizenship and political freedom and was rapidly becoming a vast servile state like those of the ancient East. The battle was fought out under the shadow of the executioners' rods and axes in praetoria and amphitheatres and concentration camps from Germany to Africa and from Spain to Armenia, and its heroes were the martyrs--Martyrum candidatus exercitus.[115]

In the *First Thousand Years: A Global History of Christianity* (2012), Robert Louis Wilken confirms the influence that martyrdom exerted over the world of the early Christians. When Galerius, the Proconsul approached Cyprian of Carthage in 251 and asked whether he would perform the religious rights demanded of the most reverend emperors, Cyprian refused. According to the *Acts of Cyprian*," Galerius then sentenced him to death. "You have been convicted as the instigator and leader of a most atrocious crime, you will be an example for all those whom in your wickedness you have gathered to yourself." Here, at least, Galerius could not have been more right. "'When the executioner came,'" as Wilkin relates, quoting the *Acts*: "'Cyprian told his friends to give the man twenty-five gold pieces. His brothers spread cloths and napkins in front of him.'" They wished to soak up his blood so they could become holy objects to be venerated after his death."[116] Moreover, as Wilken shows, Cyprian certainly saw what a force martyrdom was for the spread of Christianity. For him,

> The martyrs defined the true nature of the Church. One tiny detail makes this clear. He instructed his presbyters to give special care to the bodies of the martyrs in Carthage. He wished them not only to see to their proper burial, but also to keep a record of the day on which each martyr died. "If we know the date of their martyrdom," said Cyprian, "we will be able to include the celebration of their memories in our commemoration of the martyrs." It was to this community, the company of the martyrs, that the lapsed must be reconciled. The faithful dead created a vivid memory that the living belonged to a unique fellowship.[117]

And in this way, Cyprian was convinced, the Church could preserve her primitive integrity when, as Wilken says, "To become a Christian meant a break with family and friends, neighbors, colleagues, and business associates. The norms of behavior were set very high."[118]

---

115 Christopher Dawson, *The Judgment of the Nations* (New York: Sheed & Ward, 1942), 63–4.
116 Robert Louis Wilken, *The First Thousand Years: A Global History of Christianity* (New Haven: Yale University Press, 2012), 73–4.
117 *Ibid.*, 71.
118 *Ibid.*, 74.

For Newman, "Thus was the Roman power overcome. Thus did the Seed of Abraham, and the Expectation of the Gentiles, the meek Son of man, 'take to Himself His great power and reign' in the hearts of His people, in the public theatre of the world. The mode in which the primeval prophecy was fulfilled is as marvellous, as the prophecy itself is clear and bold."[119] For Gibbon, interpreting the martyrdom of Cyprian required precisely that "philosophical ingenuity," as Newman called it, with which the historian would regard all aspects of the Church.

> It was in the choice of Cyprian either to die a martyr or to live an apostate, but on that choice depended the alternative of honour or infamy. Could we suppose that the bishop of Carthage had employed the profession of the Christian faith only as the instrument of his avarice or ambition, it was still incumbent on him to support the character which he had assumed; and, if he possessed the smallest degree of manly fortitude, rather to expose himself to the most cruel tortures than by a single act to exchange the reputation of a whole life for the abhorrence of his Christian brethren and the contempt of the Gentile world. But, if the zeal of Cyprian was supported by the sincere conviction of the truth of those doctrines which he preached, the crown of martyrdom must have appeared to him as an object of desire rather than of terror.[120]

The Gibbon scholar David Womersley furnishes an admiring gloss on Gibbon's interpretation of Cyprian and his martyrdom, which shows how, for the liberal academy, Gibbon's cynicism, far from being any defect in the historian, is part and parcel of the merits of his literary and historical achievement: "Gibbon's whole account of Cyprian's martyrdom is calculated to keep in play ... the interpretation which here he seems to raise only to dismiss for its orthodox alternative; namely, that 'the bishop of Carthage had employed the profession of the Christian faith only as the instrument of his avarice and ambition;' and that therefore his martyrdom was an instance of a paradoxical aspect of human nature—heroic hypocrisy."[121] In contrast, Lord Brougham's gloss may not be quite as nuanced as Womersley's but it has the ring of truth. Having given it as his opinion that Gibbon's "sixteenth chapter must for ever be, in an especial manner, a monument of [the historian's] gross injustice or incurable prejudice," the Whig reformer goes on to take radical issue with the particular interpretation that Womersley is content to see in merely literary terms. For Brougham,

---

119 *Grammar of Assent*, 311–12.
120 *Decline and Fall*, II, 109–10.
121 David Womersley, *Gibbon and the "Watchmen of the Holy City": The Historian and his Reputation, 1776–1815* (Oxford: Oxford University Press, 2002), 115–16.

> [Gibbon's] account of Cyprian's martyrdom is as unfair as it could be without deceit and positive falsehood—casting a veil over all the most horrible atrocities practised on that amiable and innocent personage, and magnifying into acts of clemency exercised towards him every insignificant attention that was paid him—perverting, too, the truth of history, in order to feign circumstances which really do not appear vouched by any kind of authority. But nothing can be more preposterous than the elaborate description which he gives of the comforts derived by the sufferers in these cruel scenes from the glory of martyrdom, and from the great preference which they must have given it over the disgrace of apostasy.[122]

Unsurprisingly, for Gibbon, the commemoration of the martyrs envisioned by Cyprian only proved that "In the long period of twelve hundred years, which elapsed from between the reign of Constantine and the Reformation of Luther, the worship of saints and relics corrupted the pure and perfect simplicity of the Christian model; and some symptoms of degeneracy may be observed even in the first generation which adopted and cherished this pernicious innovation."[123] Nevertheless, for the historian of Christianity, the historian whom even Newman acknowledged as England's "sole authority for subjects as near the heart of a Christian as any can well be," this was still an arresting admission.[124] As Algernon Cecil justly observes:

> The purity, the enthusiasm, the calm serenity of the Primitive Church passed before his eyes. He treated of them with the same cold and critical indifference as he meted out to the vices of Elagabalus;[125] unaware, apparently, that he was reviewing the rise of a movement, the like of which had never been seen before, nor ever will be again ... It is not that he misstates facts, but that the facts as we know them admit of two possible explanations, and that he has preferred to adopt, apparently without a shadow of regret, the baser one. Fifty years later, from the pulpit of St Mary's, Newman surveyed the same ground with an eye trained to discern spiritual things.[126]

---

122 *The Works of Henry, Lord Brougham*, II, 426–7. Those of my readers familiar with Newman's deep dislike of Brougham and his indefatigable Whiggery might see my citing him to throttle Gibbon as rather comical, but we must take our cudgels where we find them.

123 *Decline and Fall*, III, 221.

124 Newman, "Milman's View of Christianity," in *Essays Critical and Historical*, II, 186.

125 "The richest wines, the most extraordinary victims, and the rarest aromatics were profusely consumed on [Elagabalus's] altar. Around the altar a chorus of Syrian damsels performed their lascivious dances to the sound of barbarian music, whilst the gravest personages of the state and army, clothed in long Phoenician tunics, officiated in the meanest functions, with affected zeal and secret indignation." *Decline and Fall*, I, 158.

126 Algernon Cecil, *Six Oxford Thinkers* (London: John Murray, 1909), 38.

The founder of *The Economist*, Walter Bagehot (1826–77) shared Cecil's reservations about Gibbon's understanding of the history he so meticulously documented. For Bagehot, the style was the man: Gibbon was

> a bachelor ... equable and secular; cautious in his habits, tolerant in his creed, as Porson said, "never failing in natural feeling except when women were to be ravished and Christians to be martyred."[127] His writings are in character. The essence of the far-famed fifteenth and sixteenth chapters is, in truth, but a description of unworldly events in the tone of this world, of awful facts in unmoved voice, of truths of the heart in the language of the eyes. The wary sceptic has not even committed himself to definite doubts.[128]

Even Virginia Woolf, the daughter of the impeccably skeptical Leslie Stephen, found something distasteful about Gibbon's assaults on the integrity of Christians. "However grave and temperate are Gibbon's irony at its best, however searching his logic and robust his contempt for the cruelty and intolerance of superstition, we sometimes feel, as he pursues his victim with incessant scorn, that he is a little limited, a little superficial, a little earthly, a little too positively and imperturbably a man of the eighteenth century."[129]

Apropos this crucial question of martyrdom, Gibbon's definitive biographer, Patricia Craddock (who could not show her subject more judicious sympathy) makes a vital point:

> In addition to reducing the exaggerated traditional claims about the numbers of early Christian martyrs to something more factual, chapter 16 sought to analyze the conflict between the old Empire and the new Church so as to give a sympathetic appreciation of the former ... It was a bold move to denounce Christian intolerance

---

[127] Richard Porson (1759–1809) was an English classical scholar, who, referring to Gibbon's ribald sense of humor, wrote: "Nor does his humanity slumber, unless when women are ravished, or the Christians persecuted ... A less pardonable fault [is] a rage for indecency ... If the history were anonymous, I should guess that these disgraceful obscenities were written by some debauchee, who having from age, or accident, or excess, survived the practice of lust, still indulged himself in the luxury of speculation." Richard Porson, *Letter to Mr. Archdeacon Travis* (London, 1790), xxviii–xxxi. After entering Lincoln's Inn, Lord John Campbell, the judge who presided over Newman's Achilli trial, would often go to the Cider Club, where he enjoyed "the company of an inebriated Porson." See the article on Campbell in *The Oxford Dictionary of National Biography* (Oxford: Oxford University Press, 2004).

[128] Walter Bagehot, "Edward Gibbon" (1856), in *The Collected Works of Walter Bagehot*, ed. Norman St. John-Stevas (London: The Economist, 1965), I, 386. Cf. "style is the image of character," and "The style of an author should be the image of his mind." *Memoirs of Edward Gibbon*, 36 and 166.

[129] Virginia Woolf, "The Historian and 'The Gibbon'" (1937), in *The Death of the Moth and Other Essays* (New York: Harcourt Brace Javonovich, 1970), 89.

in the context in which Christians most clearly were being victimized, and it is clear that Gibbon's effort to dramatize the outrage of Christian intolerance by contrasting it with the rational and humane requirements of the pagan state religion ... failed on two counts. First, he allows himself to seem to treat real sufferings callously and therefore puts himself and his cause in the wrong ... Second, he totally fails to understand the reasons for the martyrs' actions. He thinks of them as defending opinions; martyrs, by definition, think of themselves as defending truths.[130]

Nothing in the mountainous secondary literature surrounding Gibbon and his history exposes his failure to enter into the reality of martyrdom more persuasively than this, especially since it comes from a source so entirely partial to the historian. But there is another observation that Prof. Craddock makes about her subject that is also worth keeping in mind. "Certainly Christians had every reason to object to his contemptuous tone," she writes, "and they might also have complained about his rhetorical strategies, for in this section of the history [Chapter XVI] he does not depend on narrative or argument alone to carry his points, but attempts to discredit the Christian positon with his readers by arousing their anti-Semitism and snobbery."[131]

V

When the first volume of Gibbon's *Decline and Fall* appeared in 1776, there was a certain outcry from pulpits across the country. The response that Gibbon makes in his *Memoirs* to this indignation shows that he had a fairly good sense of the peculiar audience whose sensitivities he meant to rattle. "Had I believed that the majority of English readers were so fondly attached even to the name and shadow of Christianity—had I foreseen that the pious, the timid, and the prudent would feel, or affect to feel, with such exquisite sensibility—I might perhaps have softened the two invidious chapters, which would create many enemies and conciliate few friends. But the shaft was shot, the alarm was sounded, and I could only rejoice that if the voice of our priests was clamorous and bitter, their hands were disarmed from the powers of persecution."[132] This was fair mockery from

---

130 Craddock, *Edward Gibbon, Luminous Historian,* 64.

131 *Ibid.*. Speaking of the Jews in the years before the birth of Christ, the great admirer of the tolerance of Antonine Rome remarks: "The sullen obstinacy with which they maintained their peculiar rites and unsocial manners, seemed to mark them out a distinct species of men, who boldly professed, or who faintly disguised, their implacable hatred to the rest of human-kind." *Decline and Fall,* II, 3.

132 *Memoirs of Edward Gibbon,* 173.

an author who knew how threadbare the faith of the English National Church had become by the eighteenth century. Yet what Womersley makes of the historian's gibe points to an important aspect of rationalist history.

> Gibbon's ideas on the origin and progress of Christianity were at many points identical to, or derivable from, the work of the most orthodox toilers in the vineyard of the protestant Enlightenment, such as Johann Lorenz von Mosheim.[133] What shocked many of Gibbon's readers was the way chapters 15 and 16 demonstrated how easily that same work could support irreligious beliefs. It was his very proximity to the orthodox which made Gibbon's book both so offensive and so difficult to demolish. Yet its implication, that the governing oligarchy of Hanoverian England, to which the *Decline and Fall* was addressed and from within which it was composed, was a cadre of tolerant but unbelieving magistrates, and its rule a government of the credulous by the indifferent, could not pass unchallenged.[134]

Womersley cites Mosheim's *sola scriptura* portrayal of the rise of Christianity because he imagines it somehow validates Gibbon's decision to focus on the externals of the Church at the expense of her substance. After all, as Pocock writes, "Since truth [according to Mosheim] was in the Scriptures and not in the Church, there was no obstacle to presenting the Church as a human association located in history, exposed to the contingencies and displaying the characteristics common to other human associations whose histories could be narrated."[135] Here, however, we can see the blatantly anachronistic character of rationalist history. If history largely consists in "facing the facts," as the rationalist historian is fond of reminding his readers, no historian can write a factual history of the rise of Christianity based on an understanding of the Christian Faith that would have meant nothing to the early Christians themselves.

The definitive biographer of Newman, Ian Ker is witty on the wrongheadedness of imagining that Christianity can be understood through any *sola scriptura* lens:

---

[133] Johann Lorenz von Mosheim (1693–1755), a *sola scriptura* Lutheran church historian. In 1831, Newman wrote a correspondent: "I am engaged in a history of the Principal Councils as illustrative of the doctrines of the Articles. It is a truly interesting work, and I am led to fancy I may be able to throw some lights upon the subject. — The standard Divines are magnificent fellows, but then they are Antiquarians or Doctrinists, not Ecclesiastical Historians — Bull, Waterland, Petavius, Baronius and the rest — of the historians I have met with I have a very low opinion — Mosheim, Gibbon, Middleton, Milner, etc." Newman to Samuel Rickards (30 October 1831), in *LD*, II, 371.

[134] David Womersley, "Gibbon, Edward (1737–94)," in *The Oxford Dictionary of National Biography*.

[135] Pocock, *Barbarism and Religion*, V, 166.

> Those Christians ... who claim that they get their beliefs from the Bible as opposed to any church, might reasonably have expected to find the central Protestant doctrine of justification by faith alone categorically and specifically stated by Jesus. If one thinks that everything depends on the written Scriptures, it is hard not to convict Jesus of a certain willful negligence. It is not as if He was some unlettered teacher; He could certainly read and write as the Gospels make plain. If Jesus' message and mission were intended to be carried on and propagated by means of written texts, it is hard not to conclude that the job was strangely botched.

Instead, it is clear that Our Lord was not a scribbler: he was a doer. "On one occasion, for example," Father Ker reminds his readers, "He cured a blind man not by words but by spitting on the ground and making a paste with the spittle, which He applied to the man's eyes. This mysterious teacher and miracle-worker by no means relied only on words. There was a strange earthiness attached to much of what He did, which sits uncomfortably with any concept of a religion bound up exclusively with the written word of the Bible."[136]

Another reason why Womersley and Pocock cite Mosheim is because they wish to suggest that the *sola scriptura* historian vindicates Gibbon's depiction of what he saw as the defining corruption of the Church in the fourth and fifth centuries, even though Mosheim paints this corruption to show how Lutheranism was the necessary reform of Catholic corruption; while for Gibbon, all Christian history, Catholic and Protestant was corrupt. Nevertheless, the historian Owen Chadwick was right when he observed that "Sometimes the reader of Gibbon half fancies that he is reading a reflection of historical theory among Protestant warriors: "the triumph of barbarism and religion" meaning what the Protestant historians conceived as "the triumph of barbarism and superstition."[137] Certainly one can see English Protestant warriors reveling in this well-known passage from Chapter XLIX of the *Decline and Fall*:

> In the long night of superstition, the Christians had wandered far away from the simplicity of the gospel; nor was it easy for them to discern the clue, and tread back the mazes, of the labyrinth. The worship of images was inseparably blended, at least to a pious

---

136 Ian Ker, *Mere Catholicism* (Steubenville: Emmaus Road Publishing, 2006), 29–30.

137 Chadwick, "Gibbon and the Church Historians," 114. Chadwick also quotes Gibbon's estimate of Leclerc to suggest that the Enlightenment historian might have had more self-knowledge than he usually let on; perhaps even a penchant for self-mockery, which is not untypical of learned exiles: "He reduces the reason or folly of the ages to the standard of his private judgment," Gibbon wrote of Leclerc, "and this impartiality is sometimes quickened, and sometimes tainted, by his opposition to the fathers." *Ibid.*, 115.

fancy, with the Cross, the Virgin, the saints, and their relics; the holy ground was involved in a cloud of miracles and visions; and the nerves of the mind, curiosity and scepticism, were benumbed by the habits of obedience and belief. Constantine himself is accused of indulging a royal licence to doubt, or deny, or deride the mysteries of the Catholics, but they were deeply inscribed in the public and private creed of his bishops; and the boldest Iconoclast might assault with a secret horror the monuments of popular devotion, which were consecrated to the honour of his celestial patrons. In the reformation of the sixteenth century, freedom and knowledge had expanded all the faculties of man, the thirst of innovation superseded the reverence of antiquity, and the vigour of Europe could disdain those phantoms which terrified the sickly and servile weakness of the Greeks.[138]

While much is made of Gibbon's irony, it hardly mitigates or refines his thoroughgoing contempt for the Church, and it certainly never attains to anything like the satirical force of Newman's irony. In *Lectures on the Present Position of Catholics in England* (1851), in which the newly converted Newman got at the root of the Protestant Englishman's fanciful notions about his national identity by locating them squarely in his even more fanciful notions of the progress of the Christian faith. There, Newman explains that for English Protestants, "Christianity was very pure in the beginning, was very corrupt in the middle age, and is very pure again in England now, though still corrupt everywhere else." Moreover, as Newman explains, "in the middle age, a tyrannical institution called the Church arose and swallowed up Christianity." Fortunately, however, "the Church is alive still, and has not yet disgorged its prey, except, as aforesaid, in our own favoured country." The reason this should be the case is simple. As Newman describes it, "in the middle age, there was no Christianity anywhere at all, but all was dark and horrible, as bad as paganism, or rather much worse. No one knew anything about God, or whether there was a God or no, nor about Christ or His atonement; for the Blessed Virgin, and Saints, and the Pope, and images, were worshipped instead; and thus, so far from religion benefitting the generations of mankind who lived in that dreary time, it did them infinitely more harm than good."[139]

Here Newman's satirical wit nicely exposes how English Protestants resolutely refused to consider the real course of ecclesiastical history, a refusal first exhibited by Gibbon's *Decline and Fall*, where scoffing and mockery take the place of any equitable criticism of Christianity's true progress. Yet what Newman found most objectionable about Gibbon's

---

138 *Decline and Fall*, V, 270–1.
139 *Present Position of Catholics*, 12–13.

polemical treatment of Christianity was not that it could be made to tally with unorthodox theology—that was a given—but that it prefigured the widespread infidelity to which liberalism would give rise in the nineteenth century, and not only infidelity but what was even more distressing to Newman, rank, unreflecting unbelief. In considering Gibbon's personal life, Leslie Stephen showed how the historian contributed to this unbelief.

> If such a life has less vivid passages, is there not something fascinating about that calm, harmonious existence, disturbed by no spasmodic storms, and yet devoted to one achievement grand enough to extort admiration even from the least sympathetic? Surely it is a happy mean: enough genius to be in the front rank, if not in the highest class, and yet that kind of genius which has no affinity to madness or disease, and virtue enough to keep up to the respectable level which justifies a comfortable self-complacency without suggesting any awkward deviations in the direction of martyrdom.[140]

After Gibbon, many Englishmen would join Stephen in seeing a "comfortable self-complacency" as the end of life and martyrdom as an "awkward deviation." And for literary men this usually meant that the thing to which they aspired most was literary fame. Indeed, in the eighteenth century, as the historian Keith Thomas points out, "it was unbelievers, like the philosopher David Hume and the historian Edward Gibbon, who were most concerned with literary fame. There was a close association between religious scepticism and the attempts of the Hanoverian aristocracy to preserve their memory by constructing great mausoleums, set in parks or on hillsides, deliberately detached from any religious context."[141] Gibbon was convinced that this "lust for fame" was so general that he cited it as an agent of martyrdom:

> It is not easy to extract any distinct ideas from the vague though eloquent declamations of the Fathers or to ascertain the degree of immortal glory and happiness which they confidently promised to those who were so fortunate as to shed their blood in the cause of religion. They inculcated with becoming diligence that the fire of martyrdom supplied every defect and expiated every sin; that, while the souls of ordinary Christians were obliged to pass through a slow and painful purification, the triumphant sufferers entered into the immediate fruition of eternal bliss, where, in the society of the

---

140 Leslie Stephen, "Autobiography," in *Hours in a Library* (London: Folio Society, 1991), III, 252.

141 Keith Thomas, *The Ends of Life: Roads to Fulfilment in Early Modern England* (Oxford: Oxford University Press, 2009), 241.

patriarchs, the apostles, and the prophets, they reigned with Christ, and acted as his assessors in the universal judgment of mankind. The assurance of a lasting reputation upon earth, a motive so congenial to the vanity of human nature, often served to animate the courage of the martyrs. The honours which Rome or Athens bestowed on those citizens who had fallen in the cause of their country were cold and unmeaning demonstrations of respect, when compared with the ardent gratitude and devotion which the primitive church expressed towards the victorious champions of the faith.[142]

Needless to say, the scientific historian in Gibbon never shares with his readers the evidence on which he bases his claim that "The assurance of a lasting reputation upon earth, a motive so congenial to the vanity of human nature, often served to animate the courage of the martyrs." Nonetheless, precisely because of his own "lust for fame," Gibbon must have been pleased when David Hume wrote to congratulate him on the completion of his *Decline and Fall*:

> Whether I consider the dignity of your style, the depth of your matter, or the extensiveness of your learning, I must regard the work as equally the object of esteem; I own, that if I had not previously had the happiness of your personal acquaintance, such a performance, from an Englishman in our age, would have given me some surprise. You may smile at this sentiment; but as it seems to me that your countrymen, for almost a whole generation, have given themselves up to barbarous and absurd faction, and have totally neglected all polite letters, I no longer expected any valuable production ever to come from them.[143]

This was welcome praise because, as Nicholas Phillipson observes, Hume's groundbreaking essay, "Of Superstition and Enthusiasm" (1741), had had a profound influence on Gibbon. "Indeed, it is the starting point for nearly all subsequent secular thinking about the history of religion. Its main purpose was to analyze the political implications of religious thought and to show that both superstition and enthusiasm had potentially disastrous consequences for political stability. Psychologically, religious superstition was the natural offspring of 'weakness, fear, melancholy, together with ignorance,' and that in turn encouraged priestcraft."[144] — the most frightful of Enlightenment bugbears, the source of all pious oppression and sacerdotal chicane.

---

142 *Decline and Fall*, II, 110–11.
143 David Hume to Edward Gibbon (18 March 1776), in *Life and Correspondence of David Hume*, ed. John Hill Burton (Edinburgh: W. Tait, 1846), II, 484.
144 Nicholas Phillipson, *David Hume: The Philosopher as Historian* (New Haven: Yale University Press, 2012), 66.

Yet, despite the anticlerical views that he shared with Hume, Gibbon appeared to side with Edmund Burke when his *Reflections of the Revolution in France* (1790) were published. To Lord Sheffield, he wrote in May of 1791, "Should you admire the National Assembly, we shall have many an altercation, for I am as high an aristocrat as Burke himself; and he has truly observed that it is impossible to debate with temper on the subject of that cursed Revolution."[145] However, what exactly Gibbon thought when he read Burke contending, as he does here, that it was the *philosophes'* attack on religion that led to the confiscatory anarchy and bloodshed of the Revolution is not so clear.

> In the long series of ages which have furnished the matter of history, never was so beautiful and so august a spectacle presented to the moral eye, as Europe afforded the day before the Revolution in France. I knew indeed that this prosperity contained in itself the seeds of its own danger. In one part of the society it caused laxity and debility; in the other it produced bold spirits and dark designs. A false philosophy passed from academies into courts; and the great themselves were infected with the theories which conducted to their ruin. Knowledge, which in the two last centuries either did not exist at all, or existed solidly on right principles and in chosen hands, was now diffused, weakened, and perverted. General wealth loosened morals, relaxed vigilance, and increased presumption. Men of talent began to compare, in the partition of the common stock of publick prosperity, the proportions of the dividends with the merits of the claimants. As usual, they found their portion not equal to their estimate (or perhaps to the publick estimate) of their own worth. When it was once discovered by the Revolution in France, that a struggle between establishment and rapacity could be maintained, though but for one year, and in one place, I was sure that a practicable breach was made in the whole order of things and in every country. Religion, that held the materials of the fabrick together, was first systematically loosened. All other opinions, under the name of prejudices, must fall along with it; and property, left undefended by principles, became a repository of spoils to tempt cupidity, and not a magazine to furnish arms for defence. I knew, that, attacked on all sides by the infernal energies of talents set in action by vice and disorder, authority could not stand upon authority alone. It wanted some other support than the poise of its own gravity.[146]

---

145 *Memoirs of Edward Gibbon*, 235. Cf. Brougham: "Even when Burke's violence had spurned all bounds of moderation, we find [Gibbon], in reference to the famous debate of May 1791, in his letters exclaiming, 'Poor Burke is the most eloquent and rational madman that I ever knew. I love Fox's feelings, but I doubt the political principles of the man and of the party.'" *Works of Henry, Lord Brougham*, II, 407.

146 Edmund Burke, "Letter to William Elliot, Esq." (26 May 1795), in *The Writings and Speeches of Edmund Burke* (Boston: Little Brown, 1901), V, 121–2.

Did Gibbon own to any personal responsibility when he read Burke making these points? After all, the historian had been England's most consistent proponent of the ideas of the *philosophes*. Although fond of what he referred to as Burke's "profuse and philosophic fancy," he did not make any specific references to Burke's insistence that the Revolution's anti-Christian character was of its essence.[147] To Lord Sheffield in wrote in February 1791: "Burke's book is a most admirable medicine against the French disease, which has made too much progress even in this happy country. I admire his eloquence, I approve his politics, I adore his chivalry, and I can even forgive his superstition."[148] Then, again, he wrote in his *Memoirs*: "I beg leave to subscribe my assent to Mr. Burke's creed on the revolution in France ... I have sometimes thought of writing a dialogue of the dead in which Lucian, Erasmus and Voltaire should mutually acknowledge the danger of exposing an old superstition to the contempt of the blind and fanatic multitude."[149] This was assent to a peculiar version of Mr. Burke's creed. It also shows that the anti-Christian snob in Gibbon understood the French Revolution no more profoundly than he understood Christianity, though he remained faithful to the Antonine Roman Empire, which, in his view, knew at least how to qualify its skepticism in order to pander to the multitude's insatiable appetite for superstition. ("Gibbon," as Dean Church remarked, "in his taste for majesty and pomp, his moral unscrupulousness, and his scepticism, reflected the genius of the Empire of which he recounted the fortunes."[150])

In his entry on Gibbon in *The Oxford Dictionary of National Biography*, Womersley touches on Gibbon's reaction to Burke's interpretation of the Revolution, but sidesteps the issue of culpability.[151]

> Burke's analysis of the French Revolution, which allotted a causal and villainous role to the French *philosophes*, had imparted new

---

147 *Memoirs of Edward Gibbon*, 167.
148 *The Letters of Edward Gibbon. Volume Three. 1784–1794. Letters 619–878*, ed. J. E. Norton (London: Cassell, 1956), 216.
149 *Memoirs of Edward Gibbon*, 198.
150 Church, *The Gifts of Civilization*, 137.
151 Charlotte Roberts has nothing of Womersley's tentativeness when it comes to Gibbon's response to the French Revolution. While she might deplore the fact that "In the last years of his life, Gibbon, always suspicious of power in the hands of the 'unwieldy multitude' ... began to articulate a renewed and somewhat reactionary commitment to the traditional values of monarchical and aristocratic privilege and even organized religion," he can still be safely exonerated on both counts. Why? "It is perfectly possible to condemn both the dangerous influence of revolutionary freedom and the cruel consequences of absolute monarchy, and indeed Gibbon did deplore both with some consistency throughout his life." Roberts, *Edward Gibbon and the Shape of History*, 172. Nevertheless, Roberts, like Womersley, dodges the question of Gibbon's culpability for touting ideas that led to so much consequential bloodshed and havoc.

energy and new direction to the drama of Gibbon's reputation. Gibbon had sent for Burke's *Reflections* as soon as it was published, and on reading it he had been immediately converted to Burke's point of view. It was, however, a poignant conversion, since Gibbon cannot have been unaware that Burke's diagnosis of the toxins which had created the revolutionary infection was full of implication for himself, as the most prominent—perhaps the only—embodiment of Enlightenment in England. Suddenly the number of publications attacking him, which had gradually subsided during the 1780s, increased. In the final five years of Gibbon's life we see him obliged to re-enter the lists he thought he had quitted for good in 1779 with the publication of the *Vindication*, and contend once again over his reputation, albeit silently.[152]

If Womersley is right, Gibbon was interested in Burke's damning assessment of the ant-Christian ideas of the *philosophes* only insofar as it affected his reputation. If this were indeed the case, it would not say much for the historian's intellectual honesty, not to mention his ability to extricate himself from the adamantine rationalism that governs so much of his work. Newman's Catholic rebuttal to Gibbon, on the other hand, is directly trained on the question of religion, which Burke's interpretation correctly identified as central to any understanding of the practical impact of the Enlightenment and its ideas. "Revelation begins where Natural Religion fails," Newman writes.

> The Religion of Nature is a mere inchoation, and needs a complement,—it can have but one complement, and that very complement is Christianity. Natural Religion is based upon the sense of sin; it recognizes the disease, but it cannot find, it does but look out for the remedy. That remedy, both for guilt and for moral impotence, is found in the central doctrine of Revelation, the Mediation of Christ ... Thus it is that Christianity is the fulfilment of the promise made to Abraham, and of the Mosaic revelations; this is how it has been able from the first to occupy the world and gain a hold on every class of human society to which its preachers reached; this is why the Roman power and the multitude of religions which it embraced could not stand against it; this is the secret of its sustained energy, and its never-flagging martyrdoms; this is how at present it is so mysteriously potent, in spite of the new and fearful adversaries which beset its path. It has with it that gift of staunching and healing the one deep wound of human nature, which avails more for its success than a full encyclopedia of scientific knowledge and a whole library of controversy, and

---

152 David Womersley, "Gibbon, Edward (1737–1794)," in *The Oxford Dictionary of National Biography*.

> therefore it must last while human nature lasts. It is a living truth which never can grow old.[153]

In this defense of the Christianity that Gibbon and the *philosophes* worked so aggressively to discredit Newman shows how attuned he was to the problem of apostasy first broached by Burke, a problem Gibbon leaves unaddressed. After all, conceding Burke's point would have required him to disavow much of the thinking on which his own work was based. In his letters during this period to Lord Sheffield he may express support for the monarchy that the ideas of the *philosophes* helped to topple, but he is careful never to mention his own support of those ideas.

> [I]f you do not resist the spirit of innovation in the first attempt, if you admit the smallest and most specious change in our parliamentary system, you are lost. You will be driven from one step to another; from principles just in theory to consequences most pernicious in practice; and your first concessions will be productive of every subsequent mischief, for which you will be answerable to your country and to posterity. Do not suffer yourselves to be lulled into a false security; remember the proud fabric of the French monarchy. Not four years ago it stood founded, as it might seem, on the rock of time, force, and opinion, supported by the triple aristocracy of the Church, the nobility, and the Parliaments. They are crumbled into dust; they are vanished from the earth. If this tremendous warning has no effect on the men of property in England, if it does not open every eye and raise every arm, you will deserve your fate. If I am too precipitate, enlighten; if I am too desponding, encourage me.[154]

Clearly, Gibbon could not bring himself to acknowledge that he not only shared but touted the anti-Christian ideas of the *philosophes* that brought down the "proud fabric of the French monarchy." His anti-Christianity was as unshakeable as it was unrepentant.

In all events, that Protestant England, in the short span of less than a century after the publication of the *Decline and Fall*, should have produced in Newman someone who could take issue with Gibbon in such distinctly Catholic terms was lively proof of the accuracy of what the convert had preached so eloquently at St. Mary's, Oscott in the wake of the restoration of the English Catholic hierarchy in 1850: "what is it, my Fathers, my Brothers, what is it that has happened in England just at this time? Something strange is passing over this land, by the very surprise, by the very commotion, which it excites."[155] If the restoration of the English hierarchy

---

153 *Grammar of Assent*, 312–13.
154 *Memoirs of Edward Gibbon*, 253.
155 Newman, "The Second Spring" (1852), in *Sermons on Various Occasions*, 167–9.

upset history as Gibbon and the Enlightenment understood history—after all, their rationalist progeny referred to the restoration as mere "papal aggression"—the prophetic historian in Newman saw in it something entirely different:

> We should judge rightly in our curiosity about a phenomenon like this; it must be a portentous event, and it is. It is an innovation, a miracle, I may say, in the course of human events. The physical world revolves year by year, and begins again; but the political order of things does not renew itself, does not return; it continues, but it proceeds; there is no retrogression. This is so well understood by men of the day, that with them progress is idolized as another name for good. The past never returns—it is never good;—if we are to escape existing ills, it must be by going forward. The past is out of date; the past is dead. As well may the dead live to us, as well may the dead profit us, as the past return. *This*, then, is the cause of this national transport, this national cry, which encompasses us. The past *has* returned, the dead lives. Thrones are overturned, and are never restored; States live and die, and then are matter only for history. Babylon was great, and Tyre, and Egypt, and Nineveh, and shall never be great again. The English Church was, and the English Church was not, and the English Church is once again. This is the portent, worthy of a cry. It is the coming in of a Second Spring.[156]

And it is striking, *vis-à-vis* Newman's criticisms of Gibbon, that what this Second Spring should have most impressed upon him was the power of holy martyrdom. One is often struck by the unity of Newman's thinking, but, here, in his history, a history compared to which the history of Edward Gibbon is so much bravura trifling, the unity is profound.

> Yes, my Fathers and Brothers, and if it be God's blessed will, not Saints alone, not Doctors only, not Preachers only, shall be ours—but Martyrs, too, shall reconsecrate the soil to God. We know not what is before us, ere we win our own; we are engaged in a great, a joyful work, but in proportion to God's grace is the fury of His enemies. They have welcomed us as the lion greets his prey. Perhaps they may be familiarized in time with our appearance, but perhaps they may be irritated the more. To set up the Church again in England is too great an act to be done in a corner. We have had reason to expect that such a boon would not be given to us without a cross. It is not God's way that great blessings should descend without the sacrifice first of great sufferings. If the truth is to be spread to any wide extent among this people, how can we dream, how can we hope, that trial and trouble shall not accompany its going forth?

---

156 *Ibid.*, 168–9.

> And we have already, if it may be said without presumption, to commence our work withal, a large store of merits. We have no slight outfit for our opening warfare. Can we religiously suppose that the blood of our martyrs, three centuries ago and since, shall never receive its recompense? Those priests, secular and regular, did they suffer for no end? or rather, for an end which is not yet accomplished? The long imprisonment, the fetid dungeon, the weary suspense, the tyrannous trial, the barbarous sentence, the savage execution, the rack, the gibbet, the knife, the cauldron, the numberless tortures of those holy victims, O my God, are they to have no reward? Are Thy martyrs to cry from under Thine altar for their loving vengeance on this guilty people, and to cry in vain? Shall they lose life, and not gain a better life for the children of those who persecuted them? Is this Thy way, O my God, righteous and true? Is it according to Thy promise, O King of saints, if I may dare talk to Thee of justice? Did not Thou Thyself pray for Thine enemies upon the cross, and convert them? Did not Thy first Martyr win Thy great Apostle, then a persecutor, by his loving prayer? And in that day of trial and desolation for England, when hearts were pierced through and through with Mary's woe, at the crucifixion of Thy body mystical, was not every tear that flowed, and every drop of blood that was shed, the seeds of a future harvest, when they who sowed in sorrow were to reap in joy?[157]

If one wishes to understand the depth of Newman's understanding of history, here it is. Here is his foresight and aftersight; his recognition of the terrible dignity of history; his empathy for those who bear history's sacrificial weight. Gibbon may have been right to remind his readers that history is often "little more than the register of the crimes, follies, and misfortunes of mankind."[158] Yet what Newman shows is that history is also the register of man's need for salvation—indeed, his hope for salvation—which is why Newman's own history is always so full of prayer, as here, for priests, who have the responsibility of souls on them till the day of their death—the same priests who were anathema to Voltaire, Hume and Gibbon.

> My Fathers, my Brothers in the priesthood, I speak from my heart when I declare my conviction, that there is no one among you here present but, if God so willed, would readily become a martyr for His sake. I do not say you would wish it; I do not say that the natural will would not pray that that chalice might pass away; I do not speak of what you can do by any strength of yours;—but in the strength of God, in the grace of the Spirit, in the armour of justice, by the consolations

---

157 *Ibid.*, 178–9.
158 *Decline and Fall*, I, 84. Cf. "En effect, l'histoire n'est que le tableaux des crimes et des malheurs." Voltaire, *L'Ingénu* (1767).

and peace of the Church, by the blessing of the Apostles Peter and Paul, and in the name of Christ, you would do what nature cannot do. By the intercession of the Saints on high, by the penances and good works and the prayers of the people of God on earth, you would be forcibly borne up as upon the waves of the mighty deep, and carried on out of yourselves by the fulness of grace, whether nature wished it or no. I do not mean violently, or with unseemly struggle, but calmly, gracefully, sweetly, joyously, you would mount up and ride forth to the battle, as on the rush of Angels' wings, as your fathers did before you, and gained the prize. You, who day by day offer up the Immaculate Lamb of God, you who hold in your hands the Incarnate Word under the visible tokens which He has ordained, you who again and again drain the chalice of the Great Victim; who is to make you fear? what is to startle you? what to seduce you? who is to stop you, whether you are to suffer or to do, whether to lay the foundations of the Church in tears, or to put the crown upon the work in jubilation?[159]

VI

Newman's insistence on martyrdom as the essential cause of the rise of Christianity was bound up with his appreciation for the ubiquity of what he called God's "kind Providence," which, as he shows in the *Apologia*, always accompanied him in his own religious development. In the case of the furor caused by *Tract 90*, for example, which was one factor that led him to rethink his allegiance to the Church of England, he remarks:

> I saw indeed clearly that my place in the Movement was lost; public confidence was at an end; my occupation was gone. It was simply an impossibility that I could say any thing henceforth to good effect, when I had been posted up by the marshal on the buttery-hatch of every College of my University, after the manner of discommoned pastry-cooks, and when in every part of the country and every class of society, through every organ and opportunity of opinion, in newspapers, in periodicals, at meetings, in pulpits, at dinner-tables, in coffee-rooms, in railway carriages, I was denounced as a traitor who had laid his train and was detected in the very act of firing it against the time-honoured Establishment ... Confidence in me was lost;—but I had already lost full confidence in myself. Thoughts had passed over me a year and a half before in respect to the Anglican claims, which for the time had profoundly troubled me. They had gone: I had not less confidence in the power and the prospects of the Apostolical movement than before; not less confidence than before in the

---

159 "The Second Spring," 180–1.

grievousness of what I called the "dominant errors" of Rome: but how was I any more to have absolute confidence in myself? how was I to have confidence in my present confidence? how was I to be sure that I should always think as I thought now? I felt that by this event a kind Providence had saved me from an impossible position in the future.[160]

Then, again, on a much more fundamental level, Newman was convinced, especially once he became a Roman Catholic and found his will to succeed thwarted at every turn, that it is "the rule of Providence that we should succeed by failure."[161] After all, we become saints by allowing God to make us saints, not by delivering ourselves up to the direction of our own insistent, often misguided self-will, which is all too often beguiled by false notions of success.[162] Moreover, Newman's understanding of the providential blessing of failure gives his sense of history its depth and richness. Like Christopher Dawson, he understood that "The true progress of history is a mystery which is fulfilled in failure and suffering and which only will be revealed at the end of time. The victory that overcomes the world is not success but faith and it is only the eye of faith that understands the true value of history."[163] The faith in human progress, the faith in human perfectibility, to which so many of Newman's contemporaries subscribed, held no allure for the tough-minded convert. When it came to the Church herself, Newman agreed with Dawson, who understood that she "wins not by majorities but by martyrs ... the cross is her victory."[164] Newman, for his part, in a letter to his dear friend Mother Mary Imelda Poole, put the matter in terms that would never have endeared him to his own or, indeed, Dawson's rationalists: "I think either Antichrist is coming, or that a great

---

160 *Apologia*, 88.

161 "Now what can I say in answer to your letter? First, that your case is mine. It is for years beyond numbering—in one view of the matter for these 50 years—that I have been crying out 'I have laboured in vain, I have spent my strength without cause and in vain: wherefore my judgment is with the Lord, and my work with my God.' Now at the end of my days, when the next world is close upon me, I am recognized at last at Rome. Don't suppose I am dreaming of complaint—just the contrary. The Prophet's words, which expressed my keen pain, brought, *because* they were his words, my consolation. It is the rule of God's Providence that we should succeed by failure, and my moral is, as addressed to you, Doubt not that He will use you—be brave—have faith in His love for you—His everlasting love—and love Him from the certainty that He loves you." Newman to Lord Braye (29 October 1862), in *LD*, XXX, 141–2.

162 Cf. Jacques Philippe, *In the School of the Holy Spirit*, trans. Helena Scott (New York: Scepter, 2007).

163 Christopher Dawson, "The Kingdom of God and History" (1938), in *The Dynamics of World History*, 286.

164 *Ibid*.

and purifying trial, which may last centuries, is coming on the Church. The course of God's Providence is as glorious as it is awful."[165]

For Gibbon, Providence tended to be a blind, inscrutable, fatal force.[166] "By the wise dispensation of Providence," he remarks in one passage in the sixteenth chapter of the *Decline and Fall*, "a mysterious veil was cast over the infancy of the church, which, till the faith of the Christians was matured and their numbers were multiplied, served to protect them not only from malice, but even from the knowledge of the Pagan world."[167] Examples of such glib references to Providence could be easily multiplied throughout the *Decline and Fall*. Yet, curiously enough, the historian did have a strong sense of Providence in his personal life, even if he did not attribute it to any divine source. In his autobiography, for example, he writes:

> If my childish revolt against the religion of my country had not stripped me in time of my academic gown, the five important years, so liberally improved in the studies and conversation of Lausanne, would have been steeped in port and prejudice among the monks of Oxford. Had the fatigue of idleness compelled me to read, the path of learning would not have been enlightened by a ray of philosophic freedom. I should have grown to manhood ignorant of the life and language of Europe, and my knowledge of the world would have been confined to an English cloister. But my religious error fixed me at Lausanne in a state of banishment and disgrace. The rigid course of discipline and abstinence to which I was condemned invigorated the constitution of my mind and body; poverty and pride estranged me from my countrymen. One mischief, however, and in their eyes a serious and irreparable mischief, was derived from the success of my Swiss education: I had ceased to be an Englishman. At the flexible period of youth, from the age of sixteen to twenty-one, my opinions, habits, and sentiments were cast in a foreign mould.[168]

---

165 Newman to Mother Mary Imelda Poole (28 December 1872), in *LD*, XXVI, 222.

166 Cf. "What, in fact, was [Gibbon] writing about? In his own words, the 'vicissitudes of fortune, which spares neither man nor the proudest of his works, which buries empires and cities in a common grave.' But there is more than the blind goddess who seems to rule over history: there is human strength and human weakness, and the principle that 'all that is human must retrograde if it does not advance.'" Anthony Burgess, "Mr. Gibbon and the Huns," *New York Times* (28 February 1988). Burgess, in the same article, takes exception to Waugh's strictures against the malign influence of the famous style, about which the author of *A Clockwork Orange* nicely observes: "It is an English of very black ink, sharp quills and fine handmade paper."

167 *Decline and Fall*, II, 88.

168 *Memoirs of Edward Gibbon*, 104.

Here, Gibbon boasts of being exile's beneficiary, even though he concedes that it left him *deraciné*. It might be that displacement from his countrymen explains more about his failure to enter into the love of God's particular Providence than any reference to the ideas of the Enlightenment. For all of his delight in the society of his few but lasting friends, he never seems to have known real love. And this seems to have left him indifferent to the love of God. In any case, when in the *Decline and Fall* he speaks of "the stubborn mind of an infidel ... guarded by secret incurable suspicion," he was clearly speaking of himself.[169] Then, again, the historian Lord Acton is worth quoting on this score: "Unbelievers of the class of Hume and Gibbon did not *suffer* on account of being without faith; their turn of mind was Epicurean; the world of sense and intelligence furnished them with as much enjoyment as they required, and they had no quarrel with the social order which secured to them the tranquil possession of their daily pleasures."[170] This frivolous, Epicurean strain in the historian might also have accounted for the irresponsible superficiality with which he regarded the cataclysm of the French Revolution.

For Newman, Divine Providence betokens the particular, loving interest that a personal Creator takes in each of His creatures, and this, in turn, helps shape and transform history.

> When Hagar fled into the wilderness from the face of her mistress, she was visited by an Angel, who sent her back; but, together with this implied reproof of her impatience, gave her a word of promise to encourage and console her. In the mixture of humbling and cheerful thoughts thus wrought in her, she recognized the presence of her Maker and Lord, who ever comes to his servants in a two-fold aspect, severe because He is holy, yet soothing as abounding in mercy. In consequence, she called the name of the Lord that spake unto her, "Thou God seest me."[171]

Ruskin famously complained of the hammers of geologists smashing up his Bible Christianity. "You speak of the flimsiness of your own faith," the art historian wrote one correspondent. "Mine, which was never strong, is being beaten into mere gold leaf, and flutters in weak rags from the letter of its old forms ... the only letters it can hold by at all are the old Evangelical formulae. If only the Geologists would let me alone, I could do very well, but those dreadful Hammers! I hear the clink of them at the end of every cadence of the Bible verses."[172] Newman met with something other

---

169 *Decline and Fall*, IV, 91–2.
170 *Selected Writings of Lord Acton: Volume I: Essays in the History of Liberty*, ed. J. Rufus Fears (Indianapolis: Liberty Fund, 1985), 144.
171 "A Particular Providence as Revealed in the Gospel" (1835), Sermon 9, in *PPS*, III.
172 Ruskin, quoted in John Batchelor, *John Ruskin: No Wealth but Life* (London: Chatto

than the hammers of geologists when he opened his Bible: he met with the New Covenant, and its profound implications for history are always alive to him, as they never were to Gibbon.

> Such was the condition of man before Christ came, favoured with some occasional notices of God's regard for individuals, but, for the most part, instructed merely in His general Providence, as seen in the course of human affairs. In this respect even the Law was deficient, though it abounded in proofs that God was a living, all-seeing, all-recompensing God. It was deficient, in comparison of the Gospel, in evidence of the really-existing relation between each soul of man and its Maker, independently of everything else in the world. Of Moses, indeed, it is said, that "the Lord spake unto him *face to face*, as a man speaketh unto his friend." [Exod. 33:11.] But this was an especial privilege vouchsafed to him only and some others, as to Hagar, who records it in the text, not to all the people. But, under the New Covenant, this distinct regard, vouchsafed by Almighty God to every one of us, is clearly revealed. It was foretold of the Christian Church; "*All thy children shall be taught of the Lord; and great shall be the peace of thy children.*" [Isa. 54:13.] When the Eternal Son came on earth in our flesh, men saw their invisible Maker and Judge. He showed Himself no longer through the mere powers of nature, or the maze of human affairs, but in our own likeness to Him. "God, who commanded the light to shine out of darkness, hath shined in our hearts, to give the light of the knowledge of the glory of God in the face of Jesus Christ;" [2 Cor. 4:6.] that is, in a sensible form, as a really existing individual being. And, at the same time, He forthwith began to speak to *us* as individuals ... Thus it was in some sense a revelation face to face.[173]

And, for Newman, it follows that rejection of the reality of God's personal Providence accounts for a good deal of the actual state of the fallen world. "We know He is in heaven, and forget that He is also on earth," he wrote. "This is the reason why the multitude of men are so profane. They use light words; they scoff at religion; they allow themselves to be lukewarm and indifferent; they take the part of wicked men; they push forward wicked measures; they defend injustice, or cruelty, or sacrilege, or infidelity; because they have no grasp of a truth, which nevertheless they have no intention to deny, that God sees them."[174]

Of course, Newman appreciates that the very gravity of this truth makes it difficult to apprehend, and this is why he sees the Incarnation, in part, as

& Windus, 2000), 157.
173 Sermon 9, in *PPS*, III, 114–15.
174 *Ibid.*, 116–17.

the Creator's way of sparing His creatures the futility of trying to resort to rationalism to make sense of His Love. Indeed, for Newman, Our Savior charitably anticipated the "infirmity" of our rationalist impulses and sought by assuming human form to show their wrongheadedness.

> Now, at first sight, it is difficult to see how our idea of Almighty God can be divested of these earthly notions, either that His goodness is imperfect, or that it is fated and necessary; and wonderful indeed, and adorable is the condescension by which He has met our infirmity. He has met and aided it in that same Dispensation by which He redeemed our souls. In order that we may understand that in spite of His mysterious perfections He has a separate knowledge and regard for individuals, He has taken upon him the thoughts and feelings of our own nature, which we all understand *is* capable of such personal attachments. By becoming man, He has cut short the perplexities and the discussions of our reason on the subject, as if He would grant our objections for argument's sake, and supersede them by taking our own ground.[175]

God's love for Judas is a good example of the way God's Providence operates in the fallen world:

> Judas was in darkness and hated the light, and "went to his own place;" yet he found it, not by the mere force of certain natural principles working out their inevitable results—by some unfeeling fate, which sentences the wicked to hell—but by a Judge who surveys him from head to foot, who searches him through and through, to see if there is any ray of hope, any latent spark of faith; who pleads with him again and again, and, at length abandoning him, mourns over him the while with the wounded affection of a friend rather than the severity of the Judge of the whole earth.[176]

Moreover, Newman understands that such direct, personal solicitude from a loving Creator is difficult to credit, even by those who would acknowledge His Providence.

> God beholds thee individually, whoever thou art. He "calls thee by thy name." He sees thee, and understands thee, as He made thee. He knows what is in thee, all thy own peculiar feelings and thoughts, thy dispositions and likings, thy strength and thy weakness. He views thee in thy day of rejoicing, and thy day of sorrow. He sympathises in thy hopes and thy temptations. He interests Himself in all thy anxieties and remembrances, all the risings and fallings of thy spirit. He has numbered the very hairs of thy head

---

175 *Ibid.*, 120.
176 *Ibid.*, 121.

and the cubits of thy stature. He compasses thee round and bears thee in his arms; He takes thee up and sets thee down. He notes thy very countenance, whether smiling or in tears, whether healthful or sickly. He looks tenderly upon thy hands and thy feet; He hears thy voice, the beating of thy heart, and thy very breathing. Thou dost not love thyself better than He loves thee. Thou canst not shrink from pain more than He dislikes thy bearing it; and if He puts it on thee, it is as thou would put it on thyself, if thou art wise, for a greater good afterwards. Thou art not only His creature (though for the very sparrows He has a care, and pitied the "much cattle" of Nineveh), thou art man redeemed and sanctified, His adopted son, favoured with a portion of that glory and blessedness which flows from Him everlastingly unto the Only-begotten. Thou art chosen to be His, even above thy fellows who dwell in the East and South. Thou wast one of those for whom Christ offered up His last prayer, and sealed it with His precious blood. What a thought is this, a thought almost too great for our faith![177]

The rise of Christianity, for Newman, primarily involved those who accepted and cooperated with God's particular Providence and those who rejected and spurned it.[178] Faith is the means by which the individual, with God's providential grace, enters into the reality of history, which, for Newman, is not simply something that concerns historians or savants. Gibbon, on the other hand, regarded ordinary people and their engagement with these graces from an aloof, seigneurial, condescending remove. "The decline of ancient prejudice exposed a very numerous portion of human kind to the danger of a painful and comfortless situation," he writes of the desuetude into which devotion to the imperial gods fell before the Incarnation:

> A state of scepticism and suspense may amuse a few inquisitive minds. But the practice of superstition is so congenial to the multitude that, if they are forcibly awakened, they still regret the loss

---

177 Ibid., 124–6.
178 Cf. "As fresh circumstances arise, with their attendant obligations, fresh actual graces are offered us in order that we may derive the greatest spiritual profit from them. Above the succession of external events that go to make up our life, there runs a parallel series of actual graces offered for our acceptance ... This succession of actual graces which we either agree to make use of for our spiritual benefit, or, on the other hand, neglect to do so, constitutes the history of each individual soul as it is written down in the book of life, in God, to be laid open some day for our inspection. It is thus that our Lord continues to live in His mystical body, and especially in His saints, in whom He continues a life that will know no end, a life that at every moment requires new graces and new activities." Reginald Garrigou-Lagrange, *Providence: God's Loving Care for Men and the Need for Confidence in Almighty God* (Rockford, Illinois: TAN Books, 1998), 247-8.

of their pleasing vision. Their love of the marvellous and supernatural, their curiosity with regard to future events, and their strong propensity to extend their hopes and fears beyond the limits of the visible world, were the principal causes which favoured the establishment of Polytheism. So urgent on the vulgar is the necessity of believing that the fall of any system of mythology will most probably be succeeded by the introduction of some other mode of superstition.[179]

Compared to this contemptuous view of "the vulgar" and their susceptibility to what Gibbon regarded as mere superstition, nothing could be more refreshing than Newman's view of the ordinary faithful.

> Religion has its own enlargement, and an enlargement, not of tumult, but of peace. It is often remarked of uneducated persons, who have hitherto thought little of the unseen world, that, on their turning to God, looking into themselves, regulating their hearts, reforming their conduct, and meditating on death and judgment, heaven and hell, they seem to become, in point of intellect, different beings from what they were. Before, they took things as they came, and thought no more of one thing than another. But now every event has a meaning; they have their own estimate of whatever happens to them; they are mindful of times and seasons, and compare the present with the past; and the world, no longer dull, monotonous, unprofitable, and hopeless, is a various and complicated drama, with parts and an object, and an awful moral.[180]

Here, Newman might have been describing the case of Charles Devas, who, had it not been for his eyes being opened to the one true fold of the

---

179 *Decline and Fall*, II, 59.

180 *The Idea of a University*, 120. Ian Ker, in his brilliant biography of G. K. Chesterton, shows how Newman's great successor shared his respect for the common man, quoting that memorable passage from *Heretics* (1905): "Mr. Shaw cannot understand that the thing which is valuable and lovable in our eyes is man—the old beer-drinking, creed-making, fighting, failing, sensual, respectable man. And the things that have been founded on this creature immortally remain; the things that have been founded on the fancy of the Superman have died with the dying civilizations which alone have given them birth. When Christ at a symbolic moment was establishing His great society, He chose for its cornerstone neither the brilliant Paul nor the mystic John, but a shuffler, a snob, a coward—in a word, a man. And upon this rock He has built His Church, and the gates of Hell have not prevailed against it. All the empires and the kingdoms have failed, because of this inherent and continual weakness, that they were founded by strong men and upon strong men. But this one thing, the historic Christian Church, was founded on a weak man, and for that reason it is indestructible. For no chain is stronger than its weakest link." Chesterton, quoted in Ian Ker, *G. K. Chesterton: A Biography* (Oxford: Oxford University Press, 2011), 152.

Redeemer might have spent his days utterly unaware of this "various and complicated drama."

In his sermon on God's particular Providence, Newman shows how each of us makes his own history in embracing, or refusing to embrace God's direct, personal Love.

> These are the meditations which come upon the Christian to console him, while he is with Christ upon the holy mount. And, when he descends to his daily duties, they are still his inward strength, though he is not allowed to tell the vision to those around him. They make his countenance to shine, make him cheerful, collected, serene, and firm in the midst of all temptation, persecution, or bereavement. And with such thoughts before us, how base and miserable does the world appear in all its pursuits and doctrines! How truly miserable does it seem to seek good from the creature; to covet station, wealth, or credit; to choose for ourselves, in fancy, this or that mode of life; to affect the manners and fashions of the great; to spend our time in follies; to be discontented, quarrelsome, jealous or envious, censorious or resentful; fond of unprofitable talk, and eager for the news of the day; busy about public matters which concern us not; hot in the cause of this or that interest or party; or set upon gain; or devoted to the increase of barren knowledge! And at the end of our days, when flesh and heart fail, what will be our consolation, though we have made ourselves rich, or have served an office, or been the first man among our equals, or have depressed a rival, or managed things our own way, or have settled splendidly, or have been intimate with the great, or have fared sumptuously, or have gained a name! Say, even if we obtain that which lasts longest, a place in history, yet, after all, what ashes shall we have eaten for bread! And, in that awful hour, when death is in sight, will He, whose eye is now so loving towards us, and whose hand falls on us so gently, will He acknowledge us any more? or, if He still speaks, will His voice have any power to stir us? rather will it not repel us, as it did Judas, by the very tenderness with which it would invite us to Him?[181]

After Newman's animadversions on what, for Christians, must be the most important decision of life—whether to accept or reject God's Love[182]—

---

181 Sermon 9, in *PPS*, III, 126–7.
182 In his sermon, "Love, the One Thing Needful" (1839), Newman describes the compunction Christians feel for failing to respond adequately to God's Love—not the sort of thing that kept Edward Gibbon awake at night. "I suppose the greater number of persons who try to live Christian lives, and who observe themselves with any care," Newman writes, "are dissatisfied with their own state on this point, viz. that, whatever their religious attainments may be, yet they feel that their motive is not the highest;—that

Gibbon's defense of the skepticism that governed Antonine Rome provides a striking contrast to the response of Christians to the Incarnation, which, as we have seen, the historian scarcely credited. "In their writings and conversation," Gibbon observes approvingly, "the philosophers of antiquity asserted the independent dignity of reason, but they resigned their actions to the commands of law and custom. Viewing with a smile of pity and indulgence the various errours of the vulgar, they diligently practiced the ceremonies of their fathers, devoutly frequented the temples of the gods, and, sometimes condescending to act a part on the theatre of superstition, they concealed the sentiment of an Atheist under the sacerdotal robes." Indeed, for the Enlightenment historian, "Reasoners of such a temper were scarcely inclined to wrangle about their respective modes of faith or of worship. It was indifferent to them what shape the folly of the multitude might choose to assume; and they approached, with the same inward contempt and the same external reverence, the altars of the Libyan, the Olympian, or the Capitoline Jupiter."[183] For Gibbon, the polytheistic religion of paganism was

> not merely a speculative doctrine professed in the schools or preached in the temples. The innumerable deities and rites of polytheism were closely interwoven with every circumstance of business or pleasure, of public or of private life, and it seemed impossible to escape the observance of them, without, at the same time, renouncing the commerce of mankind, and all the offices and amusements of society. The important transactions of peace and war were prepared or concluded by solemn sacrifices, in which the magistrate, the senator, and the soldier were obliged to preside or to participate. The public spectacles were an essential part of the cheerful devotion of the Pagans, and the gods were supposed to accept, as the most grateful offering, the games that the prince and people celebrated in honour of their peculiar festivals.[184]

---

the love of God, and of man for His sake, is not their ruling principle. They may do much, nay, if it so happen, they may suffer much; but they have little reason to think that they love much, that they do and suffer for love's sake. I do not mean that they thus express themselves exactly, but that they are dissatisfied with themselves, and that when this dissatisfaction is examined into, it will be found ultimately to come to this, though they will give different accounts of it. They may call themselves cold, or hard-hearted, or fickle, or double-minded, or doubting, or dim-sighted, or weak in resolve, but they mean pretty much the same thing, that their affections do not rest on Almighty God as their great Object. And this will be found to be the complaint of religious men among ourselves, not less than others; their reason and their heart not going together; their reason tending heavenwards, and their heart earthwards." Sermon 23, in *PPS*, V, 327–9.
183 *Decline and Fall*, I, 34.
184 *Ibid.*, II, 17–18.

By contrast, for Gibbon, the "Christian, who with pious horror avoided the abomination of the circus or the theatre, found himself encompassed with infernal snares in every convivial entertainment."[185] That the "pious horror" of the Christians should stem from their readiness to obey their Maker's commandment against idolatry never enters Gibbon's astringently rationalist calculus.

The intellectual historian J. W. Burrow nicely captures how Gibbon viewed the two religions.

> Into ... [the] venerable, gently assimilative world of established but varied cults and unsystematic but traditionally channeled beliefs, Christianity erupted as an alien and destructive force: intolerant, exclusive, dogmatically theological and fiercely zealous, tightly organized, ascetic and contemptuous of the world around it. Gibbon's attitude to the transformation this wrought, like his attitude to the "barbarizing" of the Roman army and the Orientalizing of the Roman polity, was conservative. It was a conservatism shaped by eighteenth-century notions of reason, toleration, and moderation, and above all by the characteristic distaste and suspicion of the high culture of his age towards "enthusiasm", a word which then carried strong suggestions of fanaticism.[186]

What Burrow omits to remark—it would be outside the charge of any brief overview of the life and work of Gibbon—is how much the skeptical ethos he describes resembles the nineteenth-century Broad Church—where all faiths were welcome, except the one that had any legitimate claim to be true—which Newman spent so much of his life decrying. If we read Newman's sermon, "The Religion of the Day" (1832) and compare it to Gibbon's paeans to the polytheism of paganism, we shall see very little difference between the two. For Newman, pagans were not the only ones with a taste for idolatry.

> What is the world's religion now? It has taken the brighter side of the Gospel,—its tidings of comfort, its precepts of love; all darker, deeper views of man's condition and prospects being comparatively forgotten. This is the religion *natural* to a civilized age, and well has Satan dressed and completed it into an idol of the Truth. As the reason is cultivated, the taste formed, the affections and sentiments refined, a general decency and grace will of course spread over the face of society, quite independently of the influence of Revelation. That beauty and delicacy of thought, which is so attractive in books, then extends to the conduct of life, to all we have, all we do, all we are. Our manners are courteous; we avoid giving

---

185 *Ibid.*, II, 18.
186 J. W. Burrow, *Gibbon* (Oxford: Oxford University Press, 1985), 53.

pain or offence; our words become correct; our relative duties are carefully performed. Our sense of propriety shows itself even in our domestic arrangements, in the embellishments of our houses, in our amusements, and so also in our religions profession. Vice now becomes unseemly and hideous to the imagination, or, as it is sometimes familiarly said, "out of taste." Thus elegance is gradually made the test and standard of virtue, which is no longer thought to possess an intrinsic claim on our hearts, or to exist, *further than* it leads to the quiet and comfort of others. Conscience is no longer recognized as an independent arbiter of actions, its authority is explained away; partly it is superseded in the minds of men by the so-called moral sense, which is regarded merely as the love of the beautiful; partly by the rule of expediency, which is forthwith substituted for it in the details of conduct. Now conscience is a stern, gloomy principle; it tells us of guilt and of prospective punishment. Accordingly, when its terrors disappear, then disappear also, in the creed of the day, those fearful images of Divine wrath with which the Scriptures abound. They are explained away. Every thing is bright and cheerful. Religion is pleasant and easy; benevolence is the chief virtue; intolerance, bigotry, excess of zeal, are the first of sins. Austerity is an absurdity;—even firmness is looked on with an unfriendly, suspicious eye.[187]

In the same year, in the seventh of his Oxford University Sermons, "Contest between Faith and Sight," Newman would return to this theme of the world's religion, which, now, as then, attracts many devotees:

The palmary device of Satan is to address himself to the pride of our nature, and, by the promise of independence, to seduce us into sin. Those who have been brought up in ignorance of the polluting fashions of the world, too often feel a rising in their minds against the discipline and constraint kindly imposed upon them; and, not understanding that their ignorance is their glory, and that they cannot really enjoy both good and evil, they murmur that they are not allowed to essay what they do not wish to practise, or to choose for themselves in matters where the very knowledge seems to them to give a superiority to the children of corruption. Thus the temptation of becoming as gods works as in the beginning, pride opening a door to lust; and then, intoxicated by their experience of evil, they think they possess real wisdom, and take a larger and more impartial view of the nature and destinies of man than religion teaches; and, while the customs of society restrain their avowals within the bounds of propriety, yet in their hearts they learn to believe that sin is a matter of course, not a serious evil, a failing in

---

187 "The Religion of the Day" (1930), Sermon 24, in *PPS*, I, 311–12.

which all have share, indulgently to be spoken of, or rather, in the case of each individual, to be taken for granted, and passed over in silence; and believing this, they are not unwilling to discover or to fancy weaknesses in those who have the credit of being superior to the ordinary run of men, to insinuate the possibility of human passions influencing them, this or that of a more refined nature, when the grosser cannot be imputed, and, extenuating at the same time the guilt of the vicious, to reduce in this manner all men pretty much to a level.

Yet simply to express such unsparing strictures was not enough for Newman: it was also necessary to cite the "historian of the last century, who, for his great abilities, and, on the other hand, his cold heart, impure mind, and scoffing spirit, may justly be accounted as, in this country at least, one of the masters of a new school of error, which seems not yet to have accomplished its destinies, and is framed more exactly after the received type of the author of evil, than the other chief anti-Christs who have, in these last times, occupied the scene of the world."[188]

Despite its prescience, such an estimate of Gibbon and his work might very well have only compounded the contempt that many nineteenth-century historians had of Newman's historical sense. A good example of this dismissive attitude can be seen in something that the Whig historian William Edward Hartpole Lecky (1838–1903) said of Newman after his death:[189]

> In an age remarkable for brilliancy of style he was one of the greatest masters of English prose. His power of drawing subtle distinctions and pursuing long trains of subtle reasoning made him one of the most skilful of controversialists, and he had a great insight into spiritual cravings and an admirable gift of interpreting and appealing to many forms of religious emotion. But though he was a man of rare, delicate, and most seductive genius, we have sometimes doubted whether any of his books are destined to take a perma-

---

188 Newman, "Contest between Faith and Sight" (1832), Sermon 7, in *University Sermons*, 95. This is reminiscent of how Hannah More (1745–1833), the bluestocking and friend of Samuel Johnson, responded to the death of Gibbon: "How many souls have his writings polluted! Lord preserve others from their contagion!" Thomas Taylor, *Memoir of Mrs. Hannah More* (London: Joseph Rickerby, 1838), 159.

189 Newman's dear friend Emily Bowles recalled meeting Lecky at a dinner party to honor Tennyson one evening in London in 1869: "I was ... last night, to a great assembly to meet Tennyson—whom I was very glad to see and know. Otherwise it was painful. Mr. Lecky was there whose 'Morals' [*History of European Morals* (1869)] you have no doubt seen—and who is certainly a remarkable man—25—and looking like a ... dreamy boy ... I felt the greatest *pain* to see that soul—on the threshold of life—with a ship freighted out with such gifts—without compass or rudder." Emily Bowles, quoted in *LD*, XXIV, 280, n. 3.

nent and considerable place in English literature. He was not a great scholar, or an original and independent thinker. Dealing with questions inseparably connected with historical evidence, he had neither the judicial spirit nor the firm grasp of a real historian, and he had very little skill in measuring probabilities and degrees of evidence. He had a manifest incapacity, which was quite as much moral as intellectual, for looking facts in the face and pursuing trains of thought to unwelcome conclusions. He often took refuge from them in clouds of casuistry. The scepticism which was a marked feature of his intellect allied itself closely with credulity, for it was directed against reason itself; and though he has expressed in admirable language many true and beautiful thoughts, the glamour of his style too often concealed much weakness and uncertainty of judgment and much sophistry in argument.[190]

My gentle readers must judge for themselves whether Lecky was speaking sense here, though they should also be aware that he was convinced, as he wrote to one correspondent in 1891, that "Newman's death has a good deal revived over here the interest in his books and speculations. It is a curiously wide influence in England, for there is a strong sceptical element in them which appeals to many who are far from Catholicism."[191] Like so many Victorian rationalists, Lecky was incapable of seeing Newman's embrace of Catholicism in any other than a skeptical light. My readers must also ask themselves whether the judgment of any historian is worth

---

190 William Edward Hartpole Lecky, *Historical and Political Essays* (London: Longman, Green & Co., 1908), 249–50. Lecky's own work is full of comical triumphalism, as here, where he describes Rationalism slaying the great dragon, Dogma: "there is scarcely a disposition that marks the love of abstract truth, and scarcely a rule which reason teaches as essential for its attainment, that theologians did not for centuries stigmatise as offensive to the Almighty. By destroying every book that could generate discussion, by diffusing through every field of knowledge a spirit of boundless credulity, and, above all, by persecuting with atrocious cruelty those who differed from their opinions, they succeeded for a long period in almost arresting the action of the European mind, and in persuading men that a critical, impartial, and enquiring spirit was the worst form of vice. From this frightful condition Europe was at last rescued by the intellectual influences that produced the Reformation, by the teaching of those great philosophers who clearly laid down the conditions of enquiry, and by those bold innovators who, with the stake of Bruno and Vanini before their eyes, dared to challenge directly the doctrines of the past. By these means the spirit of philosophy or of truth became prominent, and the spirit of dogmatism, with all its consequences, was proportionately weakened." W. E. H. Lecky, *History of the Rise and Influence of the Spirit of Rationalism in Europe* (London: Longman, Green & Co., 1870), II, 88. Another Dubliner, James Joyce, was fond of the heretic Bruno.
191 *A Memoir of the Right Hon. William Edward Hartpole Lecky*, ed. Elisabeth van Dedem Lecky (New York: Longman, Green & Co., 1909), 257.

crediting who could claim, as Lecky claimed, that "though ... [Newman] was a man of rare, delicate, and most seductive genius, we have sometimes doubted whether any of his books are destined to take a permanent and considerable place in English literature." Yet, for our purposes, an even more pressing question is whether Lecky was right to charge that Newman "had a manifest incapacity ... for looking facts in the face." Who looked the facts of Christianity in the face? The rationalists who convinced themselves that the facts only merited scorn? Or John Henry Newman, who urged that they take into account what he nicely called "the hypothesis of faith, hope, and charity?"

Newman and Gibbon had such different views of Christianity that they might have inhabited different worlds, though the fact that these different worlds were one and the same only made Newman's point about God's particular Providence more importunate.[192] Charles Devas was right to praise Newman for being someone who, as he said, "looking before and after, foresaw the intellectual problems of the future." What he probably did not know was that one of the men who helped Newman to do this was none other than Edward Gibbon, the same man who had been the occasion of the particular Providence that made Devas himself a Catholic. And one of the most profound lessons that Newman drew from the work of the eighteenth-century rationalist can be found in the third letter that he wrote to *The Times* under the pseudonym "Catholicus" and later collected in the *Tamworth Reading Room* (1841), with which I shall conclude.

> Now, independent of all other considerations, the great difference, in a practical light, between the objects of Christianity and of heathen belief, is this—that glory, science, knowledge, and whatever other fine names we use, never healed a wounded heart, nor changed a sinful one; but Christ's word is with power. The ideas which Christianity brings before us are in themselves full of influence, and they are endowed with a supernatural gift over and above, in order to meet the special exigencies of our nature. Knowledge is not 'power,' nor is glory 'the first and only fair;' but 'grace,' or

---

192 Robert Persons would certainly have understood Newman's point about the importance of God's particular Providence, the same Persons who wrote to Queen Elizabeth in 1580 about "the last tribunal seat, where we shall all be presented shortly, without difference of persons and where the cogitations of all hearts shall be revealed and examined, and in justice of judgment rightly rewarded. Now matters are craftily clouded up and false vizards put upon every action. Then all shall appear in sincerity and truth, and nothing avail but only the testimony of a good conscience. The which Catholics by suffering do seek to retain, and which God, of his infinite goodness, inspire your Majesty, graciously without enforcement, to permit unto them still." From Robert Persons, *A Brief Discourse* (1580), quoted in *The Other Face: Catholic Life under Elizabeth I*, ed. Philip Caraman (New York: Sheed and Ward, 1960), 69.

'the word,' by whichever name we call it, has been from the first a quickening, renovating, organizing principle. It has new-created the individual, and diffused and knit him into a social body, composed of members each similarly created. It has cleansed man of his moral diseases, raised him to hope and energy, given him to propagate a brotherhood among his fellowmen, to form a large family or rather kingdom of saints all over the earth, and with wonderful vigour prolonged its original impulse down to this day. Each one of us has lit his lamp from his neighbour, or received it from his fathers, and the lights thus kindled are to-day as strong and as clear as if 1,800 years had not passed since the original of the sacred flame. What has glory or knowledge done like this? Can it raise the dead? can it create a polity? can it do more than testify man's need and typify God's remedy?[193]

---

193 Appendix 3: Peel's Tamworth Reading Room Speech and the Letters of "Catholicus" to *The Times* (5–26 February 1841), in *LD*, VIII, 543–4.

✢ 2 ✢

Newman, Superstition and the Whig Historians

Monkish ignorance and superstition is a phrase that you find in every Protestant historian, from the reign of the "Virgin" Elizabeth to the present hour. It has, with time, become a sort of magpie-saying, like "glorious revolution," "happy constitution," "good old king," "envy of surrounding nations," and the like. But there has always, false as the notion will presently be proved to be, there has always been a very sufficient motive for inculcating it.

William Cobbett, A History of the Protestant
Reformation in England and Ireland (1827)

He who truly lives in the Church will also live in the first age of the Church and understand it; and he who does not live in the present Church will not live in the old and will not understand it, for they are the same.

Johann Adam Möhler, The Unity of the Church
as Exemplified in the Fathers (1825)[1]

We are in danger of unbelief more than of superstition.

John Henry Newman, Tracts for the Times, 38 (1834)

---

1 See George P. Gooch, *History and the Historians of the Nineteenth Century* (London: Longman, Green & Co., 1913), 549. The German title of Möhler's book is *Die Einheit in der Kirche, oder das Prinzip des Katholizismus dargestellt im Geist der Kirchenvater der drei ersten Jahrhunderte*.

Newman, Superstition and the Whig Historians

IN SEPTEMBER 1839, Robert Williams, an Oriel man and MP for Dorchester who would later become an ardent Evangelical, gave John Henry Newman a copy of an article from the *Dublin Review* by Nicholas Wiseman entitled "The Anglican claim of apostolical succession," in which he likened the Donatists of the fifth century to the Anglicans of the nineteenth.[2] In his diary, Newman notes how he walked out to Littlemore with Williams that afternoon and dined with him in the evening. In the course of their conversation, Williams called Newman's attention to what he described as "the palmary words of St Augustine ... which had escaped my observation: 'Securus judicat orbis terrarum,'" which Newman translated: "The universal Church is in its judgments secure of the truth." Newman recalled how at the time Williams "repeated these words again and again, and, when he was gone, they kept ringing in my ears."[3] Interestingly enough, at that time (though certainly not later), Williams was one of the young Rome-leaning Tractarians for whom Newman wrote *Tract 90*. He wrote the tract to address the "deep passionate misgiving," as his Oriel friend Samuel Francis Wood called it, that Williams and others were beginning to feel about the Church of England.[4] In a letter to Pusey, Newman remarked, apropos Williams: "what is to be done with a man who begins by assuming as a first principle ... that the Roman is the Catholic Church, that therefore the Tridentine Decrees are eternal truth, that to oppose them is heresy, that all who sign the Thirty-Nine Articles do oppose them, and that it is a sin to be in communion with heretics?"[5] Soon, this first principle and all that flowed from it would set off in Newman himself what he called his "great revolution of mind."[6] Hearing St. Augustine's great axiom after his own

---

2 Nicholas Wiseman, "The Anglican Claim of Apostolic Succession," *Dublin Review*, 7, no. 13 (1839), 138–80.
3 *Apologia*, 110.
4 Samuel Francis Wood to Newman, 29 October 1839, in *LD*, VII, 180.
5 Newman to Edward Pusey, 28 July 1840, in *LD*, VII, 371–2.
6 *Apologia*, 90.

study of the Monophysite heresy made a profound impression on Newman. As he noted in a letter, "You see the whole history of the Monophysites has been a sort of alterative, and now comes this dose at the end of it. It certainly does come upon one that we are not at the bottom of things."[7] A month later, Henry Wilberforce recalled walking with Newman in the New Forest, and his dear friend turning to him and saying: "that for the first time since I began the study of theology, a vista has been opened before me, to the end of which I do not see."[8] From that point on, when he was scarcely thirty-eight, this was a vista that Newman would spend the rest of his long life endeavoring to understand, and it turned him into an unusually brilliant historian.

One can study John Henry Newman in many different ways. One can study him as a member of that wonderfully dissentient thing, the Newman family; as a Trinity undergraduate; as an Oriel don; as at once the founder and saboteur of the Oxford Movement. One can study him as a convert; an Oratorian; a fisher of men. One can study him as a writer, a preacher, a philosopher, a theologian, a teacher, a poet, even as a journalist. One can study him as a prophet. One can study him as a saint. But in studying him as an historian one can study him in all of these aspects and yet in a light in which he is rarely considered. In this essay, I shall endeavor to show how the historian in Newman approaches what he calls the "realms of superstition"[9] to show not only what a profoundly good historian he is but how his understanding of the past informs his understanding of the present—ours as well as his own. I shall also look at these matters in the context of the Whig historians, whose views of superstition were so pronouncedly different from those of Newman.

That Newman is a good historian is a contention with which many have disagreed. George Malcolm Young (1882–1959), one of the more exuberant chroniclers of Victorian England, wrote frequently of Newman and always with panache. In one essay, he spoke of how Newman

> is always skimming along the verge of a logical catastrophe, and always relying on his dialectical agility to save himself from falling: always exposing what seems to be an unguarded spot, and always revealing a new line of defence when the unwary assailant has reached it. I am not sure it is not a general characteristic of Oxford: we are not the children of Ockham for nothing: and we are all, I think, more ready to take intellectual risks than they are at "the less ancient and splendid" place.

---

7 Newman to Frederic Rogers, 22 September 1839, in *LD*, VII, 154.
8 Gerard Tracey. Introduction to *LD*, VII, xvii–xviii.
9 Newman, *Essay on Development*, 240.

Young's appreciation for Newman's dialectical deftness notwithstanding, he was convinced that his "fatal defect" was his "want of historic learning."[10] This was an estimate that he shared with William Ewart Gladstone, who held that Newman might have "done an incomparable and immeasurable work for the Church of England," but that he "never placed the English Church upon its historical ground. I doubt if he was even tolerably acquainted with the history of the sixteenth century."[11] In this, Gladstone echoed criticisms of Newman expressed by Johann Joseph Ignaz von Döllinger (1799–1890), the liberal opponent of papal infallibility, who said about the author of *A Letter to the Duke of Norfolk*: "Whole stretches of Church history and the history of European culture are unknown to him, as the darkest Africa. There is no way of explaining his naïve and daring assertions."[12] While Döllinger was prepared to concede that Newman "is an uncommonly gifted and also deeply religious man" and "writes excellently," he was nonetheless convinced that "his insights into Church history are too scanty." Indeed, for the German theologian, "with [Newman's] theory of development he transplants Darwinism into religion except that where Darwin lets the ape develop into Caucasian man, in Newman's case in contrast man gradually degenerates into ape."[13] Benjamin Disraeli was equally convinced of the dubiousness of the historical thinking that animated Newman's conversion. In the general preface that he wrote for his various novels in 1870, the prime minister who had so effectively identified himself with the ecclesiastical interests of the Tory party observed:

> The secession of Dr. Newman dealt a blow to the Church of England under which it still reels. That extraordinary event has been "apologized" for, but has never been explained. It was a mistake and a misfortune. The tradition of the Anglican Church was powerful. Resting on the Church of Jerusalem, modified by the divine school of Galilee, it would have found that rock of truth which Providence, by the instrumentality of the Semitic race, had promised to St. Peter. Instead of that, the seceders sought refuge in mediaeval

---

10 George M. Young, "The Schoolmen of Downing Street," in *Daylight and Champaign: Essays* (London: Rupert Hart-Davis, 1937), 57.

11 Gladstone to Richard Holt Hutton, 6 October 1890, in *Correspondence on Church and Religion of William Ewart Gladstone*, ed. Daniel C. Lathbury (London: Macmillan, 1910), I, 406.

12 Döllinger to Gladstone, 17 February 1875, BL Add. 44140/348–9 (German), quoted in Roland Hill, *Lord Acton* (New Haven: Yale University Press, 2000), 271.

13 Döllinger to Lady Blennerhassett, 20 February 1875, *Ignaz von Döllinger Briefwechsel mit Lady Blennerhassett, 1865–1886*, ed. Victor Conzemius (Munich: Beck, 1963–81), 597–8 (German), quoted in Hill, *Lord Acton*, 270.

superstitions, which are generally only the embodiments of pagan ceremonies and creeds.¹⁴

For Young, Newman might have managed to get the better of the impetuous Charles Kingsley, whose attack on his veracity led to his writing of the *Apologia pro Vita Sua* (1864), but he was not so successful when it came to Henry Hart Milman (1791–1868), the Anglican historian, who, in a long review of the *Essay on the Development of Christian Doctrine* (1845), took Newman to task for what he claimed were his historical deficiencies.¹⁵ "In the hands of Milman," Young claimed, Newman "was helpless. The *Essay on Development* is, as its title declares, nothing if not historical; and of historical evidence, as of the methods of historical inquiry, it may be safely affirmed, Newman knew nothing. Firmly handled the *Essay* simply crumbles to pieces, and what is left—let us call it by its right name—is nothing but a compost of sophistry and superstition."¹⁶

In thus siding with Milman against Newman, Young was also siding with the rationalist and literary critic John Mackinnon Robertson (1856–1933), who, in his *A History of Free Thought in the Nineteenth Century* (1929), said of Milman that he "had usefully shown that in the land of Gibbon, in the thick of reaction, it was still possible even for a university man and a priest to draw some rational inferences in the field of religious history as they were being drawn in the fields of economics, jurisprudence, politics, and science, by men who had not gone through the Oxford mill."¹⁷ The Anglo-Irish historian William Edward Hartpole Lecky (1838–1903), in his *History of the Rise and Influence of the Spirit Rationalism in Europe* (1866), expressed similar contempt for Oxford:

> It has been often remarked as a singular fact, that almost every great step which has been made by the English intellect, in connection with theology, has been made in spite of the earnest and persistent opposition of the University of Oxford ... The advocates of the theory of civil liberty, in opposition to the theory of passive obedience, and the advocates of toleration as opposed to persecution, had found at Oxford their most unflinching and their most able adversaries. In our own century, when the secularisation of politics was forced upon the public mind by the discussions on the Test Act and on Catholic Emancipation, and when it had become evident

---

14 Disraeli, quoted in William F. Monypenny and George E. Buckle, *The Life of Benjamin Disraeli, Earl of Beaconsfield* (London: John Murray, 1916), IV, 350–1.

15 For a witty, well-written, and shrewd study of Newman's most famous critic, see Una Pope-Hennessy, *Canon Charles Kingsley* (London: Macmillan, 1948).

16 George M. Young, "Sophist and Swashbuckler," in *Daylight and Champaign*, 104.

17 John M. Robertson, *A History of Free Thought in the Nineteenth Century* (London: Watts, 1929), 147.

to all attentive observers that this question was destined to be the battle-field of the contest between modern civilisation and tradition, the University of Oxford showed clearly that its old spirit had lost none of its intensity, though it had lost much of its influence.[18]

If Newman was at the forefront of that contest when he worked to remove Sir Robert Peel from his Oxford seat in 1829 after his about-face on Catholic Emancipation, Lecky was dismissive of the Oxford that created what Frederick Rogers called the "great movement in the English Church,"[19] describing it as "a great reactionary movement." For Lecky, it was "directed avowedly against the habits of religious thought which modern civilisation had everywhere produced. Its supporters denounced these habits as essentially and fundamentally false. They described the history of English theology for a century and a half as a history of uninterrupted decadence. They believed, in the emphatic words of their great leader, that 'the nation was on its way to give up revealed truth.'"[20]

This "reactionary movement" in Oxford would stall after Newman's secession to Rome in 1845 and give way to a triumphant liberalism, presided over by such liberal dons as Mark Pattison (1813–84) and Benjamin Jowett (1817–93), for both of whom it was axiomatic that dogmatic Christianity was exploded precisely because it was rooted in superstition. Pattison recalled his brief stint as a Tractarian with a kind of incredulous revulsion. "Indeed, I have great difficulty with the Diary in my hand in making intelligible the exact state of my mind and opinions in the whole of the four years from 1843–7. I do not see a single page in the Diary which savours of rationalism, I mean the application of the common reason to religion. I see a great deal of degrading superstition, of fasting and attending endless religious services."[21] And this was all the more disconcerting to the Rector of Lincoln College because he had been "reared," as he said, "on the strict lines of the inductive philosophy, and … a disciple of Bacon, Locke and Dugald Stewart."[22] Jowett blamed Newman for bringing about this perfervid ethos, claiming that he "seems to have been the most artificial man of our generation, full of ecclesiastical loves and hatred." And taking these prejudices into account, Jowett considered it "wonderful what a space [Newman] has filled in the eyes of mankind. In speculation he was

---

18 Lecky, *History of the Rise and Influence of the Spirit of Rationalism*, I, 173.
19 LD, IX, 320, n. 1.
20 Hill, *Lord Acton*, 172. The quotation within this quotation is from *Difficulties Felt by Anglicans*, 57.
21 Mark Pattison, *Memoirs* (London: Macmillan, 1885), 189.
22 Ibid., 164. Dugald Stewart (1753–1828), a Scottish philosopher and mathematician, prominent in the Scottish Enlightenment. Among his pupils was one of Newman's most obliging satirical butts, Lord Brougham.

habitually untruthful and not much better in practice. His conscience had been taken out and the Church put in its place." At the same time, Jowett, for all of his strictures, had to concede that Newman was "a man of genius, and a good man in the sense of being disinterested."[23]

Newman's genius cannot be understood apart from his interest in superstition. Indeed, his works exhibit a lifelong fascination with precisely the thing that so many of his contemporaries found insupportable. In the *Apologia*, for example, he cited recollections he had put to paper in 1820 and, then, again, in 1823, of his thoughts and feelings on religious subjects when a child and boy, and in one he noted: "I was very superstitious, and for some time previous to my conversion [when I was fifteen] used constantly to cross myself on going into the dark."[24] In his sermon, "The Religion of the Day" (1832), he declared:

> I will not shrink from uttering my firm conviction, that it would be a gain to this country, were it vastly more superstitious, more bigoted, more gloomy, more fierce in its religion, than at present it shows itself to be. Not, of course, that I think the tempers of mind herein implied desirable, which would be an evident absurdity; but I think them infinitely more desirable and more promising than a heathen obduracy, and a cold, self- sufficient, self-wise tranquillity.[25]

Then, again, in a passage from another sermon, "Religious Faith Rational" (1829), Newman conceded that:

> Doubtless there is such a fault as credulity, or believing too readily and too much (and this, in religion, we call superstition); but this neither shows that *all* trust is irrational, nor again that trust is necessarily irrational, which is founded on what is but likely to be, and may be denied without an actual absurdity. Indeed, when we come to examine the subject, it will be found that, strictly speaking, we know little more than that we exist, and that there is an Unseen Power whom we are bound to obey. Beyond this we must *trust*; and first our senses, memory, and reasoning powers; then other authorities:—so that, in fact, almost all we do, every day of our lives, is on trust, i.e. *faith*.[26]

Here, incidentally, was an early foreshadowing of the epistemological preoccupations of Newman's *Grammar of Assent* (1870), written over thirty years before he wrote Charles Meynell, Professor of Philosophy at Oscott,

---

23 Benjamin Jowett to Margot Asquith, 22 May 1891, in Margot Asquith, *Autobiography* (London: Thornton Butterworth, 1920), 123–4.
24 *Apologia*, 15–16.
25 Newman, "The Religion of the Day" (1832), Sermon 24, in *PPS*, I, 320–1.
26 Newman, "Religious Faith Rational" (1829), Sermon 15, in *PPS*, I, 193.

a great admirer of Newman's treatment of faith and reason in his *Oxford University Sermons*, to tell him that he was mulling over writing what he referred to as: "a new work ... on 'the popular, practical, and personal evidence of Christianity'—i.e. as contrasted to the scientific, and its object would be to show that a given individual, high or low, has as much right (has as real rational grounds) to be certain, as a learned theologian who knows the scientific evidence."[27]

At the same time, in the introduction to the *Remains of the Late Reverend Richard Hurrell Froude* (1838), which brought together the *obiter dicta* of the true founder of the Oxford Movement, Newman took issue with those who claimed that Froude's papers were "overstrained," "fanatical," "ascetic" and "bigoted"[28] by reminding them, with a paradoxical élan that Chesterton himself might have admired, that no one could be sure that these were not qualities that "Our Lord from the beginning willed should be impressed on His Church."[29] Certainly, one can see the respect Newman felt for the superstitious in these passionate admonitions:

> If we have not the boldness to take it on ourselves, and follow the Lamb withersoever He goeth, at least let us not throw stumbling blocks in the way of those who are more courageously disposed. When a thing is fairly proved superstitious, uncharitable, ascetic in a bad sense, unwarranted by Scripture and Antiquity, then let it be blamed and rejected, not before; lest we incur such a rebuke as he did who, with more zeal than knowledge, would have prevented Our Lord Himself ... from taking up and bearing His Cross. It was in love to Christ that he remonstrated; yet what was Christ's reproof? *"Get thee behind Me, Satan; thou art an offence unto Me; for thou savourest not the things that be of God, but the things that be of men."*[30]

Moreover, Newman is insistent that understanding the early Church requires a certain sympathy, a certain readiness to enter into its "ethos," and for that, a certain humility is in order. In the preface to the *Remains*, he is eloquent about the elements of this humility, which many of his

---

27 Newman to Charles Meynell, 23 January 1860, in *LD*, XIX, 294.

28 "Preface" to *The Remains of the Late Reverend Hurrell Froude, MA*, ed. John Keble and John Henry Newman (London: J. G. & F. Rivington, 1839), I, xv–xvi. These are the adjectives Newman uses in the preface to give his readers a sampling of the response to Froude's *Remains*: "Other particulars might be mentioned, but these which have been enumerated are surely sufficient to teach persons a little caution how they apply the readily occurring words, 'overstrained, fanatical, ascetic, bigoted,' to notions and practices as have been now alluded to." Although authorship of the "Preface" is attributed to both Newman and Keble, I adduce from the character of the prose in the passages that I cite that Newman seems to have been their sole author.

29 *Ibid.*, xvi.

30 *Ibid.*

English contemporaries might have found oddly credulous in an Oxford don. "He who makes up his mind really to take Antiquity for his guide," Newman writes, "will feel that he must be continually realizing the Presence of a wonder-working God: his mind must be awake to the possibility of special providences, miraculous interferences, supernatural warnings and tokens of the divine purpose, and also unseen agency, both good and bad, relating to himself and others."[31] Indeed, for Newman, "subjects of this sort, if a man be consistent, must fill up a larger portion of his thoughts and affections, and influence his conduct far more materially than the customs and opinions of this age would readily permit."[32] Leslie Stephen, the agnostic contributor to such liberal reviews as the *Cornhill Magazine*, *Fraser's Magazine*, and the *Fortnightly Review*, as well as the founding editor of the *Dictionary of National Biography*, was probably more representative of educated opinion in Great Britain when he wrote in one of the papers he delivered to the Metaphysical Society:[33] "the tendency of men ... to believe what is pleasant rather than what is true, shows the necessity of rigidly verifying every creed, especially if it is the product of a time when erroneous conceptions of the universe were notoriously prevalent."[34]

31 Ibid., xv.
32 Ibid.
33 The Metaphysical Society was founded in 1869 by the architect and editor James Knowles (1831–1908) to give Anglicans, Roman Catholics, Unitarians and Nonconformists, as well as atheists and agnostics, the chance to discuss metaphysical issues (broadly defined) from different viewpoints. Members included Cardinal Manning, John Dalgairns, Henry Sidgwick, Thomas Huxley, William George Ward, James Fitzjames Stephen, Richard Holt Hutton and Walter Bagehot. Dining once a month from November to July at the Grosvenor Hotel in London, members listened to and discussed a paper by one of the members circulated in advance on such topics as the arguments for a future life, the theory of causation, the scientific basis of morals, and the relation of will to thought. The Society dissolved in 1880. Apropos its upshot, Christopher A. Kent writes in the *Oxford Dictionary of National Biography*: "If no great reconciliation of science and religion had been effected, members had perhaps gained a more respectful appreciation of what divided them." Christopher A. Kent, "Metaphysical Society (act. 1869–1880)," in *The Oxford Dictionary of National Biography*. See also Alan W. Brown, *The Metaphysical Society: Victorian Minds in Crisis, 1869–1880* (New York: Columbia University Press, 1947), Richard H. Hutton, "The Metaphysical Society: A Reminiscence," *Nineteenth Century* (18 August 1885), 177–96, and Priscilla Metcalf, *James Knowles: Victorian Editor and Architect* (Oxford: Clarendon Press, 1980).
34 Leslie Stephen, "Belief and Evidence," delivered at the Metaphysical Society, 12 June 1877, in *The Papers of the Metaphysical Society 1869–1880: A Critical Edition*, ed. Catherine Marshall, Bernard Lightman, and Richard England (Oxford: Oxford University Press, 2015), III, 115. Apropos Newman's attitude to the Metaphysical Society, Henry Parry Liddon, Edward Pusey's biographer, recorded in his diary on 8 July 1872: "In the evening dined at the Deanery to meet Dr. Newman. His manner was quite that of Mr. Keble, in its simplicity and intensity. He was much amused with the Metaphysical

Nevertheless, it was in light of the practical appeal of the early Church, with all its "special providences, miraculous interferences, supernatural warnings and tokens of the divine purpose," that Newman never had any doubts about the methodical thoroughness with which "the fathers and patrons of the English Reformation ... fastened on ... Catholics first the imputation, [and] then the repute of ignorance, bigotry, and superstition"[35] in order to discredit the traditional faith in the eyes of the English people. Then, again, in the "Preface to the Third Edition" of the *Via Media*, written in 1877, forty years after he had tried and failed to impart some theological respectability to Anglicanism, Newman put the matter of superstition in an even larger light:

> Taking human nature as it is, we may surely concede a little superstition, as not the worst of evils, if it be the price of making sure of faith. Of course it need not be the price, and the Church, in her teaching function, will ever be vigilant against the inroad of what is a degradation both of faith and reason: but considering ... how feeble and confused is at present the ethical intelligence of the world at large, it is a distant day, at which the Church will find it easy, in her oversight of her populations, to make her Sacerdotal office keep step with her Prophetical. Just now I should be disposed to doubt whether that nation really had the faith, which is free in all its ranks and classes from all kinds and degrees of what is commonly considered superstition.[36]

Young claims that Milman attacked Newman on the ground that he confused historical evidence with superstition, but, in fact, the one section of Newman's *Essay on Development* that Milman praised was the one in which Newman charted the rise of superstition that coincided with the rise of Christianity.[37] "The whole chapter which traces the development of this false Heathen Idea of Christianity," wrote Milman, "is the ablest in the book, full of various reading, and told with ease and perspicuity; it is not so profoundly theological as those which follow ... but it is more full of general interest—the work, in short, of an accomplished scholar."[38] Yet, as I shall

---

Society and said that they ought not to be eating any dinners." John O. Johnston, *Life and Letters of Henry Parry Liddon* (London: Longman, Green & Co., 1904), 170 note.

35 Newman, Lecture 2, "Tradition the Sustaining Power of the Protestant View," in *Present Position of Catholics*, 64–5.

36 Newman, "Preface to the Third Edition," in *Via Media*, I, lxviii–lxix.

37 Newman, ch. 6, "Application of the First Note of a True Development—Preservation of Type," §1, "The Church of the First Centuries," in *Essay on Development*, 207–47.

38 Henry H. Milman, "Review of Newman's *Essay on Development*," in *Savonarola, Erasmus and Other Essays* (London: John Murray, 1870), 332. This review first appeared in *The Quarterly Review* in March 1846.

endeavor to show, Newman used his considerable scholarship to uncover truths that are a good deal more "profoundly theological" than either Milman or indeed most subsequent historians realize. In order to identify these truths, we should take a closer look at this section of the *Essay on Development* because it is not only a bravura piece of history, but an effective polemic.

That the rise of Christianity and the rise of superstition were indissolubly linked Newman concedes as an historical fact, though one which is acknowledged only because it is misapprehended. "Upon the established religions of Europe the East had renewed her encroachments, and was pouring forth a family of rites which in various ways attracted the attention of the luxurious, the political, the ignorant, the restless, and the remorseful. Armenian, Chaldee, Egyptian, Jew, Syrian, Phrygian, as the case might be, was the designation of the new hierophant; and magic, superstition, barbarism, jugglery, were the names given to his rite by the world. In this company appeared Christianity."[39] If Newman's controversial object in the *Essay on Development* was to demonstrate historical continuity between the Early Church and the Roman Church in order to refute the Anglican claim that the latter was an illegitimate corruption of the former, he recognized that nothing could help him to accomplish this better than historical perceptions of superstition. And so this most brilliant of polemicists considers how the Early Church appeared in what he calls "the mirror of the world."[40]

> Of course it may happen that the common estimate concerning a person or a body is purely accidental and unfounded; but in such cases it is not lasting. Such were the calumnies of child-eating and impurity in the Christian meetings, which were almost extinct by the time of Origen, and which might arise from the world's confusing them with the pagan and heretical rites. But when it continues from age to age, it is certainly an index of a fact, and corresponds to definite qualities in the object to which it relates. In that case, even mistakes carry information; for they are cognate to the truth, and we can allow for them ... What to one man is magnanimity, to another is romance, and pride to a third, and pretence to a fourth, while to a fifth it is simply unintelligible; and yet there is a certain analogy in their separate testimonies, which conveys to us what the thing is like and what it is not like. When a man's acknowledged note is superstition, we may be pretty sure we shall not find him an Academic or an Epicurean ... In like manner, there is a certain general correspondence between magic and miracle, obstinacy and faith, insubordination and zeal for religion, sophistry and argumentative talent, craft and meekness.[41]

39 Newman, *Essay on Development*, 218–19.
40 *Ibid.*, 224.
41 *Ibid.*, 223–4.

From this lively insight, Ernest Renan (1823–92) may have derived his famous *aperçu* that "forgetting and even mistakes in history are an essential part of becoming a nation"[42] and James Joyce (1882–1941) the contention he has Stephen Dedalus make in *Ulysses* (1922) that errors are the "portals of discovery."[43] Both men, after all, were attentive readers of Newman.

Having established how even erroneous perceptions can help identify a thing, Newman proceeds to show how the popular consensus about the superstitious character of Christianity was adopted by some of the ancient world's most discriminating historians. Thus, when Tacitus, Pliny, and Seutonius referred to Christianity as "a superstition and a magical superstition," they were "not simply using words at random, or the language of abuse ... they were describing it in distinct and recognized terms as cognate to those gloomy, secret, odious, disreputable religions which were making so much disturbance up and down the empire."[44] Newman also stresses that "this is no accidental imputation, but ... repeated by a variety of subsequent writers and speakers":

> The heathen disputant in Minucius calls Christianity, "*Vana et demens superstitio.*" The lawyer Modestinus speaks, with an apparent allusion to Christianity, of "weak minds being terrified *superstitione numinis.*" The heathen magistrate asks St. Marcellus, whether he and others have put away "vain superstitions," and worship the gods whom the emperors worship. The Pagans in Arnobius speak of Christianity as "an execrable and unlucky religion, full of impiety and sacrilege, contaminating the rites instituted from of old with the superstition of its novelty."[45]

By way of contrast, when liberal Anglicans took up this testimony, they tended to use it to rebuke not only Roman Catholics but Romanizing Anglo-Catholics for what they regarded as their credulity. "We cannot rise above our philosophy by taking up the horn-book again," the Broad Church polemicist Julius Charles Hare (1795–1855) contended. "Dilettantism will amuse itself with antiquarian resuscitations, and deck itself out

---

42 Ernest Renan, "*Qu'est-ce qu'une nation?*" (Lecture, Sorbonne, Paris, 11 March 1882). "Forgetfulness, and I would even say historical error, are essential in the creation of a nation." Ibid.

43 James Joyce, *Ulysses* (New York: Random House, 1946), 160. In the "Scylla and Charybdis" chapter of *Ulysses*, Joyce has John Eglinton, librarian of the National Library of Ireland, "bald, eared and assiduous," claim that Shakespeare made a mistake in marrying Ann Hathaway, to which Stephen Dedalus responds: "Bosh! A man of genius makes no mistakes. His errors are volitional and are the portals of discovery."

44 Newman, *Essay on Development*, 219.

45 Ibid., 224–5.

with modern antiques. But practical life requires its own growths."[46] Indeed, for Hare, "In ages when intellectual and moral energy is almost effete ... people will ... attempt to revive exploded superstitions, even as they may affect archaisms of language. But even then the revived superstition was no more like the reality, than a skeleton is like the living body, which once clothed it. That which has once been exploded cannot again become a part of the organic structure of society. You might as well sow a husk."[47] And it was precisely what he regarded as the radical antiquatedness of superstition that convinced him never to "anticipate ... that the Church of Rome will ever triumph over ours."[48] Indeed, for Hare, to adhere to superstition was "to seek and lose the reality in the form, in the symbol, in the outward work, in the outward ordinance: and this superstition was pervading the whole Church ... when Luther arose to call it back from the worship of forms to the worship of living realities."[49] Connop Thirlwall (1797–1875), the Anglican divine and historian who made his reputation with his *History of Greece* (1847), saw in Newman's respect for superstition a willful renunciation of his own closeted skepticism, a claim that the champion of the free churches, Andrew Martin Fairbairn (1838–1912), and, later, the scurrilous Yale historian Frank Turner (1944–2010) would attempt to revive.[50] "I should be very loth to believe Newman capable of any serious untruthfulness," Thirlwall wrote a friend, "or of any that is not implied in the sceptical and sophistical character which I ascribe to his mind. But I believe him to be at bottom far more sceptical than his brother Francis, and the extravagant credulity with which he accepts the wildest Popish legends is, as it appears to me, only another side of his bottomless unbelief."[51]

In 1885, in a piece in the *Contemporary Review* entitled "Catholicism and Apologetics," Fairbairn would attempt to defend this assertion by giving it some philosophical pedigree.

> Hobbes had no place for religion in his system save as a legalized superstition, whose source was the belief in witchcraft and in ghosts. Locke was the parent of English Rationalism and Deism;

---

46 Julius C. Hare, *Charges to the Archdeaconry of Lewes Delivered at the Ordinary Visitations in the Years 1843, 1845 and 1846* (Cambridge: Macmillan & Co., 1856), II, 146.

47 Ibid.

48 Ibid., II, 146–7.

49 Julius C. Hare, *Vindication of Luther against his Recent English Assailants* (London: John W. Parker, 1855), 89.

50 See Frank Turner, *John Henry Newman: The Challenge to Evangelical Religion* (New Haven: Yale University Press, 2002), 641: "Newman emerged as the first great, and perhaps the most enduring, Victorian skeptic."

51 Connop Thirlwall, *Letters Literary and Theological of Connop Thirlwall*, ed. John J. S. Perowne and Louis Stokes (London: Richard Bentley & Son, 1881), 261.

his empiricism could not but tempt men to strip religion of all its mysteries, in order that it might be reconciled to a reason emptied of all transcendental contents. Hume had but to use Locke as modified by Berkeley in order to evolve a scepticism so universal that it did not spare even the ego. The Mills, father and son, inherited their full share of the impotences and aversions of our insular empiricism; and though it has in Spencer changed its terminology, and even boldly essayed to become constructive, yet it remains at heart what it has ever been; for Agnosticism is just scepticism become too proud or too perverse to confess to its own real nature. And so our traditional philosophy has either attempted to explain religion out of existence as a congeries of illicit or fictitious ideas, or it has presented theology with the problem which produced the distinctive apologetics of the eighteenth century—how to get religion into a mind which has no religious constitution or contents. If men would be religious under such a philosophy it must be by the help of some external authority which supplies them with a faith and becomes the guarantee of its truth. The theological evolution of such philosophy was seen in Newman, the speculative in Hume and the Mills.[52]

In other words, for Fairbairn, Newman was not immune to the same sort of skepticism that beguiled Hobbes, and the only way that he could dispute Hobbes's view that religion was "legalized superstition" was to invoke "some external authority." Yet Fairbairn did not grasp how radically Newman departed from Hobbes and his philosophical fellows in his reading of the history of the early Church.[53] Instead of simply dismissing the testimony of the first centuries as tantamount to a "belief in witchcraft and ghosts," Newman sought to understand it by asking why the imputation of superstition had been leveled at the new religion in the first place. Accordingly, he asked, "Now what is meant by the word thus attached by a *consensus* of heathen authorities to Christianity? At least, it cannot mean a religion in which a man might think what he pleased, and was set free from all yokes, whether of ignorance, fear, authority, or priestcraft."[54] Here, Newman was taking well-aimed swipes at the Broad Church, particularly its contempt for authority and the sacerdotal. And it followed from this that "When heathen writers call the Oriental rites superstitions, they evidently

---

52 Andrew M. Fairbairn, *The Place of Christ in Modern Theology* (London: Hodder & Stoughton, 1893), 204.

53 See *The Idea of a University*, 263. In Article 3, "English Catholic Literature," Newman remarks how "If we were to ask for a report of our philosophers, the investigation would not be so agreeable; for we have three of evil, and one of unsatisfactory repute. Locke is scarcely an honour to us in the standard of truth, grave and manly as he is; and Hobbes, Hume, and Bentham, in spite of their abilities, are simply a disgrace."

54 Newman, *Essay on Development*, 225.

use the word in its modern sense; it cannot surely be doubted that they apply it in the same sense to Christianity."[55] Thus Newman establishes the continuity between ancient and modern critics of Roman Catholicism by showing how their opposition to the Church is grounded in their shared impatience with what they choose to regard as superstition.

Yet rather than impose his own views on the evidence, Newman turned to Plutarch (c. 46–c. 120), and in mining the great Greek historian and biographer who provided Shakespeare with so much of his ancient history, he began to uncover the telltale human truths to which superstition attests. Thus, Newman quotes Plutarch:

> Of all kinds of fear ... superstition is the most fatal to action and resource. He does not fear the sea who does not sail, nor war who does not serve, nor robbers who keeps at home, nor the sycophant who is poor, nor the envious if he is a private man, nor an earthquake if he lives in Gaul, nor thunder if he lives in Ethiopia; but he who fears the gods fears everything, earth, seas, air, sky, darkness, light, noises, silence, sleep. Slaves sleep and forget their masters; of the fettered doth sleep lighten the chain; inflamed wounds, ulcers cruel and agonizing, are not felt by the sleeping. Superstition alone has come to no terms with sleep; but in the very sleep of her victims, as though they were in the realms of the impious, she raises horrible spectres, and monstrous phantoms, and various pains, and whirls the miserable soul about, and persecutes it.[56]

One wonders if Goya read Plutarch before he set to work on that unforgettable etching of his *The Sleep of Reason Produces Monsters* (1799). In any case, by quoting Plutarch at such length, Newman established a redoubtable authority for treating superstition as something more than an offshoot of credulity.

Passing from the subject of sleep to that of death, Newman showed how Plutarch was equally aware of how superstition transcends our mortal coil, for "while death is to all men an end of life, it is not so to the superstitious; for then 'there are deep gates of hell ... and headlong streams of ... fire and gloom ... and darkness with its many phantoms [and] ghosts presenting horrid visages and wretched voices, and judges and executioners, and chasms and dens full of innumerable miseries.'"[57] Newman also points out how, in Plutarch, we find that "in misfortune or sickness the superstitious man refuses to see physician or philosopher." Instead, quoting Plutarch directly, Newman shows how the wretched man is impelled to cry out: "Suffer me, O man, to undergo punishment, the impious, the cursed, the hated of gods and

---

55 Ibid., 225.
56 Plutarch, "On Superstition," quoted in Newman, *Development*, 226.
57 Ibid., 226–7.

spirits."⁵⁸ In such passages, one can hear something of the poet in Newman, who, in translating Plutarch, always exhibits a poet's clairvoyance and élan.

Then, again, by quoting Plutarch's comparison between the superstitious and the unbelieving man, Newman indirectly needled his complacent contemporaries. The atheist, Plutarch says, "wipes his tears, trims his hair, [and] doffs his mourning." But how, he asks, "can you address, how help the superstitious? He sits apart in sackcloth or filthy rags; and often he strips himself and rolls in the mud, and tells out his sins and offences, as having eaten and drunken something, or walked some way which the divinity did not allow ... And in his best mood, and under the influence of a good-humoured superstition, he sits at home, with sacrifice and slaughter all round him."⁵⁹ Ordinary unbelieving men delight in "festivals, banquets at the temples, initiations, orgies, votive prayers, and adorations" while "the superstitious wishes indeed, but is unable to rejoice. He is crowned and turns pale; he sacrifices and is in fear; he prays with a quivering voice, and burns incense with trembling hands, and altogether belies the saying of Pythagoras, that we are then in best case when we go to the gods; for superstitious men fare most wretchedly and evilly, approaching the houses or shrines of the gods as if they were the dens of bears, or the holes of snakes, or the caves of whales."⁶⁰

It is amusing that the note of sympathy that Newman expressed here for the god-fearing superstitious offended Milman, who asked in his review of the *Essay on Development*: "What have we to do with what Christianity seemed to the contemptuous heathen in the first centuries, to what misrepresentations or calumnies it was exposed?"⁶¹ Newman's response was that Milman and his skeptical contemporaries had more to do with these "contemptuous heathen" than they realized, since their objections to the Roman faith were no different from those of the skeptics of the first century. Moreover, although Milman, Gladstone, Döllinger, Lecky, and Young may have scoffed at Newman's historical pretensions, few nineteenth-century English historians cited the contemporary evidence pertaining to Christianity to make the fundamental point that Newman made in citing Plutarch, a point which had significant implications for Newman's contemporaries:

> Here we have a vivid picture of Plutarch's idea of the essence of Superstition ... it was the imagination of the existence of an unseen ever-present Master; the bondage of a rule of life, of a continual responsibility; obligation to attend to little things, the impossibility of escaping from duty, the inability to choose or change one's

58 Ibid., 227.
59 Ibid.
60 Ibid.
61 Milman, "Review," 331.

religion, an interference with the enjoyment of life, a melancholy view of the world, sense of sin, horror at guilt, apprehension of punishment, dread, self-abasement, depression, anxiety and endeavour to be at peace with heaven, and error and absurdity in the methods chosen for the purpose[62]

—all of the things, in other words, that the Broad Church English were encouraged to find objectionable about the Church of Rome. Moreover, as Newman shows, Plutarch was not alone in this testimony. "Such too had been the idea of the Epicurean Velleius, when he shrunk with horror from the *'sempiternus dominus'* and *'curiosus Deus'* of the Stoics. Such, surely, was the meaning of Tacitus, Suetonius, and Pliny."[63] And from this testimony, as Newman points out, it is perfectly understandable why Christians should have been perceived as "credulous, weak-minded, and poor-spirited. The heathen objectors in Minucius and Lactantius speak of their 'old-woman's tales.' Celsus accuses them of 'assenting at random and without reason,' saying, 'Do not inquire, but believe.'"[64]

Here, Newman taunts his liberal readers by reminding them that in the first, as in the nineteenth century, the people who tended to be most opposed to Christianity were the educated. "They lay it down," Newman quotes Celsus as saying. "Let no educated man approach, no man of wisdom, no man of sense; but if a man be unlearned, weak in intellect, an infant, let him come with confidence. Confessing that these are worthy of their God, they evidently desire, as they are able, to convert none but fools, and vulgar, and stupid, and slavish, women and boys." They "take in the simple, and lead him where they will." They address themselves to "youths, house-servants, and the weak in intellect." They "hurry away from the educated, as not fit subjects of their imposition, and inveigle the rustic."[65] If, in these passages, Newman was indirectly remonstrating with the atheists of his age (with the help of Celsus), when we read them, we can hear a similar reproof of our own atheists.

In drawing his conclusions from this adroitly assembled testimony, Newman confirms how perception distorted the reality of Christianity. For the world, Christianity was indeed

> one of a number of wild and barbarous rites which were pouring in upon the Empire from the ancient realms of superstition, and the mother of a progeny of sects which were faithful to the original they had derived from Egypt or Syria; a religion unworthy of an educated person, as appealing, not to the intellect, but to the fears

62 Newman, *Essay on Development*, 227–8.
63 Ibid., 228.
64 Ibid.
65 Ibid.

and weaknesses of human nature, and consisting, not in the rational and cheerful enjoyment, but in a morose rejection of the gifts of Providence; a horrible religion, as inflicting or enjoining cruel sufferings, and monstrous and loathsome in its very indulgence of the passions; a religion leading by reaction to infidelity; a religion of magic, and of the vulgar arts, real and pretended, with which magic was accompanied; a secret religion which dared not face the day; an itinerant, busy, proselytizing religion, forming an extended confederacy against the state, resisting its authority and breaking its laws.[66]

Here, Newman could almost be said to be travestying one of the favorite ploys of the Whig historian: emphasizing the benightedness of the past by contrasting it with the supposititious enlightenment of the present; yet he undermines the convention by showing how the present, in this case, has not advanced from the past: the modern world still sees Christianity in much the same benighted aspect as the ancient world saw it. And so Newman concludes:

[I]f there is a form of Christianity now in the world which is accused of gross superstition, of borrowing its rites and customs from the heathen, and of ascribing to forms and ceremonies an occult virtue;—a religion which is considered to burden and enslave the mind by its requisitions, to address itself to the weak-minded and ignorant, to be supported by sophistry and imposture, and to contradict reason and exalt mere irrational faith;—a religion which impresses on the serious mind very distressing views of the guilt and consequences of sin, sets upon the minute acts of the day, one by one, their definite value for praise or blame, and thus casts a grave shadow over the future ... a religion which men hate as proselytizing, anti-social, revolutionary, as dividing families, separating chief friends, corrupting the maxims of government, making a mock at law, dissolving the empire, the enemy of human nature, and a "conspirator against its rights and privileges";—a religion which they consider the champion and instrument of darkness, and a pollution calling down upon the land the anger of heaven;—a religion which they associate with intrigue and conspiracy, which they speak about in whispers, which they detect by anticipation in whatever goes wrong, and to which they impute whatever is unaccountable;—a religion, the very name of which they cast out as evil, and use simply as a bad epithet, and which from the impulse of self-preservation they would persecute if they could;—if there be such a religion now in the world, it is not unlike Christianity as that same world viewed it, when first it came forth from its Divine Author.[67]

66 Ibid., 240.
67 Ibid., 245–7.

After reading this salutary piece of irony, which would have amused the satirist in Jonathan Swift, it is instructive to revisit the work of the Whig historians themselves, so much of which corroborates Newman's insights into the persistence of the world's misconceptions of the Church.[68] In his constitutional history of England, for example, Henry Hallam (1777–1859) describes the medieval Church as though it had been almost exclusively given over to pious fraud. Hallam wrote:

> The devotion of the multitude was wrought to … feverish height by the prevailing system of the clergy in that singular polytheism, which had been grafted on the language rather than the principles of Christianity, nothing was so conspicuous as the belief of perpetual miracles … These superstitions arose in what are called primitive times … But successive ages of ignorance swelled the delusion to such an enormous pitch, that it was as difficult to trace, we may say without exaggeration, the real religion of the gospel in the popular belief of the laity … Every cathedral or monastery had its tutelar saint, and every saint his legend, fabricated in order to enrich the churches under his protection, by exaggerating his virtues, his miracles, and consequently his power of serving those who paid liberally for his patronage … That the exclusive worship of saints, under the guidance of an artful though illiterate priesthood, degraded the understanding, and begot a stupid credulity and fanaticism is sufficiently evident.[69]

---

68 See Edward Short, "Whigs and Namierites: The History of English History," in *Adventures in the Book Pages: Essays and Reviews* (London: Gracewing, 2015), 184–5. "The Whig history of the nineteenth and twentieth centuries, from Henry Hallam (1777–1859) to George Trevelyan (1876–1962), tended to depict English history as a triumphant tale of English fair play, progress and continuity. Its great boasts were representative government and religious toleration—though Roman Catholics and Dissenters would always question the latter claim. Its upshot was that everything had happened for a reason and that all the reasons put together spelled the superiority of liberal Protestant Whiggery. If one doubted that upshot, all one had to do was to compare Protestant England with backward Catholic Europe. In his famous book, *The Whig Interpretation of History* (1931), Herbert Butterfield (1900–79) showed how the Whig tendency to see the past as 'the ratification, if not the glorification of the present' was something to which all historians are prone. A West Riding Methodist, he also took exception to Whig historians indulging in what he nicely called 'the luxury and pleasing sensuousness of moral indignation'—something which mars too much American history." See also John W. Burrow, *A Liberal Descent: Victorian Historians and the English Past* (Cambridge: Cambridge University Press, 1983); and John Clive, *Not by Fact Alone: Essays on the Writing and Reading of History* (New York: Alfred A. Knopf, 1989).

69 Henry Hallam, *View of the State of Europe during the Middle Ages* (London: John Murray, 1856), III, 298–9.

There is a certain aptness in the fact that these were the sentiments of a man who advocated for the same reform of the Church of Ireland that gave rise to John Keble's assize sermon on national apostasy (1833) and the beginning of the Oxford Movement, though, in many respects, Hallam was only a moderate Whig; for instance, he was not entirely in favor of reforming pocket or rotten boroughs. "The Reform Bill of 1832," he admits somewhat wistfully in his *Constitutional History*, "has of course rendered a disquisition on the ancient rights of election in boroughs a matter of merely historical interest."[70] However, when it came to the medieval Church, he was at one with Holland House and the *Edinburgh Review*, considering it an institution of self-evident imposture: "For the advance that learning then made was by no means sufficient to counteract the vast increase of monasteries, and the opportunities which the greater cultivation of modern languages afforded for the diffusion of legendary tales. It was now too, that the veneration paid to the Virgin, in early times very great, rose to an almost exclusive idolatry. It is difficult to conceive the stupid absurdity, and the disgusting profaneness, of those stories, which were invented by the monks to do her honour."[71] The implicit moral of this impeccably Whig effusion could not have been clearer: medieval Catholicism was a patent sham and only Anglicanism could reform it.[72]

James Anthony Froude (1818–94), the acolyte of Thomas Carlyle and younger brother of Hurrell Froude (the Tractarian who did more than anyone to point young Newman in the direction of Rome) wrote captivating paeans to the same Protestant Establishment in his *History of England from the fall of Wolsey to the Defeat of the Spanish Armada* (1856–70) that Newman had undermined by seceding to Rome. Froude also followed Hallam in seeing Catholicism as steeped in superstition. Speaking of the continental Reformation, Froude gave it as his opinion that the hold superstition had over Catholic Europe forced the hand of many men who might otherwise have opposed anything as drastic as a break with Rome. Indeed, for Froude, Charles V,

> like other conservative princes and statesmen, disliked Lutheranism, disbelieved in religious novelties, and wished to maintain the Church, if the Church would mend its ways. But if the Church would not mend its ways, what then? The German Protestants saw

---

70 Henry Hallam, *The Constitutional History of England from the Accession of Henry VIII to the Death of George II* (London: John Murray, 1872), III, 47.

71 Hallam, *View of Middle Ages*, III, 300.

72 Considering Hallam's low view of the Church of Rome, it is ironic that it was the death of his son, Arthur that should have inspired Tennyson to write *In Memoriam* (1850), the great prayer for faith in the long, unlovely street of Victorian skepticism, which Newman saw as the inescapable outcrop of Protestantism.

their way clearly. They had a faith of their own, and for their part were determined that, come what would, they would be ruled no longer by Pope or priests. It cost them a century of fighting, but it was they and the English martyrs, and Cromwell's Ironsides afterwards, who in fact saved the Reformation, or made it what we know. The Erasmian says it ought to have been left to the thinkers; that it could have been managed better by reason and moderation. But reason and moderation are for a world which is itself reasonable and moderate; they call out no enthusiasm and generate no vital force. The Church had at its back the superstition of a thousand years, and the practical strength which that superstition could still command. Reason is no match for such an antagonist.[73]

Lecky was equally convinced that "between the sixth and thirteenth centuries ... superstitions were most numerous, and credulity most universal ... There never had been a time, in which the minds of men were more completely imbued and moulded by supernatural conceptions ... Many thousands of cases of possession, exorcisms, miracles, and apparitions of the Evil One were recorded. They were accepted without the faintest doubt."[74] Thomas Babington Macaulay (1800–59), the greatest of the Whig historians, agreed with his liberal colleagues about the presumed deficiencies of Roman Catholicism, but was at least prepared to acknowledge that the appeal of superstition was not merely to the uneducated and the feeble-minded. "A very common knowledge of history, a very little observation of life, will suffice to prove," the great historian observed, "that no learning, no sagacity, affords a security against the greatest errors on subjects relating to the invisible world. Bayle[75] and Chillingworth,[76] two of

---

[73] James A. Froude, *Lectures on the Council of Trent*, delivered at Oxford, 1892–3 (London: Longman, Green & Co., 1896), 106–7.

[74] Lecky, *History of the Rise and Influence of the Spirit of Rationalism*, I, 61.

[75] Pierre Bayle (1647–1706), French philosopher and writer, principally known for his *Historical and Critical Dictionary* (1697). Although raised a Calvinist, he entered a Jesuit college at Toulouse and became a Roman Catholic in 1669. Shortly thereafter, he reverted to Calvinism. The precise character of his Calvinism, however, is a matter of some indefinability. According to *The Stanford Encyclopedia of Philosophy*, "Bayle might have been a positivist, an atheist, a deist, a skeptic, a fideist, a Socinian, a liberal Calvinist, a conservative Calvinist, a libertine, a Judaizing Christian, a Judeo-Christian, or even a secret Jew, a Manichean, an existentialist ... there is at least some plausibility to all of these interpretations." See Thomas M. Lennon and Michael W. Hickson, "Pierre Bayle," *The Stanford Encyclopedia of Philosophy* (Fall 2014 edn), ed. Edward N. Zalta.

[76] William Chillingworth (1602–43), an English churchman and controversialist. After becoming a fellow of Trinity College, he converted to Catholicism and studied at the Jesuit College at Douai (1630–1). Later, he reverted to Anglicanism and became the great controversial voice of Broad Church English Protestantism, famously (and from Newman's perspective, rightly) declaring, "The Bible and the Bible only is the religion

the most sceptical of mankind, turned Catholics from sincere conviction. Johnson, incredulous on all other points, was a ready believer in miracles and apparitions. He would not believe in the Earthquake of Lisbon; but he was willing to believe in the Cock Lane Ghost."[77]

Whenever Newman writes of English history, he does so with these Whig historians in mind. In this regard, he works squarely in the tradition of John Lingard (1771–1851), England's great Catholic historian, whose *History of England* (1819–30) delved into the causes of English antipathy to Rome with the same searching objectivity that can be found in Newman's *Present Position of Catholics* (1851), where he wrote:

> I am neither assuming, nor intending to prove, that the Catholic Church comes from above (though, of course, I should not have become, or be, one of her children, unless I firmly held and hold her to be the direct work of the Almighty); but here I am only investigating how it is she comes to be so despised and hated among us; since a Religion need not incur scorn and animosity simply because it is not recognized as true. And, I say, the reason is this, that reasons of State, political and national, prevent her from being heard in her defence. She is considered too absurd to be inquired into, and too corrupt to be defended, and too dangerous to be treated with equity and fair dealing. She is the victim of a prejudice which perpetuates itself, and gives birth to what it feeds upon.[78]

Newman also shared Lingard's hunger for truth and his reliance on primary sources, both of which Lingard expressed so memorably when he wrote, "My object is truth, and in the pursuit of truth I have made it a religious duty to consult the original historians. Who would draw from the troubled stream, when he may drink at the fountainhead?"[79] Another of Lingard's attributes that Newman emulated was his fine satirical touch. In his wonderfully witty *Remarks on a Charge delivered by the Bishop of Durham to the Clergy of his Diocese* (1807), Lingard wrote of Bishop Shute:

> The Right Reverend Prelate builds his opinion respecting the origin of infidelity on this basis, "that Popery, from its corruptions, is liable to the objections of thinking men." If his reasoning be just, it will naturally follow, that in Catholic countries either the number

---

of Protestants." William Chillingworth, *The Religion of Protestants, A Safe Way to Salvation* (1638), in *The Works of William Chillingworth* (London: Richard Priestley, 1820), II, 450.

77 Thomas B. Macaulay, "Ranke's History of the Popes," in *Critical and Historical Essays* (London: Dent Everyman, 1907), II, 43.

78 Newman, Lecture 1, "Protestant View of the Catholic Church," in *Present Position of Catholics*, 11–12.

79 John Lingard, *The Antiquities of the Anglo-Saxon Church* (Newcastle: Edward Walker, 1806), I, 3.

of thinking men is exceedingly small, or the number of unbelievers immensely great. The latter consequence he adopts in all its latitude, and with much solemnity assures us, "that in the nations in communion with the Church of Rome, both the members of the government and the higher classes of the people are habitually insincere; and have continued for many years to profess the Popish creed, not from any opinion of its evidence, but from an utter indifference to all religious truth whatever."[80]

That this was the charge that Kingsley brought against Newman gives this added mordancy, but it is also noteworthy that Lingard proceeded to have precisely the same sort of sardonic fun with Bishop Shute that Newman would have with Kingsley.

It would, undoubtedly, be an insult to his candour and liberality, to question the truth of a fact which he thus unequivocally asserts: on his authority then we will endeavour to believe, however improbable it may appear, that for many years all the higher orders of foreign Catholics, all who have been eminent for virtue, learning, or rank, Popes, Princes, Statesmen, Nobles, and Prelates, and even the French Clergy, who in support of their religion offered themselves to proscription, exile, and death, were habitually insincere, hypocrites, sceptics, and unbelievers. This, indeed, to many readers, will appear extraordinary, and, had not the Bishop of Durham asserted it, incredible: but what to me appears more extraordinary and more incredible is, that these thinking men did not, when they discovered the errors of Popery, adopt the pure, rational, unadulterated system of Protestantism. What induced them to prefer to it the absurdities of infidelity? This is a mystery which the Bishop has thought it prudent to conceal.[81]

While Newman was as adept as Lingard at skewering Protestant bias, he also brought a psychological acuity to his reading of English history that was all his own. For instance, he did not see in modern England a rationalist triumph over superstition, but an abandonment of the truths to which superstition attests. Nor did he find any tenable Christianity in the "pure, rational, unadulterated system of Protestantism" extolled by his former Oriel colleagues, Edward Copleston, Edward Hawkins, or Richard Whately. Copleston acknowledged this divergence when he wrote in 1835, ten years before Newman converted: "I have great personal regard for Newman, which I hope is in some degree reciprocal yet can easily imagine that our opinions on matters of academical and ecclesiastical concern do not

---

80 Lingard, *Remarks on a Charge delivered by the Bishop of Durham to the Clergy of his Diocese* (London: Keating & Brown, 1807), 12.
81 Ibid., 13.

exactly coincide."[82] Although, in his magnanimous way, Newman found laudatory things to say about his former Oriel colleagues in the opening pages of the *Apologia*, particularly crediting Edward Hawkins with helping him to understand the force of Tradition *vis-à-vis* Scripture, and Whately with reinforcing his already strong anti-Erastian convictions, this does not mean that the Anglicanism of the Noetics led him to the Church of Rome.[83] To understand Newman's conversion, we must go to his correspondence with Father Charles Russell, S.J.[84] and the impact that the palpable sanctity of Father Dominic Barberi[85] had on him, both of which enabled him to see that it was the traditional faith of the English, not the anti-Romanism imposed on them by the Henrician and Elizabethan Reformations, that was the true faith. Indeed, in one of his most moving sermons, "Christ upon the Waters," which he wrote after the English hierarchy was restored in 1850, Newman gave eloquent expression to what he saw as England's tragic betrayal of her traditional faith. After a thousand years, the English "grew tired of the heavenly stranger who sojourned among them":

> [They] had had enough of blessings and absolutions, enough of the intercession of saints, enough of the grace of the sacraments, enough of the prospect of the next life. They thought it best to secure this life in the first place, because they were in possession of it, and then to go on to the next, if time and means allowed. And they saw that to labour for the next world was possibly to lose this; whereas, to labour for this world might be, for what they knew, the way to labour for the next also. Anyhow, they would pursue a temporal end, and they would account any one their enemy who stood in the way of their pursuing it. It was a madness; but madmen are strong, and madmen are clever.[86]

---

82 William J. Copleston, *Memoir of Edward Copleston, D.D.* (London: John W. Parker, 1851), 160.

83 *Apologia*, 22 and 24–5.

84 For the vital part that Father Russell played in Newman's conversion, see *Apologia*, 176: "Dr. Russell, the present President of Maynooth … had perhaps, more to do with my conversion than any one else." See also Newman, in *LD*, VIII, 171–5, 180–3, 186–8, 288; and Newman, in *LD*, IX, 154, 155, 156, 162, 164, 165, 210, 228, 448, 450, 451, and 462.

85 For Father Dominic Barberi's influence, see Newman to Cardinal Parocchi, 2 October 1889, in Newman, in *LD*, XXXI, 277: "Certainly Fr Dominic of the Mother of God was a most striking missioner and preacher and he had a great part in my own conversion and in that of others. His very look had a holy aspect which when his figure came in sight in my circle most singularly affected me, and his remarkable *bonhomie* in the midst of his sanctity was in itself a real and holy preaching. No wonder, then, I became his convert and penitent. He was a great lover of England."

86 *University Sermons*, 130–2.

This worldly madness, for Newman, was of a piece with England's new "temporal end." And here it was ironic that he should recall the persecution of the Catholic clergy in England by making pointed references to the same Scripture that the Anglican Church would invoke in the wake of the Henrician Reformation to replace the authority of outlawed Rome.

> So with the sword and the halter, and by mutilation and fine and imprisonment, they cut off, or frightened away from the land, as Israel did in the time of old, the ministers of the Most High, and their ministrations: they "altogether broke the yoke, and burst the bonds." "They beat one, and killed another, and another they stoned," and at length they altogether cast out the Heir from His vineyard, and killed Him, "that the inheritance might be theirs." And as for the remnant of His servants whom they left, they drove them into corners and holes of the earth, and there they bade them die out; and then they rejoiced and sent gifts either to other, and made merry, because they had rid themselves of those "who had tormented them that dwelt upon the earth." And so they turned to enjoy this world, and to gain for themselves a name among men, and it was given unto them according to their wish. They preferred the heathen virtues of their original nature, to the robe of grace which God had given them: they fell back, with closed affections, and haughty reserve, and dreariness within, upon their worldly integrity, honour, energy, prudence, and perseverance; they made the most of the natural man, and they "received their reward." Forthwith they began to rise to a station higher than the heathen Roman, and have, in three centuries, attained a wider range of sovereignty; and now they look down in contempt on what they were, and upon the Religion which reclaimed them from paganism.[87]

This triumphal progress of the nineteenth-century English found one of its more emblematic milestones in Prince Albert's Great Exhibition of 1851. Indeed, in *The Great Exhibition Spiritualized* (1851), the Congregationalist minister Henry Birch hailed Albert as the "Prince of Peace" and welcomed what he was convinced would be the religious benefits of the Exhibition. "We are not without hope that the Exhibition of 1851 will subserve the interests of Christianity itself," Birch wrote, "and advance the kingdom of our common Lord and Saviour."[88] For Birch, Chillingworth's Bible Christianity and the Victorians' delight in material progress went hand in hand.

---

87 *Ibid.* The Bible verses Newman quotes, in order of appearance, are as follows: "altogether broke the yoke, and burst the bonds" (Jeremiah 5:5); "They beat one, and killed another, and another they stoned" (Matthew 12:5); "who had tormented them that dwelt on the earth" (Revelation 11:10); "received their reward" (Matthew 6:2).
88 Henry Birch, *The Great Exhibition Spiritualized* (London: John Snow, 1851), 6.

We know that "the government of the world is upon his shoulders;" we know that he has "all power in heaven and earth;" we know that he can make even "the wrath of man to praise him;" and if he can overrule the malice and plots of his enemies, and make even them subservient to his cause, much more may we suppose that this auspicious event, which bids fair to do so much to spread commerce and civilization, peace and happiness among men, shall be rendered instrumental in advancing the cause of truth and righteousness in the earth; shall do much to hasten the downfall of heathen idolatry, of Mahommedan delusion, of Jewish prejudice, of antichristian error, and of everything that exalteth itself against the pure and simple Gospel of Jesus Christ.[89]

No Victorian reading this would have been in any doubt as to what Birch had in mind when he referred to "antichristian error." Newman's friend Thomas William Allies, the short, natty, pugnacious convert, known as the "Bantam Cock," who would later teach history at the Catholic University in Dublin, responded to such No Popery innuendoes by claiming that the inspiration of the Exhibition came from "that proud, that myriad-minded Protestantism, ranging over earth and sea, from China to California, to gather their treasures for its place and hour of pride."[90] Amusingly enough, the man most responsible for mounting this testament to England's material prowess, Sir Henry Cole, was a great admirer and friend of Newman; he also had the peculiar distinction of having invented the Christmas card.[91]

In all events, for Newman, it was no cause for complacency that the modern English had left their superstition behind with their Catholic faith. Indeed, he was convinced that to be contemptuous of superstition was to be contemptuous of religion *per se*. The Whig historians, by contrast, regarded superstition as deplorably crude, unenlightened and backward. Herbert Albert Laurens Fisher (1865–1940), who together with George Trevelyan (1876–1962) constituted something of the last hurrah of the Whig tradition

---

89 *Ibid.*, 7. See also Jonathan Cohn, "Who is Out of Line in the March of Progress? Perspectives on Religion and Industry around the Great Exhibition of 1851" (Ph.D. diss., Georgetown University, 2010), 17. Cohn quotes more of the extravagant praise heaped on Albert by the nonconformist Birch: "Poets will celebrate thy praise, — historians shall record thy triumphs, — and the Christian Church will be ready to acknowledge thee as the harbinger of millennial glory."

90 See *LD*, XV, 11, n. 1.

91 Sir Henry Cole (1802–82), an English designer, writer, and civil servant. Cole founded the South Kensington Museum, where John Hungerford Pollen, who taught fine art at the Catholic University, became Assistant Keeper in 1863. According to the *Oxford Dictionary of National Biography*, "Although involved ... in all aspects of the management of the exhibition," Cole's "primary responsibility" was "the allocation of space for the 14,000 exhibitors from Britain, eleven colonies, and thirteen foreign countries."

in history, saw the Catholic Church as the epitome of superstition in what he called the "Medieval Empire."

> Every traveller remarked the contrast between ... Catholic and Protestant territories ... In one quarter you found ignorance, squalor, degrading superstition, in the other educational zeal, reading habits widely diffused and free thinking ... In Protestant Germany crime was extraordinarily rare, but nowhere were gallows and wheels so much in requisition as in Bavaria, and the astonishing proportion which burglary bore to other forms of crime in that country was attributed to the badness of the schools and the habits of beggary encouraged by the Roman Church.[92]

Fisher's irreproachably Whig view of the spread of Catholicism after the conversion of Constantine is evident in his three-volume history of Europe, where he remarks how

> The chaos of the Empire was the opportunity of the Church, the childish ignorance of the barbarian prepared the triumph of the priest. In an age when books were rare, everything depended on the voice and example of the teacher. The simple and superstitious barbarian was ready to tolerate a degree of interference in his private life which the cultivated Roman lady or gentleman would have resented as a vulgar intrusion.[93]

Newman saw the import of superstition differently. And here is where the historian in him shone, because he was not only scholarly and judicious: he was insistent on truths that his contemporaries had chosen to repudiate. Apropos the propitiatory sacrifices with which primitive man sought to atone for sins, Newman observed: "Doubtless these desperate and dark struggles are to be called superstition, when viewed by the side of true religion; and it is easy enough to speak of them as superstition, when we have been informed of the gracious and joyful result in which the scheme of Divine Governance issues. But it is man's truest and best religion, *before* the Gospel shines on him."[94] Here Newman was trying to make his Pelagian contemporaries see that from the oblations of primitive peoples they could learn something of that holy fear, which the "religion of civilization,"[95] as

---

[92] Hebert A. L. Fisher, *The Medieval Empire: Studies in Napoleonic Statesmanship: Germany* (London: Macmillan, 1898), II, 8–9.

[93] Hebert A. L. Fisher, *A History of Europe* (London: Eyre and Spottiswoode, 1935), II, 164.

[94] Newman, "On Justice, as a Principle of Divine Governance" (1832), Sermon 6, in *University Sermons*, 89.

[95] See Newman, ch. 10, "Inference and Assent in the Matter of Religion," in *Grammar of Assent*, 392–6.

he called it, with its flouting of conscience, so recklessly counseled them to abandon. In the *Grammar of Assent*, he had occasion to expand on this concept, which is vital to any consideration of Newman's appreciation of the nature and significance of superstition.

> It is scarcely necessary to insist, that wherever Religion exists in a popular shape, it has almost invariably worn its dark side outwards. It is founded in one way or other on the sense of sin; and without that vivid sense it would hardly have any precepts or any observances. Its many varieties all proclaim or imply that man is in a degraded, servile condition, and requires expiation, reconciliation, and some great change of nature ... the progress of which man's nature is capable is a development, not a destruction of its original state; it must subserve the elements from which it proceeds, in order to be a true development and not a perversion. And those popular rituals do in fact subserve and complete that nature with which man is born. It is otherwise with the religion of so-called civilization; such religion does but contradict the religion of barbarism; and since this civilization itself is not a development of man's whole nature, but mainly of the intellect, recognizing indeed the moral sense, but ignoring the conscience, no wonder that the religion in which it issues has no sympathy either with the hopes and fears of the awakened soul, or with those frightful presentiments which are expressed in the worship and traditions of the heathen.

In thus showing the superstitious such imaginative sympathy, and calling attention to the profound limitations of modern civilization, Newman entirely set himself apart from the Whig historians.

> If our race *be* in a fallen and depraved state, what ought our religion to be but anxiety and remorse, till God comforts us? Surely, to be in gloom,—to view ourselves with horror,—to look about to the right hand and to the left for means of safety,—to catch at every thing, yet trust in nothing,—to do all we can, and try to do more than all,—and, after all, to wait in miserable suspense, naked and shivering, among the trees of the garden, for the hour of His coming, and meanwhile to fancy sounds of woe in every wind stirring the leaves about us,—in a word, to be superstitious,—is nature's best offering, her most acceptable service, her most mature and enlarged wisdom, in the presence of a holy and offended God.[96]

Besides being a piece of characteristically brilliant prose, this was Newman's most moving tribute to the dignity of superstition, which he followed with an admonition that is as applicable to our age as it was to his own. "They

---

[96] Newman, "On Justice, as a Principle of Divine Governance" (1832), Sermon 6, in *University Sermons*, 89–90.

who are not superstitious without the Gospel, will not be religious with it: and I would that even in us, who have the Gospel, there were more of superstition than there is; for much is it to be feared that our security about ourselves arises from defect in self-knowledge rather than in fullness of faith, and that we appropriate to ourselves promises which we cannot read."[97] Moreover, Newman saw superstition confirming one of the "seven Notes," as he called them, "of fidelity in intellectual developments to ... Christian Doctrine," the note pertaining to "identity of type." In defining this note, he argued that "whereas all great ideas are found, as time goes on, to involve much which was not seen at first to belong to them, and have developments, that is enlargements, applications, uses and fortunes, very various, one security against error and perversion in the process is the maintenance of the original type, which the idea presented to the world at its origin, amid and through all its apparent changes and vicissitudes from first to last."[98] To ascertain what the original type of Catholic Christianity was, Newman asks his readers to make a comparative test. "Let us take it as the world now views it in its age; and let us take it as the world once viewed it in its youth; and let us see whether there be any great difference between the early and the later description of it."[99] And to make the test clearer still, as to whether there is any difference between the way that the Catholic Church was perceived in the first century and the way that it is perceived in the nineteenth century, Newman urged his readers to consider the following statement.

> There is a religious communion claiming a divine commission, and holding all other religious bodies around it heretical or infidel; it is a well-organized, well-disciplined body; it is a sort of secret society, binding together its members by influences and by engagements which it is difficult for strangers to ascertain. It is spread over the known world; it may be weak or insignificant locally, but it is strong on the whole from its continuity; it may be smaller than all other religious bodies together, but is larger than each separately. It is a natural enemy to governments external to itself; it is intolerant and engrossing, and tends to a new modelling of society; it breaks laws, it divides families. It is a gross superstition; it is charged with the foulest crimes; it is despised by the intellect of the day; it is frightful to the imagination of the many. And there is but one communion such.[100]

---

97 *Ibid.*, 90.
98 Newman, *Essay on Development*, 207.
99 *Ibid.*
100 *Ibid.*, 208.

Having dispatched this lively salvo, Newman concluded: "Place this description before Pliny or Julian; place it before Frederick the Second or Guizot. 'Apparent dirae facies.' Each knows at once, without asking a question, who is meant by it. One object, and only one, absorbs each item of the detail of the delineation."[101]

Yet Newman saw the perception of superstition as more than a means of reaffirming the continuity between the Church in the first century and the Church in the nineteenth century. In the contempt that Anglicans felt for what they alleged was the superstition of Catholicism, Newman saw a telltale skepticism. "They laugh at the notion itself of men pinning their faith (as they express themselves) upon Pope or Council; they think it simply superstitious and narrow-minded to profess to believe just what the Church believes, and to assent to whatever she will say in time to come on matters of doctrine ... They call it priestcraft to insist on this surrender of the reason, and superstition to make it."[102] From this, Newman recognized that liberal Anglican critics shared with their first-century counterparts a fundamental impatience

> with the very state of mind which all Christians had in the age of the Apostles; nor is there any doubt (who will deny it?) that those who thus boast of not being led blindfold, of judging for themselves, of believing just as much and just as little as they please, of hating dictation, and so forth, would have found it an extreme difficulty to hang on the lips of the Apostles, had they lived at their date, or rather would have simply resisted the sacrifice of their own liberty of thought, would have thought life eternal too dearly purchased at such a price, and would have died in their unbelief. And they would have defended themselves on the plea that it was absurd and childish to ask them to believe without proof, to bid them give up their education, and their intelligence, and their science, and in spite of all those difficulties which reason and sense find in the Christian doctrine, in spite of its mysteriousness, its obscurity, its strangeness, its unacceptableness, its severity, to require them to surrender themselves to the teaching of a few unlettered Galilæans, or a learned indeed but fanatical Pharisee.[103]

Reading this, we can appreciate how Newman's intimate familiarity with this deeply skeptical ethos inspired him to write one of his most moving passages, which Graham Greene would use as an epigraph to his brilliant meditation on modern skepticism, *The Lawless Roads* (1939):

---

101 Ibid.
102 Newman, Discourse 10, "Faith and Private Judgment" (1849), in *Discourses to Mixed Congregations*, 214.
103 Ibid., 214–15.

> Starting then with the being of a God, (which ... is as certain to me as the certainty of my own existence, though when I try to put the grounds of that certainty into logical shape I find a difficulty in doing so in mood and figure to my satisfaction), I look out of myself into the world of men, and there I see a sight which fills me with unspeakable distress. The world seems simply to give the lie to that great truth, of which my whole being is so full; and the effect upon me is, in consequence, as a matter of necessity, as confusing as if it denied that I am in existence myself. If I looked into a mirror, and did not see my face, I should have the sort of feeling which actually comes upon me, when I look into this living busy world, and see no reflexion of its Creator. This is, to me, one of those great difficulties of this absolute primary truth, to which I referred just now. Were it not for this voice, speaking so clearly in my conscience and my heart, I should be an atheist, or a pantheist, or a polytheist when I looked into the world. I am speaking for myself only; and I am far from denying the real force of the arguments in proof of a God, drawn from the general facts of human society and the course of history, but these do not warm me or enlighten me; they do not take away the winter of my desolation, or make the buds unfold and the leaves grow within me, and my moral being rejoice. The sight of the world is nothing else than the prophet's scroll, full of "lamentations, and mourning, and woe."[104]

Here is a good example of how unflinchingly Newman could take up what Gerard Manley Hopkins called the "last strands of man,"[105] though the historian in him drew a moral from "the general facts of human society and the course of history" that at once baffled and repulsed many of his contemporaries. In a passage that explodes the Whig faith in progress and rationalism, Newman wrote:

> To consider the world in its length and breadth, its various history, the many races of man, their starts, their fortunes, their mutual alienation, their conflicts, and then their ways, habits, governments, forms of worship; their enterprises, their aimless courses, their random achievements and acquirements, the impotent conclusion of long-standing facts, the tokens so faint and broken of a superintending design, the blind evolution of what turn out to be great powers or truths, the progress of things, as if from unreasoning elements, not towards final causes, the greatness and littleness of

---

104 *Apologia*, 216–17. The Scripture verse quoted by Newman is Ezekiel 2:9–10.

105 This is from Hopkins's poem known as "Carrion Comfort," which begins: "Not, I'll not, carrion comfort Despair, not feast on thee / Not untwist—slack they may be—these last strands of man." Gerard Manley Hopkins, *The Poems of Gerard Manley Hopkins*, 4th edn (Oxford: Oxford University Press, 1967), 99.

man, his far-reaching aims, his short duration, the curtain hung over his futurity, the disappointments of life, the defeat of good, the success of evil, physical pain, mental anguish, the prevalence and intensity of sin, the pervading idolatries, the corruptions, the dreary hopeless irreligion, that condition of the whole race, so fearfully yet exactly described in the Apostle's words, "having no hope and without God in the world," —all this is a vision to dizzy and appal; and inflicts upon the mind the sense of a profound mystery, which is absolutely beyond human solution.[106]

The Whig historians did many things superlatively well: they wrote brisk, lively, engaging narrative; they knew how to mine character for pathos and drama; they followed a teleological logic that never left their histories void of coherence. Nevertheless, there was one thing with which they were never comfortable, and that was mystery, which the superstitious may misinterpret, but always acknowledge. Speaking of man's separation from God, Newman asked: "What shall be said to this heart-piercing, reason-bewildering fact?" The answer he gave could not be less Whiggish:

I can only answer, that either there is no Creator, or this living society of men is in a true sense discarded from His presence. Did I see a boy of good make and mind, with the tokens on him of a refined nature, cast upon the world without provision, unable to say whence he came, his birthplace or his family connexions, I should conclude that there was some mystery connected with his history, and that he was one, of whom, from one cause or other, his parents were ashamed. Thus only should I be able to account for the contrast between the promise and the condition of his being. And so I argue about the world; —*if* there be a God, *since* there is a God, the human race is implicated in some terrible aboriginal calamity. It is out of joint with the purposes of its Creator. This is a fact, a fact as true as the fact of its existence; and thus the doctrine of what is theologically called original sin becomes to me almost as certain as that the world exists, and as the existence of God.[107]

For Newman, human history was defined not by the Glorious Revolution or the prejudices of Whig magnates but by the creature's rejection of his Creator. In this respect, as Monsignor H. Francis Davis, the first postulator of Newman's cause for canonization realized, "Most men were not as he was. So many of his fellow-countrymen were content to live as though this world were the whole of reality, as though they were not creatures, as though the voice of conscience had no significance." For Davis, Newman's vocation arose from his need "to discover the God ... to which

---

106 *Apologia*, 216–17. The Bible verse Newman quotes is Ephesians 2:12.
107 *Apologia*, 217–18.

his conscience drove him ... In the name of God, in the name of reason, it was the deepest desire of his life to learn humbly but surely and deeply that divine philosophy committed by the Son of God to His Church."[108] In this, he realized what a sign of contradiction his own work posed to men contemptuous of superstition. "Those who will not receive Baptism as the token of God's election," he wrote in his *Lectures on the Doctrine of Justification* (1838), "have recourse to certain supposed experiences of it in their hearts. This is the idolatry of a refined age, in which the superstitions of barbarous times displease, in consequence of their grossness. Men congratulate themselves on their emancipation from forms and their enlightened worship, when they are but in the straight course to a worse captivity, and are exchanging dependence on the creature for dependence on self."[109] That Newman was called out from his Protestant people as St. Paul had been called out from his Jewish people to attest to the promises of the Catholic Church was clear even to those who were not members of that Church. Richard Holt Hutton (1826–97), the High Church editor of the *Spectator* and one of Newman's best contemporary critics, rightly attributed the appeal of Newman's courageous witness, in part, to his appreciation for superstition. Hutton wrote that:

> It is a strange and not a discreditable characteristic of the days in which we live, that, in spite of the ardour with which the English people have devoted themselves to material progress and the scientific studies which have ministered to material progress, one man at least has been held to be truly great by the nation, who has crossed all its prejudices and calmly ignored all its prepossessions; who has lived more than half his life in what Protestants at least would call a monastery,—for his home at Littlemore as well as at Edgbaston was more than half monastic;—who has loved penance, who has always held up the ascetic life to admiration, who has haunted our imaginations with his mild and gentle yet austere figure, with his strong preference even for superstition as compared with shallow, optimistic sentiment; and has impressed upon us even more by his practice than by his teaching, that "the

---

108 H. Francis Davis, "The Catholicism of Cardinal Newman," in *John Henry Newman: Centenary Essays*, ed. Tristram, 36–7. Monsignor Davis, Professor of Theology at Oscott College, played a lively part in Newman's own history by extolling his sanctity in a piece called "Newman's Cause," which he wrote in response to Louis Bouyer's book, *Newman: sa vie, sa spiritualité* (Paris: Éditions du Cerf, 1952). He introduced Newman's cause for canonization on 28 February 1955. See *Cause of Canonization of the Servant of God John Henry Cardinal Newman (1801–1890), Founder of the English Oratories, Positio super Virtutibus* (Rome, 1989), I, xvii.

109 Newman, *Lectures on the Doctrine of Justification* (London: J. G. & F. Rivington, 1838), 371.

lust of the flesh, and the lust of the eyes, and the pride of life, are not of the Father but of the world."[110]

Yet for all his recognition of the power of superstition—indeed, he would have preferred, as he told Newman in a letter of 1872, "to see England bigoted, superstitious, gloomy, almost cruel, to seeing her without faith in the supernatural"—Hutton was enough of a Victorian rationalist to write, after reading Newman's *Grammar of Assent*, by which he was not persuaded: "The duty of restraining one's belief within the limits of what is warranted by evidence, seems to me to have been hardly at all understood in the first days of the Church, and though it is the most painful of duties surely it is a duty?"[111] Newman saw Christian duty from a different perspective. As he wrote to Louisa, the daughter of his good friend Sir John Simeon,[112] who had written to him in 1869 of her doubts with respect to this same evidence:

> Here we find ourselves in this world, with an instinct telling us that it is our duty to serve God, yet without the means of doing so as certain as the instinct is certain. As in the natural order of things a man would starve, if he did not find the means of living, so in like manner it is incumbent on us to look out for, to labour for, and so to gain the spiritual means, by which our souls may live—and this is the very end of our lives.[113]

110 Richard H. Hutton, *Cardinal Newman* (London: Methuen, 1891), 1–2.
111 Richard H. Hutton to Newman, 20 February 1872, in *LD*, XXVI, 38–9.
112 Sir John Simeon (1815–70), naval officer and MP, converted to Catholicism in 1851. He gave stalwart support to Newman's Oratory School. After his death, *The Month* observed: "No one who had seen him in his daily home life could fail to have been edified by it. He constantly attended at Mass, however ill, or tired, or late overnight; and when there was no Mass he would read prayers in his chapel. He had a great delight, as he often said, in little services, as in singing the English hymns, or saying the Rosary or Litany with his children and servants. He went with great regularity and humility to the holy Sacraments, and observed with great conscientiousness the laws of the Church. Of this he gave example at the outset of his Catholic life, when for the first time he came to know that the society of Freemasons to which, like many other young men at the Protestant Universities, he had belonged, was condemned by the Church, and instantly renounced it. His charity and kindness to the poor and to all in need and sorrow were very great. He went familiarly among them, and visited the sick in their cottages. The sweetness and tenderness of his nature attracted all those who came within its influence, and is shown by the sorrow expressed at his loss from men in public life down to a poor woman who was found in great grief some days after his death in Eaton Place, begging to be shown the house where he had lived who was the kindest friend she had ever had." (See *The Month* (December 1870), 481–4.) Lord Tennyson, a neighbor of Simeon's on the Isle of Wight, wrote one of his loveliest lyrics in memory of his dear friend: "Nightingales sang in his woods: / The Master was far away: / Nightingales warbled and sang / Of a passion that lasts but a day; / Still in the house in his coffin the Prince of courtesy lay."
113 Newman to Louisa Simeon, 24 May 1869, in *LD*, XXIV, 259.

✢ 3 ✢
Travesties of Newman

Travesties of Newman

Receptions of Newman, edited by Frederick Aquino and Benjamin King. Oxford University Press, 264 pages

No Englishman—or only Lord Byron—ever fascinated his countrymen more than John Henry Cardinal Newman. Lord Macaulay was convinced that the British public's fascination with Byron was mostly pharisaical. For the great Whig historian, the man whom Sir Walter Scott called "the Champion of the English Parnassus"[1] was held up "as a sort of whipping boy" to show how superior English morals were to "the Parisian laxity"; he was also "guilty of the offence, which, of all offences, is punished most severely; he had been overpraised." Yet, Macaulay clearly relished the irony that after "the savage envy of aspiring dunces" had done all it could to discredit the prolific poet, his work "became more popular than it had ever been."[2] The appeal Newman held for his compatriots was of an entirely different order. In 1883, Matthew Arnold might have spoken for some Protestants and some unbelievers when he said that Newman "adopted, for the doubts and difficulties which beset men's minds to-day, a solution which, to speak frankly, is impossible." Indeed, Arnold was convinced that the nineteenth-century Englishman who had sought to offer the truest solution to these "doubts and difficulties" was none other than Byron. In his preface to the *Poetry of Byron* (1881), Arnold contended that "As the inevitable break-up of the old order comes, as the English middle-class slowly awakens from its intellectual sleep of two centuries, as our actual present world, for which this sleep has condemned us, shows itself more clearly,—our world of an aristocracy materialised and null, a middle-class purblind and hideous, a lower class crude and brutal,—we shall turn out eyes again, and to more purpose, upon this passionate and dauntless soldier of a forlorn hope."[3] Yet, notwithstanding this quixotic

---

[1] Sir Walter Scott, "Review of *Childe Harold*, Canto III," *The Quarterly Review* (1816).
[2] Lord Macaulay, "Essay on Byron," *The Edinburgh Review* (1831).
[3] Matthew Arnold, "Preface to *Poetry of Byron*" (1881), in *Essays in Criticism* (London: Macmillan & Co., 1888).

plug for the cultural savior in Byron, even for those who did not follow Newman into the Church of Rome, the great convert remained a source of intense interest precisely because of the steadfastness with which he affirmed and reaffirmed his faith in the ancient Church. In 1890, Richard H. Hutton, the High Church editor of the *Spectator*, captured this aspect of Newman's appeal perhaps better than anyone in his brief biography of the Cardinal. After marveling at the esteem and affection held by "all the English Churches and all the English sects for the man who had certainly caused the defection of a larger number of cultivated Protestants from their Protestant faith than any other English writer or preacher since the Reformation," Hutton observed that, "In a century in which physical discovery and material well-being have usurped and almost absorbed the admiration of mankind, such a life as that of Cardinal Newman stands out in strange and almost majestic, though singularly graceful and unpretending contrast." For Hutton, who wrote over thirty pieces about Newman over the course of his long critical career, "No life known to me in the last century of our national history can for a moment compare with it, so far as we can judge of such deep matters, in unity of meaning and constancy of purpose. It has been carved, as it were, out of one solid block of spiritual substance."[4]

In his unsurpassed intellectual biography of Newman, first published in 1988 and reissued with an afterword in 2009, Ian Ker brilliantly mined this "solid block of spiritual substance" in Newman's books and correspondence to show how all of his life's work had culminated in what his subject had inscribed on his gravestone, "Ex umbris et imaginibus in veritatem," which Father Ker nicely translated: "Out of Unreality into Reality."[5] In any consideration of Newman's reception by his contemporaries or posterity, the nature of this uncompromising course has to be taken into account. Newman left the unreality of the Anglo-Catholic party within the National Church that he had been so instrumental in setting up because he hungered for the reality that only the Church of Rome could supply. To insist on this may grate on those who wish to present Newman as an ecumenical figure or, more mischievously still, a liberal *malgré lui*. Yet there was nothing ecumenical or liberal about what Newman had to say about the National Church or the Anglo-Catholic party that he had done so much to set up in his *Lectures on Certain Difficulties Felt by Anglicans in Submitting to the Catholic Church* (1850) or *Lectures on the Present Position of Catholics in England* (1851). On the contrary, in the former, he could not have been more forthright in his impatience with the unreality of the National Church, for all of its power and appeal.

---

4 Hutton, *Cardinal Newman*, 250–1.
5 Ian Ker, *John Henry Newman: A Biography* (Oxford: Clarendon Press, 1988), 745.

> If ... "life" means strength, activity, energy, and well-being of any kind whatever, in that case doubtless the national religion is alive. It is a great power in the midst of us; it wields an enormous influence; it represses a hundred foes; it conducts a hundred undertakings. It attracts men to it, uses them, rewards them; it has thousands of beautiful homes up and down the country, where quiet men may do its work and benefit its people; it collects vast sums in the shape of voluntary offerings, and with them it builds churches, prints and distributes innumerable Bibles, books, and tracts and sustains missionaries in all parts of the earth. In all parts of the earth it opposes the Catholic Church, denounces her as antichristian, bribes the world against her, obstructs her influence, apes her authority, and confuses her evidence. In all parts of the world it is the religion of gentlemen, of scholars, of men of substance, and men of no personal faith at all. If this be life,—if it be life to impart a tone to the court and houses of parliament, to ministers of state, to law and literature, to universities and schools, and to society,—if it be life to be a principle of order in the population, and an organ of benevolence and almsgiving towards the poor,—if it be life to make men decent, respectable, and sensible, to embellish and refine the family circle, to deprive vice of its grossness, and to shed a gloss over avarice and ambition,—if indeed it is the life of religion to be the first jewel in the Queen's crown, and the highest step of her throne, then doubtless the National Church is replete, it overflows with life; but the question has still to be answered, Life of what kind? Heresy has its life, worldliness has its life. Is the Establishment's life merely national life, or is it something more? Is it Catholic life as well? Is it a supernatural life?[6]

One might say that these were the avowals of a recent convert, eager to attest to the Faith that he had sacrificed so much to embrace. Yet in August of 1870, at the height of the papal infallibility crisis leading up to the First Vatican Council, when the rumor surfaced that Newman was contemplating returning to the Anglican Church, he responded to an Anglican clergyman named Henry Thomas Ellacombe with a letter full of the same conviction that had animated those ebullient books of his in the 1850s.

> Don't let me hurt you, my dear Ellacombe, by thus smiling over your letter, for I am not hurt at you—"make up my mind to return"— Why, I could as easily "make up my mind" to be a Garibaldian or a Siamese twin. Be sure there is as much chance of my turning an Anglican again as of my being the Irish Giant or the King of Clubs. Don't let impertinent Pamphleteers delude you. I am as certain that the Church in communion with Rome is the successor and

---

6 *Difficulties Felt by Anglicans*, 40–1.

representative of the Primitive Church, as certain that the Anglican Church is not, as certain that the Anglican Church is a mere collection of men, a mere national body, a human society, as I am that Victoria is Queen of Great Britain. Nor have I once had even a passing doubt on the subject, ever since I have been a Catholic. I have all along been in a state of inward certainty and steady assurance on this point, and I should be the most asinine, as well as the most ungrateful of men, if I left that Gracious Lord who manifests Himself in the Catholic Church, for those wearisome Protestant shadows, out of which of His mercy he has delivered me.

It is a pity that no response survives to this splendid letter. If Ellacombe had any sense of fun he must have enjoyed the charm with which Newman disabused him of his wild misapprehensions. If Newman could be fierce in public controversy, he was always gentle to those who took issue with him in private. "This is why I cannot help smiling at your invitation," Newman wrote to Ellacombe, "though it comes out of so kind a heart, as I should have laughed if I had been the chicken, to whom the good-wife said, 'Chick, chick, come and be killed.'"[7] The unity that Hutton and Ker saw in Newman's life and work is here amusingly confirmed by Newman himself.

What strikes one initially upon opening *Receptions of Newman*, a collection of academic essays edited by Dr. Frederick Aquino and Dr. Benjamin King, is that it is dedicated, in part, to Frank Turner, the stridently anti-Catholic author of *John Henry Newman The Challenge of Evangelical Religion*, which the editors laud for "opening up new historical and philosophical lines of inquiry." If Hutton and Ker saw admirable integrity in Newman, Turner saw only depravity and imposture. Indeed, for the unaccountably assertive Yale Professor, Newman only converted to the Catholic Church to mask his manifold skepticism. That Turner should be regarded by the majority of contributors here as an admirable revisionist says a good deal about their own historical pretensions, especially since Turner's revisionism, such as it is, was neither new nor substantiated by any historical evidence. After all, many of Newman's contemporary critics—from Leslie Stephen to A. M. Fairbairn—had contrived to see skepticism behind Newman's conversion to Catholicism. Indeed, by Newman's death, it had become something of a defamatory axiom among these critics, though none of them had succeeded in making their aspersions stick. To read Stephen and Fairbairn struggling to implicate Newman in skepticism is a pathetic spectacle. Their misunderstanding of the relationship between faith and reason could not have been more thoroughgoing. Indeed, if anything, they only proved that the critic of the ultra-Protestant principle in Newman was right: four hundred years of Protestantism had left English thought well-nigh irredeemably

---

7 Newman to Henry Thomas Ellacombe (23 August 1870), in LD, XXV, 195.

muddled and jejune. Moreover, Turner's charge that Newman's long-stated opposition to liberalism was somehow duplicitous and in reality an opposition to Evangelicalism—a duplicity undertaken once he had become a Catholic to hornswoggle those Ultramontane critics at Rome who had convinced themselves that Newman was not orthodox but a crypto-liberal—is demonstrably false. Some historians of nineteenth-century English history might be said to exaggerate the role Evangelicals played in that history—the work of Boyd Hilton and David Bebbington comes to mind—but neither of those otherwise good historians goes to the lengths Turner goes to try to argue that Tractarian Oxford, let alone Newman, was somehow obsessed with Evangelicals. Indeed, Hilton expressly rejects the central tenet of Turner's scurrilous book by arguing that "Turner's claim that Newman was originally driven by opposition to the evangelicalism of his upbringing rather than by opposition to liberalism is mistaken. Certainly, he loathed evangelical Dissent and Bulteel's style of apocalyptic evangelicalism, and he disapproved of orthodox evangelicals' reluctance to oppose them head on, but liberalism was always the enemy."[8]

Nevertheless, following Turner, the editors begin their introduction by asking, "Was John Henry Newman an agnostic?" The justification they give for thus inaugurating their volume with this peculiar query does not inspire confidence.

> First, Newman's writings on matters of faith continue to inform the study of theology, philosophy, and history ... Second, division over agnosticism show the contradictory ways in which Newman's readers have understood him ... Third, by beginning this introduction with one example among the many subjects on which Newman wrote, the editors want to be clear from the start that this volume is not an exhaustive account of the receptions of his work.[9]

However odd a defense for giving their collection so tendentious a turn, this does at least have the merit of showing readers how the liberal academy currently regards Newman and his legacy. If, after *Tract 90*, Newman found himself "posted up by the marshal on the buttery-hatch of every College of my University, after the manner of discommoned pastry-cooks, and ... denounced as a traitor ... against the time-honoured Establishment," the true Catholic convert is no more welcome today in most of our own colleges and universities.[10] Of course, the false agnostic Newman might

---

8 Boyd Hilton, *A Mad, Bad, and Dangerous People: England 1793–1846* (Oxford: Clarendon Press, 2006), 471.

9 *Receptions of Newman*, ed. Frederick D. Aquino and Benjamin J. King (Oxford: Oxford University Press, 2015), 1.

10 *Apologia*, 88.

be welcome for various purposes dear to the liberal prejudices of those colleges and universities, but that is a different story.

What is also striking about this collection is that the editors and their contributors only acknowledge in passing the Victorian rationalists who first brought the charge of agnosticism against Newman, most notably Thomas Huxley, Leslie Stephen, James Fitzjames Stephen, and Martin Fairbairn. Given the editors' stated interest in the charge of agnosticism, why there is no proper discussion anywhere in the volume of these polemicists and the character of their attacks on Newman's faith is a lively question. Were these Victorian rationalists ever successful in demonstrating that Newman did, indeed, succumb to agnosticism? Or did they deliberately misrepresent Newman and his work to justify their own agnosticism? Readers will find no answers to such questions in these unbalanced pages. If, as Prof. Colin Barr claims, the aim of the collection was to establish "the Newman of history," he and his academic friends might have included some discussion of the thinkers from whom their own thinking stems.[11]

When it comes to failing to acknowledge debts to past authors, however, no one can match Dr. Peter Nockles, who in his essay here on the Tractarian response to Newman refuses to admit that he took his thesis for his deeply misleading study, *The Oxford Movement in Context* (1994) from Frederick Meyrick (1827–1906), the Church of England clergyman who argued as early as the 1870s that much of the Anglican High Church had already begun to accomplish in the eighteenth what Newman set out to accomplish in the Tractarian Movement in the nineteenth century. Instead, he has the effrontery to charge that "Meyrick's extraordinary attempt to deny Newman was ever central to or even necessary to the life of the Tractarian movement finds a muted echo in Owen Chadwick."[12] Of course, Chadwick was remorselessly hostile to the convert who had so much satirical fun with the die-hards of the Anglo-Catholic party, but for Nockles to try to deflect attention away from his own failure to acknowledge his debt to Meyrick by calling attention to someone else's takes the biscuit for impudence.

Cyril O'Regan, the Catherine F. Huisking Professor of Theology at Notre Dame, contributes what is probably the least coherent piece in the collection. In "Receptions of Newman the Saint," we meet the usual defamatory innuendoes in which detractors of Newman have always specialized, though the professor, like so many of Newman's Victorian detractors, is not always careful to verify his claims. "Not all Catholics are possessed of a sensorium for sanctity; often the perceptual default for Catholics is

---

11 Colin Barr, "Historical (Mis)Understandings of the Idea of a University," in *Receptions of Newman*, ed. Aquino and King, 120.

12 Peter Nockles, "Newman's Tractarian Receptions," in *Receptions of Newman*, ed. Aquino and King, 154.

more nearly ethical," the professor writes in his characteristically barbarous English. "Some Catholic readers of Newman could conceivably find him wanting in justice with respect to his adversaries and insufficiently attentive to the ills of society at large. Others again, who have a capacity for recognizing sanctity, might not find Newman compelling in the way they find Francis of Assisi is or even John Paul II."[13] Newman's sanctity, in other words, is dubious because he did not treat his controversial opponents with kid gloves. And this despite the fact that any even cursory reading of Newman the controversialist will show that he tended to treat his opponents with remarkable forbearance and fairness, indeed suavity. One need only recall the patience with which he debated the issue of papal infallibility and civil allegiance with Gladstone. And if Newman did not comport with twenty-first-century notions of "social justice," he did win the hearts and minds of the Birmingham poor, who flocked to his funeral at the Oratory in the thousands. And as for Newman not putting one in mind of St. Francis or St. John Paul the Great, well, he was rightly insistent on the inalienable uniqueness of each individual, and this would necessarily obtain in something as personal as sanctity. On this score, Father Jacques Phillipe—whose solicitude for the salvation of souls is so deeply Newmanian—is worth quoting: "there are as many forms of holiness, and hence ways to holiness, as there are people. For God, each person is absolutely unique. Holiness is not the realization of a given model of perfection that is identical to everyone. It is the emergence of an absolutely unique reality that God alone knows and that he alone brings to fruition ... What God wants is always different, always disconcerting; but ultimately it is infinitely beautiful because only God is capable of creating unique masterpieces."[14] And certainly, most readers would agree, without fear of being thought unduly "hagiographical," that Newman is one of God's "unique masterpieces."

Still, it is comical that Prof. O'Regan should try to make invidious comparisons between Newman and Pope John Paul II because the Polish pope was warmly appreciative of Newman's sanctity. Indeed, on 22 January 2001, the Pope wrote an Apostolic Letter to the Bishop of Birmingham, confirming his admiration for the great convert:

> "Lead kindly light amid the encircling gloom, lead Thou me on," Newman wrote in "The Pillar of the Cloud"; and for him Christ was the light at the heart of every kind of darkness. For his tomb he chose the inscription: *Ex umbris et imaginibus in veritatem*; and it was clear at the end of his life's journey that Christ was the truth he

---

[13] Cyril O'Regan, "Receptions of Newman the Saint," in *Receptions of Newman*, ed. Aquino and King, 230.
[14] Philippe, *In the School of the Holy Spirit*, 17–18.

had found. But Newman's search was shot through with pain. Once he had come to that unshakeable sense of the mission entrusted to him by God, he declared: "Therefore, I will trust Him ... If I am in sickness, my sickness may serve Him, in perplexity, my perplexity may serve Him ... He does nothing in vain ... He may take away my friends. He may throw me among strangers. He may make me feel desolate, make my spirits sink, hide the future from me. Still, He knows what He is about" (*Meditations and Devotions*). All these trials he knew in his life; but rather than diminish or destroy him they paradoxically strengthened his faith in the God who had called him, and confirmed him in the conviction that God "does nothing in vain." In the end, therefore, what shines forth in Newman is the mystery of the Lord's Cross: this was the heart of his mission, the absolute truth which he contemplated, the "kindly light" which led him on.[15]

Another fundamental problem with the collection is that it pointedly ignores the one book of Newman's that attracted the most attention from his contemporaries, his *Apologia pro Vita Sua* (1865), which Newman wrote to defend himself and the development of his religious views against the calumnies of Charles Kingsley. This is particularly egregious in any book dedicated to Turner because the whole thrust of Turner's vituperative attack on Newman's integrity proceeds from the historian's revisionist misreading of the *Apologia*. If the editors and their contributors were as truly committed to establishing the historical Newman as they claim, surely they would have devoted some critical attention to ascertaining whether Turner's polemical attack on the reliability of the *Apologia* is tenable. Instead, with the exception of a few passing asides, they are almost entirely mum on that scurrilous, historically indefensible attack.

Prof. O'Regan may uncritically accept Turner's claim that the *Apologia* is little more than an exercise in self-vindication, but no impartial reader can revisit Newman's account without seeing that the autobiography teems with self-criticism. After all, Newman is unsparing when it comes to his ill-advised formulation of the *via media*. He also quotes at length from the many abusive references to Rome that he penned when he was still within the Anglican ministry. Where the self-vindication lies in these recantations is rather inscrutable. After one citation of a particularly robust anti-Roman salvo, the chastened autobiographer is constrained to admit: "No one ought to indulge in insinuations; it certainly diminishes my right to complain of slanders uttered against myself, when, as in this passage, I had already spoken in disparagement of the controversialists of that religious body,

---

15 *Letter of the Holy Father John Paul II on the Occasion of the Second Centenary of the Birth of Cardinal John Henry Newman* (Vatican, 22 January 2001).

to which I myself now belong."[16] Then, again, Newman expressly faults himself for helping usher in the triumph of liberalism at Oxford following his defection to Rome, a triumph which Dean Church would make the centerpiece of his classic *History of the Oxford Movement 1833–45* (1891), published twenty-seven years after Newman's account.[17] If disciples of Turner like Prof. O'Regan wish to claim that Newman's account is nothing more than a tissue of self-serving lies, they must also charge Church with the same uncritical mendacity, for he incorporated all of Newman's interpretive insights into his own history.

What the Newman scholar Stanley Jaki referred to as Turner's "colossal mischief" is also rubberstamped by Prof. William Abraham, who in his essay, "Reception of Newman on Revelation" exhaustively recounts Turner's numerous libels against Newman only to conclude that their truth or falsehood is ultimately unascertainable. Why? "We all fall back on our best judgments," the professor explains, "assembled in the light of all the relevant evidence." In other words, we can repeat libels in scrupulous detail but we cannot determine whether or not they are true. That the Albert Cook Outler Professor of Wesley Studies in the Perkins School of Theology at Southern Methodist University should follow up this startling claim by revealing in a footnote that his "work on the epistemology of divine revelation is deeply indebted to Newman" gives his discussion of the epistemologist in Newman added comic absurdity.[18]

In light of their unwillingness to engage Turner with any critical rigor, the liberal bias of the book's contributors will come as no surprise to readers. In their essay on "The Roman Catholic Reception of the Essay on Development," for example, Dr. Kenneth Parker and Dr. Michael Shea applaud Newman for prescience in his *Essay* but also "willful hopefulness." Why? "Development did indeed become central to the Catholic understanding of the Christian past, though not in a smooth teleological trajectory. There were many twists and turns on the journey." Although Cardinal Walter Kasper is only mentioned once in a footnote, his cynical misuse of Newman's idea of development hovers over nearly everything discussed in the essay. The "smooth teleological trajectory" for which the authors yearn may not have been in the cards, but they are not without hope. As they write in their conclusion,

> In the 2010 dialogue with Rabbi Abraham Skorka, Cardinal Jorge Mario Bergoglio, SJ, Archbishop of Buenos Aires—now Pope

---

16 *Apologia*, 120.

17 Richard William Church, *The Oxford Movement, 1833–1845* (London: Macmillan & Co., 1891).

18 William J. Abraham, "Newman on Divine Revelation," in *Receptions of Newman*, ed. Aquino and King, 212.

Francis—also affirmed the principle of development. He stated, "Religious truth does not change, but it does develop and grow. It is like with the human being, we are the same as a baby and in old age, but in the middle there is a whole journey."[19]

In other words, the truths of the Catechism may never change, but their pastoral application certainly may. What the "whole journey" envisioned by the ineffable Jorge Mario Bergoglio may entail is anyone's guess, though it is unlikely to include the principle of *semper eadem* so essential to Newman's understanding of legitimate development, not to mention the Magisterium's understanding of the Church's unalterable commitment to the moral law. In any case, the authors show their own affinities clearly enough when they write:

> Catholic receptions of Newman's *Essay* may be understood in the context of decisions that—like the tacking of a sailboat in a strong headwind—have moved forward even when zigging and zagging in opposite directions. Leo XIII launched the Thomistic revival, yet made Newman a cardinal and commended his works. In 1910, priests and seminary professors around the world were required to swear, "I flatly reject the heretical invention of the evolution of dogmas." However, Pius X earlier exempted Newman from the anti-modernist censure and commended him as a great teacher.[20]

Reading between the lines, we can see that what the authors are saying here is that Leo XIII and Pius X did not know their man. Far from being the sympathetic figure they thought they were commending, Newman was a liberal, the same liberal that the Modernists and their sympathizers have been trying to fob off as the real Newman ever since the Dublin-born Father George Tyrell, S.J. (1861–1908) tried to defend what he called "the right of each age to adjust the historico-philosophical expression of Christianity to contemporary certainties." Another Irishman beguiled by "contemporary certainties," Eamon Duffy, in his review of John Cornwell's potboiler, *Newman's Unquiet Grave* for *The New York Review of Books*, even went so far as to suggest that Benedict XVI beatified a false conservative Newman to repress the true liberal one.[21] In such ahistorical assertions, poor Newman

---

19 Kenneth Parker and Michael Shea, "Roman Catholic Receptions of the *Essay on Development*," in *Receptions of Newman*, ed. Aquino and King, 49.

20 Ibid.

21 William Oddie, the former editor of the *Catholic Herald* and author of the excellent *Chesterton and the Romance of Orthodoxy: The Making of GKC, 1874–1908* (Oxford: Oxford University Press, 2008), is good on Duffy's often laborious efforts to present Newman as a misunderstood liberal. "In his defence of Professor Beattie, Professor Duffy quotes John Henry Newman, predictably perhaps, woefully out of context: claiming Newman in this way is, of course, an established liberal tactic; usually, it is the *Letter to the Duke of*

is not only presented as at odds with Thomism, he is claimed to have been a proto-Modernist. Of course, none of these contentions is new, but that the authors should write of them as though they were minted yesterday says a good deal about their historical pretensions.

To be fair, there is one excellent essay in the collection by Father Keith Beaumont, entitled "The Reception of Newman in France," which puts Newman and the Modernists in proper critical perspective. "The regular misquotation of Newman's brilliantly pithy formula in the *Essay on Development*, almost always taken out of context, is revealing," he writes.

> Most modernists quoted, often with their own variations, only the *last* sentence of the relevant passage: "In a higher world it is otherwise, but here below to live is to change, and *to be perfect is to have changed often.*" But the sentence which *precedes* is equally important, and determines the meaning of that which follows: "It [the idea] changes with them [new forms which continually appear] *in order to remain the same.*"²²

Here, again, is the insistence on *semper eadem* that Kasper and his liberal friends refuse to acknowledge, or only acknowledge to disparage. This solitary piece, however, for all of its insight, learning and good judgment, cannot salvage an otherwise deeply misguided collection.

In 1991, after the centennial of Newman's birth, the English Dominican Fergus Kerr edited a collection of essays with David Nicholls entitled *John Henry Newman: Reason, Rhetoric, and Romanticism* which had many of the same polemical hobby horses as King and Aquino's collection. Precisely because of its strenuous denigration of Newman and his work, the book met with total oblivion. Trusting in Newman's understanding of accumulated probabilities, we should expect the same fate for *Receptions of Newman*. What Lord Macaulay called the "savage envy of aspiring dunces" is no match for the man about whom the *Staffordshire Gazette* wrote, with welcome good sense: "The strength and dignity, the simplicity and sweetness of his character were conspicuously reflected in his writings, but these qualities

---

Norfolk which is thus abused in an attempt to paint Newman, that wonderfully acerbic doctrinal rigorist and scourge of liberalism (which he describes in the *Apologia* as 'false liberty of thought') as being a liberal himself." William Oddie, "Eamon Duffy talks of 'the Sovietisation of Catholic intellectual life' and quotes Newman in defence of Tina Beattie: Newman would disagree," *Catholic Herald* (14 November 2012). Tina Beattie, Professor of Catholic Studies at Roehampton University, was disinvited to teach in an American Catholic college after it emerged that her antinomian books tout not only sodomy but killing children in the womb. Duffy had argued that Newman would have somehow approved of the college hiring Beattie.

22 Keith Beaumont, "Receptions of Newman in France," in *Receptions of Newman*, ed. Aquino and King, 174.

and virtues appealed less powerfully to his countrymen than the grandeur of his soul which made him content to find in a life of self-sacrifice and obscurity the truest opportunities for dutiful service to God and man."[23]

Yet perhaps the point that most needs to be made about receptions to Newman and his work is that, early and late, whether hostile or sympathetic, brilliant or obtuse, they never shook him from his profound, unbiddable faith. The staunchly Tractarian Frederick Rogers, who felt he had no alternative but to cut off all relations with Newman after he converted to Rome, captured something of the disarray his secession caused the Anglo-Catholic party: "Newman had joined Rome, and left those who had adhered to him headless, unorganized, suspected by others, and suspecting each other; for nobody yet knew who would follow where he led. For a time a kind of perplexed hopelessness prevailed."[24] Then, in 1868, five years after reconciling with Newman after an estrangement of twenty years, Rogers, now Lord Blachford, wrote his old Oriel friend about an Anglican vicar named Bartholomew, who could never think of Newman *sine summo desiderio*, and Newman responded with all of his accustomed fellow feeling:

> Pray convey my best thanks to Mr. Bartholomew ... for his kindness in writing for me the letter you send me ... I feel also the great kindness of what he says to you about me. It is pleasant, while it is painful to me, to have left a lasting regret in the minds of such as him—yet I have reciprocated it, though my own deep wound was before I left them, and in leaving them; and it was healed, when the deed was done, as far as it was personal, and not from the reflection of their sorrow.

Of course, this was the response of one who had played the lead part in the shattering of Tractarianism. Yet there was another response, and it continues to appeal to anyone interested in the historical Newman, rather than the Newman of liberal polemics. "To-day is the twentieth anniversary of my setting up the Oratory in England," Newman told Rogers, "and every year I have more to thank God for, and more cause to rejoice that he helped me over so great a crisis." And then he left his old friend with a parting reassurance.

> Since Mr. Bartholomew obliges me to say it, this I cannot omit to say. I have found in the Catholic Church abundance of courtesy, but very little sympathy, among persons in high place, except a few— but there is a depth and a power in the Catholic religion, a fulness of satisfaction in its creed, its theology, its rites, its sacraments, its

---

23 Obituary of Cardinal Newman in *Staffordshire Chronicle*, in LD, XXXII, 631.
24 *Letters of Frederic, Lord Blachford* (London: John Murray, 1896), 118.

discipline, a freedom yet a support also, before which the neglect or the misapprehension about oneself on the part of individual living persons, however exalted, is as so much dust, when weighed in the balance. This is the true secret of the Church's strength, the principle of its indefectibility, and the bond of its indissoluble unity. It is the earnest and the beginning of the repose of Heaven.[25]

---

25 Newman to Sir Frederic Rogers (2 February 1868), in *LD*, XXIV, 4–5.

4

Newman and the Liberals

I much fear society is rotten, to say a strong thing. Doubtless there are many specimens of excellence in the higher walks of life, but I am tempted to put it to you, whether the persons you meet generally are—I do not say seriously religious, we never can expect that in this world—but believers in Christianity in any true sense of the word. No, they are Liberals, and in saying this I conceive I am saying almost as bad of them as can be said of anyone.

John Henry Newman to John Bowden (March 1831)

From the age of fifteen, dogma has been the fundamental principle of my religion: I know no other religion: I cannot enter into the idea of any other sort of religion; religion, as a mere sentiment, is to me a dream and a mockery.

John Henry Newman, Apologia pro Vita Sua (1864)

Newman and the Liberals

I

ONE OF THE MORE ARRESTING CLAIMS of those who write of Newman from the liberal standpoint—and here I am thinking not only of the rebarbative Frank Turner but his acolytes in the liberal academy—is to claim that Newman's lifelong campaign against liberalism was somehow mistaken because he never adequately understood or defined the words *liberal* or *liberalism* and, therefore, what definitions he did offer are unreliable.[1] Turner, for those who may not know, was the John Hay Whitney Professor of History at Yale, whose scurrilous book, *John Henry Newman: The Challenge to Evangelical Religion* accused the principled convert of having been a "quasi schismatic priest and typical Victorian religious seeker,"[2] who only claimed to oppose liberalism, when, in fact, what he really opposed was the Evangelical religion to which he had subscribed briefly in his youth. Turner brought many more wildly unsubstantiated charges against Newman but it is his persistent attempt to discredit Newman's opposition to liberalism that continues to win his otherwise historically derisory work the good opinion of liberals. In this chapter, I shall endeavor to see whether Turner's claims have any merit by revisiting how Newman and his contemporaries understood the matter. In an age like ours, where liberalism continues to exert considerable sway, not only in the political but

---

1 See Turner, *John Henry Newman: The Challenge to Evangelical Religion*, 9–11, 23, 133–4, 142, 223, 277, 289. According to an obituary that appeared in *Yale News* on the distinguished Yale professor: "His wife, Ellen Tillotson, notes that there are three things that Turner wanted to be remembered for: As provost, he played a key role in the creation of the endowment for Lesbian, Gay, Bisexual, and Transgender Studies, and approved the funding for the construction of the WIYN telescope at Kitt's Peak Observatory in Arizona, a collaboration between Yale, Indiana and Wisconsin universities, and the National Optical Astronomy Observatories. Also, under his directorship, the Beinecke Library purchased its Islamic Collection." No one could possibly have questioned Turner's liberal credentials.

2 *Apologia pro Vita Sua and Six Sermons*, ed. Frank Turner (New Haven: Yale University Press, 2008), 114–15.

the ecclesiastical, educational, and judicial spheres, ascertaining whether one of the great critics of liberalism knew what he was about may not be an entirely useless undertaking.

Like so many other words that have come down in the world, the adjective "liberal," which came into the language in the late fourteenth century, began its life a perfectly respectable word, signifying, according to the *Oxford English Dictionary*, "the instinctive epithet of those 'arts' or 'sciences' that were considered *worthy of a free man*, opposed to *servile* or *mechanical*"—or, as Samuel Johnson defined the word in his great *Dictionary*, "not mean, not low in birth, not low in mind; becoming a gentleman; munificent, generous, bountiful, not parsimonious." By the mid-fifteenth century, the word had grown to mean not only *bountiful, generous* and *open-hearted* but *made without stint, abundant, ample*. It was only in the eighteenth century, under pressure from the anti-Catholic animus of the Enlightenment, that the word began to take a turn for the worse, when it acquired the new, dubious meaning of *free from narrow prejudice, open-minded, candid*. Unsurprisingly, for this newly acquired meaning, the author chosen to illustrate it was Edward Gibbon, who, for all of his incontestable brilliance, was probably one of the most prejudiced, closed-minded and devious historians who ever drew breath. Then, by the middle of the nineteenth century, the word became corrupter still, meaning *free from bigotry or unreasonable prejudice in favor of traditional opinions or established institutions; open to the reception of new ideas or proposals of reform*. And here James Murray, the *Oxford English Dictionary*'s first editor, could not resist showing his own prejudice by calling upon the American jurist Oliver Wendell Holmes to illustrate this meaning from his book, *A Rhymed Lesson* (1846): "Thine eyes behold / A cheerful Christian from the liberal fold." From these adjectival meanings, the noun "liberal" comes to denote *one who holds liberal views in politics or theology*. Thus, while it might have started its days meaning *worthy of a free man*, it ended up meaning *free from unreasonable prejudice in favor of traditional opinions or established institutions*. Its degradation was complete.

In May of 1927, G. K. Chesterton wrote a column in *The London Illustrated News* entitled "The Falling Value of Words," which nicely explains why even the best words come to grief. "I read a phrase in a newspaper the other day," Chesterton wrote, "printed in very large letters at the top of a column, which ran as follows: 'Crusade to Reform Auction Bridge.' And I mused, in a slightly melancholy mood, upon the destiny and the decline of human words, and how clearly the fate of words illustrates the fall of man." For the inspired rhetorician in Chesterton, it was hardly news that many words became playthings of thoughtless expediency, but for the student of history in him they were nevertheless reminders of truths that even the most thoughtless could never entirely expel. And this use of the noble word *crusade* was a case in point. "Surely anyone will see something a little strange in that remarkable combination of terms and topics—anyone, at least, who knows what has been for mankind the meaning of the Crusade, not to speak of the meaning of the Cross. Indeed, it is quite equally incongruous whether our sympathies are with the Cross or the Crescent ... If we have any sense of the historic influence of these images among men, of how Godfrey blazed among the Nine Worthies or what it was that lingered on the lyre of Tasso, we shall perhaps repeat to ourselves in a curious and meditative voice those simple words, "Crusade to Reform Auction Bridge."[3] In "this fall of man's chosen symbols," Chesterton saw that "there may well be a symbol of his own fall." Yet, in his conclusion to the piece—which shows how he could wrest wisdom from his most casual columns—the paradoxical convert made an arresting confession: there might be some to whom this continual degradation of language might "seem a sombre version of human existence, but not to me, for I have long believed that the only really happy and hopeful faith is a faith in the Fall of Man."[4]

The "Fall of Man" is something that we should keep in mind when revisiting Newman's understanding of liberals and liberalism because he saw the evils of liberalism in precisely those defining terms. That the *Oxford English Dictionary* does not see it in that light is perhaps not something that should surprise us. As the poet Geoffrey Hill (1932–2016) pointed out, neither does the *Oxford English Dictionary* recognize Newman's use of the word *aboriginal* in his brilliant description of original sin as the "aboriginal calamity."[5] However, for its definition of "liberalism," which it defines as the "holding of liberal views in politics or theology," the *Oxford English Dictionary* does quote from Newman's *Apologia pro Vita Sua* (1864): "The more serious thinkers among us are used ... to regard the spirit of Liberalism as the destined Anti-Christ."[6]

---

3 Gilbert Keith Chesterton, *Collected Works, Volume 34: Illustrated London News, 1926–1928*, 309–10.

4 Ibid., 313–14.

5 "Most of what one wants to know, including much that it hurts to know about the English language is held within these twenty volumes. To brood over them and in them is to be finally persuaded that sematology is a theological dimension: the use of language is inseparable from that 'terrible aboriginal calamity' in which, according to Newman, the human race is implicated. Murray, in 1884, missed the use of 'aboriginal': it would have added a distinctly separate signification to the recorded examples. In 1989 it remains unacknowledged. In what sense or senses is the computer acquainted with original sin?" Hill, quoted in Edward Short, *Newman and his Contemporaries* (London and New York: T. & T. Clark, Continuum, 2011), 391. See also Geoffrey Hill, "Common Weal, Common Woe," in *Collected Critical Writings* (Oxford: Oxford University Press, 2008), 279.

6 *Apologia*, 174.

Newman defined the liberalism that took shape over the nineteenth century in England on many different occasions, in his letters and in his published writings, over a period that spanned over sixty years, from the 1820s to the 1880s, but perhaps his most succinct definition appeared in his famous *Biglietto* speech, which he gave in Rome after Leo XIII made him a cardinal on 12 May 1879.

> Liberalism in religion is the doctrine that there is no positive truth in religion, but that one creed is as good as another, and this is the teaching which is gaining substance and force daily. It is inconsistent with any recognition of any religion, as *true*. It teaches that all are to be tolerated, for all are matters of opinion. Revealed religion is not a truth, but a sentiment and a taste; not an objective fact, not miraculous; and it is the right of each individual to make it say just what strikes his fancy. Devotion is not necessarily founded on faith. Men may go to Protestant Churches and to Catholic, may get good from both and belong to neither. They may fraternise together in spiritual thoughts and feelings, without having any views at all of doctrine in common, or seeing the need of them. Since, then, religion is so personal a peculiarity and so private a possession, we must of necessity ignore it in the intercourse of man with man. If a man puts on a new religion every morning, what is that to you? It is as impertinent to think about a man's religion as about his sources of income or his management of his family. Religion is in no sense the bond of society.[7]

He also gave a more expanded definition of liberalism in his autobiography, *Apologia pro Vita Sua* (1864). As he explained there,

> I have been asked to explain more fully what it is I mean by "Liberalism," because merely to call it the Anti-dogmatic Principle is to tell very little about it. An explanation is the more necessary, because such good Catholics and distinguished writers as Count Montalembert and Father Lacordaire use the word in a favorable sense, and claim to be Liberals themselves. "The only singularity," says the former of the two in describing his friend, "was his Liberalism. By a phenomenon, at that time unheard of, this convert, this seminarist, this confessor of nuns, was just as stubborn a liberal, as in the days when he was a student and a barrister."

That Newman should have opened his most comprehensive definition of liberalism with reference to Charles-Forbes-René Montalembert (1810–70), the Catholic publicist, historian and orator, who was born in London of an *emigré* father and Scots mother and became a leader of French Catholics

---

[7] *Addresses to Cardinal Newman with his Replies*, ed. Neville (London: Longman, Green & Co., 1905), 64–5.

during the Second Empire, was apt because Montalembert spent a good deal of his life trying to rehabilitate French liberalism from the disrepute into which it had fallen as a result of being associated with the more radical aspects of the French Revolution. Certainly, as Newman appreciated, the Revolution constituted one of the great seedbeds of the liberalism that would spread throughout England in the nineteenth century. In trying to disentangle liberalism from radicalism, Montalembert made a famous distinction between the two, which, even allowing for the many political and religious differences between France and England in the nineteenth century, still sheds a good deal of light on Newman's understanding of how liberalism inherently inclines towards radicalism.

> "Let no one say, as certain generous but blind spirits have said, that radicalism is the exaggeration of liberalism," [Montalembert declared,] "no, it is its antipodes, its extreme opposite. Radicalism is nothing more than an exaggeration of despotism; and never has despotism taken a more odious form. Liberty is reasonable and voluntary toleration; radicalism is the absolute intolerant, which is arrested only by the impossible. Liberty imposes unusual sacrifices on none; radicalism cannot put up with a thought, a word, even a prayer, contrary to its will. Liberty consecrates the right of minorities; radicalism absorbs and annihilates them. To say everything in one word, liberty is respect for mankind, while radicalism is scorn of mankind pushed to its highest degree. No; never Muscovite despot, never Eastern tyrant, has despised his fellows as they are despised by those radical clubbists, who gag their vanquished adversaries in the name of liberty and of equality!"[8]

Here, in seeing radicalism as a travesty of liberty, Montalembert anticipated many of Newman's own animadversions on liberalism. Mrs. Oliphant, that heroically prolific authoress, gives the historical context in which Montalembert made this distinction in her biography of the French Catholic. Apropos the thoroughly Erastian[9] nature of French Catholicism, she

---

8 Margaret Oliphant, *Memoir of Count de Montalembert: A Chapter of Recent French History* (Leipzig: Bernard Touchnitz, 1872), II, 63–4. In response to Montalembert's warm appreciation of the *Apologia pro Vita Sua*, Newman wrote to him: "It gives me very great pleasure to receive from such a person as yourself so kind an expression of your sympathy. From whom could such an expression be so valuable to me as from one who has been himself so emphatically an example all through his life of a noble and illrequited devotion to the Catholic cause? You are one of those in an eminent way to whom a Gracious Providence has refused in this life the reward of his good deeds, that he may receive them in superabundant measure in the world to come." Newman to Montalembert (9 March 1868), in *LD*, XXIV, 48.

9 An adherent of the doctrine of Erastus, one who maintains the complete subordination of the ecclesiastical to the secular power. Erastus, or Liebler, was a physician

writes: "Even the men who were content to risk their lives for the integrity of their Parliament and for their right to elect it, saw no harm—nay, the reverse—considered it right and necessary that all ecclesiastical dignitaries should be appointed by Government, and denied to the clergy the right to elect their representatives, the bishops." Yet, as Oliphant shows, these were not the only fetters put on the liberty of the French Church. "Prejudice and impiety had imposed upon her a much heavier yoke than the English heretics had imposed upon the Catholic Church in England. At the very time of which we speak it was dangerous for a priest to go about the streets *en soutane*, in the costume of his class; and when the cholera appeared in Paris, the services of priests, volunteered on all hands, were refused at the hospitals, and they had to be smuggled in privately in the dress of laymen to administer the last sacraments to such expiring sufferers as desired their services. Everything was free, except religion; nor does it seem to have occurred to the generality of men that the Church had any right to ask the freedom which every other institution had secured."[10]

English Erastianism may never have been so blunt as the French variety: the country's political and religious order recognized the advisability of giving the National Church at least an occasional appearance of autonomy, if only to avoid the sort of conspicuous defections that arose as the result of the Gorham Case, in which the Privy Council overruled a bishop as to whether Anglicans were obliged to believe in baptismal regeneration. Yet, below the dissembling surface, English Protestantism was just as Erastian as French Catholicism. That this shocked many otherwise well-informed Englishmen only revealed the extent to which they were willing to connive in what amounted to a self-evident sham. William Gladstone was not untypical of certain fastidiously loyal Anglicans when he shared with Henry Edward Manning his memorandum stating that "acquiescence in the principles of the Report in the Gorham Case would be fatal to ... [the] life and authority [of the Church of England] as a Branch of the Catholic Church."[11] Of course, it was "fatal" to Manning, who would be one of the most prestigious Anglicans to bolt after the Gorham judgment was passed, but it was not "fatal" to Gladstone, who remained within the Anglican fold despite the Gorham judgment.

Wilfrid Ward, certainly one of Newman's most incisive biographers, saw how Erastianism encouraged the liberals in their presumptuous mischief. In the Oxford Movement, Ward writes:

---

of Heidelberg in the sixteenth century, to whom has been attributed the theory of State supremacy in ecclesiastical affairs.

10 Oliphant, *Memoir of Count de Montalembert*, I, 104–5.

11 William Ewart Gladstone to Edward Henry Manning (20 May 1850), in *The Correspondence of Edward Henry Manning and William Ewart Gladstone* (Oxford: Oxford University Press, 2013), II, 359.

Newman and the Liberals

Newman saw the great hope for the preservation of the Christian inheritance. The liberalism which it opposed was shallow in its intellectual principles and shallow in its utilitarian policy. The Erastianism which dominated it judged of utility by the standards of an unbelieving State. Its projected intellectual reforms measured theology by the standards of human science. They left out of account in what they planned to correct or abolish, the imperfections inevitable in a science of Divine things built up of human notions. The liberals destroyed the tares with the wheat, for they assumed a power which our intellect does not possess, of accurate discrimination in a sacred tradition whose sources were mixed and obscure, partly Divine, partly human. "Liberalism" Newman defined as "the exercise of thought upon matters in which from the constitution of the human mind thought cannot be brought to any successful issue. Among such matters," he adds, "are first principles of whatever kind, and of these, the most sacred and momentous are especially to be reckoned the truths of revelation."[12]

These discriminations notwithstanding, most Anglicans agreed with the Broad Churchman, Julius Charles Hare (1795–1855), a close friend of Manning at the time of his conversion, who regarded the intrusion of the State into matters of dogma as perfectly acceptable:

> That there would be nothing monstrous or unheard of in the allowance of such a latitude, we may learn from what Horsley has said in his Charge for the year 1800, concerning the spirit of our Church, with regard to another main question of theological debate. "I know not what hinders but that the highest Supralapsarian Calvinist may be as good a Churchman as an Arminian; and if the Church of England in her moderation opens her arms to both, neither can with a very good grace desire that the other should be excluded." Would that all the members of our Church, more especially the Clergy,—whose occupations naturally render them tenacious of their peculiar opinions,—were rightly imprest with the same conviction, enforced as it is by a number of sayings in the New Testament, and that they knew how to apply it to the other topics of dispute! For this has ever been the course of true wisdom.[13]

The Erastian nature of English Christianity was important because it was out of the National Church's subordination to the State that the Broad Church arose, and, in turn, it was out of the non-dogmatical accommodations of the Broad Church that liberalism in religion arose—the conviction,

---

12 Wilfrid Ward, *Ten Person Studies* (London: Longman, Green & Co., 1908), 237–8.
13 Julius Charles Hare, *A Letter to the Hon. Richard Cavendish: On the Recent Judgement of the Court of Appeal, as Affecting the Doctrine of the Church* (London: J. W. Parker, 1850), 6.

as Newman famously wrote, that "No theological doctrine is any thing more than an opinion which happens to be held by bodies of men" and "Therefore ... no creed, as such, is necessary for salvation."[14] Of course, in this calculus, it was axiomatic that "No one can believe what he does not understand" and "Therefore ... there are no mysteries in true religion."[15] James Fitzjames Stephen (1829–94), the circuit judge and legal historian,[16] nicely confirmed this when he announced in *The Saturday Review* in 1865 in a piece entitled "Dr. Newman and Liberalism": "The great majority of Liberals in the present day would admit that they are perfectly willing to believe any doctrines which can be proved to their satisfaction to have been revealed to men by God. All that they contend for is that the question whether, in fact, alleged revelations are real is a question of evidence, to be decided by the common rules of evidence, and that the moral character of the alleged revelation is one item of the evidence to be considered."[17]

The arrogance of this effusion may be comical; but it was an arrogance shared by many skeptical Englishmen for whom the evidentiary claims of Christianity were bogus. Of course, one has to keep in mind that since these same Englishmen had only known a Protestant counterfeit of Christianity, it was not entirely surprising that they should have considered it bogus. Indeed, one of the reasons why the English came round to admiring Newman as they did, despite what they regarded as his incomprehensibly foreign Catholicism, was precisely because he refused to embrace a National Church that most of his English contemporaries knew, in their

---

14 *Apologia*, 260.

15 Ibid., 261.

16 Rosemary Ashton, in a joint review of Ian Ker's biography of Newman and K. J. M. Smith's biography of James Fitzjames Stephen, makes a perceptive point about Stephen's attitude towards religious faith: Stephen's "first love was the law, his second literary journalism. But no Victorian could ignore the question of religion. Stephen approached it from a rationalist, utilitarian point of view. As a law-giver and law-reformer, he viewed religion as a possible ally in enforcing justice. As Frederick Harrison said of him, he 'clung to Hell for its utility as a moralising agent in deterring the weak and the vicious from sin and crime.' Stephen himself gives a minimalist view in *Liberty, Equality, Fraternity* (1873): 'If there is a future state, it is natural to suppose that that which survives death will be that which is most permanent in life ... That is to say, mind, self-consciousness, conscience or our opinion of ourselves.' Here is the rationalist position put in the bleakest terms. For Stephen, Protestantism, 'in the form stated by Paley and others,' was the only form of Christianity which 'rational men' could seriously consider. Yet he himself seemed to prove Newman's rule that rational Protestantism led inevitably to unbelief." Rosemary Ashton, "Leaving It," *The London Review of Books* (16 February 1989).

17 James Fitzjames Stephen, "Dr. Newman and Liberalism" (1863), in *Selected Writings of James Fitzjames Stephen: On Society, Religion and Government* (Oxford: Oxford University Press, 2015), 184.

heart of hearts, was bogus.[18] (Here, one cannot resist quoting the witty Duff Cooper, who had occasion to observe in his autobiography that for the English "there are only two religions: Roman Catholicism, which is wrong; and all the rest, which don't matter.")[19]

There were, it is true, some, like Fitzjames Stephen, who insisted that a kind of perverse mendacity lay behind Newman's conversion: no one in good conscience could creditably convert from one bogus Christianity to another. Indeed, as K. J. M. Smith shows in his critical biography of the judge, Fitzjames Stephen saw Newman's entire career as a kind of evasion, a kind of slinking away from rational thinking. In Stephen's piece, "Newman on the Universities" (1859), Newman's career is presented as having been dedicated to "giving excellent reasons for untenable opinions" and arguing that one "must believe something because peace of mind is the reward of belief, and uneasiness is inseparable from doubt ... Unless this is truth, there is no truth; but as I cannot do without truth, this must be truth."[20] For Smith, Fitzjames Stephen sought "to ensure that metaphysics was purged and kept at a safe distance from English theology, and that whatever beliefs might survive could be honestly held without intellectual gymnastics."[21] What Smith appears not to realize is that this is not only an evasion but a mockery of metaphysics.

For Fitzjames Stephen and so many men like him, the only acceptable course for Newman after he found the Anglican Church untenable would have been to join Fitzjames Stephen and his friends in honest, foursquare skepticism. In their eyes, that Newman persevered in what they could only regard as groundless credulity was proof of his dishonesty. And that Newman was clearly aware of this himself is plain from the fourth and

---

18 It is important to say with respect to this admittedly arguable conjecture that the bogus nature of the National Church never bred in Englishmen any contempt for Anglicanism: on the contrary its very invalidity was one of the reasons why most Englishmen felt affection for it. In no other national church, after all, was there such a thing as the "sporting parson," about which the biographer of Peel, Norman Gash, is so amusing. "In November, 1882 Mrs. Oliphant's Oxonian son, reading Greek philosophy with a Devonshire vicar, described to his mother how on the day of the meeting of the Dartmoor hounds, his host and tutor (it being All Saints Day) held an early service before breakfast—a sort of 'hunting mass'—after which he breakfasted hastily in his cassock, disappeared for a few minutes, then reappeared in full hunting garb, 'entirely transmogrified from the priest of the sanctuary to the sportsman eager for the chase ...'" Norman Gash, *Robert Surtees and Early Victorian Society* (Oxford: Oxford University Press, 1993), 122–3.

19 Duff Cooper, *Old Men Forget* (London: Faber & Faber, 1953), 128.

20 Fitzjames Stephen, quoted in K. J. M. Smith, *James Fitzjames Stephen: Portrait of a Victorian Rationalist* (Cambridge: Cambridge University Press, 1988), 220.

21 Ibid., 222.

fifth propositions of the definition that he furnished of liberalism in the *Apologia*: "4. It is dishonest in a man to make an act of faith in what he has not had brought home to him by actual proof ... [and] 5. It is immoral in a man to believe more than he can spontaneously receive as being congenial to his moral and mental nature."[22] With respect to these aspects of liberalism, if our own liberal critics are to hold that Newman was mistaken, they must also hold that Fitzjames Stephen was mistaken, for Newman contends nothing that Fitzjames Stephen had not contended before him, even though the canny judge saw fit to omit any mention of propositions 4 and 5 in his response to that section in Newman's *Apologia*, doubtless realizing how self-incriminating such mention would be.

Fitzjames Stephen's point is reminiscent of a point John Stuart Mill makes in *On Liberty*, that "If a person assents undoubtingly to what they think true, though he has no knowledge whatever of the grounds of the opinion ... this is not knowing the truth. Truth thus held, is but one superstition more."[23] As Robert Pattison points out in *The Great Dissent: John Henry Newman and the Liberal Heresy* (1991): "With modifications, Mill's version of truth leads to the positivist doctrine that 'a sentence says nothing unless

---

22 *Apologia*, 260.

23 John Stuart Mill, *On Liberty* (New York: Norton Critical Edition, 1975), 35. Newman was not overly impressed by Mill's *On Liberty* (1859), remarking of its promotion of "false liberty": "there are writers who ... maintain doctrines which carried out consistently would reach that *deliramentum* which ... [Pius IX] speaks of [in his Encyclical of 1864], if they have not rather already reached it," and for Newman Mill was one of them: "We are a sober people; but are not the doctrines of even so grave and patient a thinker as the late Mr. J. S. Mill very much in that direction? ... Of course he does not allow of a freedom to harm others, though we have to consider well what he means by harming: but his is a freedom which must meet with no 'impediment from our fellow-creatures, so long as what we do does not harm them, even though they should think our conduct foolish, perverse, or wrong.' 'The only freedom,' he continues, 'which deserves the name is that of pursuing our own good in our own way, so long as we do not attempt to deprive others of theirs, or impede their efforts to obtain it. Each is the proper guardian of his own health, whether bodily, or mental and spiritual.' That is, no immoral doctrines, poems, novels, plays, conduct, acts, may be visited by the reprobation of public opinion; nothing must be put down, I do not say by the laws, but even by society, by the press, by religious influence, merely on the ground of shocking the sense of decency and the modesty of a Christian community. Nay, the police must not visit Holywell Street, nor a licence be necessary for dancing-rooms: but the most revolting atrocities of heathen times and countries must for conscience-sake be allowed free exercise in our great cities. Averted looks indeed and silent disgust, or again rational expostulation, is admissible against them, but nothing of a more energetic character." John Henry Newman, "Postscript" § 6, "A Letter to the Duke of Norfolk," in *Certain Difficulties Felt by Anglicans in Catholic Teaching* (London: Longman, Green & Co., 1900), II, 363–4.

it is empirically verifiable.'"[24] Neither Fitzjames Stephen nor Mill would grant Newman's idea of truth precisely because it was not verifiable by what Fitzjames Stephen called "the common rules of evidence." Fitzjames Stephen may have rejected Comtean positivism, seeing it, as many saw it, as "a sort of atheistical parody of Roman Catholic ritual," but he never seemed aware of how his own insistence on "the common rules of evidence" in judging metaphysical matters condemned him to precisely the same positivism that he deplored in Comte.[25] Nevertheless, for both Mill and Stephen, Newman's truth amounted to little more than credulity. For his part, Newman rejected the Cartesian contention that doubt could advance knowledge. The critical epistemologist in him spent a fair amount of time revisiting how we actually believe or disbelieve things, and it was clear after those painstaking researches that only credulity made knowledge possible.[26] Indeed, he would meet his skeptical critics' objections in *Grammar of Assent* (1870) by assuming "nothing but what has universal reception" and citing the existence of conscience as an example of something that might not be susceptible of any indubitable rational proof but which nevertheless everyone accepted as real:

> This condition is abundantly fulfilled as regards the authority and religious meaning of conscience;—that conscience is the voice of God has almost grown into a proverb. This solemn dogma is recognized as such by the great mass both of the young and of the uneducated, by the religious few and the irreligious many. It is proclaimed in the history and literature of nations; it has had supporters in all ages, places, creeds, forms of social life, professions, and classes. It has held its ground under great intellectual and moral disadvantages; it has recovered its supremacy, and ultimately triumphed in the minds of those who had rebelled against it. Even philosophers, who have been antagonists on other points, agree in recognizing the inward voice of that solemn Monitor, personal, peremptory, unargumentative, irresponsible, minatory, definitive.[27]

For Newman's liberal critics, his submission to an infallible Church was emblematic of what they regarded as his unacknowledged skepticism. For Newman himself, such defamatory charges were a kind of whistling in

---

24 Pattison, *The Great Dissent*, 190.

25 Stephen, quoted in K. J. M. Smith, *James Fitzjames Stephen: Portrait of a Victorian Rationalist* (Cambridge: Cambridge University Press, 1988), 220.

26 Newman had "no antecedent difficulty in often seeing the hand of Providence in the history of the world and of human life. And he never forgot that readiness of belief was enjoined by the Gospels." Wilfred Ward, *The Life of John Henry Cardinal Newman* (London: Longman, Green & Co., 1912), 343.

27 *Grammar of Assent*, 83–4.

the dark. Here, as is so often the case, Newman captured the thinking of his opponents better than they captured it themselves.

> That there can be peace, and joy, and knowledge, and freedom, and spiritual strength in the Church, is a thought far beyond the world's imagination; for it regards her simply as a frightful conspiracy against the happiness of man, seducing her victims by specious professions, and, when they are once hers, caring nothing for the misery which breaks upon them, so that by any means she may detain them in bondage. Accordingly, it conceives we are in perpetual warfare with our own reason, fierce objections ever rising within us, and we forcibly repressing them. It believes that, after the likeness of a vessel which has met with some accident at sea, we are ever baling out the water which rushes in upon us, and have hard work to keep afloat; we just manage to linger on, either by an unnatural strain on our minds, or by turning them away from the subject of religion. The world disbelieves our doctrines itself, and cannot understand our own believing them. It considers them so strange, that it is quite sure, though we will not confess it, that we are haunted day and night with doubts, and tormented with the apprehension of yielding to them. I really do think it is the world's judgment, that one principal part of a confessor's work is the putting down such misgivings in his penitents. It fancies that the reason is ever rebelling, like the flesh; that doubt, like concupiscence, is elicited by every sight and sound, and that temptation insinuates itself in every page of letter-press, and through the very voice of a Protestant polemic. When it sees a Catholic Priest, it looks hard at him, to make out how much there is of folly in his composition, and how much of hypocrisy.[28]

Another point regarding propositions 4 and 5 that is important to make is that they were largely defensive. Throughout Newman's letters, one can see how reluctant he was to parry the often egregious attacks made on his intellectual and, indeed, moral integrity. He only answered Kingsley and Gladstone, for example, because their charges involved his Roman Catholics co-religionists as a whole, not merely himself. Indeed, Leslie Stephen is amusing when it comes to Newman's disinclination to involve himself in controversy with liberals. "Did I tell you, by the way, about Archdeacon Allen," he asked his good friend, Charles Eliot Norton, the American social critic and professor of art in 1877, referring to John Allen (1810–66), an Evangelical Anglican and friend of Fitzgerald, Thackeray and Tennyson.

> He—a respectable, kindly, hot-headed old parson—wrote to ask me a string of questions: Whether I held Christ to be an impostor,

---

28 Newman, "Faith and Doubt," in *Discourses to Mixed Congregations*, 221–2.

&c. &c. I replied frankly, though civilly, as he was really a friend of my father and mother, in which character he addressed me. He then sent my letter to J. H. Newman, begging the great man to come out and slay the Philistine. J. H. N. replied that he was too old for controversy, and, in fact, civilly shunted the question. Then Allen wrote to (of all people!) Thompson, the Master of Trinity, sending him both letters. Thompson in reply, said nothing whatever of me and my atrocities, but said that Newman's letter was so beautiful that he would willingly give for it all the money in his pocket, viz., £3 10s. Allen accepted the offer, and presented the cash to the Zanzibar Mission—which is so far the total result of his labours.[29]

In the letter to which Stephen refers, Newman did express his unwillingness to enter the controversy enjoined by Allen, but he also expressed the futility of entering into any controversy where the controversialists could not bring themselves to acknowledge each other's first principles. "The religion of Comte, which is spreading, is an atheism," Newman told Allen, and this had fundamental consequences for Christians who wished to debate with those who regarded the first principles of Christianity as inherently untenable.

> We two mainly agree with each other, viewed relatively and in contrast to your correspondent [Stephen]. *His* difference from each of *us* is radical. We dissent from his first principles. What is the good of arguing with a man whom we cannot join issue with? It is beating the air—For instance, what an utter ignoring of what we hold as our starting points, what an assumption of what we deny, what an organic defect in logic, what an impotence to comprehend us and our views is evidenced in his urging upon us, "Cannot we believe that our race can produce a great moral type without the actual incarnation of deity?" Which incarnation he calls "blasphemous to mankind!" We have nothing in common with him. You and I think, judge, and argue in (on the whole) one and the same medium; but he inhabits, breathes, and moves in an element of his own. We must pray—we can do nothing else.[30]

In the case of Fitzjames Stephen, Newman had received the disputatious judge at the Oratory unexpectedly in October of 1865—he had come to discuss his *Saturday Review* article attacking Newman's propositions on liberalism in the *Apologia*—but, as Newman told his friend W. S. Lilly in 1881, the meeting had not gone well:

---

29 Leslie Stephen to Charles Eliot Norton (16 March 1877). in Frederic William Maitland, *The Life and Letters of Leslie Stephen* (London: Duckworth & Co., 1906), 299.
30 Newman to John Allen (17 December 1876), in *LD*, XXVIII, 146.

> He came here years ago to ferret out my answer to his objections … After hearing his arguments I had said to him "It is no good our disputing; it is like a battle between a dog and a fish—we are in different elements," meaning what I have said at *Grammar of Assent*, p. 416. He went away and told his friends that I had acknowledged that I had been unable to answer what he had said. This great misinterpretation of my words he has since thrown into the formula "his only defence of Catholicity is that atheism is its alternative." After this misstatement was brought home to me by the persons to whom he had made it, he proposed to come to me to have another conversation, and to ascertain whether I thought now "what I thought ten years ago," but I declined his proposal.[31]

The passage to which Newman refers in *Grammar of Assent* (1870) nicely accounts for why there could be no meeting of the minds between the founder of the English Oratory and James Fitzjames Stephen: "I have no scruple in beginning the review I shall take of Christianity by professing to consult for those only whose minds are properly prepared for it; and by being prepared, I mean to denote those who are imbued with the religious opinions and sentiments which I have identified with Natural Religion," Newman wrote.

> I do not address myself to those, who in moral evil and physical see nothing more than imperfections of a parallel nature; who consider that the difference in gravity between the two is one of degree only, not of kind; that moral evil is merely the offspring of physical, and that as we remove the latter so we inevitably remove the former; that there is a progress of the human race which tends to the annihilation of moral evil; that knowledge is virtue, and vice is ignorance; that sin is a bugbear, not a reality; that the Creator does not punish except in the sense of correcting; that vengeance in Him would of necessity be vindictiveness; that all that we know of Him, be it much or little, is through the laws of nature; that miracles are impossible; that prayer to Him is a superstition; that the fear of Him is unmanly; that sorrow for sin is slavish and abject; that the only intelligible worship of Him is to act well our part in the world, and the only sensible repentance to do better in future; that if we do our duties in this life, we may take our chance for the next; and that it is of no use perplexing our minds about the future state, for it is all a matter of guess. These opinions characterize a civilized age; and if I say that I will not argue about Christianity with men who hold them, I do so, not as claiming any right to be impatient or peremptory with any one, but because it is plainly absurd to attempt to prove a second proposition to those who do not admit the first.[32]

---

31 Newman to W. S. Lilly (17 February 1881), in *LD*, XXIX, 337–8.
32 *Grammar of Assent*, 267–8.

Leslie Stephen, James's brother, would hardly have disputed the futility to which Newman refers. "I had an odd experience in controversy the other night," he wrote Norton in the same letter in which he related the anecdote about Allen. "I went to the Metaphysical Club and read a paper of my brother's ... Some clever—some very able—men were there: James Martineau, Mivart, Huxley, Lord Selborne, Prof. Robertson, Hutton, etc.; but when the paper was read they had an inarticulate wrangle over things in general, which could not have been more rambling."[33] Six months later, his view was no more favorable. "I was at the Metaphysical Society two days ago and listened to a most rambling controversy between Hutton of the *Spectator*, Huxley, Dr. Ward, and others. Oh! What rot people talk, and will talk, I suppose, to the end of the chapter! If anybody finds my books on a stall a century hence, I suppose that they will make the same remark about me."[34]

Newman might have been averse to engaging in controversy with those who could not enter into his first principles. After all, from the beginning of his long, deliberative departure from everything and everyone that he had held dear in Oxford he came to appreciate that: "When men understand what each other mean, they see, for the most part, that controversy is either superfluous or hopeless."[35] Yet he was not averse to controversy *per se*, as he explained to one of his more exuberant antagonists, George William Ward (1812–82), the opera-loving Ultramontane, for whom he would always have a soft spot:

> I thank you very much for the present of your volume and for your kind letter—but far more of course for your prayers. I do not feel our differences to be such a trouble, as you do; for such differences always have been, always will be, in the Church, and Christians would have ceased to have spiritual and intellectual life, if such differences did not exist. It is part of their militant state. No human power can hinder it; nor, if it attempted it, could do more than make a solitude and call it peace. And, thus thinking that man cannot hinder it, however much he try, I have no great anxiety or trouble. Man cannot, and God will not. He means such differences to be an exercise of charity.[36]

For Newman, this "exercise of charity" would also extend to those whom he saw liberalism lead astray. Here, the most affecting example was his brother, Francis Newman, who might have begun a devout Anglican, but

---

33 Maitland, *The Life and Letters of Leslie Stephen*, 299.
34 Ibid., 303.
35 Newman, "Faith and Reason, Contrasted as Habits of Mind" (1839), Sermon 10, in *University Sermons*, 142.
36 Newman to W. G. Ward (18 February 1866), in *LD*, XXII, 157.

ended a muddled Unitarian, certain of little more than of the "right" of euthanasia, a clear casualty of what Newman memorably called the "all-corroding, all-dissolving scepticism of the intellect in religious enquiries."[37]

Newman's dear friend, Blanco White (1775–1841), was another casualty. He had met White, the gifted poet, novelist, critic and political journalist in the 1820s at Oriel, where they shared a delight in playing Beethoven's sonatas on the violin. In addition, they would often talk of Catholicisim, the faith from which Blanco had seceded in Spain before converting to Anglicanism and to which Newman was drawn after finding Anglicanism an untenably human concoction. When Newman learned that this lovable man had given up Christianity for Unitarianism, he was deeply dismayed. To his dear friend, Henry Wilberforce, he shared this dismay with an intensity that shows how seriously he took such matters.

> B. [Blanco] White's Autobiography, which is just published, is the most dismal horrible work I ever saw. He dies a Pantheist, denying that there is an ultramundane God, apparently denying a particular Providence, doubting, to say the least, the personal immortality of the soul, meditating from Marcus Antoninus, and considering that St Paul's epistles are taken from the Stoic philosophy. As to Christianity he seems thoroughly to agree with Strauss, and rejects the gospels as historical documents.[38]

These were the facts of White's apostasy, but for Newman the facts could scarcely convey the tragedy that had befallen his restless friend. "His biographer calls him a *Confessor*," he veritably wailed, "Confessor to what? Not to any opinions, any belief whatever, but to the search after truth, ever wandering about and changing … Is this the *end* of Life? can there be a greater paradox than that? But what a view does it give one of the Unitarians and *id genus omne*? They really do think it is no harm whatever being an Atheist, so that you are sincerely so, and do not cut people's throats and pick their pockets!" Some of the dismay Newman felt with regard to White's apostasy was the result of his solicitude for a man who, by rights, ought to have had the sense to steer clear of such patent pitfalls. Nevertheless, another source of his dismay was much more radically personal. Newman read White's autobiography attesting to the loss of his Christian faith in April of 1845, a bare six months before he would take his momentous final step and convert to Rome, and, in these circumstances, White's liberalism seemed a terrible cautionary tale.

> Here is Blanco White, sincere and honest. He gives up his country, and then his second home—Spain, Oxford, Whately's family, all

---

37 *Apologia*, 142.
38 Newman to Henry Wilberforce (27 April 1845), in *LD*, X, 639–40.

for an idea of truth, or rather for liberty of thought. True I think a great deal of morbid restlessness was mixed with his sincerity, an inability to keep still in one place, a readiness to take offence and be disgusted, an inward irritability and a fear of not being independent, and other bad feelings. But then the thought forcibly comes upon one, why may not the case be the same with me? I see Blanco White going wrong, yet sincere; Arnold going wrong, yet sincere; *they* are no puzzle to *me*. I can put my finger on this or that point in their character, and say, *Here* was the fault. But *they* did not know the fault—and so it comes upon me, How do I know that I too have not my weak points which occasion me to think as I think? how can I be sure that I have not committed sins which bring this unsettled state of mind on me as a judgment? This is what is so very harassing, as you may suppose.[39]

As this passage vividly shows, liberalism was not an abstraction for Newman. A ragbag of ideas purporting to guide men in the search for the truth, it actually misled them into contempt for the truth. He had seen gifted young men whom he had known at Oxford—Mark Pattison and Anthony Froude come to mind—beguiled by the same false philosophy. But Blanco White would always be a special case for Newman because he was so close to his heart. When Newman wrote his lectures on the *Present Position of Catholics in England* (1851) he had occasion to eulogize White in a section on anti-Catholic writers in England.

The Rev. Joseph Blanco White ... was a man of great talent, various erudition, and many most attractive points of character. Twenty-five years ago, when he was about my present age, I became acquainted with him at Oxford, and I lived for some years on terms of familiarity with him. I admired him for the simplicity and openness of his character, the warmth of his affections, the range of his information, his power of conversation, and an intellect refined, elegant, and accomplished. I loved him from witnessing the constant sufferings, bodily and mental, of which he was the prey, and for his expatriation on account of his religion. At that time, not having the slightest doubt that Catholicism was an error, I found in his relinquishment of great ecclesiastical preferment in his native country for the sake of principle, simply a claim on my admiration and sympathy. He was certainly most bitter-minded and prejudiced against everything in and connected with the Catholic Church; it was nearly the only subject on which he could not brook opposition; but this did not interfere in the confidence I placed in his honour and truth; for though he might give expression to a host of opinions in which it was impossible to acquiesce, and was most precipitate and unfair

---

39 Newman to Henry Wilberforce (27 April 1845), in *LD*, X, 640–1.

in his inferences and inductions, and might be credulous in the case of alleged facts for which others were the authority, yet, as to his personal testimony, viewed as distinct from his judgments and suspicions, it never for an instant came into my mind to doubt it. He had become an infidel before he left Spain. While at Oxford he was a believer in Christianity: after leaving it he fell into infidelity again; and he died, I may say, without any fixed belief at all, either in a God or in the soul's immortality.[40]

Many twenty-first century readers might read this and wonder why Newman made such a fuss over one troubled soul losing his faith. Yet Newman could never see the loss of anyone's faith as trifling. The fuss he made over White's loss was proof of his *caritas*, a staple of his character that liberals often insufficiently credit. Newman's opposition to liberalism and the infidelity to which it gives rise grew out of his lifelong commitment to the cure of souls, not out of any ideological animus.[41] Indeed, in this regard, it was a cry of love.

Newman's opposition to liberalism was also of a piece with his opposition to the faith in progress, to which so many of his contemporaries subscribed. "I fear, nothing but the reality of severe suffering will bring us to a right estimate of what we are," he wrote Samuel Francis Wood in 1832, "and rouse us from this indolent contemplation of our advances in the useful arts and the experimental sciences, to the thought and practice of our duties as immortal beings." For Newman, the sanguine hopes of liberals were misapplied. "The country seems to me to be in a dream—being drugged with this fallacious notion of its superiority to other countries and times.—And I think from this another mistake follows. Men see that those parts of the national system, (and those, of course, far the most important and comprehensive) which really depend on personal and private virtue do not work well—and, not seeing [where] the deficiency lies, viz. in want of personal virtue, they imagine they can put things right by applying their scientific knowledge to the improvement of the existing system."[42] Unlike so many of his contemporaries, on whom the idea of progress acted as almost an intoxicant, Newman would always look askance at the promises

---

40 *Present Position of Catholics*, 142–3. See also Martin Murphy, *Blanco White: Self-Banished Spaniard* (New Haven: Yale University Press, 1989).

41 White's skepticism can be seen in all of its sad incoherence in his sonnet, "To Night" (1828), which Coleridge thought the best sonnet in the language. Walter Bagehot blamed White's inability to believe on idleness. Like Newman, Bagehot considered action indispensable to faith. Writing to his father about White in 1846, Bagehot observed: "Certain it is that the constant promise of Christ that those who *do* his will shall know of the truth of his doctrine is unaccompanied by any promise of success to inactive speculation however earnest and conscientious." *The Collected Works of Walter Bagehot*, XV, 260).

42 Newman to Samuel Francis Wood (4 September 1832), in *LD*, III, 90.

of science and knowledge. The historian Michael Aeschliman shows how far-sighted Newman was in his criticism of this aspect of liberalism.

> In his prescient critique of optimistic nineteenth-century progressivism, which was to be so catastrophically disproved after the summer of 1914, Newman was one of the few major Western intellectuals of his time to see how delusory and destructive a faith it was, and how fraught with those future ill consequences ... In this sense Newman, usually seen as a believer in an age of growing skepticism, might more revealingly be seen as a skeptic in an age of growing belief—belief in the idea of the progress of mankind as a whole. He is a skeptic about the credulous faith that H. R. Trevor-Roper has called "the unwarranted assumption that man only needs freedom from ancient restraints in order to realize his inherent perfection."[43] Whatever Newman's later problems with ecclesiastical intrigue and authoritarianism, throughout a long life he remained remarkably consistent in his mistrust of the flatteries of liberalism, whether philosophical, political, or religious.[44]

In that unbearably beautiful summer of 1914, Henry James would describe the *dénouement* of this melancholy tale in a letter to his old friend, Rhoda Broughton, the Welsh novelist and short story writer, which nicely confirmed Newman's worst fears. "Black and hideous is the tragedy that gathers," the aggrieved American exile wrote, "and I'm sick beyond cure to have to lived on to see it. You and I, the ornaments of our generation, should have been spared this wreck of our belief that through the long years we had seen civilization grow and the worst become impossible. The tide that bore us along was then all the while moving to *this* as its grand Niagara." From his charming Georgian home, Lamb House in Rye on the Sussex coast, James gave voice to an entire civilization's irremediable lament. "The country and the season here are of a beauty of peace and loveliness of light, and summer grace, that make it inconceivable that just across the Channel, blue as *paint* today, the fields of France and Belgium are being ... given up to unthinkable massacre and misery."[45]

One far-sighted contemporary who entirely understood what Newman meant when he warned of the dangers of liberalism was Leo XIII (1878–1903). Indeed, it was partly with these dangers in mind that he instituted the Feast of the Holy Family and consecrated all the peoples of the world to the Sacred Heart of Jesus. He also issued the encyclical, *On the Nature of*

---

43 Hugh Trevor Roper, "Introduction," in Lord Acton, *Lectures on Modern History* (London: Fontana, 1960).

44 M. D. Aeschliman, "The Prudence of Newman," *First Things* (August 1994).

45 Henry James to Rhoda Broughton (10 August 1914), in *Henry James Letters, Volume IV, 1895–1916*, ed. Leon Edel (Cambridge, Mass.: Harvard University Press, 1984), 713–14.

Human Liberty (1888) insisting that the true custodian of liberty, properly understood, was the Church herself. Regarding his last encyclical, *The Evils of the Time and their Remedies* (1901), Wilfrid Ward makes the connection to Newman explicit:

> With solemn pathos the Holy Father depicts in this remarkable Encyclical the sufferings of the Church, and the share of her ministers in those Beatitudes which promise a reward for the endurance of present sorrow and injustice. In language suggestive of that used by Cardinal Newman he describes the war of the age in which we live on truths the most sacred, the inroads of secularism on our daily life, and the failure of the boasted progress of civilisation to take the place of that religion which it has despised and persecuted. The Encyclical is an earnest plea, not against modern progress, but against the forgetfulness of the laws of nature and society which has accompanied it. It is only so far as it is the foe to religion that the modern movement is decried. We are (the Pope says) to welcome and use "the advantages which flow from education, from science, from civilisation, from a wise and peaceful liberty." But liberty has passed into licence, and has questioned the truths on which the life of society depends. And science has not known its place, but has tried, with ludicrous unsuccess, to be a substitute for religion. "Man has been able to subdue matter, but matter has not been able to give him what it does not possess. To the great questions which concern our highest interests science has given no answer." Comfort and material civilisation are dearly bought at the cost of lost hope, lost ideals, lost coherence of principles, the loss of the realisation of the necessary laws of social life. "A law of Providence confirmed by history shows that man cannot strike at the first principles of religion without sapping the foundations of social order and prosperity." To the vindication, then, of these old and simple truths—truths of common-sense which the eccentricity of modern thought has forgotten—he devotes himself; to their restoration to true perspective, which undisciplined discussion and an exaggeration of the place occupied by science in the scheme of true wisdom had destroyed. The Pontiff asks that his message may be listened to not by Catholics only, but by all who have at heart the interests of the race. "May it be received as the testament which, standing, as we do, so near the gates of eternity, we wish to leave to the people of the earth, as a presage of the salvation which we desire for all." This Encyclical is perhaps the most touching of the whole Pontificate and breathes in every page the unearthly wisdom of the Christian Church. It is the fitting farewell of a great Pontiff to the people of Christ at the termination of a memorable reign.[46]

46 Wilfrid Ward, *Ten Personal Studies* (London: Longman, Green & Co., 1908), 182–3.

Newman and the Liberals

What gives Leo's encyclical its cogency, especially with regard to its criticism of liberalism, is that it is not the work of a reactionary or small-minded man. As Ward reminds his readers, "Pius IX began with a certain sanguine trust in the generous features of modern Liberalism. Disappointment led to reaction, and made him the *intransigeant* opponent of all that savoured of Liberalism. Leo never idealized Liberalism, and, consequently, he was kinder to it."[47] Like Newman, however, he was keenly aware that false liberty bred infidelity, and it was this aspect of liberalism that he could never abide. Newman, for his part, treated the consequences of the heterodoxy that liberalism breeds with the gravity they deserve. In *The Arians of the Fourth Century* (1833), he does not mince his words on this score:

> Many a man would be deterred from outstepping the truth, could he see the end of his course from the beginning. The Arians felt this, and therefore resisted a detection, which would at once expose them to the condemnation of all serious men. In this lies the difference between the treatment due to an individual in heresy, and to one who is confident enough to publish the innovations which he has originated. The former claims from us the most affectionate sympathy, and the most considerate attention. The latter should meet with no mercy; he assumes the office of the Tempter, and, so far forth as his error goes, must be dealt with by the competent authority, as if he were embodied Evil. To spare him is a false and dangerous pity. It is to endanger the souls of thousands, and it is uncharitable towards himself.[48]

After reading this, those who imagine that the author of the demonstrably heterodox *Amoris Laetitia* (2016) is somehow not responsible for the consequences of his published heterodoxy might wish to think again.

The ideas that Newman associated with liberal infidelity are nicely set out in the propositions that he defined in an appendix to the *Apologia*.[49] He also spoke of the same ideas in a series of Advent sermons he gave in November and December of 1835 on "The Patristical Idea of Anti-Christ," in one of which he wrote:

> Is the enemy of Christ, and His Church, to arise out of a certain special falling away from GOD? And is there no reason to fear that some such Apostasy is gradually preparing, gathering, hastening on in this very day? For is there not at this very time a special effort made almost all over the world, that is, every here and there, more or less in sight or out of sight, in this or that place, but most visibly

---

47 Ibid., 192–3.
48 John Henry Newman, *The Arians of the Fourth Century*, 3rd edn (London: Longman, Green & Co., 1908), 234–5.
49 *Apologia*, 260–2.

or formidably in its most civilized and powerful parts, an effort to do without Religion? Is there not an opinion avowed and growing, that a nation has nothing to do with Religion; that it is merely a matter for each man's own conscience?—which is all one with saying that we may let the Truth fail from the earth without trying to continue it on after our time. Is there not a vigorous and united movement in all countries to cast down the Church of Christ from power and place? Is there not a feverish and ever-busy endeavour to get rid of the necessity of Religion in public transactions? for example, an attempt to get rid of oaths, under a pretence that they are too sacred for affairs of common life, instead of providing that they be taken more reverently and more suitably? an attempt to educate without Religion?—that is, by putting all forms of Religion together, which comes to the same thing;—an attempt to enforce temperance, and the virtues which flow from it, without Religion, by means of Societies which are built on mere principles of utility? an attempt to make *expedience*, and not *truth*, the end and the rule of measures of State and the enactments of Law? an attempt to make numbers, and not the Truth, the ground of maintaining, or not maintaining, this or that creed, as if we had any reason whatever in Scripture for thinking that the many will be in the right, and the few in the wrong? An attempt to deprive the Bible of its one meaning to the exclusion of all other, to make people think that it may have an hundred meanings all equally good, or, in other words, that it has no meaning at all, is a dead letter, and may be put aside? an attempt to supersede Religion altogether, as far as it is external or objective, as far as it is displayed in ordinances, or can be expressed by written words,—to confine it to our inward feelings, and thus, considering how variable, how evanescent our feelings are, an attempt, in fact, to destroy Religion?[50]

For those who quibble over Newman's definitions of liberalism, the definitions that he supplies here of the ideas that have consistently animated the evil of liberalism can have no persuasive force. Newman's twenty-first century detractors either refuse to acknowledge the evil, or are so implicated in its furtherance, whether in the academy or within or outside the Catholic Church, that they are naturally interested in glossing over or even denying the evil. Yet, no one who pays even cursory attention to how liberal ideas continue to vitiate our social order—whether in their assault on the integrity of marriage or the other norms of the natural law vital to the flourishing of civil society—can deny that Newman's understanding of the evil was prophetic. Here, he describes not only the nineteenth-century

---

[50] Newman, "The Patristical Idea of Antichrist" (1835), in *Discussions on Various Subjects*, 59–60.

liberalism that overtook his poor addled brother Frank but the liberalism that has now overtaken the entire Western world in the twenty-first century:

> Surely, there is at this day a confederacy of evil, marshalling its hosts from all parts of the world, organizing itself, taking its measures, enclosing the Church of Christ as in a net, and preparing the way for a general Apostasy from it. Whether this very Apostasy is to give birth to Antichrist, or whether he is still to be delayed, as he has already been delayed so long, we cannot know; but at any rate this Apostasy, and all its tokens and instruments, are of the Evil One, and savour of death. Far be it from any of us to be of those simple ones who are taken in that snare which is circling around us! Far be it from us to be seduced with the fair promises in which Satan is sure to hide his poison! Do you think he is so unskilful in his craft, as to ask you openly and plainly to join him in his warfare against the Truth? No; he offers you baits to tempt you. He promises you civil liberty; he promises you equality; he promises you trade and wealth; he promises you a remission of taxes; he promises you reform. This is the way in which he conceals from you the kind of work to which he is putting you; he tempts you to rail against your rulers and superiors; he does so himself, and induces you to imitate him; or he promises you illumination,—he offers you knowledge, science, philosophy, enlargement of mind. He scoffs at times gone by; he scoffs at every institution which reveres them. He prompts you what to say, and then listens to you, and praises you, and encourages you. He bids you mount aloft. He shows you how to become as gods. Then he laughs and jokes with you, and gets intimate with you; he takes your hand, and gets his fingers between yours, and grasps them, and then you are his.[51]

II

If opposing the Erastian subordination of the Church to the State made Montalembert a liberal in France, it made Newman a conservative radical in England.[52] In August of 1833, Newman wrote his good friend and fellow Tractarian, Frederic Rogers,

---

51 *Ibid.*, 60–1.
52 Cf. "Newman was anti-liberal but he was no mere conservative." Ian Ker, *Newman on Vatican II* (Oxford: Oxford University Press, 2014), 9. Robert Pattison makes a similar point: "properly understood, Newman's is not a view of life that will win many friends among those who now pass for Western conservatives." Pattison, *The Great Dissent*, 209. The "never-say-die" Marxist Terry Eagleton, on the other hand, sees Newman as heartlessly, indeed frivolously, reactionary. "Most other Victorian sages from Carlyle to Morris were keenly engaged with the Condition of England

> Tory as I still am, theoretically and historically, I begin to be Radical practically. Do not let me misrepresent myself. I, of course, think that the most natural and becoming state of things is for the aristocratical power to be the upholder of the Church; yet I cannot deny the plain fact that in most ages the latter has been based on a popular power. It was so in its rise, in the days of Ambrose and in the days of Becket, and it will be so again. I am preparing myself for such a state of things, and for this simple reason, *because* the State has deserted us and we cannot help ourselves.[53]

While both Montalembert and Newman were one in supporting not only the integrity but the autonomy of the Roman Church, Newman realized that his own anti-liberal stance with regard to the Anglican Church had made him particularly anomalous. To capture this anomalousness, he compared himself to Montalembert's great confrere, Jean-Baptiste-Henri Lacordaire (1802–61):

> If I might presume to contrast Lacordaire and myself, I should say, that we had been both of us inconsistent;—he, a Catholic, in calling himself a Liberal; I, a Protestant, in being an Anti-liberal; and moreover, that the cause of this inconsistency had been in both cases one and the same. That is, we were both of us such good conservatives, as to take up with what we happened to find established in our respective countries, at the time when we came into active life. Toryism was the creed of Oxford; he inherited, and made the best of, the French Revolution.

---

question, appalled by the predatory nature of industrial capitalism and unsparing in their moral denunciations of it. With Newman, by contrast, we find a mind loftily aloof from Chartism, bread riots and the Factory Acts, more preoccupied with the Arian heresy of the fourth century than with typhoid epidemics in English slums." Terry Eagleton, "Washed in Milk," *London Review of Books*, 32, no. 15 (5 August 2010), 10–11. What Eagleton does not mention—his knowledge of the convert and his world is not extensive—is that Newman, like Charles Kingsley, ministered to those suffering from cholera. When the disease broke out in Bilston in 1849, for example, Newman relieved one of the local Catholic priests who had been left prostrate by the disease. The following year, Newman wrote his sister Jemima: "the cholera is very shocking to see. We went over for a time to Bilston, where it raged so, that the priests were unequal to it. Multitudes crowded for reception into the Church ... They did not send for us till one priest was ill abed, and by that time the disease was abating—but the sight of the sick in the hospitals was terrible—and brought before one most awful thoughts." Newman to Mrs. John Mozley (9 January 1850), in *LD*, XIII, 378. Still, to suggest, as Eagleton does, that it is more meritorious to combat typhoid than heresy is an unbalanced view of human endeavor: some of us would be more profitably employed in sorting out the Arian heresy, especially since it continues to destroy an incalculable number of souls.

53 Newman to Frederic Rogers (31 August 1833), in *LD*, IV, 35.

In delineating the most influential source of English liberalism, Newman pointed to without actually naming Oxford's early nineteenth-century reformers—John Everleigh and Edward Copleston of Oriel, Cyril Jackson of Christ Church, John Parsons of Balliol, and Dr. Routh of Magdalen—each of whom, in separate but related ways, helped to put Oxford on the road to a triumphal liberalism. Here, too, is the backdrop for Newman's admission that in the late 1820s, as he said himself, "I was beginning to prefer intellectual excellence to moral; I was drifting in the direction of the Liberalism of the day."[54] In the *Apologia*, he ascribes his coming to this pivotal realization as the result of "illness and bereavement:"[55]

> When, in the beginning of the present century, not very long before my own time, after many years of moral and intellectual declension, the University of Oxford woke up to a sense of its duties, and began to reform itself, the first instruments of this change, to whose zeal and courage we all owe so much, were naturally thrown together for mutual support, against the numerous obstacles which lay in their path, and soon stood out in relief from the body of residents, who, though many of them men of talent themselves, cared little for the object which the others had at heart. These Reformers, as they may be called, were for some years members of scarcely more than three or four Colleges; and their own Colleges, as being under their direct influence, of course had the benefit of those stricter views of discipline and teaching, which they themselves were urging on the University. They had, in no long time, enough of real progress in their several spheres of exertion, and enough of reputation out of doors, to warrant them in considering themselves the *élite* of the place; and it is not wonderful if they were in consequence led to look down upon the majority of Colleges, which had not kept pace with the reform, or which had been hostile to it. And, when those rivalries of one man with another arose, whether personal or collegiate, which befall literary and scientific societies, such disturbances did but tend to raise in their eyes the value which they had already set upon academical distinction, and increase their zeal in pursuing it. Thus was formed an intellectual circle or class in the University,—men, who felt they had a career before them, as soon as the pupils, whom they were forming, came into public life; men, whom non-residents, whether country parsons or preachers of the Low Church, on coming up from time to time to the old place, would look at, partly with admiration, partly with suspicion, as being an honour indeed to Oxford, but withal exposed to the temptation of ambitious views, and to the spiritual evils signified in what is called the "pride of reason."[56]

54 *Apologia*, 26.
55 Ibid.
56 Ibid., 254–5.

Identifying one source of liberalism in England in reformed Regency Oxford was characteristic of Newman's readiness to turn an objective eye on his own allegiances, even when close to his heart, if they proved unworthy of allegiance. In Newman's passage, we can also see the author of the *Oxford University Sermons* (1843), *The Idea of a University* (1875) and *An Essay on the Grammar of Assent* (1870), pondering the paradox of how the development of reason often issues in the shipwreck of reason, a paradox to which universities, then, as now, were eminently susceptible, "for, as they were following out the proper idea of a University, of course they suffered more or less from the moral malady incident to such a pursuit." For Newman, "The very object of such great institutions lies in the cultivation of the mind and the spread of knowledge" and "if this object, as all human objects, has its dangers at all times, much more would these exist in the case of men, who were engaged in a work of reformation." And, thus, Newman concluded, "In this select circle or class of men, in various Colleges, the direct instruments and the choice fruit of real University Reform, we see the rudiments of the Liberal party."

Newman defined those rudiments with acuity, proof that he had contemplated their genesis with care. "Whenever men are able to act at all, there is the chance of extreme and intemperate action," he wrote, "and therefore, when there is exercise of mind, there is the chance of wayward or mistaken exercise. Liberty of thought is in itself a good; but it gives an opening to false liberty." In other words, Newman traced the rise of liberalism not to Catholic Emancipation (1829), the First Reform Bill (1832), or even the Church Temporalities Bill (1833), which suppressed ten bishoprics in the Church of Ireland, but to the arrogance of the unshriven intellect.

> Now by Liberalism I mean false liberty of thought, or the exercise of thought upon matters, in which, from the constitution of the human mind, thought cannot be brought to any successful issue, and therefore is out of place. Among such matters are first principles of whatever kind; and of these the most sacred and momentous are especially to be reckoned the truths of Revelation. Liberalism then is the mistake of subjecting to human judgment those revealed doctrines which are in their nature beyond and independent of it, and of claiming to determine on intrinsic grounds the truth and value of propositions which rest for their reception simply on the external authority of the Divine Word.[57]

Apropos this "false liberty of thought," Newman is shrewd about how such evil does not necessarily need to be expressly championed or even understood by those who accept it in order for it to take hold and spread;

---

57 Ibid., 255–6.

"certainly," he says, "the party of whom I have been speaking, taken as a whole, were of a character of mind out of which Liberalism might easily grow up, as in fact it did; certainly they breathed around an influence which made men of religious seriousness shrink into themselves." Yet Newman was careful to qualify. Then, as now, most of those with liberal points of view held them without any understanding of what they portended.

> I have no intention whatever of implying that the talent of the University, in the years before and after 1820, was liberal in its theology, in the sense in which the bulk of the educated classes through the country are liberal now. I would not for the world be supposed to detract from the Christian earnestness, and the activity in religious works, above the average of men, of many of the persons in question. They would have protested against their being supposed to place reason before faith, or knowledge before devotion; yet I do consider that they unconsciously encouraged and successfully introduced into Oxford a licence of opinion which went far beyond them.[58]

Once this "license of opinion" ramified, it was inevitable that more and more would incline towards liberal notions in religion, even though many might have balked at considering themselves liberals *per se*. "In their day they did little more than take credit to themselves for enlightened views, largeness of mind, liberality of sentiment, without drawing the line between what was just and what was inadmissible in speculation, and without seeing the tendency of their own principles; and engrossing, as they did, the mental energy of the University, they met for a time with no effectual hindrance to the spread of their influence." It was only "the thorough-going Toryism and traditionary Church-of-Englandism of the great body of the Colleges and Convocation" that could hold them in check. Accordingly, the man who took the first stand against what became known as the "march of mind" was Newman's great friend and confidant John Keble, who, as Newman wrote, "brought the talent of the University round to the side of the old theology."[59] Rosemary Ashton, in her instructive account of Victorian Bloomsbury is good on "the march of mind":

> Bloomsbury was the main London location for the activities collectively known as "the march of mind" or the "march of intellect." The phrases were used regularly in the 1820s to describe the efforts of leading progressives, many of whom were associated both with the agitation for parliamentary and electoral reform which culminated in the first great Reform Act of 1832 and with the education movement. The latter took the form at the highest level of founding

---

58 Ibid., 256.
59 Ibid., 56–7.

a university in London to right the obvious wrong that the greatest metropolis in the world possessed no university, unlike Paris, Berlin, Florence, and many other cities. The avowedly secular university, known variously in journals such as the Tory organ John Bull as "the godless institution in Gower Street," the "radical infidel college," and the "Cockney College," was viewed with suspicion by orthodox churchmen, as well as by anti-reform politicians and journalists.[60]

One of these churchman was John Henry Newman, who referred to the London University in a letter to Archbishop Manning in 1873 as "a body which has been the beginning and source, and symbol of all the Liberalism existing in the educated classes for forty years."[61]

Ashton, to give her readers a still more vivid sense of how the place was perceived by contemporaries quotes the comic poet Winthrop Mackworth Praed, who contributed verses entitled "The London University: A Discourse delivered by a College Tutor at a Supper Party" to the *Morning Chronicle* in July 1825:

> Ye Dons and ye doctors, ye Provosts and Proctors
> Who are paid to monopolize knowledge
> Come make opposition by voice and petition
> To the radical, infidel college.[62]

In *The Tamworth Reading Room* (1841), a series of letters that Newman wrote to the *Times* satirizing the library that Henry Brougham and Sir Robert Peel had established from which all works of theology would be banned, Newman took aim at one of the main tenets of liberalism enshrined in the "godless place in Gower Street": apropos an address that Peel gave for the library, Newman wrote:

> On the occasion in question, Sir Robert gave expression to a theory of morals and religion, which of course, in a popular speech, was not put out in a very dogmatic form, but which, when analyzed and fitted together, reads somewhat as follows:—Human nature, he seems to say, if left to itself, becomes sensual and degraded. Uneducated men live in the indulgence of their passions; or, if they are merely taught to read, they dissipate and debase their minds by trifling or vicious publications. Education is the cultivation of the intellect and heart, and Useful Knowledge is the great instrument of education. It is the parent of virtue, the nurse of religion; it exalts man to his highest perfection, and is the sufficient scope of his most earnest exertions.[63]

---

60 Rosemary Ashton, *Victorian Bloomsbury* (New Haven: Yale University Press, 2012), 21.
61 Newman to Archbishop Manning (24 November 1873), in *LD*, XXVI, 390.
62 Ashton, *Victorian Bloomsbury*, 21–2.
63 Newman, "Tamworth Reading Room" (1841), in *Discussions on Various Subjects*, 255.

Newman and the Liberals

The historian George Malcolm Young (1882–1959) is particularly good at describing what amounted to the Victorian idolatry of knowledge. "A generation which has come to take invention for granted," Young writes, referring to the first readers of his classic *Portrait of an Age* (1936), "and is, perhaps, more sensitive to its mischief than its benefits, cannot easily recover the glory of an age when knowledge, and with it power, seemed to have been released for an illimitable destiny." Certainly, one gets this sense from reading of the prodigious accomplishments of Isambard Kingdom Brunel (1806–59), the heroic engineer of the Great Western Railway, who personified the faith in knowledge that Young describes so vividly:

> The Englishman might reluctantly allow that in social amenity the French, in care for the well-being of the people the Prussians, went beyond him. He might at moments be chilled by the aesthetic failure of his time, so profuse and yet so mean: alienated by its ethical assurance, at once so pretentious and so narrow. In a petulant mood, he would talk, like Grote,[64] of the Age of Steam and Cant, but all the while he knew that in the essential business of humanity the mastery of brute nature by intelligence, he had outstripped the world, and the Machine was the emblem of and the instrument of his triumph.[65]

In the *Apologia*, Newman would summarize this brave view still further by giving as his eighteenth proposition of liberalism:

> Virtue is the child of knowledge, and vice of ignorance.
> Therefore, e.g. education, periodical literature, railroad traveling, ventilation, drainage, and the arts of life, when fully carried out, serve to make a population moral and happy.[66]

What rankled Turner was Newman's perfectly defensible claim that opposition to "the march of mind" in Oxford could only come from a representative of the old High Church, like Keble, because "the party called Evangelical never has been able to breathe freely in the atmosphere of Oxford, and at no time has been conspicuous, as a party, for talent or learning." Then, again, if Turner could not abide Newman's occasional jibes at Evangelicals (which were rarely harsh), it is amusing to think of what

---

64 George Grote (1794–1871), an English historian whose claim to fame was his *History of Greece* (1846–56), about which Ruskin is amusing: "If you know—and I think you know— ... that the only two works of value on Rome and Greece are by a polished infidel, Gibbon, and a vulgar materialist, Grote—you may wonder that I have not had fever of the very scarletest, long ago." Ruskin to Henry Acland (1864), quoted in Tim Hilton, *John Ruskin: The Later Years* (New Haven: Yale University Press, 2000), 77.

65 *Early Victorian England*, ed. G. M. Young, 2nd impression (Oxford: Oxford University Press, 1951), II, 419.

66 *Apologia*, 262.

he would have made of Robert Surtees's view of them. In *Hillingdon Hall or the Cockney Squire* (1845) the great comic novelist describes his Evangelical James Blake as "one of those desperately over-righteous, cushion-thumping, jump-Jim-Crow breed of parsons, so sanctified that he could hardly suffer the light of heaven to shine upon him, and he ate cold roast potatoes to save his servant the sin of cooking on Sunday."[67] Certainly, Vivian Green, the Rector of Lincoln College and a historian of Oxford, on whom John Le Carré based his character George Smiley, corroborated Newman's account of the nineteenth-century Oxford Evangelicals with characteristic panache:[68]

> The Evangelical movement in the University tended to become by the 1830s a matter of theological sympathies rather than a distinctive party. It numbered a few senior members among its supporters, notably the layman Dr. J. D. Macbride, who held the principalship of Magdalen Hall and Lord Almoner's professorship of Arabic from 1813 to 1868, and his successor as Principal, Richard Mitchell, fellow of Lincoln and critic of Pattison, who became subsequently the first Principal of Hertford; Pusey's brother-in-law, the pusillanimous Dr. Cotton, Provost of Worcester from 1839 to 1880 and one of the chief promoters of the Martyrs Memorial in 1841: and the rumbustious Ben Symons, Warden of Wadham from 1831 to 1871, whose Sunday gatherings were known to undergraduates as "tea and hassocks" and who had been known to threaten his listeners, when they misbehaved at his lectures on the Thirty-nine Articles delivered in hall between 1.0 and 2.0 p.m., that "Twenty years ago, Sir, I should have had you flogged at the buttery-hatch!" Symons managed to secure the election of a group of like-minded fellows in the college, which became known as a centre for Evangelical teaching. Daniel Wilson sent his son there in 1822 rather than to St Edmund's Hall. R. W. Church, Dean of St. Paul's, was sent there for a similar reason in 1833. "Wadham," young Francis Chavasse commented in 1863, "is the Evangelical College of Oxford—none the worse for that." The Warden, it was said, timed evening prayers to prevent undergraduates from going to St. Mary's to hear Newman preach at four. There were others who held similar views; the militant chaplain of New College and All Souls, Peter Maurice, who sought to awaken his sympathizers to the threat represented by the Tractarians with his pamphlet Popery at Oxford; or the clerical gadfly C. P. Golightly. There were even more eccentric deviationists

---

67 R. S. Surtees, *Hillingdon Hall or the Cockney Squire* (London: Folio Society, 1983), 181.

68 "Green was always erudite, readable and scholarly, but was not the sort to espouse radical new theories or seek notoriety. His insights and discoveries were incremental, and he always acknowledged his debt to his predecessors. In a field strewn with denominational mines and partisanship, no one ever accused him of bias." See Green's obituary in the *Daily Telegraph* (26 January 2005).

on the left wing, among them a young fellow at Exeter, Henry Bulteel, who perturbed his listeners at St. Mary's by preaching a Calvinistic sermon and had his license withdrawn by Bishop Bagot for itinerant preaching, subsequently founding a sect of his own Evangelical thinking in the very shadow of St. Aldate's, of which he had once been curate; his colleague, J. L. Harris of Exeter, became a Plymouth Brother.[69]

All of these figures might be of interest from the standpoint of Oxford history but they were hardly members of any redoubtable party. Indeed, Green, who is nothing if not a sympathetic historian, shows that they were never capable of mounting a coherent, compelling program, which was precisely the point about them that Newman made.

> Although the Evangelicals continued to have their supporters in the University, there is little to suggest that they presented a positive lead in the heated religious atmosphere of the time. They were in the main critics of Tractarianism, readily penning pamphlets not always distinguished by Christian charity, and occasionally, as it would appear, sponsoring means to undo their opponents, whom they believed sincerely to be endangering the Church of England, which were not wholly scrupulous. They were perfectly willing to ally with the "high and dry" majority to push their progamme; and appeared to smell popery in every Tractarian line. Maurice expressed his horror at Newman's chapel at Littlemore. Golightly massed his supporters to sponsor the erection of the Martyrs Memorial, the one surviving relict of protest; but there was no society through which they could attract an undergraduate following. They were as averse to reform of the University and to liberal thought as their critics. It can hardly have been an accident that Wadham reacted against the rough rule of its Evangelical Warden by becoming a nest of early positivist thought under the lead of Frederic Harrison and Richard Congreve; or that many of those brought up in their hot-house tradition ultimately deserted it.[70]

As Greene so clearly shows, Newman was simply acknowledging an historical truism when he wrote that the Evangelicals were never a party in Oxford "conspicuous for talent or learning," the sort of truism which is simply immune to any sensible revisionism. Moreover, Greene shows that Turner was writing demonstrable nonsense when he claimed that Newman's real complaint was not with liberalism but with Evangelicalism. This has never deterred Simon Skinner, Colin Barr, Peter Nockles,

---

69 V. H. H. Green, *Religion at Oxford and Cambridge* (London: SCM Press, 1964), 215–16.
70 Ibid., 216.

Kenneth Parker and Benjamin King from praising Turner's work.⁷¹ Nockles, whom too many uncritical readers imagine a reliable intellectual historian, is particularly culpable on this score, repeating Turner's groundless calumny, that, as he puts it, "Newman reinterpreted his Tractarian life in order to curry favor with his Roman Catholic co-religionists by retrospectively making liberalism to be his guiding *bête noir*" without comment, as though the "argument," as he calls it, had some genuine, evidentiary basis.⁷²

What Green does not show—it is beyond the scope of his study of religion in Oxford and Cambridge—is how wrong Turner was with regard to Newman's attitude towards Evangelicals. Instead of Turner's typically ill-informed suppositions, readers can consult the history of the Anglican Church that Newman supplied for the French edition of the *Apologia* (1866), in which he wrote:

> The Evangelical party ... maintains all the biblical societies and most of the associations for protestant missions throughout the world. The origin of this party may be traced back to the puritans, who began to show themselves in the last years of Queen Elizabeth's reign. It was almost entirely thrown out of the Church of England at the time of the restoration of Charles II in 1660. It took refuge among the dissenters from that Church and was expiring little by little when its doctrines were revived with great vigour by the celebrated preachers Whitfield and Wesley, both pastors of the Anglican Church and founders of the powerful sect of the Methodists. These doctrines, while creating a sect outside the established Church, exercised at the same time an important influence in the bosom of that Church itself, and developed there little by little until it formed

---

71 That Barr should have claimed that Turner's edition of the *Apologia pro Vita Sua* is "the standard scholarly edition of a classic of Victorian literature" nicely defines the severe limits of his critical judgment. See Barr's review of the edition in the *Journal of Ecclesiastical History*. King shows even worse judgment by commending Turner's claim that "Conversion for Newman was a confession of failure both to secure latitude for Catholics in the English Church and to define a Catholic faith that could hold a congregation." Turner, quoted in Benjamin King, *Newman and the Alexandrian Fathers: Shaping Doctrine in Nineteenth-Century England* (Oxford: Oxford University Press, 2012), 49. Skinner goes so far as to refer to Turner's *John Henry Newman: The Challenge to Evangelical Religion* (2002) as "a major contribution to nineteenth-century British history ... empirically exhaustive, contextually assured and critically rigorous." Simon Skinner, "History versus Hagiography: The Reception of Turner's Newman," *Journal of Ecclesiastical History*, 61, no. 4 (October 2010), 764. And the comical Parker calls the book "magisterial." See Kenneth Parker, Review of *The Cambridge Companion to John Henry Newman*, ed. Ian Ker and Terrence Merrigan, *Church History*, 82, no. 2 (June 2013).

72 Peter Nockles, "Newman's Tractarian Responses," in *Receptions of Newman*, ed. Aquino and King, 152.

the evangelical party, which is to-day by far the most important of the three schools which we are trying to describe.⁷³

The other two schools Newman described in his precis were the "apostolic or Tractarian party" and the "Liberal party."

Thus, *pace* Turner, Newman was not simply dismissive of Evangelicals; he was always ready to concede that Evangelical "teaching had been a great blessing for England" particularly because "it had brought home to the hearts of thousands the cardinal and vital truths of Revelation"; he was also appreciative of the importance that Evangelicals placed on conversion, even though he took issue with their understanding of the nature of conversion, believing that they underestimated the often incalculable workings of grace inseparable from its progress by placing undue emphasis on feeling. After all, Newman himself had been transformed by two conversions in his own life, the first in 1816 to dogmatic religion; and the second, in 1845, to Roman Catholicism.⁷⁴ Moreover, David Newsome persuasively shows how Newman's lifelong "quest for holiness" can be said to have had Evangelical origins. After all, Samuel Wilberforce might have found Newman's early sermons too harsh, too austere, but as Newman reminded him: "We require the 'Law's stern fires.' We need a continual Ash Wednesday."⁷⁵ And in another context, Newman was refreshingly adamant that "Those who make comfort the great subject of their preaching seem to mistake the end of their ministry. Holiness is the great end. There must be a struggle and a trial here. Comfort is a cordial, but no one drinks cordials from morning to night."⁷⁶ In this insistence on holiness, Newman was carrying on what he had learned as a young man from Thomas Scott (1747–1821), the great Biblical commentator, one of whose maxims was "Holiness rather than peace."⁷⁷ Scott's autobiography, *The Force of Truth* (1814) might also have

---

73 John Henry Newman, Appendix to French edition of *Apologia pro Vita Sua* (1866) quoted in *Newman's Apologia pro Vita Sua*, ed. Wilfrid Ward (Oxford: Oxford University Press, 1913), xxiv.

74 For an excellent overview of Newman's response to Evangelical Christianity, see Ian Ker, *Newman and the Fullness of Christianity* (Edinburgh: T. & T. Clark, 1993), 19–30, 123–45.

75 David Newsome, "The Evangelical Sources of Newman's Power," in *Rediscovery of Newman: An Oxford Symposium*, ed. John Coulson and A. M. Allchin (London and Melbourne: Sheed and Ward, 1967), 25.

76 John Henry Newman, *Autobiographical Writings*, ed. Henry Tristram (New York: Sheed & Ward, 1957), 172.

77 *Apologia*, 19. Unlike the tributes Newman wrote to his Oriel colleagues in the *Apologia pro Vita Sua*, which abound in a strenuously charitable magnanimity, his tribute to Scott is *ex corde*: he refers to the author as one "who made a deeper impression on my mind than any other, and to whom (humanly speaking), I almost owe my soul." *Apologia*, 18.

given Newman his idea for writing his own autobiography in his *Apologia*.[78] Evangelicals, in other words, had had a profound influence on Newman, even if it had been a limited one. Nevertheless, despite this clear evidence to the contrary, Turner convinced himself that Newman was categorically hostile to Evangelicals, and this typically unhistorical misapprehension only exacerbated his hostility to Newman.

In judging Turner's work on Newman, Eamon Duffy makes his reservations against the wild biases of the Yale professor plain enough.

> [Simon] Skinner assures us that Turner's book was written out of "a conviction of Newman's towering importance." But the Newman whom Turner portrays is a spiritual pygmy, the prisoner of a dysfunctional psycho-pathology, mean-spirited and small-minded in all his doings. No one reading Turner's book would suspect that in the period it deals with its subject established himself as the most austerely eloquent preacher of the nineteenth century, or that, in his Oxford University sermons, he had composed one of the most searching studies ever written of the relationship between faith and reason, or that the Essay on development ... has remained one of the seminal works of modern ecclesiology. And it is hard to see how so unredeemed a bundle of vindictiveness and spite could ever have attracted and held the devoted admiration of so many of his contemporaries ... Simon Skinner deplores the hagiographical reverence which he thinks has blinded Newman's admirers to the momentousness of Turner's scholarly achievement. But loathing is just as insidious an enemy of objectivity as adulation, and whatever lip-service Turner may have paid to Newman's greatness, his book is manifestly informed by loathing.[79]

Duffy is right: Turner was motived by "loathing." And while it is true that Yale might not have seen this loathing as disqualifying Turner from teaching nineteenth-century intellectual history—indeed, the ardently liberal university might even have seen it as an asset—this same loathing was hardly capable of giving Turner any creditable insights into the development of Newman's highly nuanced religious convictions, or his understanding of the force of tradition, which Keble personified in so many fundamental ways.

Understanding Newman's paean to Keble in the *Apologia* is essential to understanding his rejection of the arid, ahistorical, mandarin faith of the Noetics. It is also essential to understanding Newman's recognition of the liberalism that has only become more puissant, more destructive and,

---

78 Martin J. Svalgic makes this point. See *Apologia*, 481.
79 Eamon Duffy, "The Reception of Turner's Newman: A Reply to Simon Skinner," *Journal of Ecclesiastical History*, 63, no. 3 (July 2012), 547–8.

indeed, more pathological since his death. "Keble was a man who guided himself and formed his judgments, not by processes of reason, by inquiry or by argument, but, to use the word in a broad sense, by authority," Newman wrote.

> Conscience is an authority; the Bible is an authority; such is the Church; such is Antiquity; such are the words of the wise; such are hereditary lessons; such are ethical truths; such are historical memories, such are legal saws and state maxims; such are proverbs; such are sentiments, presages, and prepossessions. It seemed to me as if he ever felt happier, when he could speak or act under some such primary or external sanction; and could use argument mainly as a means of recommending or explaining what had claims on his reception prior to proof ... What he hated instinctively was heresy, insubordination, resistance to things established, claims of independence, disloyalty, innovation, a critical, censorious spirit. And such was the main principle of the school which in the course of years was formed around him; nor is it easy to set limits to its influence in its day; for multitudes of men, who did not profess its teaching, or accept its peculiar doctrines, were willing nevertheless, or found it to their purpose, to act in company with it.[80]

Here was the traditional thinking that Keble and Newman and all of their contemporaries had seen the Jacobins of the French Revolution overturn, with ramifications that are with us still. Edmund Burke may now be viewed in certain quarters as though he were the reverse of a conservative in these matters, but there was never any ambiguity in his understanding of the ineradicably anti-Christian essence of those French *philosophes* that gave England's radicals so many of their governing principals.[81] Speaking of the Jacobins whose anti-Christian fervor animated the French Revolution, Burke wrote of how this "literary cabal had some years ago formed something like a regular plan for the destruction of the Christian religion. This object they pursued with a degree of zeal which hitherto had been discovered only in the propagators of some system of piety.[82] They were possessed with a

---

80 *Apologia*, 257.
81 For a different reading of Burke, see Emily Jones, *Edmund Burke and the Invention of Modern Conservatism 1830–1914: An Intellectual History* (Oxford: Clarendon Press, 2017). Jones makes her argument despite J. M. Robertson's contention that in the wake of the French Revolution, Burke's ideas became "more conservative than ever." J. M. Robertson, *The Meaning of Liberalism* (London: Methuen, 1912), 16.
82 John Stuart Mill would echo Burke when he referred to Auguste Comte's work in his *Autobiography*: "M. Comte lived to carry out ... in his last work, the *Système de Politique Positive*, the completest system of spiritual and temporal despotism, which ever yet emanated from a human brain, unless possibly that of Ignatius Loyola: a system by which the yoke of general opinion, wielded by an organized body of spiritual

spirit of proselytism in the most fanatical degree; and from thence, by an easy progress, with the spirit of persecution according to their means."[83] If this was a reading of the nature of the anti-Christian revolution under the shadow of which Newman had been born, he would live to see a recrudescence of the same revolution, as Burke so vividly attested:

> What was not to be done towards their great end by any direct or immediate act, might be wrought by a longer process through the medium of opinion. To command that opinion, the first step is to establish a dominion over those who direct it. They contrived to possess themselves with great method and perseverance, of all the avenues to literary fame. Many of them indeed stood high in the ranks of literature and science. The world had done them justice; and in favour of general talents forgave the evil tendency of their peculiar principles. This was true liberality, which they returned by endeavouring to confine the reputation of sense, learning, and taste to themselves or their followers. I will venture to say that this narrow, exclusive spirit has not been less prejudicial to literature and to taste, than to morals and true philosophy. Those Atheistical fathers have a bigotry of their own; and they have learnt to talk against monks with the spirit of a monk. But in some things they are men of the world. The resources of intrigue are called in to supply the defects of argument and wit. To this system of literary monopoly was joined an unremitting industry to blacken and discredit in every way, and by every means, all those who did not hold to their faction. To those who have observed the spirit of their conduct, it has long been clear that nothing was wanted but the power of carrying the intolerance of the tongue and of the pen into a persecution which would strike at property, liberty, and life.[84]

It is precisely because this revolution is still unfolding in our own time, when the liberal state, the liberal academy and the liberal judiciary enjoy precisely the same influence that Burke described in his great anatomy of revolution, that we should appreciate Newman's prophetic warnings against it in his own time. Refusing to heed these warnings on the grounds that Newman somehow did not understand liberalism is not

---

teachers and rulers, would be made supreme over every action, and as far as is in human possibility, every thought, of every member of the community, as well in the things which regard only himself, as in those which concern the interests of others." John Stuart Mill, *The Collected Works of John Stuart Mill, Volume I - Autobiography and Literary Essays*, ed. John M. Robson and Jack Stillinger, introduction by Lord Robbins (Toronto: University of Toronto Press, London: Routledge and Kegan Paul, 1981), 221.

83 Edmund Burke, *Reflections on the Revolution in France: A Critical Edition*, ed. J. C. D. Clark (Stanford: Stanford University Press, 2001), 276.

84 Ibid., 276–7.

only intellectually dishonest, in light of the mountainous evidence to the contrary: it is ahistorical.

In response to the nascent liberalism that Newman saw forming in Oxford, he embraced the apostolic Fathers, about whom he writes (in the third person) in his autobiographical memoir, written from 1874 to 1876:

> "A cold Arminian[85] doctrine, the first stage of Liberalism was the characteristic aspect, both of the high and dry Anglicans of that day and of the Oriel divines. There was great reason then to expect that on Newman's leaving the crags and precipices of Luther and Calvin, he would take refuge in the flats of Tillotson and Barrow, Jortin and Paley ... but the ancient Fathers saved him from the danger that threatened him. An imaginative devotion to them and to their times had been the permanent effect upon him of reading at School an account of them and extracts from their works in Joseph Milner's Church History, and even when he now and then allowed himself as in 1825 in criticisms of them, the first centuries were his *beau idéal* of Christianity."[86]

Newman would also confirm this in the *Apologia*, where he remarks: "In proportion as I moved out of the shadow of that liberalism which had hung over my course, my early devotion towards the Fathers returned; and in the Long Vacation of 1828 I set about to read them chronologically, beginning with St. Ignatius and St. Justin. About 1830 a proposal was made to me by Mr. Hugh Rose, who with Mr. Lyall (afterwards Dean of Canterbury) was providing writers for a Theological Library, to furnish them with a History of the Principal Councils. I accepted it, and at once set to work on the Council of Nicæa. It was to launch myself on an ocean with currents innumerable; and I was drifted back first to the ante-Nicene history, and then to the Church of Alexandria ... the historical center of teaching in those times."[87] Here, it is clear, that Newman's revulsion from liberalism led him not only to the Fathers but, by 1839, to an understanding of the historical untenability of what had been his own fanciful justification of the National Church while still a Tractarian. "For a mere sentence, the words of St. Augustine struck me with a power which I never had felt from any words before ... 'Securus judicat orbis terrarum!' By those great words of the ancient Father, interpreting and summing up the long and varied course of ecclesiastical history, the theory of the *Via Media* was absolutely pulverized."[88]

---

85 Relating to, characteristic of or following the doctrines of the Dutch Protestant theologian Jacobus Arminius (1560–1609), who rejected the Calvinist doctrine of predestination.
86 Newman, *Autobiographical Writings*, 83.
87 *Apologia*, 35–6.
88 *Ibid.*, 110–11. Newman translated St. Augustine's "palmary words" thus: "The universal Church is in its judgements secure of the truth." See *Apologia*, 543, n. 110.11.

In his lecture, "On the Patristic Idea of Anti-Christ" (1835), Newman set out how the French Jacobins had provided the boilerplate for the liberalism that would enter England in its wake:[89]

> [I]n the Capital of that powerful and celebrated nation, there took place, as we all well know, within the last fifty years, an open apostasy from Christianity; nor from Christianity only, but from every kind of worship which might retain any semblance or pretence of the great truths of religion, atheism was absolutely professed;—and yet in spite of this, it seems a contradiction in terms to say it, a certain sort of worship, and that, as the prophet expresses it, "a strange worship," was introduced. Observe what this was.
>
> I say, they avowed on the one hand Atheism. They prevailed upon a wretched man, whom they had forced upon the Church as an Archbishop, to come before them in public and declare that there was no God, and that what he had hitherto taught was a fable. They wrote up over the burial-places that death was an eternal sleep. They closed the churches, they seized and desecrated the gold and silver plate belonging to them, turning, like Belshazzar, those sacred vessels to the use of their impious revellings; they formed mock processions, clad in priestly garments, and singing profane hymns. They annulled the divine ordinance of marriage, resolving it into a mere civil contract to be made and dissolved at pleasure. These things are but a part of their enormities.
>
> On the other hand, after having broken away from all restraint as regards God and man, they gave a name to that reprobate state itself into which they had thrown themselves, and exalted it, that very negation of religion, or rather that real and living blasphemy, into a kind of god. They called it LIBERTY, and they literally worshipped it as a divinity. It would almost be incredible, that men who had flung off all religion should be at the pains to assume a new and senseless worship of their own devising, whether in superstition or in mockery, were not events so recent and so notorious. After abjuring our Lord and Saviour, and blasphemously declaring Him

---

89 Radical societies proliferated in England after the outbreak of the French Revolution. "The London Corresponding Society was started in January 1792 by a Scottish Dissenter, Thomas Hardy, who owned a shoe shop in Piccadilly. It began campaigning for manhood suffrage and solidarity with the French Revolution, and attracted several hundred members across the country ... A high proportion were Dissenters, including Methodists and Millenarians. Socially, these 'English Jacobins,' as they were sometimes called, were similar to the French Jacobins and Sans Culottes they admired: a middle-class leadership, including both solid businessmen and sometimes marginal intellectuals (writers, artists, preachers, lawyers) and a rank and file of tradesmen and skilled workers." Robert Tombs, *The English and their History* (New York: Knopf, 2014), 388.

to be an impostor, they proceeded to decree, in the public assembly of the nation, the adoration of Liberty and Equality as divinities: and they appointed festivals besides in honour of Reason, the Country, the Constitution, and the Virtues. Further, they determined that tutelary gods, even dead men, may be canonized, consecrated, and worshipped; and they enrolled in the number of these some of the most notorious infidels and profligates of the last century. The remains of the two principal of these were brought in solemn procession into one of their churches, and placed upon the holy altar itself; incense was offered to them, and the assembled multitude bowed down in worship before one of them—before what remained on earth of an inveterate enemy of Christ.[90]

Here was the historical context that Newman supplied for his concerns over liberalism—a revolutionary context in which liberalism became not only anti-religion but a religion in itself. In the *Apologia*, he recounts how in 1833, when traveling in the Mediterranean, before the launching of the Oxford Movement, he could scarcely contain his detestation for the new liberal religion. "It was the success of the Liberal cause which fretted me inwardly," he confessed. "I became fierce against its instruments and its manifestations. A French vessel was at Algiers; I would not even look at the tricolour. On my return, though forced to stop twenty-four hours at Paris, I kept indoors the whole time, and all that I saw of that beautiful city was what I saw from the Diligence."[91] Grounds for regarding this revolutionary context as genuinely menacing abounded. "The Gallican Church was necessarily a prime revolutionary target," Prof. Nick Groom of Exeter University points out in his introduction to the classic Gothic novel, *The Italian* (1797) by the radical Unitarian, Anne Radcliffe (1763–1823), which draws on the conflict between the Jacobins and the Catholic Church for much of its characters and plot. The Catholic Church in France was being ruthlessly plundered even while Burke was writing his *Reflections on the Revolution in France* (1790), "losing property, revenue, and a state role, and being ceaselessly and mercilessly attacked in revolutionary propaganda." Indeed, "the September Massacres of 1782 exterminated some 200 priests, and in 1793 and 1794, the Revolutionary Tribunal pursued a deliberate policy of state atheism ... through movements such as the Cult of Reason. Scores of priests and nuns were charged, tried, and convicted for counter-revolutionary activities such as possessing elements used in celebrating the Mass."[92] For the intellectual historian, Jonathan Clark these

---

90 Newman, "The Religion of Antichrist," in *Discussions on Various Subjects*, 69–70.
91 *Apologia*, 42.
92 Nick Groom, "Introduction," in Anne Radcliffe, *The Italian* (Oxford: Oxford World's Classics, 2017), xxviii–xxix.

were the revolutionary events that compelled Burke to come to the realization that "The great conflict was not between Popery and Protestantism ... but between Christianity and Jacobinism."[93] Burke was clear about this in a letter of 1792 that he wrote his son, Richard, in which he warned that:

> If ever the Church and the Constitution of England should fall in these Islands, (and they will fall together), it is not Presbyterian discipline, nor Popish hierarchy, that will rise upon their ruins. It will not be the Church of Rome nor the Church of Scotland—not the Church of Luther, nor the Church of Calvin. On the contrary, all these Churches are menaced, and menaced alike. It is the new fanatical Religion, now in the heat of its first ferment, of the Rights of Man, which rejects all Establishments, all discipline, all Ecclesiastical, and in truth all Civil order, which will triumph, and which will lay prostrate your Church ... If the present establishment should fall, it is this religion which will triumph in Ireland and in England, as it has triumphed in France. This religion, which laughs at creeds and dogmas, and confessions of faith, may be fomented equally amongst all descriptions and all sects; amongst nominal Catholics, and amongst nominal churchmen; and amongst those dissenters, who know little and care less about a presbytery, or any of its discipline, or any of its doctrine.[94]

If, as Newman thought, the liberalism threatening the Anglican and the Catholic Church alike from the 1820s on had antecedents in the Jacobinism of the French Revolution, this letter of Burke's would have nicely corroborated his apprehensions. Yet it was not only past critics of the Revolution who shared Newman's reading of its malign influence. In 1856, more than twenty years after Newman had written his Advent sermons, calling attention to how the Jacobins had sought to deify their revolutionary State, the great historian of the French Revolution, Alexis de Tocqueville, would also echo Newman's concerns:

> Because the Revolution seemed to be striving for the regeneration of the human race even more than for the reform of France, it lit a passion which the most violent political revolutions had never before been able to produce. It inspired conversions and generated propaganda. Thus, in the end, it took on the appearance of a religious revolution that so astonished its contemporaries. Or, rather,

---

93 Burke, quoted by Groom, "Introduction," xxix. Jonathan Clark, *English Society, 1688–1832: Ideology, Social Structure and Political Practice during the Ancien Regime* (Cambridge: Cambridge University Press, 1991), 252.

94 Groom quotes a briefer portion of this letter, xxix. Edmund Burke to Richard Burke, Esq. (n.d.), in *The Works and Correspondence of the Right Honourable Edmund Burke*, 8 vols. (London: Francis and John Rivington, 1852), VI, 59.

it itself became a new kind of religion, an incomplete religion, it is true, without God, without ritual, and without life after death, but one which nevertheless, like Islam, flooded the earth with its soldiers, apostles and martyrs.[95]

Five years after writing his Advent sermons, in February of 1840, Newman wrote his sister Jemima—a close confidant at the time—of what he saw as a coming showdown between Christianity and the sort of unbelief being sown by such liberals as Henry Hart Milman and Thomas Arnold:

> I begin to have serious apprehensions lest any religious body is strong enough to withstand the league of evil but the Roman Church. At the end of the first Millenary it withstood the fury of Satan—and now the end of a second is drawing on. It has [[possesses]] *tried* strength; what it *has* endured during these last centuries! and it is stronger than ever. We on the other hand have never been tried and come out of trial without practical concessions. I cannot see that we *can* receive [[sustain]] the assault of the foe. We are divided among ourselves, like the Jews in their siege. So that it seems to me as if there were coming on a great encounter between infidelity and Rome, and that we should be smashed between them.[96]

III

What makes Turner's claims about Newman's portrayals of nineteenth-century liberalism so surprising, coming as they do from someone who claimed to have some scholarly understanding of nineteenth-century intellectual history, is that they would have been rejected by Newman's contemporaries, most of whom recognized the accuracy of his portrayals, even if they did not always put the same prophetic construction on them as he did.

One of these was Benjamin Disraeli (1804–81), the Tory prime minister, about whom his biographers Monypenny and Buckle wrote: "Faith in the genius of Toryism; a conviction of the possibility of restoring it to vigour by a recurrence to its historic traditions, and a reconstruction of the party on a popular basis; a desire to maintain and strengthen the influence of the upper orders, combined with a readiness to trust the masses of the people and a genuine interest in their well-being; above all, dislike of the Whigs, and of the middle-class Liberalism in which Whiggery was merging—these things Disraeli and his younger friends had in common ... When Disraeli was a youth, romanticism had been flowing in

---

95 Alexis de Tocqueville, *The Old Regime and the French Revolution*, ed. François Furet and Françoise Mélonio (Chicago: University of Chicago), I, 101.
96 Newman to Mrs. John Mozley (25 February 1840), in *LD*, VII, 245.

the revolutionary channel prepared for it by Byron; it was now flowing strongly in the channel of reaction. That memorable revolt against the domination of liberalism in politics and religion, which had issued from Oxford early in the thirties, and taken thence its name, had soon won a footing in the sister University." There, Disraeli and his friends "prayed and fasted and swore by Laud and Strafford." Moreover, reading the Tractarians "gave a seventeenth-century colour to their political ideals." In addition to discovering Pitt and Canning and making them their "model Tory statesmen," they drew "inspiration from the age and writings of Bolingbroke" and "went behind the glorious Revolution sacred to the Whigs, and sought the fountain-head of Toryism in the reign of Charles I." Indeed, "in the matter of the Church, the Oxford movement completed their emancipation from the thraldom of Erastian ideas; in the matter of the Crown it transmuted their sentimental Jacobitism into a reasoned political theory and a serious political purpose; and working through them it produced parallel effects in the mind of Disraeli."[97] The Tory dandy's contempt for liberalism arose, in part, from his profound identification with his ancestral Judaism, even though his definitive biographer Lord Blake was convinced that he was "surprisingly ignorant of Jewish observances, and seems to have had only very vague notions about the content of Judaism."[98] Still, he went to his grave convinced that "The Jews represent the Semitic principle, all that is spiritual in our nature ... They are a living and most striking evidence of the falsity of that pernicious doctrine of modern times—the natural equality of man ... The native tendency of the Jewish race ... is against the doctrine of the equality of man ... All the tendencies of the Jewish race are conservative. Their bias is to religion, property, and natural aristocracy."[99] Newman might have deplored what became Gladstone's radical liberalism, telling Lord Blachford in 1877 that the Liberal Party that their mutual friend led was "as openly unbelieving and as consciously uniting politics and infidelity as Gambetta's," but he could never have made the same complaint about Gladstone's fiercest rival.[100] Disraeli knew exactly what Newman meant by liberalism and shared his deep distaste for it.

Another good example of a contemporary who understood what Newman meant by liberalism was the historian James Anthony Froude (1818–

---

97 William Flavelle Monypenny and George Earle Buckle, *Life of Benjamin Disraeli, Earl of Beaconfield* (London: Macmillan Company, 1910–20), II, 170.
98 Robert Blake, *Disraeli* (London: Eyre & Spottiswoode, 1966), 503.
99 Benjamin Disraeli, *Lord George Bentinck* (London: Routledge, 1858), 356. John Vincent quotes this in his excellent little study of Disraeli. John Vincent, *Disraeli* (Oxford: Oxford University Press, 1990), 43.
100 Newman to Lord Blachford (25 May 1877), in *LD*, XVIII, 199.

94), the brother of Hurrell Froude, Newman's best friend in his Tractarian days.[101] Froude points out:

> When the Oxford theologians began, in 1832, their attempt to unprotestantise the Church of England, they were roused to activity chiefly by the Latitudinarianism of the then popular Whig philosophy. The Whigs believed that Catholics had changed their nature and had grown liberal, and had insisted on emancipating them. The Tractarians looked on emancipation as the fruit of a spirit which was destroying Christianity, and would terminate at last in atheism. They imagined by reasserting the authority of the Anglican Church, they could at once stem the encroachments of Popery and arrest the progress of infidelity.[102]

Froude goes on to argue that both the Whigs and the Tractarians deluded themselves. The Whigs would never make proper Whigs of emancipated Irish Catholics and the Tractarians would never stop Rome-leaning Anglicans from defecting to the Church of Rome. Yet no one reading this could ever creditably argue that Froude did not understand why Newman and the Tractarians opposed the Latitudinarianism of the liberals.

Yet another contemporary who corroborated Newman's understanding of liberalism was George William Erskine Russell (1853–1919), the Liberal politician and Evangelical author, who, curiously enough, attended University College, Oxford but only graduated with a pass degree. As an Evangelical, he was influenced in his youth by the Christian socialists, F. D. Maurice and Charles Kingsley, though in taking part in purity missions he pointedly parted ways from the libidinous Kingsley. In addition to being one of the founders of the Liberal Club, Russell was a prolific author, writing biographies of Gladstone, Sydney Smith, Edward Pusey, and Pusey's biographer Henry Parry Liddon. He also edited the letters of Matthew Arnold and gathered his weekly *Manchester Guardian* pieces into a lively book of essays entitled *Collections and Recollections* (1898), which provides an entertaining overview of the religious, political and literary landscape of the late nineteenth century.

---

101 In a letter to Hurrell Froude (1803–36), Newman addressed his dear friend as Ἀδελφὲ φιλοκαθολικώτατε — "Most Catholic-Hearted Brother." Newman to Hurrell Froude (9 August 1836), in *LD*, V, 118. The aptness of Newman's epithet is clear from something Froude once wrote regarding the architects of the English Reformation: "I never mean if I can help it to use any phrases even, which can connect me with such a set. I shall never call the Holy Eucharist 'the Lord's supper,' nor God's priests 'Ministers of the Word,' nor the Altar 'the Lord's Table,' etc. etc." Froude to Newman (January 1835), in *LD*, V, 18.

102 James Antony Froude, "The Revival of Romanism," in *Short Studies of Great Subjects*, 3rd series (New York: Charles Scribner's Sons, 1888), 95.

In his life of Pusey, Russell clearly shows that, although a liberal himself, and an Evangelical liberal, he had no hesitation in conceding the reality of the liberalism that Newman deplored throughout his life. If Turner found Newman's idea of liberalism unacceptable, he would have found Russell's idea equally so—or, perhaps, even more so, considering Russell's deep Evangelical sympathies. Here, very much like Newman, Russell does not hesitate to acknowledge that liberalism in religion spanned the entire nineteenth century, from Richard Whately to John Colenso, without ever losing its defining opposition to the traditional faith of Christians so important to Newman and Keble.

> The "Liberal" school in theology (so termed by a curious misnomer, for nothing on earth can be less Liberal than the attitude of Latitudinarians towards Catholicity), had of late years made great advances. [Russell is speaking of the mid to late nineteenth century.] Richard Whately was already an Archbishop. His favorite henchman, Samuel Hinds, had now been made a bishop; so had Hampden, who lay under the censure of the University for supposed heresy; and so had Lee, a Greek scholar free from all theological prepossessions. Thus encouraged, the smaller fry took heart of grace. Benjamin Jowett, Fellow of Balliol and Professor of Greek, denied the Atonement, the inspiration of the Bible, and the Personality of the Holy Spirit. Arthur Stanley denied nothing, but mystified everything, by the joint working of a most inaccurate mind and a most fascinating style. Bishop Colenso, who was neither accurate nor fascinating, found the Pentateuch full of arithmetical blunders. F. D. Maurice (who had the hardihood to charge Pusey with "ambiguity"), explained away the Eternity of Punishment. The writers of *Essays and Reviews*, a rough hash of heresies and platitudes, disturbed the faith of some, and were upheld by the Judicial Committee of the Privy Council, which, by the mouth of its presiding officer, spoke of "the inferior Persons of the Trinity."[103]

Whately, Hinds, Hampden, Lee, Jowett, Stanley, Colenso, and Maurice may all be accurately accounted liberals in religion. Another Evangelical who corroborated Newman's understanding of liberalism in religion was Ronald Knox's father, Edmund Arbuthnott Knox (1847–1937), the fourth Bishop of Manchester. Apropos Newman's defection from the Anglican ministry, Knox observed: "He was handing over, as he well knew, Oxford education to Liberalism from which he had laboured to defend it. He was breaking the hearts of his most intimate friends."[104]

---

103 George William Erskine Russell, *Dr. Pusey* (London: A. R. Mowbray & Co., 1907), 103–4.

104 E. A. Knox, *The Tractarian Movement 1833–1845* (London: Putnam, 1933), 331.

Newman and the Liberals

There were others, as we have seen, like Leslie Stephen, whose liberalism was more of a positivist cast, though there has always been a close affinity between liberalism and positivism. Certainly, there was nothing in Newman's definitions of liberalism—which are at once precise and comprehensive—that did not take this peculiar type of liberalism into consideration. Apropos this "irreligious" liberalism, Mark Francis is incisive.

> Like [G. H. Lewes], Stephen grasped the idea that it was evolutionists who had made positivism into a workable doctrine. Instead of parroting Comte, they had brought positivism into a more thoroughly scientific condition than it had been when under his control. When Stephen referred to himself as a Darwinist, as he frequently did when dramatically enunciating views on agnosticism, he was not offering allegiance to a particular evolutionary theory; he was signaling to his secular readers that he wanted to confound Christians. For him, as for many Victorians, the proclamation of faith in Darwinism was a sign that he had thrown off the shackles of orthodox religion.[105]

Turner and his acolytes claim that Newman's understanding of liberalism is unreliable because he does not offer a different definition for liberals and liberalism for each of the decades of the nineteenth century in which liberals worked, as though from decade to decade they fundamentally changed their thinking. As Turner asserts, "throughout the *Apologia*, Newman had great difficulty establishing a substantial link other than the term itself between what he designated as liberalism in the 1830s and 1840s and that of the 1860s."[106] To try to substantiate this, Turner quotes another assertion, this time from Owen Chadwick: "The fact is, what Newman denounced as liberalism, no one else regarded as liberalism."[107] This would have been news to Pusey, Keble, Hurrell Froude, James Mozley, Cardinal Manning, Bishop Ullathorne, Dean Church, Henry Parry Liddon and many other Anglicans and Catholics, who not only knew what Newman meant by liberalism but shared his

---

105 Mark Francis, "The Evolutionary Turn in Positivism," in *The Oxford Handbook of British Philosophy in the Nineteenth Century*, ed. W. J. Mander (Oxford: Oxford University Press, 2014), 302.

106 *Apologia pro Vita Sua and Six Sermons*, ed. Turner, 56–7.

107 Turner omitted to cite Chadwick's full point. In fact, he wrote: "what Newman regarded as liberalism, no one else regarded as liberalism. And this led to misunderstandings. Men supposed that Newman was illiberal because he kept saying so, and because he refused to recant when he was pressed. People supposed the young bigot of 1834 must be the essential Newman. But no one who reads his later work, or ponders his private letters, can possibly think this to be true." Owen Chadwick, *Newman* (Oxford: Oxford University Press, 1983), 74.

apprehensions about it. Yet having made this unsubstantiated charge with respect to Newman's contemporaries, Turner turns to Newman's commentators and insists that "none of his well-informed commentators has been able to assign the concept substantial content or meaning because they have left it alienated from the historical and religious contexts."[108] This is another false assertion. If we revisit Newman's "well-informed commentators," whether Richard Holt Hutton, Wilfrid Ward, Henry Tristram, Charles Stephen Dessain, Meriol Trevor or Ian Ker, we can see that all of them put Newman's fight against liberalism in historical and religious context. Indeed, they give it center stage. For Father Tristram, the "supreme mission" of Newman's life was "to stem, as far as it lay in his power, the tide of unbelief and to dissipate what seemed to him to be the 'terrible deceit of these latter days.'" Accordingly, in his own excellent anthology of Newman's work, published in 1948, he focused on Newman's "protracted struggle against the 'doctrine that there is no positive truth in religion,' or 'liberalism,' as [Newman] called it, which from tentative beginnings in his earlier years continued to gather strength during the course of his life, and has become the great menace of to-day."[109] To substantiate his point, Father Tristram quotes the philosopher Alfred North Whitehead (1861–1947), who had no axes to grind in these matters.

> The witness of history and of common sense tells us that systematic formulations are potent engines of emphasis, of purification, and of stability. Christianity would long ago have sunk into a noxious superstition, apart from the Levantine and European intellectual movement, sustained from the very beginning until now. This movement is the effort of Reason to provide an accurate system of theology ... Thus the attack of the liberal clergy and laymen, during the eighteenth and nineteenth centuries, upon systematic theology was entirely misconceived. They were throwing away the chief safeguard against the wild emotions of superstition.[110]

Here, in approving "the effort of Reason to provide an accurate system of theology," Whitehead might be describing the work of the early Church Fathers, which meant so much to Newman's religious development and, indeed, paved the way for his conversion. Here, too, Whitehead shows one reason why Newman always extolled the dogmatic principle inherent in Roman Catholicism over against the latitudinarianism inherent in Protestantism.

---

108 *Apologia pro Vita Sua and Six Sermons*, ed. Turner, 57.
109 *The Living Thoughts of Cardinal Newman*, ed. Henry Tristram (London: Cassell & Co., Limited, 1948), xii.
110 Alfred North Whitehead, *Adventures of Ideas* (New York: Simon and Schuster, 1933), 161–2.

Turner's assertion that Newman was somehow confused about his understanding of liberalism because he did not supply a different definition for liberals in the 1830s, 1840s and 1860s can also be refuted by consulting Newman's vast correspondence: if one looks at Newman's letters, spanning as they do over 32 volumes, one can see how his understanding of liberals and liberalism did evolve over the different decades of the nineteenth century, from the 1820s to the 1880s, in response to different aspects of liberalism, without his ever losing sight of its core, abiding features. The charge made by Turner—that Newman only retrospectively claimed to be opposed to liberalism in order to endear himself to Ultamontanes in Rome—could only be made by someone either ignorant of or heedless of Newman's correspondence, let alone his other voluminous writings, where his opposition to liberalism is at once long-standing and consistent. Indeed, for anyone familiar with Newman's correspondence, which exhibits the evolution of his religious convictions with documentary fidelity, Turner's claim can have no validity whatever.

Whenever we revisit Newman's long opposition to liberalism, we have to keep Turner's claim in mind, because when Newman was still an Anglican minister he had occasions to attack the liberalism he saw not only in the Anglican Church but in the Catholic Church as well—hardly something that corroborates Turner's theory that Newman only claimed to be opposed to liberalism to win favor with the Catholic Church in Rome when he was given his red hat. In 1840, Newman deplored what he thought the readiness of the Catholic Church to ally herself with the worst agents of liberalism and infidelity:

> "By their fruits ye shall know them." When we go into foreign countries, we see superstitions in the Roman Church which shock us; when we read history, we find its spirit of intrigue so rife, so general, that "'jesuitism'" has become a bye-word; when we look us round at home, we see it associated everywhere with the low democracy, pandering to the spirit of rebellion, the lust of change, the unthankfulness of the irreligious, and the enviousness of the needy. We see its grave theologians connecting their names with men who are convicted by the common sense of mankind of something very like perjury, and its leaders in alliance with a political party notorious in the *orbis terrarum* as a sort of standard in every place for liberalism and infidelity. We see it attempting to gain converts among us, by unreal representations of its doctrines, plausible statements, bold assertions, appeals to the weaknesses of human nature, to our fancies, our eccentricities, our fears, our frivolities, our false philosophies. We see its agents smiling and nodding and ducking to attract attention, as gipsies make up to truant boys, holding out tales for the nursery, and pretty pictures, and gold gingerbread, and physic concealed in jam, and sugarplums for good children.

Who can but feel shame when the religion of Ximenes, Borromeo, and Pascal is so overlaid? Who can but feel sorrow when its devout and earnest defenders so mistake its genius and our capabilities? We Englishmen like manliness, openness, consistency, truth. Rome will never gain on us till she learns these virtues.[111]

Then, again, in 1835, Newman responded to a letter from Sir James Stephen (1789–1859), the colonial undersecretary and abolitionist who was also the father of James Fitzjames and Leslie Stephen, in which Sir James had suggested that the Vicar of St. Mary's was unfairly opposed to Evangelicalism in his sermons. Newman responded by pointing out that he was not hostile to Evangelicalism *per se*: he was simply concerned that some strains of Evangelicalism led to "liberalism and Socinianism":

I am very much obliged by your note received this morning—or rather ... I do really feel myself to be quite unworthy of it, as being far too kind. The only thought I had ... after reading your remarks to S. Wilberforce, was, how disheartening it was to find the time and space it took in writing to explain one's meaning. I felt that my Sermons only gave one side of my opinions, and I said in consequence to him something of this kind; "if Mr. Stephen knew more of me or of my doctrine, he would not think that I despised the so-called Evangelicals." Indeed I have every reason the other way. When I was a youth of 19 and 20, I held their opinions myself, as far as I had any. I have friends among them, and revere some of them. Nothing I believe in my Sermons is against them except so far forth as they hold certain opinions, which they hold more or less, some in name, others consistently. Against the *spirit* of their school certainly I have spoken strongly; and, while I believe (as I do now, whether rightly or wrongly,) that that spirit tends to liberalism and Socinianism, I ever must. This is the reason for my strong language, my fear of a system of doctrine which eats out the heart of godliness, where truer and holier instincts do not exclude it from producing its legitimate results. If this be so, it is no question of taste, whether to suffer or denounce it, but a matter of duty to hinder (if it be possible) excellent men from what may prove a snare to them, and what on the long run certainly (as it seems to me, and as history seems to show,) tends to one form or other of infidelity.[112]

Over four decades later, in the speech he gave after receiving his red hat—his famous *Biglietto* speech—he echoed the same sentiments that he had shared with Stephen: "For thirty, forty, fifty years I have resisted to

---

111 John Henry Newman, "Catholicity of the English Church," *British Critic*, 27 (January 1840), 86–8, in *LD*, VII, 197–8.
112 Newman to James Stephen (27 February 1835), in *LD*, V, 31–2.

the best of my powers the spirit of liberalism in religion. Never did Holy Church need champions against it more sorely than now, when, alas! it is an error overspreading, as a snare, the whole earth; and on this great occasion, when it is natural for one who is in my place to look out upon the world, and upon Holy Church as in it, and upon her future, it will not, I hope, be considered out of place, if I renew the protest against it which I have made so often." If Newman had declared instead, as Turner contends his true, concealed sentiments obliged him to declare, that for thirty, forty, fifty years, he had resisted to the best of his powers Evangelicalism, his auditors would have rightly thought him gaga. Nevertheless, Turner insisted that "Liberalism in religion was Evangelicalism."[113]

Stephen responded to Newman with a letter that might have kept his sons James Fitzjames and Leslie from the rationalist blind alleys in which they frittered away so many of their considerable talents. "How much is said by our Saviour, and how much by St. Paul," the occasionally lucid old lawyer declared, "in depreciation of human Wisdom ... To the Poor the Gospel is preached—to the intellectually poor—to those who have become as little children."[114]

Dean Church shows how even those most opposed to Newman's religious development, whether as a Tractarian or as a Roman Catholic, were not necessarily at variance with his opposition to liberalism. Edward Hawkins (1789–1882), the Provost of Oriel while Newman was a Fellow of Oriel, is a good example. Church observed in 1874 in a piece on Hawkins in the *Guardian* (which was then an Anglican paper):

> [T]he times in which we live and what they bring with them mould most of us and the times shaped the course of the Provost of Oriel, and turned his activity into a channel of obstinate and prolonged antagonism, of resistance and protest, most conscientious but most uncompromising, against two great successive movements, both of which he condemned as unbalanced and, recoiled from as revolutionary—the Tractarian first, and then the Liberal movement in Oxford.

If Hawkins opposed the Oxford Movement because, as Church related, "he detested ... its dogmatic assertions; he resented its taking out of his hands a province of theology which he and Whately had made their own ... he thought its tone of feeling and its imaginative and poetical side exaggerated or childish; and he could not conceive of its position except as involving palpable dishonesty," he was equally contemptuous of what Church referred to as "the great Liberal tide," which succeeded the defeat

---

113 *Apologia pro Vita Sua and Six Sermons*, ed. Turner, 63.
114 James Stephen to Newman (16 March 1835), in *LD*, V, 43.

of Tractarianism at Oxford, with "its demands for extensive and immediate change, its anti-ecclesiastical spirit, its scarcely disguised scepticism, its daring philosophical and critical enterprises."[115]

Hawkins's opposition to the rise of liberalism in Oxford would be echoed by Henry Parry Liddon (1829–90), Pusey's biographer, who may have thoroughly opposed Newman's Romanism but never underestimated the convert's abilities, not to mention his sanctity—something at which Turner and his school tend to scoff.[116] In thanking Newman for a copy of his *Historical Sketches*, Liddon wrote, "I wish it were possible to avoid making some painful contrasts between the Oxford which is in your mind and the Oxford of today … like many other younger men who did not know you at Oxford, I owe you a very great moral and intellectual debt." Their differences with regard to dogma notwithstanding, they both saw eye to eye on the fundamental threat posed by liberalism to Christianity. "The Tractarian Movement has generally been described as an attempt to effect a High Church revival, by reasserting those portions of the Church's teaching which the popular Evangelicalism was in danger of overlooking," Liddon remarked in his life of Pusey. "This indeed was its immediate and most obvious result; but the Tractarians were not ultimately concerned with the deficiencies of Evangelicalism. They were chiefly thinking of the assaults of 'Liberalism' upon the institution and faith of the Church. They were convinced that the only adequate protection against such assaults was to be found in strengthening a position which Evangelicalism had not thought it worthwhile to occupy." Here, again, the acolytes of Turner will need to add another of Newman's contemporaries to their list of muddled schismatics, for, together with Newman, Russell, Hawkins and Church, Liddon clearly did not share their understanding of the roles played by liberals and Evangelicals in nineteenth-century England. On the contrary, Liddon saw them in the same light in which Newman saw them.

> Cardinal Newman has told us that these fears filled his mind during his foreign tour in 1832 and 1833: "I had," he wrote, "fierce thoughts against the Liberals." The letters of that date from Keble, Newman, Froude, Rose, Perceval and all who took part in the 'Association of Friends of the Church' show that they were keenly alive to the

---

115 Richard William Church, "The Retirement of the Provost of Oriel" (1874), in *Occasional Papers Selected from the Guardian, the Times, and the Saturday Review 1846–1890* (London: Macmillan & Co.), II, 346–7.

116 "The temptation to dismiss the assessment of Pope Benedict XVI in relation to the beatification of Newman as a partisan advocate of conservative Catholicism will be strong among those who do not believe the claims about divine revelation so carefully worked out by Newman." William J. Abraham, "Reception of Newman on Revelations," in *Receptions of Newman*, ed. Aquino and King, 212.

reality of this danger. But the ordinary Englishman was far from being aware of the principles and tendency of the Liberal school of theology. He heard proposals in Parliament and elsewhere for abolishing Irish bishoprics, and for strange changes in English Cathedrals; but he knew nothing of the theological and ecclesiastical presuppositions which underlay these changes. Newman alluded to this connexion between "Liberal" theology and some of the Parliamentary measures of 1832 in a retrospective passage of the Advertisement to the third volume of the Tracts. "Irreligious principles and false doctrines which had hitherto been avowed only in the closet, or on paper, had just been admitted into public measures on a large scale." Already in 1835, the practical questions had fallen into the background, but the question of theological principle was becoming more apparent. The subject is discussed by Newman at the close of that year in a lengthy Tract (No. 73) "On the Introduction of Rationalistic Principles into Religion"; at the end of this Tract he calls attention to the "subjectivity" of Evangelicalism, which he considered its great weakness, and which, to his mind, rendered it useless as a defence of Church doctrine.[117]

Considering this acknowledgment of the serious limitations of Evangelicalism, it is surprising that Turner never turned his considerable powers of vituperation against Liddon. Certainly, everything that Turner found reprehensible about Newman's opposition to the rationalism of the liberals was taken up and championed by the anti-rationalist Anglican churchman. Apropos the concluding paragraph of *Tract 73*, for example, Liddon observes:

> While exposing Rationalism, [Newman] was looking round for traces of its spirit nearer home. He says that the Evangelical appeal to the heart alone shared the fatal defect of one-sidedness that belonged also to that exclusive appeal to reason against which the early Evangelicals had nobly revolted. "I will conclude by summing up in one sentence, which must be pardoned me if in appearance harsh, what the foregoing discussion is intended to show. There is a widely spread though variously admitted school of doctrine among us, within and without the Church, which intends and professes peculiar piety, as directing its attention to the heart itself, not to anything external to us, whether creed, actions, or ritual. I do not hesitate to assert that this doctrine is based upon error, that it is really a specious form of trusting man rather than God, that it is in its nature Rationalistic, and that it tends to Socinianism. How the individual supporters of it will act as time goes on is another

---

[117] Henry Parry Liddon, *Life of Edward Bouverie Pusey* (London: Longman, Green & Co., 1897), IV, 2.

matter,—the good will be separated from the bad, but the school, as such, will pass through Sabellianism to that "God-denying Apostasy," to use the ancient phrase, to which in the beginning of its career it professed to be especially opposed." The following year witnessed the first skirmish of the coming struggle in the agitation which sprang up against the appointment of Hampden as Regius Professor of Divinity.[118]

Liddon's conclusion would only have exasperated Turner more:

> The influence of Newman, and in his own way of Pusey also, during the twelve years between 1833 and 1845 did not a little to check this spirit of Rationalism, and to prepare the Church to resist it if it should grow stronger. Many of the ablest and most highly cultured minds found refuge from this tendency in the fuller restatement of the whole Catholic creed which the Tractarians set before them; and it was a common saying when the Heads of Houses were taking their measures against Newman, "You may crush Tractarianism, but then you will have to deal with Germanism." This was very soon found to be true. After the Academical overthrow of the Tractarians as a party in 1845, and the consequent suspicion and discredit which fell on them, a new and more vigorous school of Liberal Theologians began to gain a wider influence in Oxford.[119]

Moreover, Liddon makes a rather incisive point when he argues that "Tractarianism was sufficiently definite to have been crushed by direct attack; but it was difficult to find any weapons to wield against this new foe." Why? "'Germanism' in fact in those days was by its own nature peculiarly able to evade assault. Its weapons were questionings, hints, doubts, suspicions, undigested and exaggerated criticism and distorted historical analogies."[120]

IV

"Germanism," as Liddon nicely put it, would take triumphant possession of the field in Oxford once Newman effaced himself. He confirmed this in the *Apologia*, confessing how he had terrible inklings of what effect his conversion would have.

> The most oppressive thought, in the whole process of my change of opinion, was the clear anticipation, verified by the event, that it would issue in the triumph of Liberalism. Against the Anti-dogmatic principle I had thrown my whole mind; yet now I was doing more than any one else could do, to promote it. I was one of those who

118 *Ibid.*, 2–3.
119 *Ibid.*, 4.
120 *Ibid.*, 5.

had kept it at bay in Oxford for so many years; and thus my very retirement was its triumph. The men who had driven me from Oxford were distinctly the Liberals; it was they who had opened the attack upon Tract 90, and it was they who would gain a second benefit, if I went on to abandon the Anglican Church.[121]

In light of this admission, it is baffling how Turner and his friends can continue to charge that the *Apologia* is little more than an exercise in mendacious self-vindication. Here, Newman was admitting to having willy-nilly advanced the very thing that he had spent most of his life before and after his conversion working to combat. And yet where many might see self-deprecatory honesty, the Turner camp persists in seeing calculated imposture. Nockles, citing the work of the wobbly Anglican Frank L. Cross, contends that "We have in Cross's analysis a hint of what Frank Turner was later to argue—that the opposition to Tract 90 brought out a latent spirit of *ressentiment* in Newman, with theological considerations playing only a part in his conversion and that personal psychological weaknesses had a key role."[122] Readers unfamiliar with the term, *ressentiment* will doubtless be startled to learn that it means, "a psychological state arising from suppressed feelings of envy and hatred that cannot be acted upon, frequently resulting in some form of self-abasement." (Could it be that Nockles, when not penning his footling attacks on Newman, moonlights as an amateur psychologist?) Then, again, Cyril O'Regan actually commends Turner for "taking up Kingsley's cause and supplying the answer that Kingsley did not or was unable to supply to Newman's magisterial self-exoneration tendered in the *Apologia*."[123] Yet if Newman was somehow throwing dust in his readers' eyes when he admitted that his conversion had opened the door to the "triumph of Liberalism," what could have motivated Dean Church to mount the same interpretation of events twenty-seven years after the publication of the *Apologia*?

---

121 *Apologia*, 184.

122 Peter Nockles, "Newman's Tractarian Receptions," in *Receptions of Newman*, ed. Aquino and King, 152.

123 Cyril O'Regan, "Reception of Newman the Saint," in *Receptions of Newman*, ed. Aquino and King, 220. Obviously, neither Nockles nor O'Regan credits what the reliable eye-witness Frederick Oakeley had to say of what lay behind his own and Newman's conversions: "Instead of a disposition to appreciate the sacrifices which many converts have made, at any rate in the cause of conscience if they will not admit it to be the cause of truth, we have often met with an inclination to attribute to some unworthy motive—such as personal pique, intellectual conceit, love of religious externals, and the like—an act which has, at any rate, stood the test of time, and ought, as that time has proceeded, to have cleared itself, in the judgment of equity, from the suspicion of shallowness and inconsiderateness." Frederick Oakeley, *Historical Notes on the Tractarian Movement 1833–1845* (London: Longman, Green; Longman, Roberts & Green, 1865), 105.

> The decisive breach between the old parties in the Church, both Orthodox and Evangelical, and the new party of the movement, with the violent and apparently irretrievable discomfiture of the latter as the rising force in Oxford, opened the way and cleared the ground for the formation and the power of a third school of opinion, which was to be the most formidable rival of the Tractarians, and whose leaders were eventually to succeed where the Tractarians had failed, in becoming the masters and the reformers of the University. Liberalism had hitherto been represented in Oxford in forms which though respectable from intellectual vigour were unattractive, sometimes even repulsive. They were dry, cold, supercilious, critical; they wanted enthusiasm; they were out of sympathy with religion and the religious temper and aims. They played, without knowing it, on the edge of the most dangerous questions.[124]

O'Regan takes his cue from Simon Skinner's polemics[125] when he says that Turner had a tougher time of it than Kingsley in trying to unmask the true historical Newman because he had "to contend with over a century of hagiographical treatment of Newman's life in which his religious opinions are always sound, his motives pure, his treatment of those with whom he disagrees above reproach, and his religious life exemplary and edifying in every way."[126] It is true that Newman's best biographers see their subject through a lens that might be called "hagiographical" in the true sense of that word. After all, Richard Holt Hutton, Wilfrid Ward, Meriol Trevor, Stephen Dessain and Ian Ker all had the sense to see that their subject's sanctity was central to his character. How could it not be for the man who saw the creature's relationship to the Creator in such stark terms as these?

> Earth must fade away from our eyes, and we must anticipate that great and solemn truth, which we shall not fully understand until we stand before God in judgment, that to us there are but two beings in the whole world, God and ourselves. The sympathy of others, the pleasant voice, the glad eye, the smiling countenance, the thrilling heart, which at present are our very life, all will be away from us, when Christ comes in judgment. Every one will have to think of himself. Every eye shall see Him, every heart will be full of Him. He will speak to every one; and every one will be rendering to Him his own account. By self-restraint, by abstinence, by prayer, by meditation, by recollection, by penance, we now anticipate in our measure that dreadful season. By thinking of it beforehand, we hope to mitigate its terrors when it comes. By humbling ourselves now, we hope to escape humiliation then. By owning our faults now,

---

124 Church, *The Oxford Movement, 1833–1845*, 337–8.
125 Skinner, "History versus Hagiography."
126 O'Regan, "Reception of Newman the Saint," 220.

we hope to avert the disclosures of that day. By judging ourselves now, we hope to be spared that judgment which mercy tempers not. We prepare now to meet our God; we retire, as it were, to our sick room, and put our house in order. We "remember our Creator in the days of our youth" and strength, "while the evil days come not, nor the years draw nigh, in which is no pleasure;" ere "the keepers of the house tremble, and the strong men bow themselves, and the doors are shut in the streets, and the daughters of music are brought low, and desire fails: or ever the silver cord be loosed, or the golden bowl be broken, or the pitcher be broken at the fountain, or the wheel broken at the cistern." We leave the goods of earth before they leave us.[127]

For O'Regan to suggest that treating the writer of this passage with sympathy and admiration must result in insipid panegyric exhibits not only his bias but his superficiality. Dean Church, in his various writings on Newman, shows that one can take a thoroughly sympathetic approach to Newman without considering him as "beyond reproach" or treating his different positions on various matters as "always sound." After all, Church was convinced that Pusey had the better of the debate over devotional excesses amongst the Catholic faithful that inspired Newman's *Letter to Pusey* (1866).[128] Similarly, Walter K. Firminger (1870–1940), who was at Merton College before becoming archdeacon of Calcutta and a historian of India (he was the first editor of *Bengal, Past & Present*, the journal of the Calcutta Historical Society) never let his objections to Newman's Catholic convictions get in the way of his acknowledging the integrity of the man who wrote the *Apologia*.

> If we look back on Newman's history, we shall, I think, be convinced of the slight evidence on which most of the criticism [of him and his work] depends, and indeed this is perhaps the most fitting way of dealing with those who sceptically cry, shew us some token for good. At any rate, it is the method the Cardinal chose in dealing with Mr. Kingsley, who, like his Hereward,[129] possessed an untiring

---

127 Newman, "Our Lord's Last Supper and His First," in *Sermons on Subjects of the Day*, 44–5.

128 "If Dr. Newman is able, as we doubt not he is desirous, to elevate the tone of his own communion and put to shame some of its fashionable excesses, he will do a great work, in which we wish him every success, though the result of it might not really be to bring the body of his countrymen nearer to it. But the substance of Dr. Pusey's charges remain after all unanswered, and there is no getting over them while they remain." R. W. Church, "Dr. Newman on the Eirenicon," in R. W. Church, *Occasional Papers* (London: Macmillan, 1897), II, 437.

129 See *Hereward the Wake: Last of the English* (1866), a novel by Charles Kingsley. In his *Companion to British History* (1996), the magnificent Charles Arnold-Baker identifies

energy for hitting furiously at what he believed wrong, and, once more like Hereward, found his match at last. In passing on to our story, we can hardly help paying homage to the sincerity without which the *Apologia* could never have won its cause with the English world as it has done, which alone made possible that wonderfully objective autobiography to be found among the letters in Miss Mozley's volumes.[130] The secret of the completeness of the self-revelation is the love of truth which has never been sinned against. Newman is describing himself not in order that he may win what he always despised and over and over again sacrificed—the admiration of his contemporaries, he is stating what conscience tells him to be the plain history of his religious experience, and he cares little what men may think when God is Judge. "Commit thy way to the Lord and trust in Him, and He will do it. And He will bring forth thy justice as the light, and thy judgment as the noon day."[131]

Unlike O'Regan, who tends to see his opponents as men of straw, Church saw liberals, not simply as adherents of a flawed philosophical or religious system but as real people, with real convictions, however inimical to his own. "The older Oxford Liberals," he writes, "were either intellectually aristocratic, dissecting the inaccuracies or showing up the paralogisms of the current orthodoxy, or they were poor in character, Liberals from the zest of sneering and mocking at what was received and established, or from the convenience of getting rid of strict and troublesome rules of life. They patronized Dissenters; they gave Whig votes; they made free, in a mild way, with the pet conventions and prejudices of Tories and High

---

Hereward as "a partly legendary Saxon landowner, who led an English insurrection at Ely and sacked Peterborough with Danish help in 1070. He was joined by Earl Morcar, Bishop Aethelwine of Durham and other northern dignitaries and held out in the Ely marshes for some time but eventually escaped to the Continent when the others submitted. He is said to have been killed by the Normans in Maine."

130 *Letters and Correspondence of John Henry Newman during his Life in the English Church with a Brief Autobiography*, 2 vols., ed. Anne Mozley (London: Longman, Green & Co., 1890).

131 Walter K. Firminger, *Some Thoughts on the Recent Criticism of the Life and Works of John Henry Cardinal Newman* (London: James Parker & Co., 1892), 19–20. A good example of Newman's ability to discount the world's misjudgments of him can be seen in his response to Thomas Mozley's *Reminiscences* (1882), which contained offensively erroneous references to Newman's father "As to Mr. Mozley's volumes, I was so offended at the inaccuracies which met my eye when I first took it up, that I threw it down. I feel that his inaccuracies cannot be all set right without almost my writing a book, which I cannot do. And what right had he to put in a letter of mine without asking my leave? It is one of those incidents which are intended I believe by a good Providence to deepen one's indifference as to what the world thinks of one." Newman to George T. Edwards (22 February 1884), in *LD*, XXX, 312.

Newman and the Liberals

Churchmen."[132] Certainly, Oriel's Edward Copleston and Richard Whately would have fit a good deal of this bill. Yet Church was also appreciative of "a younger set of men brought, mainly from Rugby and Arnold's teaching," who, together, constituted "a new kind of Liberalism." And here, one can see the intellectual historian in Church at his best, precisely because he is willing to show what the Turner camp rarely show: sympathy for his opponents. Speaking of this "new kind of Liberalism," Church remarks:

> It was much bolder and more independent than the older forms, less inclined to put up with the traditional, more searching and inquisitive in its methods, more suspicious and daring in its criticism; but it was much larger in its views and its sympathies, and, above all, it was imaginative, it was enthusiastic, and, without much of the devotional temper, it was penetrated by a sense of the reality and seriousness of religion. It saw greater hopes in the present and the future than the Tractarians. It disliked their reverence for the past and the received as inconsistent with what seemed evidence of the providential order of great and fruitful change. It could not enter into their discipline of character, and shrank from it as antiquated, unnatural, and narrow. But these younger Liberals were interested in the Tractarian innovators, and, in a degree, sympathized with them as a party of movement who had had the courage to risk and sacrifice much for an unworldly end.[133]

This ambivalent attitude to the Tractarians—and especially the Tractarian in Newman—turned Arthur Hugh Clough (1819–61), Arnold's best pupil, into one of Queen Victoria's greatest poets, though the same ambivalence that helped him to find his poetic voice would also be the source of his abiding spiritual distress. "*ACTION will furnish belief,*—but will that belief be the true one? / This is the point, you know."[134] Arnold's son Matthew was another of this brilliant band, who, for all of his strenuous agnosticism, not only rhapsodized about Newman's sermons at St. Mary's but commended a political speech in one of his letters for setting its young orator apart "from the old stagers, whose stock vulgar Liberalism will not satisfy even the middle class, whose wants it was originally modelled to meet."[135] Newman shared Church's respect for Oxford's younger liberals, even if he shuddered to think of where their liberalism was leading them. "The Liberal party grew all the time I was in Oxford," he wrote in his *Apologia*,

---

132 Church, *The Oxford Movement, 1833–1845*, 338.

133 Ibid., 338–9.

134 Arthur Hugh Clough, "Amours de Voyage" (1849–58), in *The New Oxford Book of Victorian Verse*, ed. Christopher Ricks (Oxford: Oxford University Press, 1987), 257.

135 Matthew Arnold to Mrs. Forster (January 1864), in *The Letters of Matthew Arnold, 1848–1888*, ed. George William Erskine Russell (London: Macmillan & Co., 1895), I, 249.

"even in numbers, certainly in breadth and definiteness and power. And what was a far higher consideration, by the accession of Dr. Arnold's pupils it was invested with an elevation of character which claimed the respect even of its opponents."[136]

Despite this admiration for his pupils, Arnold himself felt nothing but contempt for Newman and those whom he called the "Newmanites." "Not living in Oxford, and seeing only the books of the Newmanites, and considering only their system," Arnold wrote, "any mind that can turn towards them ... with anything less than unmixed aversion, appears to be already diseased; and do what I will I cannot make allowance enough for the peculiar circumstances of Oxford, because I cannot present them to my mind distinctly."[137] As Dean Stanley shows in his biography of Arnold, this inability to understand how Newman's opposition to liberalism could have taken hold in Oxford was the result of shock. After all, for Arnold, Tractarianism was the "unexpected revival of what he conceived to be the worst evils of Roman Catholicism," which was shocking enough; but what was perhaps even more shocking was that all Newman and the Tractarians seemed concerned with in the first volumes of the "Tracts for the Times" (1833–6) was the Apostolical Succession and the concomitant claim of the Church of England to be regarded as the only true Church in England. "In other words," to quote Stanley again, "the one doctrine which was then put forward as the cure for the moral and social evils of the country, which [Arnold] ... felt so keenly, was the one point in their system, which he always regarded as morally powerless and intellectually indefensible."[138]

When Newman and the Tractarians joined a total of over eighty Oxford dons in 1836 to protest Renn Dickson Hampden's appointment by the Whig Melbourne government to the Regius Chair of Divinity, Arnold wrote his famous piece in the *Edinburgh Review*, "The Oxford Malignants and Dr. Hampden" (1836) in which he likened Newman and those whom he referred to as the "Oxford conspirators" to the superannuated High Church:

> Unlike the political Tories, who are only analogously like the Tories of the Revolution, by being as much in the rear of the existing generation as the old Tories were in the rear of theirs, these Church Tories have stirred neither actually nor relatively; they are the very Nonjurors and High Church clergy of King William's, and Anne's, and George the First's reign, reproduced, with scarcely a shade of difference. Now, as then, this party is made up of two elements ... the mere low worldly clergy, careless and grossly ignorant,—

---

136 *Apologia*, 258.

137 Arnold, quoted in Arthur Penryn Stanley, *Life of Thomas Arnold, D.D., Head-Master of Rugby* (London: John Murray, 1904), 380.

138 *Ibid.*, 378.

ministers not of the Gospel but of the aristocracy, who belong to Christianity only from the accident of its being established by law; and of the formalist Judaizing fanatics, on the other hand, who have ever been the peculiar disgrace of the Church of England; for these High Church fanatics have imbibed, even of fanaticism itself, nothing but the folly and the virulence.

Yet in quoting the specific charges brought against Hampden's heterodoxy, Arnold cannot be numbered amongst those suppositious contemporaries who somehow did not understand what Newman meant by liberalism. Here, the charges themselves echo some of Newman's most fundamental objections to liberalism. Hampden "contradicted the doctrinal truths which he was pledged to maintain" and "asserted principles which necessarily tend to subvert, not only the authority of the Church, but the whole fabric and reality of Christian truth." In fine, he was inculcating the "Philosophy of Rationalism."[139]

Of course, Newman agreed, but what he found particularly objectionable about Hampden was his undermining of the dogmatic principle, which was so essential both to the Early Fathers in articulating and safeguarding the *fidei depositum* and to the Church as a whole in understanding and preserving her doctrinal coherence and integrity. In his article on Hampden for the *Oxford Dictionary of National Biography*, Richard Brent observes how Hampden's idea of theological dogma found its fullest expression in his Bampton Lecture, *The Scholastic Philosophy Considered in its Relation to Christian Theology* (1833), where he argued that the Scholastics, as well as the early Church Fathers formulated doctrines that "were no more than deductive statements infused with human imperfection." Indeed, for Hamden, "Doctrinal statements assumed their form by the successive impressions of historical controversy: they were not themselves repositories of Christian truth." Newman's response to Hamden's interpretation of doctrine can almost be said to have given him the foundation for his criticism of liberalism.

> Dr. Hampden's views then seem at length to issue in the following theory: that there is one and one only truth, that that truth is the record of facts, historical and moral, contained in the text of Scripture; that whatever is beyond that text, even to the classifying of its sentences, is human opinion, and unrevealed; that, though a thoughtful person cannot help forming opinions and theories upon the Scripture record, and is bound to act upon and confess those opinions which he considers to be true, yet he has no right to identify his own opinion on any point, however sacred in itself,

---

139 Thomas Arnold, "The Oxford Malignants and Dr. Hampden," *Edinburgh Review* (April 1836).

with the facts of the revealed history, or to assume that a belief in it is necessary for the salvation of another, or to impose it as a condition of union with another; that, though he considers he can not be more sure of being right than another, and does not hold his own opinions to be more pious than another's.[140]

Arnold's counterattack against Newman and the Tractarians would animate the Broad Church for decades to come: "A dress, a ritual, a name, a ceremony; — a technical phraseology; — the superstition of a priesthood, without its power; — the form of Episcopal government, without the substance; a system imperfect and paralyzed, not independent, not sovereign, — afraid to cast off the subjection against which it is perpetually murmuring. Such are the objects of High Church fanaticism; objects so pitiful, that, if gained ever so completely, they would make no man the wiser or the better; they would lead to no good, intellectual, moral, or spiritual; to no effect, social or religious, except to the changing of sense into silliness, and holiness of heart and life into formality and hypocrisy." Yet, as the historian G. M. Young recognized, Arnold was facing a problem that faced most of the Tractarians as well: how to make religion appeal to "the half-barbarized population of the great towns," for whom religion meant next to nothing. "The world, as [Arnold] conceived it, needed new rulers, and the rulers needed a new faith, which was to be found in the historic record, in the Bible, doubtless, most of all, but in the Bible — and here he broke definitely with Oxford and current Protestantism alike — interpreted not by tradition, but by science, scholarship, and, above all, political insight ... He took the self-consciousness of the English gentry, benevolently authoritative, but uneasily aware that its authority was waning and gave it religious and historic justification."[141]

Arnold's criticisms of Newman are important because they reflect the criticisms that many liberals had of what they regarded as his intellectual shortcomings. Lord Acton and Ignaz von Döllinger, from their different perspectives, had similar criticisms of Newman's learning, though Mark Pattison was perhaps his most acerbic critic in this line. After asking whether Newman's "insight into character was keen enough" to see that his former pupil was succumbing to precisely the same rationalism that would soon overtake the entire university, Pattison remarked how there was "a general wonder" how Newman could associate with men like Frederick Bowles, John Dalgairns, Ambrose St. John and William Lockhart. From Pattison's point of view, they were clearly not bright enough to be proper companions for Newman. Of course, Newman himself would have found such comparisons

---

140 John Henry Newman, *Elucidations of Dr. Hampden's Theological Statements* (London: J. H. Parker and Messrs. Rivington, 1836), 53.

141 *Early Victorian England 1830–1865*, ed. G. M. Young, 2nd edn (London: Oxford University Press, 1951), II, 472–3.

invidious, though he would have seen the tragic logic of Pattison's confessing that he had left the Church to seek out better intellectual company.

> I venerated Newman himself as having been so much to me in so many ways; and I had too little knowledge to see how limited his philosophical acquirements were. The force of his dialectic, and the beauty of his rhetorical exposition were such that one's eye and ear were charmed, and one never thought of inquiring on how narrow a basis of philosophical culture his great gifts were expended. A. P. Stanley once said to me, "How different the fortunes of the Church of England might have been if Newman had been able to read German." That puts the matter in a nut-shell; Newman assumed and adorned the narrow basis on which Laud had stood 200 years before. All the grand development of human reason, from Aristotle down to Hegel, was a sealed book to him. There lay a unity, a unity of all thought, which far transcended the mere mechanical association of the unthinking members of the Catholic Church; a great spiritual unity, by the side of which all sects and denominations shrink into vanity.[142]

Whether German philosophy could supply what George Eliot had her character Mr. Casaubon refer to in her novel *Middlemarch* (1872) as the "Key to All the Mythologies" was a question that exercised many liberals besides Pattison.[143] Yet how German philosophy would have saved not only Newman but "the fortunes of the Church of England" was an even livelier question. The historian Boyd Hilton is helpful here.

> Liberal Anglicans were convinced that religion would not be able to foster national unity and heal social divisions unless it faced up to the challenges of German philosophy ... Thanks in part to Coleridge's influence, they took Lessing, Kant, Hegel, Fichte, and Schelling on board, and learned to accept that not everything in Scripture was an immutable and universal truth, or the product of divine inspiration. On the contrary, the Bible had been composed by human beings writing in given historical contexts, and expressed only so much of the truth as God had chosen to reveal in any particular generation. It followed that, if religious doctrine was to continue developing, biblical scholars everywhere must adopt German methods of inquiry, disposing of superstitious and outdated elements.[144]

---

142 Mark Pattison, *Memoirs* (London: Macmillan, 1885), 210–11.
143 See "Mr. Casaubon in *Middlemarch*," in Antony David Nuttall, *Dead from the Waist Down: Scholars and Scholarship in Literature and the Popular Imagination* (New Haven: Yale University Press, 2003), 26–71.
144 Boyd Hilton, *A Mad, Bad, and Dangerous People? England 1783–1846* (Oxford: Clarendon Press, 2006), 465.

That undermining the historical validity of the Bible would unite Victorian Englishmen was perhaps one of the oddest of all liberal contentions. Of course, it simply deprived different Englishmen of what had formerly been their only religion, which was Chillingworth's Bible Christianity.[145] Then, again, as we have already seen, Newman pointedly rejected liberal prescriptions regarding religious doctrine, seeing them as nothing more than invitations to rationalism. He broke from liberals in seeing what they regarded as "superstition" as salutary reminders of truths about the nature of the supernatural that civilized man flouted at his peril. He also disagreed with the liberal enthusiasm for the notion of national religion, as opposed to Christendom, which they took from the German poet and critic Johann Gottfried Herder (1744–1803). Peter Mandler, the cultural historian is good on this aspect of the liberal credo.

> The Liberal Anglicans were a group of liberal clerics clustered around the moral and intellectual leadership of Thomas Arnold, who wished to believe in the reality—and perhaps the inevitability—of progress for the mass of the people ... [They] were willing to take seriously Herder's proposition that a people expressed their true religion in the form of the nation—a compound of race, language, religious and political institutions ... It was the combination of race and morals that made modern history so eventual and the English so great ... And this central moral dimension meant, too, that the Liberal Anglicans also fitted themselves into a civilizational framework, for they shared not only Herder's belief in the salience of the nation but also his universalistic belief that the nation was but a transitional stage—a proving ground in the struggle for moral perfection—that would end in the holy reunion of humanity.[146]

Newman would certainly have agreed with the accuracy of Mandler's account of his liberal opponents. He would also have agreed with Hilton that Trinity College, Cambridge was a kind of seminary for liberal religion, producing not only the eccentric broad churchman, Julius Hare and the impious historian Connop Thirlwall, both of whom took issue with what they saw as the superstitious obscurantism of Newman's Romanism, but Frederick Denison Maurice (1805–72), who, together with Charles King-

---

145 When John Jordan, vicar of Enstone, read Newman's *Letter to Dr. Jelf*, he wrote a rousing pamphlet entitled *The Crisis Come* (1841), in which he exclaimed: "We have need to raise once more the banner of the Reformation, and to take our stand upon the great principle maintained by Chillingworth, the Bible, the whole Bible, and nothing but the Bible." In his book, *The Religion of Protestants* (1637), Chillingworth had made the terse observation that "The Bible and the Bible only is the religion of Protestants."

146 Peter Mandler, *The English National Character: The History of an Idea from Edmund Burke to Tony Blair* (New Haven: Yale University Press, 2006), 42–3.

sley and Thomas Hughes, founded the Christian socialist movement. "I am annoyed but not surprised about Maurice," Newman wrote to Walter Farquhar Hook in 1835.

> He is a Coleridgian and a Platonist, I believe—and so though not far from a Catholic, when contrasted with Rationalists, yet some way off too. He is of the Cambridge School—and from the little I have seen of those men, they seem to me never satisfied to take things as they find them, but to be always meddling and (as they think) improving truths which have been from the beginning—and to believe sacred doctrines, not because they have received them, but because they can prove them from philosophy. M. himself is an excellent and very deserving, as well as clever man, but I wish all those men would have something more of childlike faith.[147]

Newman would also have agreed with Hilton in seeing Trinity's counterpart in Oxford as Oriel College, which produced the Noetics Hampden, Henry Milman and Thomas Arnold, all of whom would become whipping boys for Newman's more spirited polemics against what he saw as the tendency of liberalism to give way to infidelity—indeed, in many circumstances, to be in deliberate league with infidelity.

When it comes to this tendency, no one was wittier than Lord Salisbury (1830–1903), the conservative prime minister, who, in his youth, admired the Tractarian Newman.[148] In response to John Morley's claim that "The State Church stands for *a decaying order of ideas*, and for ideas that grow narrower and more intense in proportion as they fall more out of harmony with the intellectual life of the time," and that enlightened statesmen should not, therefore, entrust the teaching of schoolchildren to "a fresh and holy army of misologists,"[149] Salisbury observed:

> [The] union of the Dissenters and the Infidels is one among the many unnatural alliances which are so potent an instrument for destruction in our day. It is easy to combine on a mere negative. Numbers who have no liking in common can agree upon what they hate: and they seem to think that such a bond of union is sufficient to justify political combination. In such monstrous partnerships there is always an element of treachery. There is always on each side a full intention that at the close of the operation the other side of the alliance shall not keep the chestnuts. The fruits of victory cannot

---

147 Newman to Walter Farquhar Hook (21 December 1835), in *LD*, V, 180.
148 See Andrew Roberts, *Salisbury: Victorian Titan* (London: Weidenfeld & Nicolson, 1999), 12, 13.
149 The quotation is from Morley's "The Struggle for National Education" (Part II), *Fortnightly Review*, new series, 14 (1873), 311. Misology means "hatred of reason or discussion; hatred of free argumentative discussion."

be divided between parties who are diametrically opposed: they must be appropriated wholly for the benefit of one ally or the other. The only interesting question is, Which will succeed in deceiving his friend? The honest Dissenter does not wish for the success of the Infidel: the Infidel assuredly has no intention of promoting the religious doctrines of the Dissenter. But they combine to assail the Church, which for different reasons is in their way; and each party flatters itself that the other has miscalculated, and the reward of their combined efforts will fall to it. No student of history can have any doubt which of these two calculations will prove correct. In a combined movement against established institutions it is not the Girondins who win.[150]

V

That false liberty begets false education no one can deny who sees the ruin to which liberalism has led our educational system, where an unholy "army of misologists," to borrow Morley's phrase, now rule the roost. And yet in all of his criticisms of liberalism in the educational sphere, Newman is at pains to stress that true liberal education is noble because its end is not utility, or, worse, subservience to the dictates of false liberty, but wisdom. And here, again, we cannot help but be reminded of Chesterton's understanding of the degradation of words being an inalienable concomitant of our aboriginal calamity. In the *Discourses on the Scope and Nature of University Education* (1852), Newman set out what he meant by the wisdom to which true liberal education, or that *befitting a free man*, should aspire.

> At first, we emerge from the state of slaves into that of children and of children only, and not yet of men. We are exercised by faith; it is our education. And in like manner children are exercised at school; they are taught the rudiments of knowledge upon faith; they do not begin with philosophy. But, as in the natural order, we mount up to philosophical largeness of mind from lessons learned by rote and the schoolmaster's rod, so too in the order supernatural, even in this life, and far more truly in the life to come, we pass on from faith and penance to contemplation. Such is the loving-kindness of the Everlasting Father ... To those who have begun with faith, He adds, in course of time, a higher gift, the gift of Wisdom, which, not superseding, but presupposing Faith, gives us so broad and deep a view of things revealed, that their very consistency is an evidence of their Author, and, like the visible world, persuades us to adore His Majesty. This endowment the Apostle speaks of, when

---

150 Lord Salisbury, "The Programme of the Radicals," in *Lord Salisbury on Politics*, ed. Paul Smith (Cambridge: Cambridge University Press, 1972), 326.

addressing the educated Corinthians. First he makes mention of that liberal knowledge or philosophy in the natural order, which is my present subject, and which in the absence of theology had been sublimated into an empty worthless speculation, and had become a mere "worldly wisdom." After warning his converts against this perversion, he proceeds to say, by way of contrast, "We speak a wisdom among the perfect, yet not the wisdom of this world, but the wisdom of God in a mystery, a wisdom, which is hidden wisdom." Such a wisdom is the whole series of Christian Evidences, the cumulative proof of the Being of a God, of the divinity of Judaism, and of the mission of the Apostles; such the course of the Divine Dispensations, the structure of Scripture Prophecy, the analogy between the systems of nature and grace; such the notes of the Church, the history of miracles, the philosophy and phenomena of the heroic life, the never-ending conflict between Christ and the world, the harmony of Catholic doctrine, and the process of its evolution. These and many other subjects of thought form a multitude, or rather a system and philosophy of divine sciences, which, rising out of Faith, tend nevertheless towards that eternal state of illumination, when Faith shall yield to sight. It is the gift of Wisdom; and of this our Lord seems to speak, and almost designates it as the liberal knowledge of His favoured ones, by contrasting it with the servile condition of mind in which we act without being able to give an account of our actions. "I will not now call you servants," He says, "for the servant knoweth not what his Lord doth; but I have called you friends, because all things, whatsoever I have heard from my Father, I have made known to you." Parallel then to this Divine Wisdom, but in the natural order, even though it takes cognisance of supernatural subjects, is that philosophical view or grasp of all matters of thought, in which I have considered Liberal Knowledge to consist, and which is desirable for its own sake, though it brought with it nothing beyond. Such knowledge is not a mere extrinsic or accidental advantage, which is ours to-day and another's to-morrow, which may be got up from a book, and easily forgotten again, which we can command or communicate at our pleasure, which we can borrow for the occasion, carry about in our hand, and take into the market; it is an acquired illumination, it is a habit, a personal possession, and an inward endowment.[151]

It is precisely because Newman saw the liberalism of the nineteenth century in the light of the "Liberal Knowledge" that he so eloquently describes here that he could describe the evils of liberalism with such authority. Those who defend Turner's attacks on Newman's criticism of liberalism

151 John Henry Newman, *Discourses on the Scope and Nature of Liberal Education* (Dublin: James Duffy, 1852), 84–7.

do so within a highly decadent liberal Establishment hostile not only to the historical Newman and the Roman Church to which he converted but to the very "Liberal Knowledge" that free scholars are called to foster and enrich. The force of Newman's critique of liberalism was certainly not lost on the liberal Robert Pattison, who sees with admirable clarity the salutary benefits of that critique, even for liberals themselves.

> The great virtue of Newman's critique of liberalism is that it should exist at all. That there should be one consistent view of the world opposed to liberalism, root and branch, sharing none of its premises and despising all of its works is an inestimable benefit, for no one more than the liberal himself. Without some honest and unforgiving voice such as Newman's, the liberal would be lost in the labyrinth of his own ideology. He would smugly assume that the paradoxical tenets of his creed are what Jefferson assured them they were: self-evident truths ... The poverty of feeling without belief, the politics that is expediency, and the humanism that denies truth all fall within the scope of Newman's invective and receive from him no quarter. He treats the ugliest manifestations of liberalism with the contempt they deserve but rarely provoke. Newman is the master of those who dissent.[152]

In his attack on scholars sympathetic to Newman, whom he dubs "hagiographical" (his preferred term of abuse), Simon Skinner shows the foolishness that can result when liberal scholars are unaware of precisely the labyrinth of ideology to which Pattison refers. One good case in point is Skinner's complaint that too few of the scholars sympathetic to Newman are properly qualified. Why? Well, for Skinner, they refuse to get on all fours and respond to Turner's more fantastic calumnies: they will not debate whether Newman was "self-deluding," "misogynistic," "egotistical," or "latently homosexual."[153] He also suggests that only university historians can write reliably about Newman, and since those sympathetic to Newman are not all university historians their work by definition cannot be sound.[154] Of course, this is risible effrontery. Still, it is ironic that Skinner and his fellow Newman detractors should preen themselves on

---

152 Pattison, *The Great Dissent*, 215.

153 Skinner, "History versus Hagiography," 779. Here, it should be noted that Ian Ker, in his epilogue to the 2009 edition of his definitive biography of Newman does address the reckless homosexual charge but only to dismiss it as unfounded.

154 Duffy's response to Skinner's absurd claim is worth quoting: "history is not an arcane discipline ... The ordinary rules of historical evidence are intelligible to anybody, and a *de haut en bas* restriction of the right to an opinion on Turner's book to the guild of professional historians runs the risk of seeming both arbitrary and condescending." Duffy, "The Reception of Turner's Newman," 534.

their credentials as academic historians because the only history they manage to present accurately is the history to which Newman refers in one of his more caustic poems—

> The Age to Come
>
> WHEN I would search the truths that in me burn,
> And mould them into rule and argument,
> A hundred reasoners cried,—"Hast thou to learn
> Those dreams are scatter'd now, those fires are spent?"
> And, did I mount to simpler thoughts, and try
> Some theme of peace, 'twas still the same reply.
> Perplex'd, I hoped my heart was pure of guile,
> But judged me weak in wit, to disagree;
> But now, I see that men are mad awhile,
> 'Tis the old history—Truth without a home,
> Despised and slain, then rising from the tomb.
>
> Palermo.
> June 9, 1833

In conclusion, Turner was wrong on all counts regarding Newman's reading of liberalism. He was wrong to charge that Newman's various definitions of liberalism did not tally with those of his contemporaries. He was wrong to charge that Newman opposed Evangelicalism, not liberalism. And he was wrong to charge that Newman only claimed to oppose liberalism to curry favor with critics of liberalism in nineteenth-century Rome.

On this last point, I shall call my readers' attention to the work of the scholar for whom Turner and his liberal friends show least respect, Ian Ker, who, by general consent, has written the most learned, elegant, and insightful books on Blessed John Henry Cardinal Newman, including the definitive biography and a number of studies of his theological and spiritual achievement. Towards the end of his admirable biography, where Newman's great *Biglietto* speech is the topic, Father Ker proves why he remains the doyen of Newman studies by getting to the very heart of Newman's understanding of liberalism. Here, he begins by sharing with his readers his subject's response to "the encroaching secularization whereby, to use Newman's phrase, 'that goodly framework of society which is the creation of Christianity, is throwing off Christianity.'"

> Instead of the Church's authority and teaching, they would substitute first of all a universal and a thoroughly secular education, calculated to bring home to every individual that to be orderly, industrious, and sober is his personal interest ... As to Religion, it is a private luxury, which a man may have if he will; but which of course he must pay for, and which he must not obtrude on others, or indulge in to their annoyance.

While many readers of Newman's work may be familiar with this passage, they will still benefit from the parish priest in Father Ker showing how what follows the passage puts the great convert's understanding of liberalism in its proper, pastoral context. Newman, it is true, does not pull his punches when he attacks what he considers the anti-Catholic character of liberalism.

> But he does not hesitate, in the heart of Catholic Rome, to introduce the important modification, "that there is much in the liberalistic theory which is good and true; for example, not to say more, the precepts of justice, truthfulness, sobriety, self-command, benevolence, which ... are among its avowed principles, and the natural laws of society." The surprise, however, lies in the conclusion: it is precisely because of the positive aspects of liberalism that "There never was a device of the Enemy, so cleverly framed, and with such promise of success." But that is not the end of the speech, which closes on the optimistic note that "Christianity has been too often in what seemed deadly peril, that we should fear for it any new trial now." It is not its survival which is in doubt, but rather the unexpected manner in which it will win through: "Consequently the Church has nothing more to do than to go on in her own proper duties in confidence and peace, to stand still and to see the salvation of God."[155]

This, by any measure, is persuasive criticism. It certainly shows Newman's fairmindedness and acuity. Yet it also shows, by contrast, what a false, ungenerous, ahistorical view Frank Turner and his friends have of Newman and his altogether warrantable opposition to the manifest evils of liberalism.

---

[155] Ian Ker, *John Henry Newman: A Biography* (Oxford: Clarendon Press, 1988), 721. See also Ian Ker, "Introduction to John Henry Cardinal Newman's *Biglietto* Speech," *Logos*, 6, no. 4 (Fall 2003), 164–70. For a good, sympathetic reading of nineteenth-century political liberalism in England, see Ian Bradley, *The Optimists: Themes and Personalities in Victorian Liberalism* (London: Faber and Faber, 1980)

5

Signs of Contradiction, Signs of Hope: A Talk at Westminster Cathedral

Signs of Contradiction, Signs of Hope: A Talk at Westminster Cathedral

"Each generation," G. K. Chesterton once said, "is converted by the saint who contradicts it most. In a world that was too stolid, Christianity returned in the form of a vagabond; in a world that has grown a great deal too wild, Christianity has returned in the form of a teacher of logic."[1]

Well, St. Francis and St. Thomas were certainly not go-along-to-get-along types. The "accommodationism" that now disgraces and enfeebles our own Catholic Church would have struck both these wonderful saints as a poor evasion of the clear Christian duty to affirm the reality of God's love, even when that affirmation is most anathema to what Newman called the "gross, carnal, unbelieving world."[2] But if Chesterton's apothegm applied to St. Francis and St. Thomas, it applies to Blessed John Henry Newman even more, for Newman's life can be seen as a continual contradiction of the reigning idolatries of his age, an age which had, for the most part, nothing

---

[1] This passage is so wonderful that I shall quote it in its entirety: "Each generation is converted by the saint who contradicts it most. St. Francis had a curious and almost uncanny attraction for the Victorians; for the nineteenth-century English who seemed superficially to be most complacent about their commerce and their common sense. Not only a rather complacent Englishman like Matthew Arnold, but even the English Liberals whom he criticised for their complacency, began slowly to discover the mystery of the Middle Ages through the strange story told in feathers and flames in the hagiographical pictures of Giotto. There was something in the story of St. Francis that pierced through all those English qualities which are most famous and fatuous, to all those English qualities which are most hidden and human: the secret softness of heart; the poetical vagueness of mind; the love of landscape and of animals. St. Francis of Assisi was the only medieval Catholic who really became popular in England on his own merits. It was largely because of a subconscious feeling that the modern world had neglected those particular merits. The English middle classes found their only missionary in the figure, which of all types in the world they most despised: an Italian beggar." G. K. Chesterton, *Saint Thomas Aquinas* (1933), in *The Works of G. K. Chesterton*, vol. 2, *The Everlasting Man, Saint Francis of Assisi, Saint Thomas Aquinas* (San Francisco: Ignatius Press, 1986), 424–5.

[2] Newman, "Wisdom and Innocence" (1843), in *Sermons on Subjects of the Day*, 300.

but contempt for what he held most dear. Indeed, in Newman's case, in a world that had seen fit to exchange sentiment for dogma, Christianity returned in the form of a most unsentimental dogmatist. If this helped convert some of his contemporaries, it puzzled and scandalized a good deal more.

In this brief talk, I should like to show how Newman's relations with his contemporaries highlighted two of his most attractive attributes: not only his readiness to oppose his contemporaries, when he was convinced that they required opposing, but his great respect for that indispensable theological virtue, hope, which he nicely defined in one of his Anglican sermons as "the patient subdued tranquil cheerful thoughtful waiting for Christ."[3] I was struck by the power of this definition the other day, when I was reading, of all improbable people, George Gissing (1857–1903), the melancholy novelist, who wrote in his diary on 3 June 1888:

> Strange how sternly I am possessed of the idea that I shall not live much longer. Not a personal thought but is coloured with this conviction. I never look forward more than a year at the utmost; it is the habit of my mind, in utter sincerity to expect no longer tenure of life than that. I don't know how this has come about; perhaps my absolute loneliness has something to do with it. Then I am haunted with the idea that I am consumptive. I never cough without putting a finger to my tongue to see if there is a sign of blood. Morbidness—is it? I only know that these forecasts are the most essential feature of my mental and moral life. Death, if it came now, would rob me of not one hope, for hopes I simply have none.[4]

When I say that Newman was ready to oppose his contemporaries, perhaps I should qualify, because I do not wish to suggest that his attitude was merely negative. In a letter to Henry Cole, the man who succeeded John Hungerford Pollen as Director of the South Kensington Museum, which would eventually become the Victoria and Albert, Newman wrote, apropos Cole's edition of the works of the now forgotten poet and litterateur, Thomas Love Peacock, "I have read a good deal of Mr. Peacock's works which you gave me. He is always brilliant and interesting—witty and original—and some of his poetry is beautiful. But he is also always critical, and never categorical—and I cannot feed on negatives. What does he hold? What does he inculcate? What is he aiming at? In consequence his volumes are books to take up and lay down again

---

3 John Henry Newman, "Sermon on the Liturgy" (March 1830), in *John Henry Newman: Sermons 1824–1843. Volume I: Sermons on the Liturgy and Sacraments on Christ the Mediator*, ed. Placid Murray (Oxford: Oxford University Press, 1992), 90.

4 *Letters of George Gissing to Members of his Family*, ed. Algernon and Ellen Gissing (London: Constable & Co., 1927), 215.

and effect nothing. Am I severe on a man whom I dare say his friends loved with much affection?"[5]

In contrast, in most of his dealings with his contemporaries, even with those who were least receptive to the faith that meant so much to him, Newman was almost punctiliously positive, and his opposition always aimed at inculcating in those he opposed practical benefits. Even Mark Pattison, the Oxford don, who looked back on his brief stint as a Tractarian with shuddering recoil, could never forget the impact that Newman had made on him before the parting of friends. "Thin, pale, and with large lustrous eyes piercing through this veil of men and things," Newman, Pattison recalled, "hardly seemed made for this world. But his influence had in it something of magic. It was never possible to be a quarter-of-an-hour in his company without a warm feeling of being invited to take an onward step ... Newman always tried to reach the heart and understanding of those with whom he had to do."[6] And this came, at least partly, from his abounding fellow feeling, which he extended most discerningly to those who chose to disbelieve. In his wonderful *University Sermons*, for example, which are some of the best he ever wrote, he conceded how: "It is indeed a great question whether Atheism is not as philosophically consistent with the phenomena of the physical world, taken by themselves, as the doctrine of a creative and governing Power." But, by the same token, he also recognized that "the practical safeguard against Atheism in the case of scientific inquirers is the inward need and desire, the inward experience of that Power, existing in the mind before and independently of their examination of His material world."[7] Here, Newman might be alluding to the irresistible faith of Francis Bacon (1561–1626), the English courtier, lawyer, philosopher and wit, who was obliged to confess in his essay, "On Atheism" (1625): "I had rather believe all the fables in the legend, and the Talmud, and the Alcoran, than that this universal frame is without a mind." Indeed, Bacon anticipated a good deal of Newman's response to the rationalism of the nineteenth century when he wrote how "A little philosophy inclineth men's minds to atheism, but depth in philosophy bringeth men's minds to religion." In *Newman and his Contemporaries* I have a chapter on the naval and railway engineer William Froude, the brother of Newman's great friend Hurrell Froude, who was so instrumental in opening his eyes to the claims of Rome, and in it I touch on this long-held conviction of Newman's that even the most skeptical must hanker for the Creator that created them, despite their

---

5 Newman to Sir Henry Cole (5 December 1877), in *LD*, XXVIII, 275.

6 Mark Pattison, Review of Thomas Mozley's *Reminiscences of Oriel College and the Oxford Movement*, *The Academy*, 22 (July–December 1882).

7 Newman, "Faith and Reason, Contrasted as Habits of Mind" (1839), Sermon 10, in *University Sermons*, 138.

doubts, though William, for all of Newman's assiduous counseling, seems to have gone to his grave unconverted.⁸

Unbelief is a theme that looms large in Newman's dealings with his contemporaries because after he converted to Rome he came to suspect that many more of his contemporaries were unbelievers than outward appearances, or their professions to the contrary, might suggest. This aspect of Newman—his acknowledgment of how three hundred years of "Church of Englandism," as Thackeray called it, had left the English practically incapable of religion—has always reminded me of some amusing entries in Samuel Johnson's diary. Some of you may recall the passages where Johnson had gone to the Anglican service on Easter Day and seen a "man meanly dressed" who yet struck him as a very pious, devout man; and so taken was he by the fellow that he actually invited him back to his house to pump him on the faith. Now, in one sense, it was not unusual for Johnson to do this: after all, he was an extraordinarily gregarious man and filled his various homes over the years with necessitous lodgers. But how telltale it was that this brilliant, God-fearing, conscientious man should have desired to gratify his zeal for religion by taking up an entire stranger for no other reason than that he looked pious! In all events, when Johnson sought to glean new insights into the faith from his arresting guest, he was disappointed. As it turned out, the fellow proved an opinionated Methodist bore.⁹

Nevertheless, Newman would have appreciated his illustrious predecessor's hunger to know more about his faith because it was a hunger that both he and his dear friend Hurrell Froude and so many others of his generation shared when they were young men and trying to learn to live the devout life themselves. I have a fairly brisk chapter on Newman and the Americans in *Newman and his Contemporaries* and there is a section there on a young man named Arthur Carey who also had something of this same Johnsonian interest in the devout life.¹⁰ There is another chapter in the book on Richard Holt Hutton, the great editor of the *Spectator* and one of Newman's best contemporary critics, and there I also show how this son of a lachrymose Dublin Unitarian prized his correspondence with Newman precisely because it enabled him to grow in his increasingly High Church Anglican faith.¹¹

---

8 Edward Short, "The Certainty of Vocation: Newman and the Froudes," in *Newman and his Contemporaries* (London and New York: T. & T. Clark, 2011), 135–63.

9 See Samuel Johnson, *Diaries, Prayers and Annals*, ed. E. L. McAdam, Jr. (Yale University Press: New Haven, 1958), 80 and 94.

10 Edward Short, "Newman and the Americans," in *Newman and his Contemporaries*, 283–302.

11 "On the Track of Truth: Newman and Richard Holt Hutton," ibid., 303–34.

Signs of Contradiction, Signs of Hope

If Newman's interactions with his contemporaries show his interest in the experience of true faith, it also shows his interest in the many ways in which the would-be faithful could be seduced into settling for counterfeit faiths. And here his own experience with the *via media*, that mediatorial half-way house between Rome and Augsburg, which he would later abandon as an untenable theory, helped him to see how susceptible we all are to succumbing to false gods. English rationalists from Thomas Arnold to A. M. Fairbairn had taken it into their heads to make a religion of knowledge. Newman is one of the most discerning of all English authors precisely because, while he never lost sight of how reason can cooperate with and indeed nourish faith, he never took it into his head to imagine that reason could somehow supplant faith. St. Thomas sets this out with his customary perspicuity. "The divine truths of faith are not closed to scientific inquiry," he writes in *de Trinitate*; "and its method of working from the unknown to the known can be applied. However, two sides are engaged. For our part, we can discover divine truths only by working from our environment, which is composed of creatures perceived through our senses. On their side, in themselves, they are the most evident of all truths, and are so beheld by God and the blessed, though not at present by us." And from this wonderfully simple truth, St. Thomas draws an analogy that one can see at work in Newman's responses to the rationalists in his midst.

> Consequently, there are two kinds of theology. One follows the reasonable course, of inferring divine truths from meanings governing the physical world; it is thus that philosophers claiming for fundamental philosophy, or metaphysics, the title of the divine science, have discussed theological truths. The other, while appreciating that at present when we are wayfarers we cannot see for ourselves the supreme evidence of divine truths, already begins through infused faith to take after and share in God's own knowledge by cleaving to his fundamental truth for its own sake.[12]

Newman, for his part, in Sermon 10 of the *University Sermons*, "Faith and Reason, Contrasted as Habits of Mind" (1839), elaborated on St. Thomas's fundamental point by distinguishing between two powers that are often confused by rationalists. Many were convinced that Newman would have made a splendid barrister. Here he makes his case with a masterly cogency.

> Now, in attempting to investigate what are the distinct offices of Faith and Reason in religious matters, and the relation of the one to the other, I observe, first, that undeniable though it be, that Reason has a power of analysis and criticism in all opinion and conduct,

---

[12] St. Thomas Aquinas, quoted in *St. Thomas Aquinas: Theological Texts*, selected and trans. Thomas Gilby (Oxford: Oxford University Press, 1955), 24–5.

and that nothing is true or right but what may be justified, and, in a certain sense, proved by it, and undeniable, in consequence, that, unless the doctrines received by Faith are approvable by Reason, they have no claim to be regarded as true, it does not therefore follow that Faith is actually grounded on Reason in the believing mind itself; unless, indeed, to take a parallel case, a judge can be called the origin, as well as the justifier, of the innocence or truth of those who are brought before him. A judge does not make men honest, but acquits and vindicates them: in like manner, Reason need not be the origin of Faith, as Faith exists in the very persons believing, though it does test and verify it. This, then, is one confusion, which must be cleared up in the question,—the assumption that Reason must be the inward principle of action in religious inquiries or conduct in the case of this or that individual, because, like a spectator, it acknowledges and concurs in what goes on;—the mistake of a critical for a creative power.[13]

This clear-sighted appreciation of the limits of reason informed Newman's criticism not only of the Noetics whom he had encountered in the Senior Common Room at Oriel in the 1820s and 1830s—men like Thomas Arnold, Renn Dickson Hampden, Richard Whately and Edward Hawkins—but of the rationalists and agnostics who would succeed them as the nineteenth century progressed.

No one saw the battle-lines forming between Roman Catholicism and its liberal enemies as clearly as Newman. The late Yale professor Frank Turner, whose scurrilous attacks on Newman still command the respect of Newman detractors intent on endearing themselves to the liberal academies that pay them their paychecks, sought to argue that Newman's very concept of liberalism was flawed because it was somehow lacking in specificity or nuance. Readers can judge for themselves whether Newman is, indeed, vulnerable on this score. Certainly, throughout his long life, he took up the evils posed by liberalism—evils that are infinitely greater today than they were in Newman's day—with powerful clarity. "I look out, then, into the enemy's camp, and I try to trace the outlines of the hostile movements and the preparations for assault which are there in agitation against us," Newman wrote in 1858. "The arming and the manœuvring, the earth-works and the mines, go on incessantly; and one cannot of course tell, without the gift of prophecy, which of his projects will be carried into effect and attain its purpose, and which will eventually fail or be abandoned."[14] Nevertheless, Newman could delineate the main lines of the liberal philosophy that

13 Newman, "Faith and Reason, Contrasted as Habits of Mind" (1839), Sermon 10, in *University Sermons*, 131.
14 Newman, "A Form of Infidelity of the Day," in *The Idea of a University*, 313.

would seek to discredit and dislodge the one holy catholic and apostolic faith. "You may have opinions in religion, you may have theories, you may have arguments, you may have probabilities," Newman portrayed his rationalist liberals arguing, "you may have anything but demonstration, and therefore you cannot have science. In mechanics you advance from sure premises to sure conclusions; in optics you form your undeniable facts into system, arrive at general principles, and then again infallibly apply them: here you have Science." But for the liberal rationalists, "it is absurd for men in our present state to teach anything positively about the next world, that there is a heaven, or a hell, or a last judgment, or that the soul is immortal, or that there is a God."[15]

In capturing the ethos of this anti-Christian rationalism so precisely, Newman captured not only the skepticism of his own age but that of ours as well.

> Well, then, if Religion is just one of those subjects about which we can know nothing, what can be so absurd as to spend time upon it? what so absurd as to quarrel with others about it? Let us all keep to our own religious opinions respectively, and be content ... upon no subject whatever has the intellect of man been fastened so intensely as upon Religion. And the misery is, that, if once we allow it to engage our attention, we are in a circle from which we never shall be able to extricate ourselves. Our mistake reproduces and corroborates itself. A small insect, a wasp or a fly, is unable to make his way through the pane of glass; and his very failure is the occasion of greater violence in his struggle than before. He is as heroically obstinate in his resolution to succeed as the assailant or defender of some critical battlefield; he is unflagging and fierce in an effort which cannot lead to anything beyond itself. When, then, in like manner, you have once resolved that certain religious doctrines shall be indisputably true, and that all men ought to perceive their truth, you have engaged in an undertaking which, though continued on to eternity, will never reach its aim; and, since you are convinced it ought to do so, the more you have failed hitherto, the more violent and pertinacious will be your attempt in time to come. And further still, since you are not the only man in the world who is in this error, but one of ten thousand, all holding the general principle that Religion is scientific, and yet all differing as to the truths and facts and conclusions of this science, it follows that the misery of social disputation and disunion is added to the misery of a hopeless investigation, and life is not only wasted in fruitless speculation, but embittered by bigotted sectarianism.[16]

15 Ibid., 314–15.
16 Ibid., 315–16.

Here, one can see not only the satirical reader of Voltaire and all his progeny but something of the genius with which Newman entered into the rationale of his opponents, and it is this critical clairvoyance that makes him such an incomparable guide to the essence of liberalism.

Nevertheless, Newman, always a very practical man, was always concerned about what the issue of this doctrinaire anti-Catholicism would be. "Where men really are persuaded of all this, however unreasonable," he asks, "what will follow?" For Newman, liberal relativism would not be inconsequential, and the accuracy of his predictions can be verified by our own increasingly tragic experience: it would issue in "A feeling, not merely of contempt, but of absolute hatred, towards the Catholic theologian and the dogmatic teacher. The patriot abhors and loathes the partisans who have degraded and injured his country; and the citizen of the world, the advocate of the human race, feels bitter indignation at those whom he holds to have been its misleaders and tyrants for two thousand years."[17]

If Newman was alive to the arguments of those consciously and indeed actively opposed to the Church, he was also aware that most people naturally excuse themselves from polemical warfare, and here he put his finger on that latitudinarian indifference that makes the work of the more deliberate enemies of the Faith so much easier. Speaking of "the multitude of men everywhere and at all times," Newman describes them as men who "do not see the Image of Almighty God before them"; they do not "ask themselves what He wishes":

> if once they did ... they would begin to see how much He requires, and they would earnestly come to Him, both to be pardoned for what they do wrong, and for the power to do better. And, for the same reason that they do not please Him, they succeed in pleasing themselves. For that contracted, defective range of duties, which falls so short of God's law, is just what they can fulfil; or rather they choose it, and keep to it, *because* they can fulfil it. Hence, they become both self-satisfied and self-sufficient;—they think they know just what they ought to do ... and in consequence they are very well content with themselves, and rate their merit very high, and have no fear at all of any future scrutiny into their conduct ... though their religion mainly lies in certain outward observances, and not a great number even of them.[18]

In my chapter on Thackeray in *Newman and his Contemporaries*, I show how the satirical novelist shared this trifling view, though never so much as to

---

17 Ibid., 317.
18 Newman, "The Religion of the Pharisee, the Religion of Mankind" (1856), in *Sermons on Various Occasions*, 28–9.

prevent his yearning for the true Faith.¹⁹ At the same time, in my chapter on the Americans, I show how Newman was fascinated by the social springs of nominal Christianity, a species of unbelief which we now see much more ostentatiously among Roman Catholics, especially moneyed Roman Catholics, than among their greatly reduced Protestant counterparts.

Speaking of Protestants, I should say something about Keble and Pusey, for I have chapters in my book on both of them. I know that it may not be altogether fair or charitable to say but I have always found these two men somewhat exasperating, for all of their undoubted merits. In an article in the *Catholic Herald*, Father Ian Ker argued that one proof of Newman's sanctity was his readiness to respond wholeheartedly to the letters of strangers. Well, I should say that an even greater proof of this sanctity lay in his readiness to correspond as patiently and as charitably as he did with Keble and Pusey. Of course, it may be necessary to revisit the elaborate shilly-shally of both men, but only because their Anglo-Catholic paralysis throws Newman's conversion into such radiant relief.

If there is anything contentious in my book, I suppose it is in my refusal to grant the Oxford Movement the favorable consideration that many Newman commentators grant it. Yes, it was an important phase in Newman's development but it was only a phase. When he broke with the *via media* and joined the Catholic Church, Newman broke with a world of illusion, even though it was in this world that he had come to see intimations of the One True Fold. Hilaire Belloc was clear-sighted about the claims of the Oxford Movement, about which so many earnest men have written so many dull books.

> In the year 1833 a group of men at Oxford, who had grown dissatisfied with the lethargy of religious feeling in the Established Church, launched a movement which aimed primarily at its revival. The theory upon which the movement was based was one more or less familiar to the Anglican writers of the seventeenth century, but one which had gone out of fashion after the Revolution and had almost entirely disappeared from men's minds during the Erastian and ultra-Protestant eighteenth century.²⁰ Its two leading principles

---

19 Edward Short, "Newman, Thackeray and Vanity Fair," in *Newman and his Contemporaries* (London and New York: T. & T. Clark, Bloomsbury, 2011), 244–82.

20 Belloc's choice of the word "ultra-Protestant" here is certainly arguable, though the question remains whether the eighteenth-century High Church truly anticipated all that Newman and the Tractarians sought to accomplish in the nineteenth century in order to revive the Anglican Church, a contention advanced most notably by Frederick Meyrick, though Peter Nockles claimed it for his own in *The Oxford Movement in Context* (Cambridge 1994). "It is an entire mistake to suppose that the religious movement in Oxford of the last century owes its origin to Newman, or required his help for its success," Meyrick wrote. "It would have taken place had Newman not existed, though

were the doctrine of Continuity and the Appeal to Antiquity. It maintained that the existing Church of England was one with the pre-Reformation Church, which in its turn was one with the Church of the Fathers. All that had happened at the Reformation was that certain popular corruptions which had grown up during the Middle Ages were cleared away, and along with them some useful but not essential customs which it might be well to restore. But the Church of England remained a branch of the one Catholic Church established from the beginning. Her bishops were true successors of the Apostles; her clergy were a true priesthood, as fully qualified to administer the Sacraments as any priests of Rome or Constantinople. Her faith was the Catholic faith as originally transmitted by the Apostles, and this was to be proved by constant reference to the Early Fathers in whose writings there was supposed to be found a complete cycle of Christian doctrine requiring no further interpreting. Both "Romanism" and popular Protestantism were to be condemned, the one for having added to the faith, the other for falling short of it. The schism between East and West, like the later schism between England and Rome, were admittedly regrettable incidents, but they did not impair the true Catholicity of every branch of the Church which mark reposed upon the possession of Apostolic authors the maintenance of the Apostolic Creed, and the continuity of Apostolic tradition in Hierarchy and in Orders. It will be clear at once that such a theory, though its supporters might call it Catholic and might be accused by their enemies of "Romanising," strikes at the very root of Catholicism as it is understood by all who acknowledge the supremacy of the Holy See not a whit less than does avowed Protestantism. No Catholic would listen for a moment either to its historical or its doctrinal assumptions. And in point of fact, with perhaps the exception of Hurrell Froude (who died quite early in the movement), all the leaders were vehemently and even ferociously anti-Roman at that time; none more so than the greatest of them, John Henry Newman.[21]

It seems to me that Newman, once he had converted, although appreciative of the appeal of those assumptions—after all, he had been instrumental in giving them expression—would have agreed. Certainly, he was never reluctant, even as an Anglican, to concede the difficulties inherent in the *via media*. In the *Lectures on the Prophetical Office of the Church* (1837), he made these difficulties plain:

the fire would not have blazed up so rapidly nor so fiercely if he had not been there to feed it." Frederick Meyrick, *Memories of Life at Oxford and Experiences in Italy, Greece, Turkey, Germany, Spain and Elsewhere* (London, 1905), 26.
21 John Lingard and Hilaire Belloc, *The History of England from the First Invasion by the Romans to the Accession of King George the Fifth* (Washington: The Catholic Publication Society of America, 1915), XI, 587–9.

> Protestantism and Popery are real religions; no one can doubt about them; they have furnished the mould in which nations have been cast: but the *Via Media*, viewed as an integral system, has never had existence except on paper; it is known, not positively but negatively, in its differences from the rival creeds, not in its own properties; and can only be described as a third system, neither the one nor the other, but with something of each, cutting between them, and, as if with a critical fastidiousness, trifling with them both, and boasting to be nearer Antiquity than either.[22]

At the same time, as he demonstrates in his *Essay on Development* (1846), Newman was aware of how an inadequate religion like the one he cobbled together in the *via media* could nonetheless lead to, if not embody the true faith:

> True religion is the summit and perfection of false religions; it combines in one whatever there is of good and true separately remaining in each. And in like manner the Catholic Creed is for the most part the combination of separate truths, which heretics have divided among themselves, and err in dividing. So that, in matter of fact, if a religious mind were educated in and sincerely attached to some form of heathenism or heresy, and then were brought under the light of truth, it would be drawn off from error into the truth, not by losing what it had, but by gaining what it had not,—not by being unclothed, but by being "clothed upon," that mortality may be swallowed up of life. That same principle of faith which attaches it at first to the wrong doctrine would attach it to the truth; and that portion of its original doctrine, which was to be cast off as absolutely false, would not be directly rejected, but indirectly, in the reception of the truth which is its opposite. True conversion is ever of a positive, not a negative character.[23]

After he converted, Newman was highly critical of the Tractarian Movement, though always solicitous towards individual Tractarians. In this respect, Newman anticipated Pope Benedict XVI and his Anglican Ordinariate. Of course, some, even now, after all of the false starts and false promises of ecumenism, wish to turn Newman into a sort of Anglo-Catholic ecumenist *malgré lui*, but there is nothing in the record to suggest that he somehow pined for a return to the ministry he had made so many sacrifices to repudiate. Indeed, in 1862, when the Irish Unionist Thomas Monsell alerted Newman to a report in the public prints suggesting that he was on

---

[22] John Henry Newman, *Lectures on the Prophetical Office of the Church* (London: J. G. & F. Rivington, 1837), 20.

[23] Newman, *Essay on Development*, 200–1. I am grateful to Dr. Giulia Marotta for calling my attention to this important passage.

the brink of returning to the Church of England, Newman could not have published a more categorical disavowal. On 27 June the *Globe* (which, as Monsell noted, had "great circulation") had run the following paragraph from the *Morning Advertiser*:

> We learn from a quarter in which we place our every reliance, that the Rev. Dr. Newman, who many years ago went over to Popery from the Church of England, has left, or is about to leave, the Oratory at Brompton, of which he has been the head for several years. We are further assured that the impression among Dr. Newman's private friends is, that this step is the preliminary to his return to the Church of England.[24]

Newman's response is worth quoting in full, not least because it shows the charitable patience with which he was always prepared to explode the misrepresentations that were continually circulated about him.

> The Oratory, Birmingham, June 28, 1862
>
> Sir,
>
> A friend has sent me word of a paragraph about me, which appeared in your paper of yesterday, to the effect that "I have left, or am about to leave, my Oratory at Brompton, of which I have been for several years the head, as a preliminary, in the expectation of my private friends, to my return to the Church of England."
>
> I consider that you have transferred this statement into your columns from those of a contemporary, in order to give me the opportunity of denying it, if I am able to do so. Accordingly I lose not an hour in addressing these lines to you, which I shall be obliged by your giving at once to the public.
>
> The paragraph is utterly unfounded in every portion of it.
>
> 1. For the last thirteen years I have been head of the Birmingham Oratory. I am head still; and I have no reason to suppose that I shall cease to be head, unless advancing years should incapacitate me for the duties of my station.
>
> 2. On the other hand, from the time that I founded the London Oratory, now at Brompton, twelve years ago, I have had no jurisdiction over it whatever; and so far from being its head, it so happens I have not been within its walls for the last seven years.
>
> 3. I have not had one moment's wavering of trust in the Catholic Church ever since I was received into her fold. I hold, and ever have held, that her Sovereign Pontiff is the centre of unity and the Vicar of Christ. And I ever have had, and have still, an unclouded faith in her creed in all its articles; a supreme satisfaction in her worship, discipline, and teaching; and an eager longing and a hope against

24 LD, XX, 215, n. 2.

hope that the many dear friends whom I have left in Protestantism may be partakers of my happiness.

4. This being my state of mind, to add, as I hereby go on to do, that I have no intention, and never have had any intention, of leaving the Catholic Church and becoming a Protestant again, would be superfluous, except that Protestants are always on the look-out for some loophole or evasion in a Catholic's statement of fact. Therefore, in order to give them full satisfaction, if I can, I do hereby profess ex animo, with an absolute internal assent and consent, that Protestantism is the dreariest of possible religions; that the thought of the Anglican service makes me shiver, and the thought of the Thirty-nine Articles makes me shudder. Return to the Church of England! no; "the net is broken, and we are delivered." I should be a consummate fool (to use a mild term) if in my old age I left "the land flowing with milk and honey" for the city of confusion and the house of bondage.

I am, Sir, your obedient servant, John H. Newman.[25]

In light of his appreciation of how "Protestants are always on the look-out for some loophole or evasion in a Catholic's statement of fact," it is unlikely that Newman would be surprised that these misrepresentations continue unabated, both from without and within the Catholic Church, though one great blessing of the record he left behind in his correspondence and his personal memoranda is that it can always be drawn on to refute these misrepresentations.

In renewing his rejection of the false religion of the National Church, Newman revealed the source of that hope that governed all of his dealings with his contemporaries, a hope that appears in his private mediations with moving conviction.

> O my God, how can I look Thee in the face when I think of my ingratitude, so deeply seated, so habitual, so immovable — or rather so awfully increasing! Thou loadest me day by day with Thy favours, and feedest me with Thyself, as Thou didst Judas, yet I not only do not profit thereby, but I do not even make any acknowledgment at the time. Lord, how long? when shall I be free from this real, this fatal captivity? He who made Judas his prey, has got foothold of me in my old age, and I cannot get loose. It is the same day after day. When wilt Thou give me a still greater grace than Thou hast given, the grace to profit by the graces which Thou givest? When wilt Thou give me Thy effectual grace which alone can give life and vigour to this effete, miserable, dying soul of mine? ... O my God, I am so fast in prison that I cannot get out.

---

25 Newman to the editor of the *Globe* (28 June 1862), in LD, XX, 216–16.

> O Mary, pray for me. O Philip, pray for me, though I do not deserve Thy pity.[26]

There, I should say, in his prayerful humility and in his penitent hope is the quintessential Newman.

Now, I suppose I should say something of how I view Newman. The other evening, I was reading Lord Dunsany's Jorkens stories, which are some of the most enchanting ever written. They all center around a peculiar fellow named Jorkens, who tells the most enrapturing tall tales from an armchair in his club in return for glasses of Irish whisky, and in the preface to *Jorkens Remembers Africa* (1933) I came upon a bit that reminded me of the true Newman. "Many a man's memory," Dunsany writes, "as he grows old loses slowly its colour and splendour, till pictures that he believed could never fade, fall from it one by one. How fortunate if the refreshments that we sometimes offer Jorkens are able to open again that closed but brilliant inner eye, till we watch it gazing once more steadfast and child-like sheer in the face of Truth."

If there is something I wished to capture in writing my book about John Henry Newman it was this ability of his to gaze "steadfast and child-like sheer in the face of Truth." Newman has a reputation for being rather formidable, intellectual in the worst way, subtle beyond subtle. Well, I see a different Newman. I see in him holy simplicity. He was not only a good man, he was a good-hearted man. He was without guile. He was as generous as he was forbearing. He loved the people he found himself among and treated them with respect, generosity and Christ-like care. He lived to cure souls; he wrote to cure souls. My book is full of instances of this *caritas*—in Newman's readiness to correspond with those with religious questions, in his readiness to condole with the bereaving, in his readiness to share with his contemporaries his great love of God and His Church.

Walter K. Firminger (1870–1940), who had been at Lancing and Merton before venturing to Calcutta, where he became Archdeacon of Calcutta and a leading member of the Calcutta Historical Society, wrote in 1892 of how Newman had met with a fair amount of criticism by those who attacked both his contributions to the Oxford Movement and his motives for converting. (It was around this time that Edwin A. Abbott published his stupefyingly tedious, two-volume assault on the Anglican Newman.) Firminger responded to Abbott and other critics by echoing the immortal Jorkens:

> Newman neither refuted Robert Elsmere, nor outsocialised the Fabian Society, and so from a *fin de siècle* point of view he is perhaps a thing of nought. To me, however, it seems that his greatness is in

---

[26] *Meditations and Devotions of the Late Cardinal Newman* (New York and London: Longman, Green & Co., 1903), 308–9.

his very power to take you from a world of burning questions, away from the noisy assertions of first-principle-despising controversialists, back, behind the hastily-drawn inferences of practical life, to the sphere where truth stares the soul in the face and refuses to be misunderstood ... He imperatively demands that you should take his point of view, and with him see the distant scene suffused with a light that never was on land or sea. He has preeminently the power of making life "real" to us, and this by reason of the subtle power by which in his own life the "real" has its being in the unseen Eternity of God.[27]

Throughout his long life, as one can see from his letters, Newman was animated by one all-important purpose: love of God, and it was this more than anything else that made him such a superlatively good friend, confidante and counselor to so many of his contemporaries. He was also animated by the conviction that faith must be lived, not merely professed. "[L]et me bid you cherish, what otherwise it were shocking to attempt," he tells his readers in one of his Anglican sermons, "a constant sense of the love of your Lord and Saviour in dying on the cross for you." And it is typical of Newman's shrewd understanding of fallen human nature that he should realize how difficult an undertaking that is. It is also typical of him that he should warn his readers against making glib professions.

> "The love of Christ," says the Apostle, "constraineth us;" not that gratitude leads to love, where there is no sympathy, (for, as all know, we often reproach ourselves with not loving persons who yet have loved us,) but where hearts are in their degree renewed after Christ's image, there, under His grace, gratitude to Him will increase our love of Him, and we shall rejoice in that goodness which has been so good to us. Here, again, self-discipline will be necessary. It makes the heart tender as well as reverent. Christ showed His love in deed, not in word, and you will be touched by the thought of His cross far more by bearing it after Him, than by glowing accounts of it.[28]

In addition to being so incomparably articulate about the Faith, Newman was humble. Francis Palgrave, the editor of the *Golden Treasury* gave vivid expression to this quality when he visited him at the Oratory in 1887, when Newman was a still spry 86.

> I was allowed an interview with Cardinal Newman at the Oratory. There sat that aged man with his snow-white hair; he rose and

---

27 Walter K. Firminger, *What then did Newman Do? Being an Inquiry into his Share in the Church Revival and a Brief Statement of the Leading Features of his Religious Teaching* (Oxford: B. H. Blackwell, 1892), 18.
28 "Love, the One Thing Needful" (1839), Sermon 23, in *PPS*, V, 338.

thanked me for coming and for caring for him with a sort of young child's gracious simplicity. He was much changed, of course, since I had last seen him many years ago: the look of almost anxious searching had passed into the look of perfect peace. His mind was not only bright as ever, but with the cheerfulness and humour of youth. He talked of his old Oxford days ... Then of [Dean] Church, "whom no one could know without loving." He spoke of his voyage long ago in the Mediterranean ... He went on to speak of Creighton's "Papacy," and the Renaissance and its evils in high places; and he broke out, with a bright smile of tenderness: "How wonderful was the revival of the Church soon after under Loyola, St Philip Neri, San Carlo Borromeo!" ... He thanked me again for what he called my kindness in caring to see him. This great and perfect humility was almost overwhelming in its strikingness. No wonder he looked up with reverence to the two Borromei, whom he mentioned with special admiration. What a strange and beautiful union of the saint and the poet! His voice has much of its old strange sweetness, such as I heard it at Littlemore in my Oxford days—how far off for both of us![29]

As a Catholic, Newman devoted a fair amount of his time to two ends: to educating English Catholics in their Catholic faith and to helping Anglicans, including his old Tractarian friends with their various Anglican difficulties, which, then, as now, were never easily resolved. Much of my book is given over to these two themes, both of which exemplify not only the charitable empathy but the abounding hope that governed Newman's dealings with his fellow men.

Henry Tristram, the last Oratorian to have known Newman at the Birmingham Oratory, and one of his greatest commentators, pinpointed the aspect of Newman that I personally find most engaging. During the Second World War, Tristram conducted impromptu tours of the Oratory for visiting American soldiers and afterwards he described how deeply moved these young men were by the emblems of Newman's sanctity. Although they knew little about the man and had read none of his works, they could see, as Tristram noted, that this was someone who "shared with the Saints one preeminent gift, given only to a few, the gift of kindling in the minds of others the sense of God's nearness; and humanity, although it may feign indifference or even contempt, will always revere, as in a class apart, those chosen souls who through the veil of the visible behold the invisible that lies beyond and reveal to others a glimpse, although only a glimpse of what they themselves have seen."[30]

---

29 See *LD*, XXXI, 184, n. 5.

30 Henry Tristram, "Introduction" to *John Henry Newman: Centenary Essays* (London: Burns, Oates and Washbourne, 1945), 14.

✣ 6 ✣

Port Middlebay: Tractarians Abroad

Port Middlebay: Tractarians Abroad

The Oxford Movement: Europe and the Wider World, 1830–1930, edited by Stewart J. Brown and Peter B. Nockles. Cambridge University Press, 273 pages

IN THE PREFACE that John Henry Newman wrote as an old man to a reissue of *Tract 90*, the pamphlet that preceded his conversion to the Church of Rome, he made some characteristically incisive points. First, he identified what he called the "all-important question" of the Tract as "whether the 39 Articles … one by one … were (as was said at the time) 'patient, though not ambitious, of a Catholic interpretation.'" Secondly, he reminded his readers that "The Tract which follows made that experiment"—which was an amusing way of alluding to the fury that the Tract inspired among English Protestants when it was first published in 1841. And finally he added a self-deprecatory aside showing how far the Catholic convert had traveled from the controversies that unsettled his Anglican priesthood. "I ought to add that, in this edition, I have not thought it necessary to insert at full length the passages of the Homilies, as they were inserted originally in the Tract. This omission weakens indeed the Author's argument, but it is better than the alternative of their lavish exhibition. It is penance enough to reprint one's own bad language, without burdening it with the blatant abuse of the Homilies."[1]

Here were the lessons Newman drew from the Tract: it proved that the National Church could never accept any Catholic reading of its formularies and it reminded a fairly fastidious author of a stylistic misjudgment that he was pleased to set right. The lessons Anglo-Catholics have drawn from the Tract are quite different. Despite their distaste for the tergiversating Newman, they have always been ready to cite his Tract as evidence of the theological legitimacy of their own party.

Then, too, after Newman seceded, Edward Pusey was careful to resurrect the Tract as a means of reasserting the Anglican Church's claim to being a branch of the Universal Church. The editors of this collection, nicely encapsulate this claim in their introduction when they speak of the

---

1 Newman, *Via Media*, II, 257.

Church of England as "an integral part of the Church Catholic that had been instituted by Christ, guided through time by the Holy Spirit, directed by the apostles and then by their episcopal successors, preserved in doctrinal truth, enriched by long centuries of tradition, venerated by generations of the faithful, infused with divine grace through the sacraments and destined to abide until the return of God in glory."[2] However vexed such claims have proven, it is good to have them presented at the very outset of this collection, even if the editors understandably ignore the fact that not only Newman but the English people as a whole roundly rejected them.

If Anglo-Catholics are as keen in the twenty-first century of laying claim to *Tract 90* as they were in the nineteenth century, they are equally adverse to making any mention of Newman's *Lectures on Certain Difficulties Felt by Anglicans in Submitting to the Catholic Church* (1850), in which Newman directly addressed his erstwhile Anglo-Catholic friends and exhorted them to repudiate a party that could make no legitimate claim to membership within the actual as opposed to the Tractarians' theoretical Catholic Church nor find any acceptable home within the Established Church.

The central claim of the collection is that English Anglo-Catholicism is not an off-shoot of the fundamental provincialism of English Protestantism but a much larger, even cosmopolitan faith, which enjoyed an appeal far beyond the shores of Albion. "Our international team of authors," the editors declare, "have viewed the Oxford Movement as an international movement within a global context."[3]

To see how the editors deliver on this claim, I turned first to the essays on the reception Tractarianism received in Australia, expecting to read of a transformation there similar to that of Wilkins Micawber, who may not have met with much success in England but found fame and fortune when he emigrated to Australia and became District Magistrate of Port Middlebay.[4] But alas the reception the Oxford Movement met with in Australia was of a piece with the reception it met with in all of the places to which it was introduced: it was distrusted by Protestants for being too "catholic" and by Catholics for being too "protestant." In the case of Australia, many

---

2 *The Oxford Movement and the Wider World*, ed. Stewart J. Brown and Peter B. Nockles (Cambridge: Cambridge University Press, 2012), 1.

3 Ibid., 3–4.

4 "The public dinner to our distinguished fellow-colonist and townsman, WILKINS MICAWBER, ESQUIRE, Port Middlebay District Magistrate, came off yesterday in the large room of the Hotel, which was crowded to suffocation. It is estimated that not fewer than forty-seven persons must have been accommodated with dinner at one time, exclusive of the company in the passage and on the stairs. The beauty, fashion, and exclusiveness of Port Middlebay, flocked to do honor to one so deservedly esteemed, so highly talented, and so widely popular" Charles Dickens, *The Personal History of David Copperfield* (Oxford: Oxford University Press, 1948), 870–1.

of its bishops might have had Tractarian sympathies—Augustus Short, Bishop of Adelaide most notably—but Gladstone was right to characterize them as a "true Anglican episcopate," which is not the same thing as a Tractarian episcopate.[5]

Since so much of the Oxford Movement turned on defining certain fiercely contested concepts—"catholicity" being, perhaps, the most disputed—it is well for the conscientious commentator to be precise about terms, especially those used by the Tractarians and their opponents themselves. Peter Nockles, one of the editors here, falls down terribly on this score when he refers to the label "Noetic" given to members of the Oriel Senior Common Room as "implying freethinkers." Since Richard Whately, Edward Hawkins and Edward Copleston prided themselves on their logical rigor, *freethinking* was precisely what they eschewed themselves and excoriated in others. Nockles, however, is right to observe that "Oriel was truly the cradle, crucible, and making of Tractarianism,"[6] though he omits to acknowledge its considerable intellectual, theological and pedagogical deficiencies. Those interested in seeing just how glaring these were should read Newman's correspondence with Whately and Hawkins.

Then there is a rather misleading essay by Rowan Strong entitled "The Oxford Movement and the British Empire," which merely discusses how the Anglican Henry Edward Manning initially welcomed the Jerusalem Bishopric before rejecting it—an odd way to claim Tractarianism for the empire. For readers unfamiliar with these recondite matters, the Jerusalem Bishopric was a scheme concocted by Baron Bunsen in 1841 to set up a joint Anglican and Lutheran bishopric in Jerusalem, which predictably fizzled out in 1886. That Manning regarded the scheme favorably hardly alters the standard view of the Anglo-Catholic party as quintessentially insular. As this collection shows, the appeal of the party's mandarin faith in or beyond the British Isles was negligible. That Nockles and his co-editor should have commissioned a band of scholars to find otherwise says something about the keenness in certain quarters to have this faith taken seriously beyond Pusey House.

Still, if the editors' main argument is unpersuasive, there is much of interest in this collection. There is a particularly lively essay by Albrecht Geck, professor of ecclesiastical history at the University of Osnabruck, entitled "The Oxford Movement in Germany," which demonstrates why the Anglo-Catholics and their exotic "catholicity" should have found so little sympathy among Germans, Protestant or Catholic. Dr. Geck cites the historian Heinrich Friedrich Fock (1819–72), who, as he says, "did not

---

5 *The Oxford Movement and the Wider World*, 113.
6 Ibid., 32.

have high hopes for the future progress of Protestantism in England."[7] Indeed, "his doubts about the national character of the English made him still more skeptical"—doubts to which the historian gave memorable expression.

> Were they capable, in the end, of finding their way in the "world of ideas"? He believed that Roman Catholicism, which was authoritarian, suited the English more than the Protestant striving for freedom in the realm of ideas. The Roman Catholic sought submission to some higher authority outside himself. The Protestant, however, sought the identity of subjectivity, of the will and the moral law, of *Wollen and Sollen*, within the individual human mind. To establish this identity was the ultimate meaning of history, and Protestantism was a decisive step in this process. It was so to speak, the ideology of the day: "Freedom! is the great watchword of our times: freedom! also in religion."[8]

This "pure Hegelianism," as Dr. Geck usefully refers to it, doubtless disinclined German Protestants from appreciating an Anglo-Catholic faith that was deeply critical of the theological freedoms of English Protestants. Newman and Hurrell Froude, after all, were fond of referring to the Evangelicals in their midst as *Peculiars*. Moreover, this Hegelian strain explains why Pusey, who began his scholarly career immersed in the anfractuosities of German theology, should have repudiated what he came to regard as a misguided respect for German piety. "I watched with deep interest and great hopefulness the early stages of revival of religious earnestness among you," Dr. Geck quotes Pusey writing the German theologian August Tholuck (1799–1877), "then ... I turned heart-sick."[9]

Geoffrey Rowell, Anglican Bishop of Gibraltar in Europe rightly stresses how important Newman's correspondence with the French Abbé Jager was to his pivotal *Prophetical Office of the Church* (1837) and his *Essay on Development* (1846), a correspondence which shows that if the Anglo-Catholics did not influence Europe, the Europeans did influence the Anglo-Catholics, at least when they were under the leadership of Newman. Still, this influence was not of a sort to reassure Anglo-Catholics of the tenability of their ground, especially since Newman eventually came away from his epistolary exchanges with Jager convinced that no idiosyncratic party within the Established Church could provide any basis for a rediscovery of the apostolic religion on which he had set his heart. As his letters make abundantly plain, by 1837, Newman had already begun to unplug from the *via media*.

7 *Ibid.*, 182.
8 *Ibid.*
9 *Ibid.*

Another good essay here is entitled "French Catholics and the Oxford Movement" by Jeremy Morris, the author of the illuminating *F. D. Maurice and the Crisis of Authority* (2005). Here, Morris shows how the readers of the major French Catholic papers, *L'Ami* and *L'Univers* "were generally tutored to read the Oxford Movement not so much for what it told them about the Church of England and the religious condition of England, as about the post-Napoleonic resurgence of the Catholic Church, and above all the imminent conversion of England." Indeed, Newman's sister Harriett, who traveled to Normandy with her husband Thomas Mozley at the same time that Newman was moving closer and closer to Rome was horrified by the extent to which their French hosts regarded this "imminent conversion" as a *fait accompli*. In this regard, she was one with Charlotte Bronte, who wrote from Brussels in 1842, "My advice to all Protestants who are tempted to do anything so besotted as turn Catholics, is, to walk over the sea on to the Continent; to attend mass sedulously for a time; to note well the mummeries thereof; also the idiotic, mercenary aspect of all the priests; and *then*, if they are still disposed to consider Papistry in any other light than a most feeble, childish piece of humbug, let them turn Papists at once."[10]

The good essays included here notwithstanding, the editors might have put together a better collection by addressing the real character of Anglo-Catholicism, whether abroad or at home. After all, at its heart, the Oxford Movement was a yearning for true faith on the part of a people that had only known a nationalist travesty of faith. G. K. Chesterton made some useful observations on this score when he noted how the "significance" of the Oxford Movement was "not quite easy immediately to define. It was certainly not aesthetic ritualism; scarcely one of the Oxford High Churchmen was what we should call a Ritualist. It was certainly not a conscious reaching out towards Rome: except on a Roman Catholic theory which might explain all our unrests by that dim desire. It knew little of Europe, it knew nothing of Ireland."

For the perceptive convert in Chesterton, who had known something of the dissatisfactions of false religion among the crapulous *bons viveurs* of Fleet Street, the more the Oxford Movement was studied, "the more it would appear that it was a movement of mere religion as such. It was not so much a taste for Catholic dogma, but simply a hunger for dogma. For dogma means the serious satisfaction of the mind. Dogma does not mean the absence of thought, but the end of thought."[11]

---

10 *Selected Letters of Charlotte Bronte*, ed. Margaret Smith (Oxford: Oxford University Press, 2007), 38.
11 G. K. Chesterton, "The Victorian Compromise and its Enemies" (1913), in *The Collected Works of G. K. Chesterton* (San Francisco: Ignatius Press, 1989), XV, 439.

This, of course, was Newman's contention as well, to which he gave such perspicacious expression in his *Anglican Difficulties*. If much about the Oxford Movement is of interest only to historians of religion, its yearning for dogma has perennial appeal, especially in an age like ours, where the abandonment of dogma in so many quarters has caused much unnecessary muddle, indeed heterodoxy, especially among confused or mutinous Catholics. Readers interested in why Tractarianism arose in England in the wake of the French Revolution and why it continues to be a reminder of the primacy of dogma should read Newman's brilliant appeal to his erstwhile Anglican companions, about which Richard Holt Hutton, his finest contemporary critic wrote: "the *Lectures on Anglican Difficulties* was the first book of Newman's generally read among Protestants, in which the measure of his literary power could be adequately taken. In the Oxford sermons there had been of course more room for the expression of religious feeling of a higher type, and frequently there had been more evidence of depth and grasp of mind; but here was a great subject with which Newman was perfectly intimate, giving the fullest scope to his powers of orderly and beautiful exposition, and opening a far greater range to his singular genius for gentle and delicate irony."[12]

---

12 Hutton, *Cardinal Newman*, 207.

✛ 7 ✛

John Henry Newman, C. S. Lewis and the Reality of Conversion

John Henry Newman, C. S. Lewis and the Reality of Conversion

To speak creditably about C. S. Lewis, John Henry Newman and the reality of conversion, we should first define terms. What would Newman and Lewis have understood by conversion, growing up in their respective worlds, Newman at the beginning of the nineteenth and Lewis at the beginning of the twentieth century?

In the case of Newman (1801–90), we might start by looking at how Samuel Johnson defined the word in his great dictionary. There, Johnson defines "convert" as to "change from one religion into another," though he supplies no illustrating quotation, doubtless because most conversions in the eighteenth century were from the Established Church to the various non-conformist or free churches, and Johnson, like many of his Tory and even Whig contemporaries, had little patience with the theological claims of such churches. In his own definition of "nonconformity," which he defines as "refusal to join the established religion," Johnson added this quote from the irreproachably Laudian Robert South (1634–1716): "Since the liturgy, rites, and ceremonies of our church, are so much struck at, and all upon the plea of conscience, it will concern us to examine the force of this plea, which our adversaries are still setting up as the grand pillar and buttress of nonconformity." Of course, for Johnson, as for South, the force of such pleas was negligible. In the dictionary's next entry for "conversion," Johnson defines the word as to "change from reprobation to grace, from a bad to a holy life." Conversion, in other words, is defined in moral terms. And here the illustrative quotation is from the Epistle of James 5:19–20:

> He who converteth the sinner from the errour of his way,
> Shall have a soul from death, and hide a multitude of sins

By the time Lewis (1898–1963) came of age in the early twentieth century, Johnson's dictionary had been supplanted by the *New English Dictionary*, which would later become *The Oxford English Dictionary*. In fact, when the first edition of the new dictionary was published in 1928, Lewis was already an English don at Magdalen, where, when not tutoring undergraduates, he was reading Chesterton, though more for his rhetoric than his Christianity. The first entry for the noun, "conversion," in the *Oxford English Dictionary* is "Turning in position, direction, destination," which nicely exhibits the loosely Calvinist strain of the dictionary's first editor, James Murray, a stalwart Congregationalist, who often preached at Oxford's George Street chapel. Murray's eighth entry for the word is also worth noting—"The bringing of any one over to a specified religious faith, profession, or party, especially to one regarded as true, from what is regarded as falsehood or error." And to illustrate this definition, Murray includes something from Bishop William Stubbs, the great constitutional historian, in which, speaking of Oxford University, he writes, "She is the Church of the National History, of the Conversion, the Constitution, the Reformation." Here, Stubbs makes no bones of how, for the English, religion is a matter not of doctrine or authority but of the Nation State, from which the Erastian National Church arose, a fact which would have an immense impact on the conversions of both Newman and Lewis. (The word "Erastian," since we are defining terms, stems from the name of the sixteenth-century Heidelberg physician Erastus, who believed that ecclesiastical should be subordinated to secular power.) Lastly, in his ninth entry for the word, Murray endeavors to define "conversion" in what he called theological terms as "The turning of sinners to God; a spiritual change from sinfulness, ungodliness, or worldliness to love of God and pursuit of holiness," and there he chooses as one of his illustrative quotations something from John Angell James (1785–1859), the Nonconformist clergyman of Birmingham, who founded both the Evangelical Alliance and the Congregational Union of England and Wales: "The first error is to mistake knowledge, impression and partial reformation, for genuine conversion." What is striking about this is that it is not a theological definition but a variation of the moral definition that Johnson had included in his dictionary, though it is telltale that Murray should have imagined a moral could somehow pass for a theological definition.

Now, the important thing about both Johnson and Murray for our purposes is that they see conversion in exclusively English terms. In none of their entries is there any reference to the Church of Rome, or, indeed, to Christendom, and this is highly emblematic of the social, religious and intellectual worlds in which both Newman and Lewis came to maturity, worlds, which, for all of their imperial sway, were still proudly provincial in their religious affiliations.

For a definition of the word as Catholics would have understood it, we can go to the *Catholic Encyclopaedia* (1913), which might have been written expressly to taunt the No Popery prejudices of the Protestant English:

> Every man [the *Encyclopaedia* states] is bound by the natural law to seek the true religion, embrace it when found, and conform his

John Henry Newman, C. S. Lewis and the Reality of Conversion

life to its principles and precepts. And it is a dogma of the Church defined by the Vatican Council that man is able by the natural light of reason to arrive at the certain knowledge of the existence of the one true God, our Creator and Lord. The same council teaches that faith is a gift of God necessary for salvation, that it is an act of the intellect commanded by the will, and that it is a supernatural act. The act of faith then is an act of the understanding, whereby we firmly hold as true whatever God has revealed, not because of it intrinsic truth perceived by the natural light of reason, but because God, who can neither deceive nor be deceived, has revealed it. It is in itself an act of the understanding, but it requires the influence of the will which moves the intellect to assent. For many of the truths of revelation, being mysteries, are to some extent obscure. Yet, it is not a blind act, since the fact that God has spoken is not merely probable but certain. The evidences for the fact of revelation are not, however, the motive of faith; they are the grounds which render revelation credible, that is to say, they make it certain that God has spoken. And since faith is necessary for salvation, that we may comply with the duty of embracing the true Faith and persevering in it, God by His only-begotten Son has instituted the Church and has adorned it with obvious marks so that it may be known by all men as the guardian and teacher of revealed truth. These marks (or notes) of credibility belong to the Catholic Church alone. Nay, the Church itself by its admirable propagation, sublime sanctity, and inexhaustible fecundity, by its Catholic unity and invincible stability, is a great and perpetual motive of credibility and irrefragable testimony of its Divine mission.

Besides echoing the case Newman made for the "notes" of the Church in the his *Essay on Development* (1845), this definition will be useful in showing how Newman and Lewis differed in their respective conversions, Newman eventually embracing the definition and Lewis embracing only parts of it.

In the case of Newman, we have to appreciate that while he converted to Roman Catholicism formally in October of 1845, he had important conversion experiences prior to that. In 1816, under the influence of the Reverend Walter Mayers, the classics master at Ealing School, he was converted, as he wrote in the *Apologia*, to "a definite Creed, and received into my intellect impressions of dogma, which, through God's mercy, have never been effaced or obscured." Then, again, when he visited Rome and witnessed the Catholic Mass for the first time in 1833, he wrote home to his French Huguenot Mother how the experience had staggered him, impelling him to ask questions of Rome and the claims of Rome that most good English Protestants simply did not ask. After referring to the "unedifying dumbshow" of the Mass and to Rome as "a doomed city ... one of the 4 monsters of Daniel's vision," he confessed to being gravely torn: "as I looked on, and saw ... the Holy Sacrament offered up, and the blessing given, and recollected I was in church, I could only say in very perplexity ... 'How shall I name thee, Light of the wide west, or heinous error-seat?'"[1]

Here, we can see Newman dramatically struggling with his ancestral allegiances in face of a religious appeal that directly opposed those allegiances. However reassuring it might have been for Mrs. Newman to hear her son speak of the "4 monsters of Daniel" and the "unedifying dumbshow" of the Mass, it could only have been profoundly unsettling for her to hear him even suggesting that the Church of Rome might be the "Light of the wide west." All of the ambivalence that Newman felt about the Church that he was sworn as a good Anglican to denounce rose to the surface in this letter, and it was an ambivalence that his Huguenot mother, let alone his Protestant siblings could only have found deeply upsetting. The Catholics of France, after all, had caused the Huguenots continual grief, culminating in the Massacre of St. Bartholomew's Day, when, on 24 August 1572, Catherine de' Medici, the mother of King Charles IX, instigated the murder of what historians estimate were anywhere from five to thirty thousand Huguenots. With such an episode of Catholic frightfulness lodged in their ancestral memory, it is no wonder Newman's conversion did not go down well with his family. When his mother died in 1836, she did so deeply disapproving of her son's Romanizing. His siblings were equally hostile. His father, a private banker in the City of London, might have been more receptive, moving as he did in the cosmopolitan world of finance, undefined by the usual English prejudices. But he died in 1824, years before his son began his substantive turn towards Rome. When Newman converted to the Church, about which he had heard only defamatory caricatures since boyhood, he converted without the sympathy, let alone understanding of his family.

Chesterton, in his clairvoyant way, exhibited his keen understanding of the inescapably incremental way in which most English conversions to Catholicism occur when he observed how the Englishman must first discover the Catholic Church before he chooses either to war against or convert to it. "This process, which may be called discovering the Catholic Church, is perhaps the most pleasant and straightforward part of the business; easier than joining the Catholic Church and much easier than trying to live the Catholic life. It is like discovering a new continent full of strange flowers and fantastic animals, which is at once wild and hospitable. To give anything like a full account of that process would simply be to discuss about half a hundred Catholic ideas and institutions in turn." A good deal of the history of the Oxford Movement could be written by

---

[1] Letter of John Henry Newman to Mrs. Jemima Newman (25 March 1833), in *LD*, III, 267–8.

John Henry Newman, C. S. Lewis and the Reality of Conversion

showing how Newman and his friends Edward Pusey, John Keble and Hurrell Froude wrestled with the discovery of this "new continent" in their own spiritual development. And Chesterton is also helpful for our purposes because he realizes how definitions *per se* always play a unique, pivotal role in converting the English. Indeed, for Chesterton, as he said,

> I might remark that much of it consists of the act of translation; of discovering the real meaning of words, which the Church uses rightly and the world uses wrongly. For instance, the convert discovers that "scandal" does not mean "gossip"; and the sin of causing it does not mean that it is always wicked to set silly old women wagging their tongues. Scandal means scandal, what it originally meant in Greek and Latin: the tripping up of somebody else when he is trying to be good. Or he will discover that phrases like "counsel of perfection" or "venial sin," which mean nothing at all in the newspapers, mean something quite intelligent and interesting in the manuals of moral theology. He begins to realise that it is the secular world that spoils the sense of words; and he catches an exciting glimpse of the real case for the iron immortality of the Latin Mass. It is not a question between a dead language and a living language, in the sense of an everlasting language. It is a question between a dead language and a dying language; an inevitably degenerating language.[2]

If this first stage of encountering the strange new definitions of Catholicism influenced the conversions of both Newman and Lewis, so too did the "adventurous and varied" second stage, as Chesterton saw it, when the convert has "numberless glimpses of great ideas, that have been hidden from [him] ... by the prejudices of his provincial culture." This, for Chesterton, was, "broadly speaking, the stage in which the man is unconsciously trying to be converted." Chesterton's third stage, however, is the one that we can apply most to Newman, since, as Chesterton remarks, it "is perhaps the truest and the most terrible. It is that in which the man is trying not to be converted." When we read Newman's day-by-day correspondence with his Anglican friends preliminary to his formally going over to Rome—a correspondence that goes on for six years and is replete with the most excruciating deliberation imaginable—we can see how right Chesterton was to characterize this stage as "the truest and the most terrible." In all events, it is a pity that Chesterton never wrote a book on Newman because if he had he would have given us marvelous insight into the crucible of conversion. Apropos his suppositious convert, Chesterton writes:

---

[2] Gilbert Keith Chesterton, *The Catholic Church and Conversion* (London: Macmillan, 1927), in *The Collected Works of G. K. Chesterton* (San Francisco: Ignatius Press, 1990), III, 91.

He has come too near to the truth, and has forgotten that truth is a magnet, with the powers of attraction and repulsion. He is filled with a sort of fear, which makes him feel like a fool who has been patronising "Popery" when he ought to have been awakening to the reality of Rome. He discovers a strange and alarming fact, which is perhaps implied in Newman's interesting lecture on Blanco White and the two ways of attacking Catholicism. Anyhow, it is a truth that Newman and every other convert has probably found in one form or another. It is impossible to be just to the Catholic Church. The moment men cease to pull against it they feel a tug towards it. The moment they cease to shout it down they begin to listen to it with pleasure. The moment they try to be fair to it they begin to be fond of it. But when that affection has passed a certain point it begins to take on the tragic and menacing grandeur of a great love affair. The man has exactly the same sense of having committed or compromised himself; of having been in a sense entrapped, even if he is glad to be entrapped. But for a considerable time he is not so much glad as simply terrified. It may be that this real psychological experience has been misunderstood by stupider people and is responsible for all that remains of the legend that Rome is a mere trap. But that legend misses the whole point of the psychology. It is not the Pope who has set the trap or the priests who have baited it. The whole point of the position is that the trap is simply the truth.[3]

One fundamental factor that Chesterton does not take into account in his calculus of conversion is the factor of self-sacrifice. Thirty years after his conversion, in a letter to Lady Margaret Heywood, Newman would vividly list the necessary sacrifices exacted by converting to a religion which in England was regarded as synonymous with ignorance, superstition, backwardness and treachery:

> Your case is the case of many others, and a very painful one. But I suppose the inward conflict of mind which was the inevitable lot of those who in the first age of the Church had to face the prospect of loss of friends, home, familiar habits, the happy and secure routine of life, life-long beliefs and opinions and human authority and favour, with the chance of persecution and death, in order to win Christ, was still more painful, but even the trial to which the soul is subjected now and in this country, ere it can get free of the world and follow Christ, is great indeed. And bystanders can only pray for souls in this distress; for it is God, and none else, who must help them.[4]

---

3 *Ibid.*, 92.
4 Newman to Lady Margaret Heywood (15 November 1876), in *LD*, XXVII, 376.

Yet, in converting and leaving not only his own people but an entire English way of life, Newman found a new life, the companions of which could not be taken away from him. "You speak of feeling drawn to the religion of Ireland by your love of Ireland," Newman wrote a Protestant Irishman drawn to Irish Catholicism, "I felt something like this as regards the Fathers. After my conversion I had a sensible pleasure in taking down the Volumes of St Athanasius, St Ambrose etc in my Library—The words rose in my mind 'I am at one with you now.' I had a feeling of family-intimacy with them then, the want of which I suffered from before, without recognising it."[5]

Newman's doubts about the tenability of the Church of England would reemerge in 1839, three years after cobbling together his *via media*, in which he sought to chart a mediatorial course between Augsberg and Rome. In September of that year, Robert Williams, an Oriel man and MP for Dorchester, who would later become an ardent Evangelical, gave Newman a copy of an article by Nicholas Wiseman, "The Anglican Claims of Apostolical Succession" from the *Dublin Review*, in which the then Vicar General likened the Donatists of the fifth century to the Anglicans of the nineteenth. In his diary, Newman notes how he walked out to Littlemore with Williams that afternoon and dined with him in the evening. In the course of their conversation, Williams called Newman's attention to what he described as "the palmary words of St Augustine... which had escaped my observation: 'Securus judicat orbis terrarum,'" which Newman translated: "The universal Church is in its judgments secure of the truth." Newman recalled how at the time Williams "repeated these words again and again, and, when he was gone, they kept ringing in my ears."[6] Soon, this first principle and all that flowed from it would set off in Newman himself what he called his "great revolution of mind."[7] Hearing St. Augustine's great axiom after his own study of the Monophysite heresy made a profound impression on him.[8] As he wrote his good friend Frederic Rogers, "You see the whole history of the Monophysites has been a sort of alterative, and now comes this dose at the end of it. It certainly does come upon one that we are not at the bottom of things. At this moment we have sprung a leak, and the worst of it is that those clever fellows Ward, Stanley and Co. will not let one go to sleep on it. Curavimus Babylonem et non est sanata was an awkward omen... How are

---

5 Newman to W. J. O'Neill Daunt (13 August 1864), in *LD*, XXI, 195.
6 *LD*, VII, xvii.
7 *Apologia*, 90.
8 The Monophysites were fifth-century heretics who believed that there is only one nature in the person of Christ. "In reaction to the Nestorian view, the Monophysites ... held that after the Incarnation Christ had but one nature, the divine absorbing the human." See *Apologia*, 540.

we to keep hot heads from going over? Let alone ourselves."[9] A month later, Henry Wilberforce recalled walking with Newman in the New Forest, and his dear friend turning to him and saying "that for the first time since I began the study of theology, a vista has been opened before me, to the end of which I do not see."[10] For the accuracy of this recollection, we have Newman's own letter to Rogers, in which he signed off by assuring his friend, who would eventually break off all relations with Newman for twenty years after he defected from the Anglican Church: "It is no laughing matter. I will not blink the question; but you don't suppose I am a madcap to take up notions so suddenly. Only there is an uncomfortable vista opened which was closed before."[11] Converting to Rome—which, hitherto, would have been a very madcap notion indeed—had suddenly became a distinct possibility.

It is striking that Newman should have had this epiphany while out walking because nearly a hundred years later, in September of 1931, Lewis would have a similarly illuminating walk of his own with his friends Hugo Dyson, a lecturer in English at Reading University and J. R. R. Tolkien, the author of *The Lord of the Rings*. After dining in Magdalen College, the three professors took a postprandial stroll along Addison's Walk, a footpath beside the River Cherwell and discussed the nature of myth. When a flurry of windswept leaves sent them back to Lewis's rooms, they resumed their discussion, though now it had evolved into a consideration of the claims of Christianity. Tolkien called it a night at 3 AM and Dyson left an hour later. In a letter to his friend Arthur Greeves, written two weeks afterwards, Lewis shared the upshot of his nocturnal chinwag: "I have just passed on from believing in God," he wrote, "to definitely believing in Christ—in Christianity. I will try to explain this another time. My long night talk with Dyson and Tolkien had a good deal to do with it." A week later, Lewis sent off the promised explanation. What had kept him from believing in Christianity was his inability to see "how the life and death of Someone Else (whoever he was) 2000 years ago could help us here and now." It was Tolkien who urged his friend to read the New Testament with the same imaginative sympathy that they both read pagan myths in their academic work. And as a result, the penny finally dropped for Lewis. Writing again to Greeves, after his talk with Tolkien and Dyson, he came to see how "The story of Christ is simply a true myth: a myth working on us in the same way as the others, but with this tremendous difference that *it really happened*."[12]

9 Newman to Frederic Rogers (22 September 1839), in *LD*, VII, 154. The "awkward omen" to which Newman refers is from Jeremiah 51:9,"We would have cured Babylon but she is not healed."
10 *LD*, VII, xvii–xviii.
11 Newman to Frederic Rogers (22 September 1839), in *LD*, VII, 154–5.
12 Alister McGrath, *C. S. Lewis: A Life: Eccentric Genius, Reluctant Prophet* (London:

John Henry Newman, C. S. Lewis and the Reality of Conversion

This revelation on Lewis's part was followed up by a trip one sunny morning to Whipsnade Zoo in September in 1931 whither he was driven in a motorcycle by his brother Warnie. "When I set out," he records in his spiritual autobiography, *Surprised by Joy* (1955), "I did not believe that Jesus Christ is the Son of Man, and when we reached the Zoo I did." Engaged in no great thought, aware of no great emotional upheaval, Lewis recalled the experience as one in which he was like "a man," who, "after long sleep, still lying motionless in bed, becomes aware that he is now awake." He also recalled "the birds singing overhead and the bluebells underfoot," a scene evocative of "Eden come again,"[13] though his latest biographer, Alistair McGrath disputes Lewis's dating of the experience, if only because bluebells do not bloom in England in September but from late April till late May, after which their leaves wither and vanish. Still, McGrath is right to stress that it was only fitting that Lewis should associate his conversion with bluebells. From childhood, he had been devoted to the Blue Flower, which symbolizes, as McGrath notes, "a longing for the elusive reconciliation of reason and imagination, the observed world outside the mind and the subjective world within."[14] An outcrop of German Romanticism, the Blue Flower was especially beloved of the poet Novalis, the pen name of Friedrich von Hardenberg (1772–1801), who, interestingly enough, called for the establishment of a renewed Christendom to restore the social, intellectual, and cultural unity of Europe, which had been shattered by the Reformation and the Enlightenment.[15] "Christendom must come alive again and be effective," the poet urged, "and, without regard to national boundaries, again form a visible Church which will take into its bosom all souls athirst for the supernatural, and willingly become the mediatrix between the old world and the new."[16] Nearly two hundred years after Hardenberg's death, Penelope Fitzgerald, the niece of the great English

---

Hodder & Stoughton, 2013), 146–51.

13 C. S. Lewis. *Surprised by Joy*. (New York: Harcourt Brace Javonovich, 1955), 237–8.

14 McGrath, *C. S. Lewis: A Life*, 154–5.

15 After the First World War, the great diplomatic historian George Peabody Gooch (1873–1968) would also see the need for a revival of Christendom, even though his understanding of what Christianity meant in doctrinal terms would almost certainly have mystified both Newman and Lewis. In his entry on Gooch in the *Oxford Dictionary of National Biography*, Frank Eyck observes how "Gooch supported the movement for the establishment of a league of nations, and recalled with approval the medieval ideal of the *respublica christiana*, which had been shattered by the doctrine of the unfettered sovereignty of the state." Here, we can see vindication from an unlikely quarter of Pius IX's prescient rejection of the state's "unfettered sovereignty" in his *Syllabus of Errors* (1864).

16 See "Christendom or Europe?" in Novalis, *Hymns to the Night and Other Selected Writings*, trans. Charles E. Passage (New York: Liberal Arts Press, 1960), 45–63.

convert, Ronald Knox, made Novalis the hero of her historical novel *The Blue Flower* (1991), in which she has him observe how, "As things are, we are enemies of the world, and foreigners to the earth. Our grasp of it is a process of estrangement"—sentiments which would have struck a deep, plangent chord in Lewis, both the grieving boy, who lost his beloved mother, and the grieving man, who lost his beloved wife.[17]

As a child, Lewis had an experience which corroborated the power and appeal of the symbolism behind the Blue Flower. He was standing by a currant bush on a summer day when suddenly he became aware of an earlier morning when his brother had brought his beloved toy garden into the nursery, a memory, as Lewis relates, which constituted "a sensation … of desire; but desire for what? Not certainly for a biscuit tin filled with moss, or even (though that came into it) for my own past." The depth and intensity of the longing was as mysterious as it was unmistakable. "Before I knew what I desired," Lewis recorded, "the desire itself was gone, the whole glimpse withdrawn, the world turned commonplace again, or only stirred by a longing that had ceased. It had taken only a moment of time; and in a certain sense everything that had ever happened to me was insignificant in comparison."[18] Here is language that goes to the very heart of conversion, and it is an eloquent foreshadowing not only of the eventual religious conversion that Lewis would undergo but his entire career as a Christian apologist. This is also a highly significant passage because although one could point to other factors in Lewis's life that might have prepared the way for his conversion—the death of his mother, perhaps, or his experiences in the trenches of the First World War—it was his longing for Paradise that was most decisive, a longing which took place in an otherwise humdrum childhood. If as a child he was given no strong religious instruction, he still managed to find what the Catholic poet Francis Thompson called "nurseries of Heaven" in the delight he took in the beauty of the created world.[19]

The account that Lewis gives to his conversion in *Surprised by Joy* is also reminiscent of his appreciation of the miraculous. In one piece that he wrote on the subject, he exclaims

> How deeply right St. Athanasius was between the miracles of Our Lord and the general order of nature. Both are a full stop for the explaining intellect. If the "natural" means that which can be fitted into a class, that which obeys a norm, that which can be paralleled, that which can be explained by reference to other events, then Nature herself as a whole is *not* natural. If a miracle means that

---

17 Penelope Fitzgerald, *The Blue Flower* (London: Harper Collins, 1995), 217.
18 McGrath, *C. S. Lewis: A Life*, 16.
19 See, "For My Godchild Francis M. W. M." (1891), in *Poems of Francis Thompson*, ed. Brigid M. Boardman (London: Continuum, 2001), 53.

> which must simply be accepted, the unanswerable actuality which gives no account of itself but simply is, then the universe is one great miracle. To direct us to that one great miracle is one main object of the earthly acts of Christ that are, as He himself said, Signs. They serve to remind us that the explanation of particular events which we derive from the given, the unexplained, the almost willful character of the actual universe, are not explanations of that character. These Signs do not take us away from the reality: they recall us to it—recall us from our dream world of "if and ands" to the stunning actuality of everything that is real. They are points at which more reality becomes visible than we ordinarily see at once.[20]

And this insistence on faith as a beckoning gateway to reality is one that Lewis shared with Newman. In *The Idea of a University*, he has occasion to speak of those "uneducated persons, who have hitherto thought little of the unseen world," as Newman described them, who on "turning to God, looking into themselves, regulating their hearts, reforming their conduct, and meditating on death and judgement, heaven and hell … seem to become, in point of intellect, different beings from what they were. Before they took things as they came, and thought no more of one thing than another. But now every event has a meaning; they have their own estimate of whatever happens to them; they are mindful of times and seasons, and compare the present with the past; and the world, no longer dull, monotonous, unprofitable, and hopeless, is a various and complicated drama, with parts and an object, and an awful moral."[21]

Lewis had glimmerings of this great drama when he was a young man reading Chesterton in his draughty rooms at Magdalen. Most of us, whether we are converts or cradle Christians, can recall the penny dropping when we first read Chesterton. In *The Everlasting Man* (1925), his account of why he came to accept the Nicene Creed is exhilarating.

> Beyond the broad suggestion of this chapter I attempt no apologetic about why the creed should be accepted. But in answer to the historical query of why it was accepted, and is accepted, I answer for millions of others in my reply; because it fits the lock; because it is like life. It is one among many stories; only it happens to be a true story. It is one among many philosophies; only it happens to be the truth. We accept it; and the ground is solid under our feet and the road is open before us. It does not imprison us in a dream of destiny or a consciousness of the universal delusion. It opens to us not only incredible heavens, but what seems to some

---

20 From "Miracles," in C. S. Lewis, *God in the Dock: Essays on Theology and Ethics*, ed. Walter Hooper (Cambridge: William B. Eerdmans, 1970), 21–2.
21 *The Idea of a University*, 120.

> an equally incredible earth, and makes it credible. This is the sort of truth that is hard to explain because it is a fact; but it is a fact to which we can call witnesses. We are Christians and Catholics not because we worship a key, but because we have passed a door; and felt the wind that is the trumpet of liberty blow over the land of the living.[22]

Here, one can see how radically Chesterton influenced Lewis, not only with his understanding of the reassuring reality but the liberating joy of the Christian faith.

Before his conversion to Christianity, Lewis had had a conversion to Theism, a somewhat torturous conversion, which he mapped out in *Surprised by Joy*, with the mordant observation, apropos Oxford in the 1920s, that "there were in those days all sorts of blankets, insulators, and insurances which enabled one to get all of the conveniences of Theism, without believing in God." The purveyors of this metaphysics included T. H. Green, Francis Herbert Bradley and Bernard Bosanquet, all of whom encouraged their acolytes to beguile their religious yearnings by believing in the existence of an Absolute Mind. Again, Lewis is trenchant about the appeal of such an impersonal, amorphous belief:

> The emotion that went with all this was certainly religious. But this was a religion that cost nothing. We could talk religiously about the Absolute; but there was no danger of Its doing anything about us. It was 'there,' safely and immovably "there". It would never come "here", never (to be blunt) make a nuisance of Itself. This quasi-religion was all a one-way street; all eros ... but no agape ... There was nothing to fear; better still, nothing to obey.[23]

Newman links theism and conversion in his *Apologia* in a way that nicely shows how he shared Lewis's need for his faith to have a strong basis in reason. In fact, he "found," as he says, "a corroboration of the fact of the logical connexion of Theism with Catholicism in a consideration parallel to that which I had adopted on the subject of development of doctrine."

> Speaking historically of what I held in 1843–4, I say, that I believed in a God on a ground of probability, that I believed in Christianity on a probability, and that I believed in Catholicism on a probability, and that these three grounds of probability, distinct from each other of course in subject matter, were still all of them one and the same in nature of proof, as being probabilities—probabilities of a special kind, a cumulative, a transcendent probability but still probability; inasmuch as He who made us has so willed, that in mathematics

---

22 G. K. Chesterton, *The Everlasting Man* (San Francisco: Ignatius Press, 1993), 248–9.
23 C. S. Lewis, *Surprised by Joy* (London: Geoffrey Bles, 1955), 209–10.

indeed we should arrive at certitude by rigid demonstration, but in religious inquiry we should arrive at certitude by accumulated probabilities;—He has willed, I say, that we should so act, and, as willing it, He co-operates with us in our acting, and thereby enables us to do that which He wills us to do, and carries us on, if our will does but co-operate with His, to a certitude which rises higher than the logical force of our conclusions. And thus I came to see clearly, and to have a satisfaction in seeing, that, in being led on into the Church of Rome, I was not proceeding on any secondary or isolated grounds of reason, or by controversial points in detail, but was protected and justified, even in the use of those secondary or particular arguments, by a great and broad principle. But, let it be observed, that I am stating a matter of fact, not defending it; and if any Catholic says in consequence that I have been converted in a wrong way, I cannot help that now.[24]

What is remarkable about this passage is how Lewis-like it is, both in its logic and its appreciation of the limitations of logic. In a discerning piece of his own called "Is Theism Important?" Lewis speaks of how learned and even unlearned converts often start their conversion by giving intellectual assent to the proposition that God exists before moving on to the more arduous business of conversion to belief in a personal Saviour. Lewis observes:

> Nearly everyone I know who has embraced Christianity in adult life, has been influenced by what seemed to him to be at least probable arguments for Theism. I have known some who were completely convinced by Descartes's Ontological Proof: that is, they received Faith A from Descartes first and then went on to seek and to find Faith B. Even quite uneducated people who have been Christians all their lives not infrequently appeal to some simplified form of the Argument from Design. Even acceptance of tradition implies an argument which sometimes becomes explicit in the form: "I reckon all those wise men wouldn't have believed in it if it weren't true."[25]

This obviously echoes Augustine's axiom, though Lewis would never go so far as to allow that the true Church was the "one, holy, catholic and apostolic Church" of Rome. If the anti-Romanism of Oxford was a barrier to Newman's converting to Rome, the even more pronounced anti-Romanism of Belfast was a barrier to Lewis even contemplating such a conversion.[26] As he lay dying, Lewis confirmed this obdurate barrier when he wrote a

---

24 *Apologia*, 180–1.
25 "Is Theism Important?" in C. S. Lewis, *God in the Dock*, 187–8.
26 For an account of English anti-Romanism as it relates to Newman, see Edward Short, *Newman and his Family* (London: Bloomsbury, 2013), 270–1.

friend named Father Guy Brinkworth, asking for "prayers that the prejudice instilled in me by an Ulster nurse might be overcome."[27]

Nevertheless, Lewis had something of Newman's appreciation for the appeal of nominal Christianity in a country where Catholic Christianity had been absent since Thomas Cromwell sold off the monasteries to enrich the Reformation gentry, those grasping, impious, unconscionable parvenus of whom the popular novelist Hilary Mantel is so fond.[28] In a piece called "The Decline of Religion" Lewis makes the observation that "the religion which has declined was not Christianity," the truth of which we can all attest from our own baleful experience. If the once widely subscribed Anglican religion of the English was not Christianity, what was it? "It was a vague Theism with a strong and virile ethical code," the Irish colonial in Lewis could see clearly enough, "which, far from standing over against the 'World,' was absorbed into the whole fabric of English institutions and sentiment and therefore demanded church going as (at best) a part of loyalty and good manners and (at worst) a proof of respectability."[29] Christopher Dawson made an ancillary point when he observed how, "We have only to compare modern ecclesiastical art with that of the past to feel that the life has gone out of it, and that what was once seen as living reality has become a dead formula. And this devitalization of modern religion goes a long way to explain the anti-Christian attitude of writers like Nietzsche and D. H. Lawrence. For there is nothing so repulsive as dead religion; it is the deadest thing there is. As the Gospel says, it is not even good enough for the dunghill."[30] Far from deploring the decline of this pinchbeck religion, Lewis welcomed it, pointing out another insight that our own experience can richly corroborate: "When no man goes to church except because he seeks Christ the number of actual believers can at last be discovered."[31]

Vis-à-vis the moral definitions for conversion given by both Johnson and Murray, it is noteworthy that both Newman and Lewis should offer their respective proofs of God, such as they were, based on moral argument. In *Mere Christianity*, Lewis argues that if we are all conscious of not behaving as we ought to behave, there must be some law outside of ourselves that makes us aware of our falling short of this law, and that this law necessarily

---

27 Father Brinkworth, quoted in Joseph Pearce, *C. S. Lewis and the Catholic Church* (San Francisco: Ignatius Press, 2003), 148.

28 Cf. William Cobbett: "For cool, placid, unruffled impudence, there has been no people in the world to equal the 'Reformation gentry.'" Cobbett, *History of the English Reformation*, 15.

29 "The Decline of Religion," in *God in the Dock*, 239.

30 Christopher Dawson, "Religion and Life," in *Enquiries into Religion and Culture*, 246.

31 "The Decline of Religion," in *God in the Dock*, 239.

presupposes a Lawgiver. Newman also saw in conscience an importunate advocate for the objectivity of the moral law, and, therefore, a Lawgiver, a reality which inspired in him a grave, Johnsonian sense of accountability. "The idea of a judgment is the first principle of religion," he wrote to his good friend and frequent correspondent, Mary Holmes, the governess, who was a sort of Catholic Jane Eyre, "as being involved in the sentiment of conscience—and, as life goes on, it becomes very overpowering. Nor do the good tidings of Christianity reverse it, unless we go into the extreme of Calvinism or Methodism with the doctrine of personal assurance. Otherwise, the more one has received, the more one has to answer for. We can but throw ourselves on the mercy of God, of which one's whole life is a long experience." Since it was on his seventy-fourth birthday that Newman imparted this grave truth he could substantiate it with ungainsayable personal experience. "A birthday," he told Miss Holmes, "is a very sad day at my age—or rather I should say a solemn day. When I call it sad, it is when it brings before me the number of friends who have gone before me—though this is a most ungrateful sadness, since I have so many affectionate and anxious friends left, who are so good to me. I think what makes me low, is the awful thought that where my departed friends are, there I must be—and that they can and do rejoice in their trial and their judgment being over, whereas I am still on trial and have judgment."[32]

What is puzzling about Lewis is how he could so plainly see the need for an orthodox Christianity and yet remain an Anglican. One of the guiding axioms of the convert in Newman—"To be deep in history is to cease to be Protestant"—was not one that seems to have ruffled Lewis, which is baffling when one considers what an otherwise sharp historical sense he had.[33] No one can doubt this sense who reads his literary criticism, especially his bravura survey of sixteenth-century English literature, where, speaking of "the ruffs, the feathers, the tapestries, the rich carvings, the mannered gardens, the elaborate courtesies" of the age of Sidney and Spenser, which mirror so the Elizabethans' elaborate, courtly verse, he writes of how "To judge between one *ethos* and another, it is necessary to have got inside both, and if literary history does not help us to do so it is a great waste of labor."[34] Many of Lewis's contemporaries condemned such verse as intolerably artificial without appreciating that such elaborate artificiality was the age's great aesthetic *donnée*.[35] To take exception to the

---

32 Newman to Mary Holmes (21 February 1875), in *LD*, XXVII, 226–7.
33 Newman, *Essay on Development*, 7.
34 C. S. Lewis, *English Literature in the Sixteenth Century* (Oxford: Oxford University Press, 1944), 330–1.
35 One of these readers was the poet Philip Larkin, who thought *The Faerie Queene* the "dullest thing" ever written. See also Henry James, "The Art of Fiction," *Longman's*

Elizabethans' ruffs would be like taking exception to the Edwardians' tea tables. Nevertheless, Lewis's historical sense, so ably deployed in the realm of literature, was absent whenever the question of the tenability of Anglicanism arose. Of course, Lewis justified his allegiance to Anglicanism by stressing that his own brand of the National Church gave him the chance to recommend "mere Christianity." But this was a phrase that he took from the *bête noir* of Hilaire Belloc, Dean Inge, not a figure to which any one would go for doctrinal depth or consistency. Then, again, even though Lewis liked to associate Anglo-Catholicism with elitism and party, charging T. S. Eliot, for example, with advocating a kind of coterie Christianity, to which ordinary people were not invited, he was fond of the doctrinal Anglo-Catholicism wrought by Richard Hooker, the Elizabethan divine who invented what Lytton Strachey (1880-1932) liked to call "the tight rope of High Anglicanism."[36] By any chalk, Lewis's allegiance to Anglicanism was fraught with inconsistency.

Indeed, if one reads Lewis's work as a whole, it teems with criticisms of precisely the sort of latitudinarianism to which Anglicanism has always been prone. In *The Screwtape Letters* (1941), for example, Wormwood's perspicacious uncle observes how "Once you have made the World an end, and faith a means, you have almost won your man, and it makes very little difference what kind of worldly end he is pursuing. Provided that meetings, pamphlets, policies, movements, causes and crusades matter more to him than prayers and sacraments and charity, he is ours—and the more 'religious' (on those terms) the more securely ours. I could show you a pretty cageful down here."[37] Then, again, Lewis has the same witty fiend make an observation that goes right to the heart of what is wrong with latitudinarianism in religion. "Talk to him about 'moderation in all things.' If you can get him to the point of thinking that 'religion is all very well up to a point,' you can feel quite happy about his soul. A moderated religion is as good for us as no religion at all—and more amusing."[38]

To give another example, in a piece called "Priestesses in the Church," Lewis is quick to reassure his readers that "No one among those who dislike the proposal is maintaining that women are less capable than men of piety, zeal, learning, and whatever else seems necessary for the pastoral office." He even goes so far as to point out that "The Middle Ages carried their reverence for one Woman to a point at which the charge could be plausibly made that the Blessed Virgin became in their eyes almost

---

Magazine (September 1884): "We must grant the artist his subject, his idea, what the French call his *donnée*; our criticism is applied only to what he makes of it."

36 Lytton Strachey, *Eminent Victorians* (London: Chatto & Windus, 1918), 19.
37 C. S. Lewis, *The Screwtape Letters* (London: Geoffrey Bles, 1941), 30.
38 Ibid., 37.

'a fourth Person of the Trinity' ... All salvation depends on the decision which she made in the words, *Ecce Ancilla*; she is united in nine months' inconceivable intimacy with the eternal Word; she stands at the foot of the cross." But when it comes to ordaining women Lewis is nonetheless adamant that administrative or even pastoral competence is not the issue: sex is, which he nicely describes as involving "not merely facts of nature but the live and awful shadows of realities utterly beyond our control and largely beyond our direct knowledge."[39] (It is writing of this calibre that prompted Flannery O'Connor, no blundering stylist herself, to say to one of her correspondents apropos Lewis: he is "deceptively simple. You have to read every sentence twice.")[40] For Lewis, a priest is "primarily a representative, who represents us to God and God to us." God is God the Father: He is not God the Mother. And for Lewis, the fact that "Christians [recognize] that God himself has taught us how to speak of Him" carries with it inviolable distinctions. "To say that it does not matter is to say either that all the masculine imagery is not inspired, is merely human imagery, or else that though inspired it is quite arbitrary and unessential. And this is surely intolerable ... it is an argument not in favour of Christian priestesses but against Christianity."[41]

Here, those who conduct their war against Christianity under the guise of feminism would have to applaud Lewis's astuteness. The feminization of the Anglican Church continues to be profoundly de-Christianizing. Why?

> The innovators are really implying that sex is something superficial, irrelevant to the spiritual life. To say that men and women are equally eligible for a certain profession is to say that for the purposes of that profession their sex is irrelevant. We are within that context, treating both as neuters. As the State grows more like a hive or ant hill it needs an increasing number of workers who can be treated as neuters. This may be inevitable for our secular life. But in our Christian life we must return to reality. There we are not homogenous units, but different and complementary organs of a mystical body.[42]

This surely is not the language of contemporary Anglicanism, or even the Anglicanism of the mid-twentieth century. In the intellectual, ethical, and spiritual travels that Lewis would undertake as a part of his lifelong conversion, he may have packed his bag in 1928 once he read Chesterton and saw that there was indeed an order to the universe that the nihilism

---

39 "Priestesses in the Church?" in *God in the Dock*, 256–7.
40 Flannery O'Connor, *The Habit of Being*, ed. Sally Fitzgerald (New York: Farrar, Straus & Giroux, 1979), 572.
41 "Priestesses in the Church?", 259.
42 *Ibid.*, 259.

of atheism could not explain, but it would be unwise to imagine that he unpacked his bag for good in an Anglicanism full of Mr. Broads. Most of my readers familiar with the work of Lewis will know to whom I refer when I refer to Mr. Broad. Of course, he is that most finely drawn character in *The Pilgrim's Regress*, with whom the hero John has such revealing conversations. In one passage, when John asks the way for the island of his longing, Mr. Broad replies: "That is a beautiful idea ... And if you trust an elder traveller, the seeking is the finding. How many happy days you have before you!" In another, John asks whether it is necessary to "cross the canyon" in order to find the island, and Mr. Broad says,

> I wouldn't for the world hold you back. At the same time, my dear boy, I think there is a very real danger at your age of trying to make these things too definite. That has been the great error of my profession in past ages. We have tried to enclose everything in formulae, to turn poetry into logic, and metaphor into dogma; and now that we are beginning to realise our mistake we find ourselves shackled by the formulae of dead men. I don't say that there were not once adequate once: but they have ceased to be adequate for us with our wider knowledge. When I became a man, I put away childish things. These great truths need to be reinterpreted in every age.[43]

Nothing could be less Catholic, more antagonistic to the principle of *semper eadem*, which is the very lifeblood of Catholic tradition. When Lewis composed an afterword for the book's third edition, ten years after the first edition, he confessed to how he regarded the book as a series of impressions, "and every one of these impressions is wrong." Indeed, he went further:

> The sole merit I claim for the book is that it is written by one who has proved them all to be wrong. There is no room for vanity in the claim: I know them to be wrong not by intelligence but by experience, such experience as would not have come way if my youth had been wiser, more virtuous, and less self-centered than it was. For I have myself been deluded by every one of these false answers in turn, and have contemplated each of them earnestly enough to discover the cheat. To have embraced so many false Florimels is no matter for boasting: it is fools, they say, who learn by experience. But since they do learn by experience they do at least learn; let a fool bring his experience into the common stock that wiser men may profit by it.[44]

And here we can identify one of the great differences between Lewis and Newman in their understanding of conversion. Lewis is preeminently

---

43 C. S. Lewis, *The Pilgrim's Regress* (London: Geoffrey Bles, 1943), 112.
44 *Ibid.*, 203.

English in his understanding of faith because it is an understanding that almost presupposes that the acquisition, exercise and nourishment of faith is largely a "do-it-yourself" affair. One can see this clearly in his conclusion to his article on the importance of theism.

> Faith, as we know it, does not flow from philosophical argument alone; nor from experience alone, nor from history alone; but from historical events which at once fulfill and transcend the moral category which link themselves with the most numinous elements in Paganism, and which (as it seems to us) demand as their presupposition the existence of a Being who is more, but not less than the God whom many philosophers think they can establish ... By Faith we hope to believe always what we hope hereafter to see always and perfectly and have already seen imperfectly and by flashes.[45]

Here, with the English lexicographers, Lewis is content to treat his subject not only without any reference to Christendom but even to any church at all. Indeed, in *Letters to Malcolm* (1964), Lewis declares that he can "well understand how a man who is trying to love God and his neighbor should come to dislike the very word *religion*, a word, by the way, which hardly ever appears in the New Testament. Newman makes my blood run cold when he says in one of the *Parochial and Plain Sermons* that Heaven is like a church because, in both, 'one single sovereign subject—religion—is brought before us.' He forgets that there is no temple in the new Jerusalem." Indeed, for Lewis, Newman "substituted *religion* for God."[46]

To determine whether this is just, one needs to see the full passage from Newman's sermon, "Holiness Necessary for Future Blessedness" (1826), where the point he makes is not that religion is a substitute for God but that it is an essential means of discovering, understanding, and honoring God.

> Heaven then is not like this world; I will say what it is much more like,—a church. For in a place of public worship no language of this world is heard; there are no schemes brought forward for temporal objects, great or small; no information how to strengthen our worldly interests, extend our influence, or establish our credit. These things indeed may be right in their way, so that we do not set our hearts upon them; still (I repeat), it is certain that we hear nothing of them in a church. Here we hear solely and entirely of God. We praise Him, worship Him, sing to Him, thank Him, confess to Him, give ourselves up to Him, and ask His blessing. And therefore, a church is like heaven; viz. because both in the one and the other, there is one single sovereign subject—religion—brought before us.[47]

---

45 Lewis, "Is Theism Important?" 191.
46 C. S. Lewis, *Letters to Malcolm* (New York: Harcourt Brace Javonovich, 1964), 29–30.
47 Sermon 1, in *PPS*, I, 4–5.

Why Lewis chose to take so unjust a swipe at Newman is not difficult to see. Lewis lashed out against the great convert because he knew that he was on indefensible ground when it came to what Newman called the "One True Fold," and in disparaging Newman he was attempting to deflect attention away from this vulnerability, which only became more nettlesome as he aged.[48] Lewis might also have never forgiven Newman for drawing up the eighth proposition in his Note on Liberalism in the *Apologia*, which states that "There is a system of religion more simply true than Christianity as it has ever been received," not a proposition which could have pleased the author of *Mere Christianity*.[49] And yet and yet, when Lewis speaks himself of his conversion he writes in a language that must deeply resonate with every Catholic, especially those aware of how reluctant the natural man is to abandon the illusions inimical to conversion. Here is a familiar passage from *Surprised by Joy*, a letter Lewis wrote to his dear friend Arthur Greeves, which merits quoting nonetheless.

> You must picture me alone in that room in Magdalen, night after night, feeling, whenever my mind lifted even for a second from my work, the steady, unrelenting approach of Him whom I so earnestly desired not to meet. That which I greatly feared had at last come upon me. In the Trinity Term of 1929 I gave in, and admitted that God was God, and knelt and prayed: perhaps, that night, the most dejected and reluctant convert in all England. I did not then see what is now the most shining and obvious thing; the Divine humility which will accept a convert even on such terms. The Prodigal Son at least walked home on his own feet. But who can duly adore that Love which will open the high gates to a prodigal who is brought in kicking, struggling, resentful, and darting his eyes in every direction for a chance of escape? The words "compelle intrare," compel them to come in, have been so abused by wicked men that we shudder at them; but, properly understood, they plumb the depth of the Divine mercy. The hardness of God is kinder than the softness of men, and His compulsion is our liberation.[50]

Newman's conversion was similarly reluctant—he dreaded unsettling the faith of his many Anglican friends—but unlike Lewis he came to believe that his very salvation depended upon his seceding from a fold about which he was otherwise deeply solicitous. As he wrote his sister Jemima, "If I thought any other body but that which I recognise to be the Catholic

---

48 See Newman's letter, "I am this night expecting Father Dominic the Passionist, whom I shall ask to admit me into the Old True Fold. This letter will not go until it is over." Newman to F. W. Faber (8 October 1845), in *LD*, XI, 7.

49 *Apologia*, 260.

50 C. S. Lewis, *Surprised by Joy* (London: Geoffrey Bles, 1955), 228–9.

to be recognised by the Saviour of the world, I would not have left that body."[51] The distinguished Lewis scholar James Como speculates that if Lewis had left the Anglican for the Catholic Church, his influence would have "declined pronouncedly."[52] When Newman's sister Jemima said the same thing to Newman after he converted, her brother's response was characteristic. "Nothing you say about my loss of influence has any tendency to hurt me, as you kindly fear it should ... The pain indeed, which I knew I was giving individuals, has affected me much—but as to influence, the whole world is one great vanity, and I trust I am not set on any thing in it."[53] If Lewis had had the same view, and acted accordingly, his far-ranging influence might have been more far-ranging still.

Then, again, it is important to stress how keenly aware Newman was of the inescapable failure that must attend his work as an Oratorian in nineteenth-century England. There was, after all, so much that needed to be done to revive the Catholic Church in England and so little time in which to do it. In his "Reformation of the Eleventh Century" (1841), Newman could have been writing of himself when he wrote of the great reformer Pope Gregory VII (1020–85):

> On the 25th of May, 1085, [Gregory] peacefully closed his earthly career; just rallying strength, amid the exhaustion of his powers, to utter, with his departing breath, the words, "I have loved justice and hated iniquity; and therefore I die in exile."
>
> "In exile!" said a prelate who stood by his bed, "... in exile thou canst not die! Vicar of Christ and His Apostles, thou hast received the nations for thine inheritance, and the uttermost parts of the earth for thy possession."
>
> Gregory thought he had failed: so it is; often a cause seems to decline as its champion grows in years, and to die in his death; but this is to judge hastily; others are destined to complete what he began. No man is given to see his work through. "Man goeth forth unto his work and to his labour until the evening," but the evening falls before it is done. There was One alone who began and finished and died.[54]

The differences inherent in their respective conversions notwithstanding, Newman and Lewis were still kindred spirits in many ways. Certainly, there were many aspects about Lewis that Newman would have found

---

51 Newman to Mrs. Jemima Mozley (9 October 1845), in *LD*, XI, 14.
52 See James Como, "C. S. Lewis' Quantum Church," in *C. S. Lewis and the Church*, ed. Judith Wolfe and Brendan N. Wolfe (London: Bloomsbury, 2011), 93.
53 Newman to Mrs. Jemima Mozley (14 October 1845), in *LD*, XI, 16.
54 Newman, "Reformation in the Eleventh Century," in *Essays Critical and Historical*, II, 316–17.

appealing—his humility, his intellectual honesty, the bravery with which he professed his Christian faith in an Oxbridge contemptuous of Christian profession. If Newman thought that there were only two ultimate positions that one could take with respect to Christian faith—Catholicism or atheism—he also recognized that many were necessarily in transit between the two opposite poles. The Enlightenment's assault on faith, which both Novalis and Newman felt so deeply, had left so many unsettled in their faith. On the uncertain circuit between Catholicism and atheism, Lewis was nearer to Catholicism than he might have wished to admit, though why he chose to stay put in a communion with which he had so many fundamental disagreements must always remain a mystery. In trying to understand what might have been the significance of his not making the final step, I have always been helped by a passage in Newman's letters. In answer to Lady Margaret Heywood, who confessed that one of the reasons she was reluctant to leave the Anglican Church was that it was so full of admirably devout Anglican Christians, Newman's response was intriguing.

> I grant the high religious excellence of men such as those you name. Far be it from me to assert that they have in wilfulness shut their eyes to light, which has been granted them and which would have led them on into the Catholic Church ... but we must look at ourselves individually, not at others. Recollect there is an election of grace. Some, and not all, are elected for the privileges and blessings of the Kingdom. We shall all be judged according to our opportunities. The question is whether you and I are called, not why others are not. "We cannot be as they." You ask, is not the fact that certain good men are contented with the Church of England a proof that that Church is part of the Catholic Church. Since their virtues and various excellences must come from God, does not therefore their teaching come from God also? Are they not raised up in order by their strong protests, such as have been made to you to hinder souls from going to Rome? This you seem to say; but surely there is another supposable reason for God's dealings with them. They are kept where they are ... being Anglicans in good faith, in order gradually to prepare their hearers and readers in greater numbers than otherwise would be possible for the true and perfect faith, and to lead hearers or readers on in due season into the Catholic Church.[55]

Is it too fanciful to number C. S. Lewis among those good Anglicans whom Newman describes here? Certainly, he sought to remind Anglicans of their historical fidelity to "mere Christianity." And of course, remaining within the Protestant pale enabled him to dispatch a lively number of converts to the Catholic Church, including Walter Hooper and Thomas

---

55 Newman to Lady Margaret Heywood (15 November 1875), in *LD*, XXVII, 377.

Howard, both of whom are capable apologists in their own right, proof that they profitably put themselves to school to one of the greatest of all twentieth-century apologists. Newman, however, could never have remained an Anglican. In fact, in one of his notebooks, after his conversion, he jotted down some amusingly candid verses.

> Any who have died Protestants through me
> Make up to them and forgive me
> The defects of my ministrations.[56]

Father Aidan Nichols, O.P., the dizzyingly prolific theologian, sees Lewis as a necessary ally in the reconversion of England, the grounds for which he sets out in three books laced with admiring references to Lewis: *Christendom, Awake* (1999), *The Realm* (2008) and *Lessons in a Rose-Garden: Reviving the Doctrinal Rosary* (2012). In *The Realm*, he has occasion to praise Lewis's "mere Christianity" for being "positive, self-consistent and inexhaustible." For Nichols, it takes both sympathy and tough-mindedness to appreciate that Lewis was not trying to "indicate that all the verities of faith and order that Jesus Christ instructed his apostles to preserve and disseminate until the world's end are comprised within these central beliefs and moral suasions." Father Nichols does not overlook the fact that "Evangelicals, Anglo-Catholics, conservative Lutherans, Orthodox and Roman Catholics have issues of substance to debate even when they remain firmly committed to the basic truths of the revelation in action of the Father through the incarnated Son and outpoured Spirit for the world's salvation—and to the moral practice which belongs with the life of the Kingdom won by Christ's atoning work."[57] Yet, for Nichols, Lewis is to be commended for encouraging different Christians to see and honor this shared commitment to "the life of the Kingdom won by Christ's atoning work." Certainly, Lewis, despite his uneasy allegiance to the National Church, was always prepared to fight the good fight, even, or perhaps one should say especially in circumstances that were far from propitious.

> In the first place, it must be admitted by anyone who accepts Christianity, that an increased interest in it, or even a growing measure of intellectual assent to it, is a very different thing from the conversion of England or even of a single soul. Conversion requires an alteration of the will, and an alteration which, in the last resort, does not occur without the intervention of the supernatural. I do not in the least agree with those who therefore conclude that the spread of

---

56 Quoted in Gerard Skinner, *Newman the Priest: A Father of Souls* (Leominster: Gracewing, 2010), 295.
57 Aidan Nichols, *Christendom Awake: On Re-energizing the Church in Culture* (London: Bloomsbury, 1999), 195–6.

an intellectual (and imaginative) climate favorable to Christianity is useless. You do not prove munition workers useless by showing that they cannot themselves win battles, however proper this reminder would be if they attempted to claim the honour due to fighting men. If the intellectual climate is such that, when a man comes to the crisis at which he must either accept or reject Christ, his reason and imagination are not on the wrong side, then his conflict will be fought out under favourable conditions. Those who help to produce and spread such a climate are therefore doing useful work: and yet no such great matter after all. Their share is a modest one; and it is always possible that nothing—nothing whatever—may come of it. Far higher than they stands the character whom, to the best of my knowledge, the present Christian movement has not yet produced—the *Preacher* in the full sense, the Evangelist, the man on fire, the man who infects. The propagandist, the apologist, only represents John the Baptist: the Preacher represents the Lord Himself. He will be sent—or else he will not. But unless he comes we mere Christian intellectuals will not effect very much. That does not mean we should down tools.[58]

Newman's idea of the conversion of England was not altogether dissimilar. In an address to the Duke of Norfolk and the Catholic Union that he gave in 1880, he asked himself what previous English Catholics "would understand now by praying for the conversion of England," and he answered "that they would contemplate an object present, immediate, concrete, and in the way of Providence; and it would be ... not the conversion of England to the Catholic Church, but the growth of the Catholic Church in England." For Newman, his Catholic predecessors

> would expect again, by their prayers, nothing sudden, nothing violent, nothing evidently miraculous, nothing inconsistent with the free will of our countrymen, nothing out of keeping with the majestic march of slow but sure triumph of truth and right in this turbulent world. They would look for the gradual, steady, and sound advance of Catholicity by ordinary means and scenes, which are properly acts and proceedings which are good and holy. They would pray for the conversion of individuals, and for a great many of them, and out of all ranks and classes, and those especially who are, in faith and devotion, nearest to the Church, and seem, if they do not themselves defeat it, to be the objects of God's election, for a removal from the public mind of all prejudices about us, for better understanding of what we hold and what we do not hold, for a feeling of goodwill and respectful bearing in the population towards our Bishops and priests, for a growing capacity in the educated classes of entering

---

58 "The Decline of Religion," in *God in the Dock*, 231.

into a just appreciation of our characteristic opinions, sentiments, ways, and principles, and, in order to effect all this, for a blessing upon our controversialists, that they may be gifted with an abundant measure of prudence, self-command, tact, knowledge of men and things, good sense, candour, and straightforwardness, that their reputation may be high, and their influence wide and deep, and as a special means, and most necessary for our success, for a larger increase in the Catholic body of brotherly love, mutual sympathy, unanimity, and high principle, rectitude of conduct, purity of life.[59]

For all of his opposition to the papacy and to what he regarded as Rome's extravagant devotion to Our Lady, Lewis would have welcomed these sentiments. So many of them, after all, coincided with his own understanding of the obligations of conversion, even though he might have been uncomfortable with the fact that they were not entirely the sort of thing that would have met with the approval of his Ulster nurse.

---

59 *Sayings of Cardinal Newman* (London: Burns & Oates, 1890), 67–8.

✢ 8 ✢
Newman Distilled

Newman Distilled

The Genius of John Henry Newman: Selections from his Writings, edited with an introduction by Ian Ker. Oxford University Press. 341 pages

WHEN JOHN HENRY NEWMAN died in 1890, English papers around the world singled out different aspects of his life and work for praise or censure but on one point they were unanimous. As the obituarist of the *Colonies and India* put it, "We question whether there is a living writer who had a command of the English tongue at once so eloquent and incisive, though often ironical."[1] The force of Newman's style may have been universally acknowledged but the content of the writing was rarely paid the attention it deserves. Then, as now, Newman had many admirers and many detractors but few critics. Indeed, for many, insisting on the beauty of Newman's style was a convenient way of ignoring the style's content altogether.

There is a parallel of this in the way that Newman's contemporaries tended to take up religion. In one of his greatest sermons, "Unreal Words" (1839), Newman observed how profession could become an evasion not only of the practice but even the apprehension of religion. "Let us never lose sight of two truths," he exhorted his readers, "that we ought to have our hearts penetrated with the love of Christ and full of self-renunciation; but that if they be not, professing that they are does not make them so." Similarly, effusing about the beauty of Newman's prose style can never be a substitute for entering into the matter that the style articulates.

If there is a tendency on the part of some to separate style from content in Newman's work, instead of seeing them, as they need to be seen, as indivisible, it might stem from the example of two other prose stylists of the nineteenth century, Ruskin and Froude, whose styles often have a life of their own, quite independent from their content. Certainly, one does not have to enter into Ruskin's quixotic attack on Renaissance Venice to enjoy the majestic music of *The Stones of Venice* or Froude's defense of Henry VIII to find the prose of his Tudor histories spellbinding. But one cannot arrive at a just estimate of Newman's prose without entering into the truths that

---

[1] LD, XXXII, 587.

the prose was written to impart. Newman was a great stylist because he had great things to say, not (as was so often the case with Ruskin) because he was simply a master of language, although he was that as well.

Newman is amusing on this subject in his *Idea of a University* (1873) where he writes of how

> We read in Persian travels of the way in which young gentlemen go to work in the East, when they would engage in correspondence with those who inspire them with hope or fear. They cannot write one sentence themselves; so they betake themselves to the professional letter-writer ... They have a point to gain from a superior, a favour to ask, an evil to deprecate; they have to approach a man in power, or to make court to some beautiful lady. The professional man manufactures words for them, as they are wanted, as a stationer sells them paper, or a schoolmaster might cut their pens. Thought and word are, in their conception, two things, and thus there is a division of labour. The man of thought comes to the man of words; and the man of words, duly instructed in the thought, dips the pen of desire into the ink of devotedness, and proceeds to spread it over the page of desolation. Then the nightingale of affection is heard to warble to the rose of loveliness, while the breeze of anxiety plays around the brow of expectation.[2]

In contrast to this "division of labour," Newman was adamant that "thought and speech are inseparable from each other. Matter and expression are parts of one: style is a thinking out into language."

One can open Ian Ker's excellent anthology, *The Genius of John Henry Newman*, at nearly any page and find examples of how the brilliance of Newman's style issues directly from the brilliance of what he has to say. On the worldly pseudo-Christianity that is as much a part of our society as it was of his, he speaks of "an existing teaching ... built upon worldly principle, yet pretending to be the Gospel, dropping one whole side of the Gospel, its austere character, and considering it enough to be benevolent, courteous, candid, correct in conduct, delicate, — though it includes no true fear of God, no fervent zeal for His honour, no deep hatred of sin." Such a mundane religion puts Newman in mind of the far more unworldly Middle Ages, which his Protestant contemporaries were disposed to regard as lost in Roman error and corruption. For Newman, "the present age is the very contrary to what are commonly called the dark ages; and together with the faults of those ages we have lost their virtues. I say their virtues; for even the errors then prevalent, a persecuting spirit, for instance, fear of religious inquiry, bigotry, these were, after

---

2 *The Idea of a University*, 233.

all, but perversions and excesses of *real virtues*, such as zeal and reverence; and we, instead of limiting and purifying them, have taken them away root and branch. Why? because we have not acted from a love of the Truth, but from the influence of the Age."[3]

Here, also, is a good example of the conversational character that Gerard Manley Hopkins commended in Newman's work. "What Cardinal Newman does is to think aloud," the poet discerned, "to think with pen and paper ... He seems to be thinking 'Gibbon is the last great master of traditional English prose; he is its perfection; I do not propose to emulate him; I begin all over again from the language of conversation, of common life.'"[4]

This was an astute insight because, for all of his dazzling attainments, Newman paid very close attention to "common life." It was an expression of his deep respect for the importunate claims of reality. Consequently, the limpidity of his prose is of a piece with the naturalness, the sincerity, the humility of the man himself. Dean Church, the author of what remains the greatest history of the Oxford Movement, made a number of observations in his obituary of Newman in the *Guardian*—an Anglican paper in the nineteenth century—which nicely corroborate Hopkins's point.

> It is common to speak of the naturalness and ease of Cardinal Newman's style in writing. It is, of course, the first thing that attracts notice when we open one of his books; and there are people who think it bald and thin and dry. They look out for longer words, and grander phrases, and more involved constructions, and neater epigrams. They expect a great theme to be treated with more pomp and majesty, and they are disappointed. But the majority of English readers seem to be agreed in recognising the beauty and transparent flow of language, which matches the best French writing in rendering with sureness and without effort the thought of the writer. But what is more interesting than even the formation of such a style—a work, we may be sure, not accomplished without much labour—is the man behind the style. For the man and the style are one in this perfect naturalness and ease. Any one who has watched at all carefully the Cardinal's career, whether in old days or later, must have been struck with this feature of his character, his naturalness, the freshness and freedom with which he addressed a friend or expressed an opinion, the absence of all mannerism and formality; and where he had to keep his dignity, both his loyal obedience to the authority which enjoined it and the half-amused, half-bored impatience that he should be the person round whom

---

[3] Newman, "The Religion of the Day" (1832), Sermon 24, in *PPS*, I, 313–14.
[4] Gerald Manley Hopkins to Coventry Patmore (20 October 1887), in *The Collected Works of Gerard Manley Hopkins, Volume II: Correspondence 1882–1889*, ed. R. K. R. Thornton and Catherine Phillips (Oxford: Oxford University Press, 2013), 898–9.

all these grand doings centred. It made the greatest difference in his friendships whether his friends met him on equal terms, or whether they brought with them too great conventional deference or solemnity of manner. He was by no means disposed to allow liberties to be taken or to put up with impertinence; for all that bordered on the unreal, for all that was pompous, conceited, affected he had little patience; but almost beyond all these was his disgust at being made the object of foolish admiration. He protested with whimsical fierceness against being made a hero or a sage; he was what he was, he said, and nothing more, and he was inclined to be rude when people tried to force him into an eminence which he refused. With his profound sense of the incomplete and the ridiculous in this world, and with a humour in which the grotesque and the pathetic sides of life were together recognised every moment, he never hesitated to admit his own mistakes.[5]

These are the qualities that make the *Apologia pro Vita Sua* (1864), Newman's great autobiography, such a special book. Far from being an exercise in self-vindication, as some have insinuated, it is full of the most guileless honesty.

If we recognize that Newman's style is the natural efflorescence of his thought, we will also see that that thought is the expression of a very versatile personality, all of whose preoccupations bespeak a rare unity of purpose. Father Ker does this unity justice by distilling Newman's vast output in terms of what he wrote as an educator, philosopher, theologian, preacher and writer.

Thus, in the education section, there are brilliant passages from *The Idea of a University*, demonstrating the perennial appeal of Newman's educational insights, especially at a time when the incoherence of our own universities could not be more patent. In the philosophy section, there are wonderfully choice extracts from *A Grammar of Assent* (1870), which provide a useful key to that otherwise difficult book. Then, again, Newman's preaching is nicely epitomized by a generous sampling of his *Parochial and Plain Sermons* (1868). In the section on his theological writings, there are extracts from both his Anglican and his Catholic periods, showing the striking cohesiveness of his theological work, as well as something that Chesterton once remarked: "All Christianity concentrates on the man at the cross-roads."[6] And lastly,

---

5 Richard William Church, "Cardinal Newman's Naturalness," in *Occasional Papers* (London: Macmillan & Co., 1897), II, 480–1.
6 "All Christianity concentrates on the man at the cross-roads. The vast and shallow philosophies, the huge syntheses of humbug, all talk about ages and evolution and ultimate developments. The true philosophy is concerned with the instant. Will a man take this road or that? that is the only thing to think about, if you enjoy thinking. The aeons are easy enough to think about, any one can think about them. The instant

Newman Distilled

there is a splendid chapter on Newman the writer, which highlights not only his polemical but his satirical genius. From Newman's caustic essay, "The Anglo-American Church" (1839), for example, Father Ker includes that wonderful passage where Newman captures the essence of our refined Unitarians: "They want only so much religion as will satisfy their natural perception of the propriety of being religious. Reason teaches them that utter disregard of their Maker is unbecoming, and they determine to be religious, not from love and fear, but from good sense."[7]

Father Ker is to be commended for choosing his selections with such consummate care. Here, in three hundred pages, he exhibits the power and the unity of Newman's work with the same critical discrimination with which he exhibited the trials and turning points of Newman's heroic life in his magisterial biography. In addition, he includes terse, shrewd, informative introductions to each of the sections. Under the section of extracts devoted to Newman the writer, for example, Father Ker observes: "Like Cicero, whom Newman greatly admired both as a controversialist and as a master of style, it is hardly possible to imagine Newman without his letters, so integral do they seem to his artistic and intellectual achievement. Not only does the corpus of correspondence provide a detailed and extended commentary on the published works, but it is in itself a marvelous manifestation of Newman's powers as an 'occasional writer.'"[8] This is true: the voluminous letters abound with Newman's impromptu splendor.

For readers seeking either an introduction or a re-introduction to the work of this wonderfully fascinating figure, Father Ker's anthology will be indispensable. Especially in an age like ours, an age of intellectual muddle and religious philistinism, an age in which liberals and neo-Modernists continue to misrepresent the work of Newman to advance their own impious purposes, it is important to have an

---

is really awful: and it is because our religion has intensely felt the instant, that it has in literature dealt much with battle and in theology dealt much with hell. It is full of *danger*, like a boy's book: it is at an immortal crisis. There is a great deal of real similarity between popular fiction and the religion of the western people. If you say that popular fiction is vulgar and tawdry, you only say what the dreary and well-informed say also about the images in the Catholic churches. Life (according to the faith) is very like a serial story in a magazine: life ends with the promise (or menace) 'to be continued in our next.' Also, with a noble vulgarity, life imitates the serial and leaves off at the exciting moment. For death is distinctly an exciting moment." Gilbert Keith Chesterton, *Orthodoxy* (1908), in *G. K. Chesterton Collected Works*, ed. David Dooley (San Francisco: Ignatius Press, 1986), I, 341.

7 John Henry Newman, "The Anglo-American Church," *The British Critic* (October 1839), *Essays Historical and Critical*, I, 349.

8 *The Genius of John Henry Newman*, ed. Ian Ker (Oxford: Oxford University Press, 1989), 284.

introduction to the full range of Newman's work that is at once sound and perceptive. Ker's anthology fits that bill. It is also worth pointing out that Oxford University Press has actually printed the book on proper paper and bound it with some eye to durability—a welcome departure from its usual egregious production standards.

9

Newman and the Law

Newman and the Law

I

IN 1866, BLESSED JOHN HENRY NEWMAN had occasion to write to a good friend of his, Lady Chatterton (1806–76), who, though converted to Rome in 1865, could not entirely reconcile herself to what she regarded as the foreignness of the Catholic faith. Born into a strong High Church family—her father was the Reverend Lascelles Iremonger, prebendary of Winchester—she had particular difficulties with those doctrines pertaining to the Real Presence and the Blessed Virgin. Newman responded to her doubts with a letter of characteristic acuteness, in which he addressed the same core difficulty that prevented so many Anglicans from even considering, much less acceding to the claims of Rome. Newman wrote:

> Every society has its own ways; it is not wonderful then, that the Catholic Church has its own way of praying, its own ceremonies, and the like. These are strange and perhaps at first unwelcome to those who come to them from elsewhere, just as foreign manners are unpleasant to those who never travelled. We all like home best, because we understand the ways of home. Abraham doubtless found his life in Canaan not so pleasant to him, as his native Mesopotamia. We ever must sacrifice something, to gain great blessings. If the Catholic Church is from God, to belong to her is a make-up for many losses. We must beg of God to change our tastes and habits, and to make us love for His sake what by nature we do not love.[1]

These were lessons peculiarly suited to English ears, for English tastes and English habits were profoundly at odds with Roman Catholicism. Indeed, as late as December 1844, Newman himself confided to his dear friend John Keble: "No one could have a more unfavorable view than I have of the present state of the Roman Catholics—so much so that any who joined them would be like the Cistercians at Fountains, living under trees till their

---

1 Newman to Lady Chatterton (Holy Thursday 1866), in *LD*, XXII, 194.

house was built."² It was only after he read St. Ignatius's *Spiritual Exercises* that he finally embraced what he would call the "one true Fold of the Redeemer," though even after he converted he still needed time to adjust to his new affiliation.³ In this essay I shall revisit Newman's letters and sermons to show how instrumental the law was in helping him to understand what it truly meant to be an English Catholic in a Protestant country.

Newman first began taking stock of the historical place of the Catholic Church in England after the reconstitution of the hierarchy in 1850 by Archbishop Wiseman. In his great sermon about this historical reconstitution, "The Second Spring" (1852), he wrote of how "Three centuries ago, the Catholic Church, that great creation of God's power, stood in this land in pride of place. It had the honours of near a thousand years upon it; it was enthroned in some twenty sees up and down the broad country; it was based in the will of a faithful people; it energized through ten thousand instruments of power and influence; and it was ennobled by a host of Saints and Martyrs." Mindful of this rich history, he could only marvel that the Church should now strike even Catholic converts as alien. And he would have been particularly conscious of this melancholy irony in the case of Lady Chatterton because she was a close friend of the Ferrers family, who had owned Baddesley Clinton, the moated manor house in what had been the Forest of Arden in Warwickshire since the fifteenth century, a manor house which epitomized English recusancy. Last year, Jack Scarisbrick, the great biographer of Henry VIII, and an indefatigable pro-lifer, gave me a guided tour of the house, with its ingenious priest-holes and portraits of Lady Chatterton and Newman. The ghosts of Catholicism can still be encountered at every turn in twenty-first-century England but they positively pullulate at Baddesley Clinton.

Here, during the Elizabethan terror, heroic Jesuits had sought to win back English souls to the traditional faith at a time when defending that faith was a capital crime. In October of 1591, at five o'clock in the morning, the manor was raided by pursuivants. Father Henry Garnet, Father Robert Southwell, Father Edward Oldcorne and six others evaded capture by standing in ankle-deep water for four hours in a sewer converted to a hiding-place. Historians debate whether the Jesuit missionaries only made matters worse for English Catholics. Penry Williams, one of the more evenhanded historians of the later Tudors, points to the poet John Donne as an instructive case in point.

> John Donne's brother Henry harboured a priest in London, was arrested, imprisoned, and died in Newgate of the plague. Donne

---

2 Newman to John Keble (29 December 1844), in *LD*, X, 476. For Newman's reading of the Spiritutal Exercises of St. Ignatius Loyola, see Newman to John Keble (15 April 1843), in *LD*, IX, 307–8.

3 Newman to Mrs. John Mozley (8 October 1845), in *LD*, XI, 9.

himself was profoundly marked and torn by the experience, for to desert the faith led to the fires of hell, while remaining within it exposed him to the fate of his brother; and, after undergoing intense internal conflict, he chose apostasy and thereafter reserved a special hatred for the Jesuits, who had, he believed, imperiled his family and forced his conversion.[4]

Such recriminations were the tragic outcrop of persecution. The extent of the late Tudor persecution was not inconsiderable: between 1581 and 1603, 131 priests and 60 lay persons were executed.[5] To blame the Jesuit missionaries for this state butchery seems hardly fair, even though Elizabeth and her councilors did succeed in using the Jesuits to brand Catholicism foreign.

If the failure of the Jesuit mission haunted subsequent English history, it put Newman in mind of the efficacy of the English Reformation. Long before the historians Geoffrey Elton, Jack Scarisbrick, Christopher Haigh and Eamon Duffy anatomized the unpopularity of the English Reformation, Newman showed how Protestantism had been imposed on the English through the power and majesty of the law. "It was plain," Newman wrote in his *Lectures on the Present Position of Catholics in England* (1851), "what had to be done to perpetuate Protestantism" in a country where Protestant ideas had not found any popular footing.

> Convoke the legislature, pass some sweeping ecclesiastical enactments, exalt the Crown above the Law and the Gospel, down with the Cross and up with the lion and the dog, toss all priests out of the country as traitors; let Protestantism be the passport to office and authority, force the King to be a Protestant, make his Court Protestant, bind Houses of Parliament to be Protestant, clap a Protestant oath upon judges, barristers-at-law, officers in army and navy, members of the universities, national clergy; establish this stringent Tradition in every function and department of the State, surround it with the luster of rank, wealth, station, name, and talent; and this people, so careless of abstract truth, so apathetic to historical fact, so contemptuous of foreign ideas, will *ex animo* swear to the truth of a religion which indulges their natural turn of mind, and involves no severe thought or tedious application.[6]

Newman also saw that the most effective way to establish this otherwise uncongenial religion was to make it inseparable from the English Sovereign. And here Newman brought his shrewd grasp of psychology to bear to show with what blithe cynicism this was accomplished. The practical, commercial

---

4 See Penry Williams, *The Later Tudors: England 1547–1603* (Oxford: Oxford University Press, 1995), 475.
5 Ibid.
6 *Present Position of Catholics*, 63.

English "would be sure to revolt from the unnatural speculations of Calvin ... and the dreamy and sensual doctrines of Luther. The emptiness of a ceremonial, and the affectation of a priesthood" could be "no bribe to its business-like habits and its ingrained love of the tangible."[7] It therefore became necessary for those whom Newman called "the ruling spirits of the English Reformation" to find another way "to make Protestantism live; and that was to embody it in the person of its Sovereign.

> English Protestantism is the religion of the throne: it is represented, realised, taught, transmitted in the succession of monarchs and an hereditary aristocracy. It is religion grafted upon loyalty; and its strength is not in argument, not in fact, not in the unanswerable controversialist, not in an apostolical succession, not in sanction of Scripture—but in a royal road to faith, in backing up a King whom men see, against a Pope whom they do not see. The devolution of its crown is the tradition of its creed; and to doubt its truth is to be disloyal towards its Sovereign. Kings are an Englishman's saints and doctors; he likes somebody or something at which he can cry "huzzah," and throw up his hat. Bluff King Hal, glorious Bess, the Royal Martyr, the Merry Monarch, the pious and immortal William, the good King George, royal personages very different from each other,—nevertheless, as being royal, none of them comes amiss, but they are all of them the objects of his devotion, and the resolution of his Christianity.[8]

Having uncovered the top-down strategy of Thomas Cromwell and his Reformation gentry, whom William Cobbett considered incomparable "for cool, placid, unruffled impudence,"[9] Newman proceeded to describe the cult of "glorious Bess," which was instrumental in consolidating the gains of the Reformation. "The Virgin Queen rose in her strength; she held her court, she showed herself to her people; she gathered round her peer and squire, alderman and burgess, army and navy, lawyer and divine, student and artisan. She made an appeal to the chivalrous and the loyal, and forthwith all that was noble, powerful, dignified, splendid and intellectual, touched the hilt of their swords, and spread their garments in the way for her to tread upon."[10] Here was the Virgin Queen's cult, which had been carefully concocted to replace devotion to the Blessed Virgin, which, in turn, had been bundled away with the Dissolution of the Monasteries. Impressive though these depredations were, they would not alone sustain

---

7 Ibid., 61–2.
8 Ibid.
9 William Cobbett, *A History of the Protestant Reformation in England and Ireland* (London: Burns Oates & Washbourne, 1896), 15.
10 *Present Position of Catholics*, 64.

the new Protestant Establishment: something else was required and, again, the law was key, as Newman appreciated.

> And first of all [Elizabeth I] addressed herself to the Law; and that not only because it was the proper foundation of a national structure, but also inasmuch as, from the nature of the case, it was her surest and most faithful ally. The Law is a science, and therefore takes for granted afterwards whatever it has once determined; hence it followed, that once Protestant, it would be always Protestant; it could be depended on; let Protestantism be recognised as a principle of the Constitution, and every decision, to the end of time, would but illustrate Protestant doctrines and consolidate Protestant interests. In the eye of the Law precedent is the measure of truth, and order the proof of reasonableness, and acceptableness the test of orthodoxy. It moves forward by a majestic tradition, faithful to its principles, regardless of theory and speculation, and therefore eminently fitted to be the vehicle of English Protestantism such as we have described it, and to co-operate with the monarchical principle in its establishment.[11]

Newman then went on to show how this "majestic tradition" would impact "a number of delicate questions which had been contested in previous centuries, and had hither-to been involved in contradictory precedents." Long-standing disputes between the Pontificate and the Regale, Rufus and St. Anselm, Henry the Second and St. Thomas, Henry of Winchester and St. Edmund—all would receive the same "Protestant solution." In every case, the king would be in the right and the saints in the wrong. Indeed, "the eighth Harry had settled [his dispute] his own way, when, on Cardinal Fisher's refusing to acknowledge his spiritual power, he had, without hesitation, proceeded to cut off his head." The new rulings would be unvarying: "whatever the Crown had claimed was to be its due, whatever the Pope claimed was to be a usurpation. What could be more simple and conclusive?"[12]

The parallels between the Protestant establishment that was put in place in the sixteenth century and the anti-life, anti-family, antinomian establishment into which it has evolved are too numerous to name but it is obvious that they both derive their otherwise tenuous coherence from the same coercive power of the law. The only difference between the two is that, in what Edmund Adamus refers to as "the epicenter of the culture of death," it is no longer merely English Protestantism that connives in the tyranny of the deified State: the English Catholic episcopate also plays its accommodationist part.[13]

---

11 *Ibid.*
12 *Ibid.*, 64–5.
13 See Edmund Adamus in *Zenit* (23 August 2010).

II

It is intriguing to think of what Newman might have made of his life if he had chosen the law over the Church. Most of his contemporaries agreed that he would have made a superb barrister. His younger brother Frank might have been eccentric in many ways—he was fond of wearing rugs instead of overcoats and a rabid foe of meat, tobacco, drink and vivisection long before such fads became *de rigueur* among subscribers to the higher atheism—but he was sound on his brother's considerable rhetorical skills. Frank noted in a memoir that he wrote after Newman's death:

> I have often heard the remark, that if he had become a barrister, whether in Common Law or Chancery, he would have been eminent among the few ... His fine taste and 'subtlety' would have suited Chancery, and from Cicero he had learned the art of pommelling broadly enough for any Jury. He urgently needed a thesis to attack or defend, some authority as the goal of his eloquence, or *concessions* made by another: then he had a start. In his conversation, as soon as he had extracted adequate concessions, he was a powerful reasoner, entangling, like Socrates, the unwary disputant.[14]

G. K. Chesterton captured this quality in Newman best: "The quality of his logic is that of a long but passionate patience, which waits until he has fixed all corners of an iron trap. But the quality of his moral comment on the age remains what I have said: a protest of the rationality of religion as against the increasing irrationality of mere Victorian comfort and compromise."[15]

Newman's father, a banker in the City, initially expected his bright, capable son to enter one of the Inns of Court. Newman, for a brief spell, was fully prepared to oblige his father, confessing in a fragment of autobiography, how, as he said, "I hoped great things for myself, not liking to go into the Church, but to the Law." But "these dreams of a secular ambition ... departed from him, never to return."[16]

Still, Newman had no illusions about what his choice would entail in terms of worldly disadvantages. To his mother, in 1829, he admitted that "The Church party ... is poor in mental endowments. It has not activity, shrewdness, dexterity, eloquence, practical powers. On what then does it depend? on prejudice and bigotry."[17] Later in life, he contrasted the Catholic Church in England with the Established Church and observed:

---

14 Francis W. Newman, *Contributions Chiefly to the Early History of the Late Cardinal Newman* (London: K. Paul, 1891), 44.

15 Gilbert Keith Chesterton, "The Victorian Age in Literature" (1903), in *G. K. Chesterton: Collected Works*, ed. Alzina Stone Dale (San Francisco: Ignatius Press, 1989), XV, 441.

16 *Autobiographical Writings*, 45.

17 Newman to Mrs. Jemima Newman (13 March 1829), in *LD*, II, 130.

we ought to realize what a small body we are. You compare and contrast us with the Church of England; but think of the numbers, the wealth, the prestige, the popularity, the political weight of that communion; of the knowledge of the world, the learning, the traditions of its three centuries. Think of its place in English history, its biographies, ecclesiastical and lay, its noble buildings, memorials often of the Catholic past but in the occupation of Protestantism — what have we to show per contra? the Gunpowder Plot, and the blundering Stuarts![18]

After deciding to enter the Church, Newman would always maintain a keen interest in the law, as his letters attest. When his good friend Henry Wilberforce, one of the Great Liberator's sons was torn between the Church and the Law, Newman wrote him: "you would have a greater field of usefulness in the Church than in the Law — you are sure of usefulness, more or less, in the former — and a bird in the hand, etc. — In the Law you cannot do religious good by it till your name is known — and then if you continue practice, it is only your name that does good, for time you have none."[19] I am sure most lawyers can vouch for that. Then, again, when Francis Wood, one of Newman's closest friends at Oriel left Oxford to pursue a career as a barrister of the Inner Temple, Newman taunted him for delighting in his new profession. "By the bye," he wrote Wood in 1832, a year before the Oxford Movement got underway, "I am amused ... to find that Law should be to you this kind of interesting study — for I always thought there were obscurities and absurdities enough in it to allay any enthusiasm which the novelty and extent of its system might else excite."[20]

Newman's first joust with the law would occur over something that came to be known as the Jubber case, when he refused to marry a Miss Jubber and her fiancé because the bride-to-be was not baptized in the Church of England. As a result of his refusal, in July 1834 Newman found himself at the center of a national controversy. There were letters to *The Times* about the case, and a question in Parliament. Supported by Keble and Pusey, though not his bishop or the local clergy, Newman refused to bow to pressure on what he regarded as his rock-solid legal ground. Something of his confidence, as well as his exasperation, can be gleaned from his letters of the time. In one, he writes:

At present the noise about the Jubber affair has died away. Whether it will be revived in any shape in the Commons, I know not ... No one is against me, but those whose opposition I should have expected, — which is a great comfort. I trust I may have done two

18 Newman to St. George Jackson Mivart (6 March 1884), in *LD*, XXX, 319.
19 JNN to Henry Wilberforce (26 February 1832), in *LD*, III, 23.
20 Newman to Samuel Francis Wood (4 September 1832), in *LD*, III, 89–90.

things in a measure; — expressed a strong opinion on the necessity of baptism — and shown the possibility of a clergyman's acting against the law. It was only last year that one of the clergy here ... was shocked at my saying that a Quaker was not a Christian.[21]

In another letter, he was even more insistent:

> As to J's argument about the Law being against me, and that I should not go into the Church unless I mean to obey the Law, I ask where in the marriage act or elsewhere am I bid to marry unbaptized persons? the Law is only against me by construction — as to the spirit of English Law that decidedly is for me. We still vow in the Ordination Service to observe the Church and Realm as one. I as a Churchman do not acknowledge as British subjects those who are not Churchmen. I do not acknowledge (that is) the acts of the Legislature where they interfere with the rules of the Church. In a Churchman's theory Church and State are one till Convocation alters the Services.[22]

The irony here is that it was precisely the constitutional inseparability of the English Church and State that would later undo the Oxford Movement. As it happened, Miss Jubber and her groom were married elsewhere. And Newman had his principled, if pyrrhic victory.

III

Newman's next brush with the law was rather more consequential. The Achilli Trial as it has come to be known grew out of a lecture that Newman gave in Birmingham, *The Present Position of Catholics in England* (1851), in which he referred to the sexual offences of a former Dominican friar named Giovanni Giacinto Achilli (c. 1803–c. 1860), who made a lifelong habit of seducing and, indeed, raping women.[23] A zealous convert to evangelical Protestantism after he was shown the door by the Dominicans, Achilli was a regular speaker on the anti-Catholic lecture circuit. In the wake of the reconstitution of the English hierarchy, during the period known as Papal Aggression (1850), Achilli was taken up by the powerful Evangelical Alliance and exhibited as an eyewitness to the sins of popery. It was after Newman referred to Achilli's "extraordinary depravity," which made him "the scandal of Catholicism," that the defrocked Dominican brought his

---

21 Newman to Harriett Newman (27 July 1834), in *LD*, IV, 311.
22 Newman to Henry Wilberforce (27 July 1834), in *LD*, IV, 313.
23 For my understanding of the legal aspects of the Achilli trial, I am heavily indebted to M. C. Mirow, "Roman Catholicism on Trial in Victorian England: The Libel Case of John Henry Newman and Dr. Achilli," *Catholic Lawyer*, 36 (1996), 401–53.

libel suit.[24] Avid to make his suit as damaging as possible, he brought it as a criminal, rather than a civil action both because it would entail the very real threat of imprisonment for the accused and because it would bar Newman from giving evidence on oath at the trial.[25] Whatever his objections to Rome, Achilli clearly recognized the inadvisability of giving so eloquent a defendant any courtroom pulpit.

On 27 October 1851, Newman was duly served with a writ charging that he had acted maliciously by publishing words that subjected Achilli to "great contempt, scandal, infamy and contempt." In addition, the writ stated that Newman's "false, scandalous, malicious, and defamatory libel" was "in contempt of our said Lady the Queen, to the evil and pernicious example of all others in the case of offending and against the peace of our said Lady the Queen, her crown and dignity."[26] In response, Newman entered pleas stating that his references to Achilli in his lectures were true and that he published them not out of malice but for the benefit of the public.

Even before the trial began, Newman's defense encountered difficulties. First, Cardinal Wiseman mislay the written evidence verifying Achilli's sexual offences, which obliged Newman to dispatch friends and fellow Oratorians to Italy to collect the necessary evidence. Secondly, Wiseman did not furnish a strong enough letter to the Neapolitan police to enlist their cooperation in gathering the evidence. Consequently, Newman and his team had difficulty obtaining the necessary documents proving Achilli's guilt. Thirdly, some of the witnesses contacted by Newman's agents refused to sign affidavits.

Nevertheless, the evidence compiled by the Oratorians Nicholas Darnell and Joseph Gordon and Newman's long-time family friend, Maria Giberne was compelling. One woman testified that she had had sexual relations with Achilli after he explained to her that it was no sin; another that he had raped and impregnated her; eighteen others swore affidavits that they had personal knowledge of Achilli's sexual offences. Even that quixotic Evangelical and factory reformer, the 7th Earl of Shaftesbury (1801–85) testified that Achilli had been relieved of his duties at St. Julian's College, Malta when his sexual misconduct came to light there.

Still, such abundant evidence was no match for the bias of the prosecution and the bench. Sir Frederick Thesiger, the lead prosecutor, told the jury when the trial opened at the Queen's Bench that whatever affidavits Newman might produce would be dubious because, as he claimed, in Catholic Italy witnesses would naturally favor the word of an English convert over an Italian apostate. Another prosecuting attorney questioned whether the

24 Newman to Edward Badeley (30 November 1851), in *LD*, XV, 444.
25 Mirow, "Roman Catholicism on Trial in Victorian England," 420.
26 *Ibid.*, 421–2.

evidence produced by Newman from the Court of the Inquisition regarding Achilli's offences could be admitted in an English court, since England did not recognize the pope's jurisdiction.

Frederick Thesiger, first Baron Chelmsford (1794–1878) was born in London, the third and youngest son of Charles Thesiger (d. 1831), collector of customs in the island of St Vincent in the West Indies, and his wife, Mary Anne (d. 1796). Educated at Dr. Charles Burney's school at Greenwich, he later enrolled in Gosport naval academy. (His uncle, Sir Frederick Thesiger, afterwards Nelson's aide-de-camp at Copenhagen, was a distinguished officer). In 1807, after a year at Gosport, he joined the frigate *Cambrian* as a midshipman and served at the seizure of the Danish fleet at Copenhagen—Britain's first strike in the Napoleonic Wars against Napoleon's "Continental System," the French emperor's abortive attempt to weaken his enemy by embargoing British trade. However, once Thesiger became heir to his father's West Indian estates after the death of his brother, he left the navy, though once in St Vincent his dreams of taking over the paternal estate were dashed when a volcanic eruption occurred in 1812, which ruined the estate and left the family impoverished. The decision was then made that Thesiger should practice as a barrister in the West Indies. Accordingly, he entered Gray's Inn on Guy Fawkes Day 1813, and read, by turns, in the chambers of a conveyancer, an equity draughtsman, and of Godfrey Sykes, a well-known special pleader, who dissuaded Thesiger from practicing in the West Indies. Instead, Thesiger decided to try his luck in England. In 1818, he was called to the bar, joining the home circuit and Surrey sessions, where he soon distinguished himself. In 1834 Thesiger became a king's counsel and was leader of his circuit for the next ten years. In 1852, he became attorney-general in Lord Derby's first administration. According to J. A. Hamilton's entry on Thesiger in the *Oxford Dictionary of National Biography*, from which I have plucked these biographical facts, Thesiger was "probably the most popular leading counsel of his day. As a lawyer he was ready and painstaking, and was a good cross-examiner, although not renowned for his intellectual abilities. Politically, he was rightwing and Conservative; however, as a judge he seems to have remained independent and principled on the whole." With regard to his record in the Derby administration, Hamilton observes: "His chancellorship was short, since the government fell in June 1859. His chief speech while in office was an opposition to the removal of Jewish disabilities, on which subject he had repeatedly been the principal speaker on the Conservative side in the House of Commons. He was very much opposed to the idea of Jews in parliament, as well as to the establishment of the Roman Catholic hierarchy in England."[27]

---

27 J. A. Hamilton, "Thesiger, Frederick, first Baron Chelmsford (1794–1878)," rev.

Newman and the Law

Newman's lead counsel, Sir Alexander Cockburn was forced to spend most of the trial defending the integrity of the evidence, rather than its truth. "Gentlemen, we have heard a great deal about the Inquisition—though the Roman must not be confounded with the Spanish—and none of the atrocities can be imputed to the former which are ascribed to the latter. It is not a court which is approved of in this free country, where religion and everything is unfettered, limited only by the laws necessary for the peace and good order and welfare of mankind. We desire no secret tribunals. But do not let us be unjust on that account!"[28] Here, the frustration of this famously adroit advocate is palpable. When Newman wrote Cockburn an effusive letter of thanks after the proceedings, there was as much condolence as gratitude in the letter.[29]

Sir Alexander James Edmund Cockburn, twelfth baronet (1802–80) was educated at Trinity Hall, Cambridge before entering the Middle Temple in 1823: he was called to the bar in 1829. As a judge, he did not have the highest of reputations. "He was not remembered as a deductive legal logician," Michael Lobban points out in his entry on Cockburn in *The Oxford Dictionary of National Biography*, "but rather as a man of the world who knew how to master detail by hard work and present a rounded picture to the jury." A friend of Charles Dickens, he was a warm, witty, charming man, with a melodious voice and a keen appreciation of music. Indeed, he liked to entertain prima donnas late into the night and often had difficulty appearing in court the next morning on time. His deep legal conviction that the law should not be invoked to question people's honour and reputation without due foundation might not have been entirely disinterested. By all accounts, Cockburn had had a wild youth. In later years, Lobban notes, he would tell boon companions: "Whatever happens I have had my whack." On one occasion he even had to evade the bailiffs by climbing out the window of the robing rooms at Exeter Castle. Always fond of the society of women, he sired two illegitimate children, a girl and a boy, to the latter of whom he left most of his fortune. That Cockburn should have been charged with defending Newman against the profligate Achilli must have struck him as a rich irony.[30]

Lord Campbell, the presiding judge, admitted the evidence from the papal court, but with such invidious reluctance as to leave the jury in no doubt as to the weight he attached to it. "It has been remarked," Campbell observed, "that this is the first time since the Reformation that the judgment

---

Sinéad Agnew, *The Oxford Dictionary of National Biography*.
28 Mirow, "Roman Catholicism on Trial in Victorian England," 430.
29 Newman to Sir Alexander Cockburn (25 June 1852), in *LD*, XV, 106.
30 Michael Lobban, "Cockburn, Sir Alexander James Edmund, Twelfth Baronet (1802–1880)," in *The Oxford Dictionary of National Biography*.

of the Court of Inquisition has been tendered in evidence in an English Court of Justice. Looking at this document, I find that it is a copy of the Court of Inquisition and that such a jurisdiction is exercised at Rome. Thank God it does not extend to this country. But this country will be ready to receive documents emanating from Courts of other countries."[31]

Lord John Campbell (1779–1861), who eventually became Lord Chancellor, was a distant relation of Sir Walter Scott, one of Newman's favorite novelists. Coincidentally enough, after the trial, Newman recuperated with his good friend, the parliamentary lawyer James Hope-Scott, who married Scott's granddaughter and lived at Abbotsford, which Scott built on the banks of the Tweed. Newman was not taken with the place, finding it too dark and too cramped. "I could shake hands with the nursery maids in the room opposite me without leaving my own room," he wrote a friend.[32] However, while awaiting sentencing in London from 18 to 25 November, Newman stayed with the Duke and Duchess of Norfolk at their residence at 11 Carlton Terrace, about which he wrote the Duchess nearly ten years later. Newman's letter bears quoting in full, if only because it so eloquently shows how much the Achilli ordeal prepared him to appreciate the appeal of those, like the Duke and Duchess, who personified the inextinguishable life of the Roman Catholic Church in an England otherwise hostile to the Catholic religion, a life Newman would eventually come to personify himself.

> The Oratory Birmingham March 13, 1861
>
> My dear Duchess,
>
> I did not dare to allude to those most sacred subjects, of which you have so kindly spoken in your letter to me. But, indeed, it was not that I do not constantly think of them. There is no one, I am sure, who has been for so little time in the sight of your past life, who has loved and revered it more.
>
> For, as you say, during the weeks you refer to, I saw a most happy home, happy in its own virtues, in its devotion and its good works, a home written doubtless in God's eternal book; and its sunshine has especially rested in my mind, because it so tenderly expressed its sympathy to me in a season of anxiety.
>
> I think the memory of it will remain with me, while I live. And to you, when the first suffering is over, it will surely be an anticipation of heaven, till you are taken thither. What will be the joy, if we are worthy, to be admitted to the Holy Family above, who in their own persons have known the sorrows of separation, and who will then repair for us our own broken ties, never again to be undone,

---

[31] Mirow, "Roman Catholicism on Trial in Victorian England," 425.
[32] Newman to John Joseph Gordon (7 January 1853), in *LD*, XV, 247.

Newman and the Law

> Give my love to Henry, and believe me, My dear Duchess of Norfolk,
>
> Ever Yours most sincerely in Xt John H Newman of the Oratory[33]

Lord Campbell, curiously enough, was an ardent Protestant who had given serious consideration to joining the Church before entering Lincoln's Inn. The old DNB pointed out another of the judge's traits: "Lord Campbell possessed in a supreme degree the art of getting on. 'If Campbell,' said Perry of the *Morning Chronicle*, 'had engaged as an opera-dancer, I do not say he would have danced as well as Deshayes, but I feel confident he would have got a higher salary.'"[34]

> Certainly, this pillar of the Establishment did not hesitate to call the jury's attention to the fact that the sentence of the papal court against Achilli was theologically motivated and therefore dubious: "Dr. Achilli says it was for heresy, and that no charge of immorality was brought against him. It is for you to say whether you believe it was for heresy or for immorality." This nicely reinforced Campbell's claim that the evidence of the papal court was tainted. "If it be meant that, because Dr. Achilli did not believe in transubstantiation or auricular confession, that he is therefore an infidel, I say—without the least levity but with strong feeling—I hope the number of such infidels will daily increase! Gentlemen, with all the trembling anxiety suited to such sacred subjects, I make only those remarks which are necessary to show that the charge is not substantiated."[35]

As it happened, the jury agreed, but only after Lord Campbell had deviously impugned Newman's integrity:

> Then, as to Dr. Newman, there is no danger of his being looked upon by you unfavourably, though he has left the Protestant religion, and is now of the Church of Rome. Gentlemen, no doubt he has acted from the purest motives, and I give him credit for the

---

33 Newman to The Duchess of Norfolk (13 March 1861), in *LD*, XXXII, 216.

34 André-Jean-Jacques Deshayes (1777–1846) was a French ballet dancer and choreographer. The son of the ballet master of the Comédie-Italienne, Jacques-Francois Deshayes, Andre-Jean-Jacques studied dance under his father, and then, from 1788, at the school of the Paris Opera Ballet, where he debuted. Hired by the Opera as principal dancer in 1794, Deshayes toured Lisbon, Milan, Naples and Vienna, before making London his base. He performed his most brilliant work at the King's Theatre in London, where, from 1804 to 1842, he was principal dancer and choreographer. During these years, he was instrumental in developing Romantic ballet in Great Britain, though the English never produced a Romantic ballerina themselves. Clara Webster (1821–44), whom London critics hoped would be the country's first great ballerina, had her career cut short when her dress caught fire on stage.

35 Mirow, "Roman Catholicism on Trial in Victorian England," 431–2.

> course he has adopted. What I dislike to see is clergymen (if there be any such) remaining in the Protestant Church, who, while they are Roman Catholics in heart, and wish to be so in their practice, remain in the Protestant Church; but when a man of piety, honour, and education (like Dr. Newman) feels that he does not belong to the Church of England and resigns his position in that Church, and all the advantages arising from it, there is no reason to cast any imputation upon him.[36]

Newman is often accused of being too subtle for his own good—when liberal critics of the Magisterium attempt to enlist him in their liberal causes they are fond of claiming that he was prone to saying and unsaying when it came to expressing his obedience to the Magisterium—though, certainly, as this summation shows, no one could say and unsay quite as deviously as Lord Campbell.

However, if in discrediting Newman, Lord Campbell was prepared to be somewhat roundabout, Thesiger was admirably direct.

> Gentlemen, who is the person from whom these charges proceed? From Dr. Newman! Was he suddenly converted? Did no doubts intrude into his mind while he was a member of our Protestant Church! Did conviction flash at once upon his soul? Did he lie down at night a satisfied and contented Protestant—disbelieving in transubstantiation, confession, and absolution—and rise up in the morning a full-blown Romanist?[37]

After being found guilty, Newman was fined a nominal £100. For Newman, the verdict constituted a moral victory—it was not a charge against him but against Roman Catholicism—and he pointedly instructed his counsel to reaffirm that he retracted nothing of what he had said against Achilli. William Francis Finlason, the barrister of the Middle Temple who was one of the trial's reporters, claimed that the verdict exhibited England's "blind and bitter prejudice against the Catholic Church," though he consoled himself with the conviction that most Englishmen would not agree with it. "They will not sanction a perversion of justice," he wrote, "in order to secure a triumph for Protestantism. They may not appreciate religious houses, but they venerate religion; they may reluctantly tolerate Popery, but they will not perpetuate iniquity."[38]

It is interesting that Thackeray did not see it in this light, for certainly, in his clubbable way, he was not unrepresentative of upper middle-class, professional society. For Thackeray, Achill was "a rascal hypocrite no doubt;

---

36 Ibid., 434.
37 Ibid., 432.
38 Ibid., 436.

but; as the law is, the verdict was right—though I think the judge's behaviour in the trial was most unfair and unworthy."[39] The *Times* agreed with Finlason: "We consider ... that a great blow has been given to the administration of justice in this country, and Roman Catholics will have henceforth only too good reason for asserting, that there is no justice for them in cases tending to arouse the Protestant feelings of judges and juries."[40] One historian of libel, as Matthew Mirow points out in his indispensable study of the trial, considered it "the most celebrated miscarriage of justice in the nineteenth century."[41]

This judgment would be more widely known and shared if Newman had been allowed to deliver a speech he had wished to give before the verdict was heard. Lord Campbell, undoubtedly aware of Newman's personal appeal, which so many of his contemporaries found so captivating, as much for his learning and piety as for his charm and what Lord Coleridge recalled as his "sweet musical, almost unearthly voice," declined to let him speak.[42] The theatrical panache of Newman's oration proves that Lord Campbell had a point.

> My Lords I am going to suffer punishment for a libel, published with an absolute conviction that its matter was true, and with an utter absence of any private motive whatever in publishing it. So certain was I of its truth, that, even up to the date of the verdict, (it would not become me to go further,) never for a moment did I feel a wish, however transient, that I had not published it. So clear was I of all personal feeling against the individual who was the subject of it, that, even since the verdict, my most jealous scrutiny has failed to detect in me one motion of resentment or indignation.
>
> My Lords my end in publishing it was a legitimate end, and my means were strictly fitted to that end. A man, already publicly named by Protestants themselves, as one whose word could not be trusted, on the credit of that word made charges, gross and false, against a religious community, which I was ... [by] my office bound to defend. I met his statements by appealing to the inveterate opinion, or rather (as I fancied it,) the almost historical judgment, of mankind, founded and expressed in specific imputations, in proof of his untrustworthiness; and (fully thinking I had evidence of each particular, at once irrefragable and immediately producible,) I argued, that he who had been so long dishonest, had no claim to

---

39 *The Letters and Private Papers of William Makepeace Thackeray*, ed. Ray (Cambridge, Mass.: Harvard University Press, 1946), III, 66.
40 Mirow, "Roman Catholicism on Trial in Victorian England," 436.
41 *Ibid.*
42 Extract from the Diary of Sir John Taylor Coleridge in Bernard Lord Coleridge. *This for Remembrance* (London: T. F. Unwin, 1925), 85–6.

be considered honest now. His veracity was the very edge of his allegations against us; his want of veracity was the very pith of my reply to them. I said, fully thinking I spoke the fact, that he had made promise before heaven to live chastely, and that he had thro' many years broken that promise by habits of deliberate profligacy ...

My Lords I cheerfully submit to the law of my country. I justly confide in your Lordships' administration of it. Religion reminds me that you are the Ministers of the Most High. History assures me of the impartiality of your Court. I have nothing to complain of, nothing to regret, nothing to fear. You, my Lordships, and I, have our respective parts to fulfil in this transitory scene. I am content with my own. A prison can but shorten my life; a fine can but drive me to beg; the world's reproach and scorn can but inflict on me what it has already inflicted for a long twenty years. Nothing can I suffer, but will be made up to me a hundred fold hereafter. I am encompassed with blessings and mercies. There is a God above us. He has never failed me; He does not fail me now.[43]

In Newman's experience—which he recreates so faithfully in his letters, journals, prayers and sermons—apparent failure often brought spiritual and other dividends. Indeed, in some respects, we could only succeed by failing, and the Achilli trial was no exception. The blessings Newman drew from the ordeal would stay with him for life. In a letter to a leading Birmingham Catholic and owner of an ecclesiastical metal works, John Hardman (1812–67), who was also one of Pugin's most trusted colleagues, Newman delineated the meaning of his suffering with brilliant incisiveness.

These proceedings, you recollect well, were directed against a certain illustration which I introduced into my lecture, of those national prejudices of which we are the victims; they have ended in furnishing me with an additional illustration in point. They were intended to prove that my charges against a distinguished champion of Protestantism were false; they have but succeeded in proving that my charge against Protestantism was true. I said that Catholics had no fair play in the Protestant world: is my statement confirmed or refuted by the trial which has followed upon it?

There is no need to enter here into particulars. The public knows them, and posterity will do justice to them. I have been running the gauntlet of Protestantism in its many varieties, from the Evangelical Alliance to the High Anglicanism of a Judge. It is a strange history; but I am not going to complain of it, though I fairly might complain. "They who play at bowls, must expect rubbers;" I acquiesce in the truth of the proverb. Good sense is sufficient to keep me from

---

43 "Appendix 2: Speech to have been delivered before Judgment, at the conclusion of the Achilli Trial," in *LD*, XV, 525–6.

complaining, let alone Christian charity or meekness. I have been too surprised at what I have undergone to be indignant, and too well satisfied with what I have done to be resentful. I have struck at the Protestant world, and the Protestant world has struck at me; and I consider I have inflicted as good as I have received, or rather better. I trust my own blows have been fair; I cannot say so much of those which have been levelled against me; but, any how, I have gained more by truth than my opponents have gained by falsehood; and I am content with my bargain.[44]

And he concluded his letter with a reference to a sermon that he had written sixteen years before, "Christ upon the Waters," which he had republished during the time known as Papal Aggression, when forces not unlike those that threatened violence before Pope Benedict XVI's visit to England were menacing the newly reconstituted English Church.[45]

I said then in that sermon, — "We love you, O men of this generation, but we fear you not. Understand well, and lay it to heart, that we will do the work of God and fulfil our mission, with your consent, if we can get it, but in spite of you if we cannot. As to ourselves, the world has long done its worst against us; long ago has it seasoned us for the encounter. We know our place and our fortunes: to give witness and to be reviled; to be cast out as evil and to succeed. Such is the law which the Lord of all has annexed to the promulgation of the truth: its preachers suffer, but its cause prevails. Joyfully have we become a party of this bargain; and as we have resigned ourselves to the price, so we intend, by God's aid, to claim the compensation." Nothing, then, from the Protestant world has been able to surprise me; what really has surprised me, what has overwhelmed me, is the generosity with which my Catholic brethren have made my cause their own, the munificence with which they have carried it forward, and the perseverance by which they have brought it to a happy termination.[46]

The Catholics Newman had most in mind in saying this were the Catholics not only of Birmingham but those of Ireland, France and America, all of whom had contributed handsomely to his defense.[47] When Archbishop

---

44 Newman to John Hardman (2 March 1853), in *LD*, XV, 318.

45 Pope Benedict XVI's visit to the United Kingdom, 16–19 September 2010, was the first state visit by a pope to the country, Pope John Paul II's visit in 1982 having been a pastoral, rather than state visit.

46 *LD*, XV, 318–19. The sermon from which Newman quotes is "Christ on the Waters" (1857), in *Sermons on Various Occasions*, 159–60.

47 As for the costs of the trial, which Newman was obliged to pay, they were considerable: £14,000, which in today's money would be as much as one hundred times this figure. In the dedication to the *Discourses on the Scope and Nature of University Education* (1852), Newman thanked his "many friends and benefactors" in Great Britain, Ireland,

Kenrick of Baltimore sent Newman extracts from a letter from Martin Spalding, Archbishop of Louisville, the last of which closed with the Archbishop saying: "in common with my colleagues, and the Clergy and Laity at large, I entertain sincere admiration of your zeal, and unqualified confidence in the integrity of your faith,"[48] Newman responded:

> Did I need a fresh proof, in addition to the many which have already been showered upon me, how the Loving Providence of God defeats evil and turns trial into joy and triumph, I should find it in the course and issue of the proceedings to which those Resolutions relate. And did I look for an evidence of the unity of object and the world-encircling charity which are the characteristics of Catholicism, I should find an instance, even more impressive than occurs in Apostolic times, (as occupying a more extensive field and carried out amid the changes of human society,) in that vigilant paternal sollicitude, which has fixed the eyes of an exalted Hierarchy, with a whole continent to engage them, upon one person, over the great ocean, who happens in a particular instance to have been made the sport of the common Enemy of Christians in every land.[49]

Here, at this pivotal point in his life, when so many of his Catholic endeavors lay before him, Newman was transformed. He was no longer simply an English convert at the mercy of the Evangelical Alliance, but an English Catholic at home in a Roman faith that stretched far beyond the pale of No Popery, and it was the law that helped him to realize the full meaning of this embattled profession. As he told another correspondent in the wake of the trial:

> What is good, endures; what is evil, comes to nought. As time goes on, the memory will simply pass away from me of whatever has been done in the course of these proceedings, in hostility to me or in insult, whether on the part of those who invoked, or those who administered the law; but the intimate sense will never fade away, will possess me more and more, of that true and tender Providence which has always watched over me for good, and of the power of that religion which is not degenerate from its ancient glory, of zeal for God, and of compassion towards the oppressed.[50]

France, Belgium, Germany, Poland, Italy, Malta, North America, and other countries for their "generous stubborn efforts" and "their munificent alms." John Hughes, the Archbishop of New York, contributed £223, which Newman used to buy Rednall, the residence outside Edgbaston, where the Oratorians are buried.

48 *LD*, XV, 212, n. 2.
49 Newman to Francis Kenrick, Archbishop of Baltimore (3 December 1852), in *LD*, XV, 212–13.
50 Newman to Robert Whitty (2 March 1853), in *LD*, XV, 320.

✟ 10 ✟

Newman in his Letters

Newman in his Letters

John Henry Newman: A Portrait in Letters, edited by Roderick Strange. Oxford University Press, 595 pages

IN *Antony and Cleopatra*, Shakespeare has his great heroine tell her attendant Iras how she foresees posterity treating her after death.

> Nay, 'tis most certain, Iras: saucy lictors
> Will catch at us, like strumpets; and scald rhymers
> Ballad us out o' tune: the quick comedians
> Extemporally will stage us, and present
> Our Alexandrian revels; Antony
> Shall be brought drunken forth, and I shall see
> Some squeaking Cleopatra boy my greatness
> I' the posture of a whore.

If saucy posterity has, on the whole, been just to Blessed John Henry Cardinal Newman, it is largely because his correspondence documents the events of his life sufficiently to forestall gross misrepresentation. And since these letters document not only the events themselves but Newman's own deeply meditated responses to events, those who would distort his life and legacy have always had a difficult time of it. In this regard, Newman agreed with Lord Acton, who told Gladstone's daughter Mary in a letter of 1880 that "history does not stand or fall with historians. From the thirteenth century we rely much more on letters than on histories written for the public."[1]

In a piece on John Chrysostom, written when he was an Anglican and later collected in his *Historical Sketches* (1872), Newman particularly praised the correspondence of the Fathers for uncovering the often elusive history of sanctity, to which we might otherwise have little access. For example, he cited the epistles of Pope Gregory, which "give us the same sort of insight into the holy solicitude for the universal Christian people ... that minute vigilance, yet comprehensive superintendence of the chief pastor, which in a very different field of labour is seen in the Duke of Welling-

---

[1] *Letters of Lord Acton to Mary, Daughter of the Right Honorable W. E. Gladstone*, ed. Herbert Woodfield Paul (London: George Allen, 1904), 32.

ton's despatches on campaign, which tell us so much more about him than any panegyrical sketch."[2] Then, again, for Newman, the letters of St. Chrysostom "are for the most part crowded into the three memorable years in which the sufferings of exile gradually ripened into a virtual martyrdom."[3] Indeed, the very decision of the Fathers to write letters to advance their catechetical purposes was illustrative because, as Newman appreciated, "Their authoritative declarations are written, not on stone tablets, but on what Scripture calls 'the fleshly tables of the heart.'"[4] And the epistolary character of these records, in turn, enabled readers to follow not only the outward lives of the saints but "the aims, the difficulties, the disappointments, under which they journeyed on heavenward," as well as "their care of the brethren" and "their anxieties about contemporary teachers of error."[5] Lastly, Newman understood that "Dogma and proof are in them at the same time hagiography. They do not write a *summa theologiae*, or draw out a *catena*, or pursue a single thesis through the stages of a scholastic disputation. They wrote for the occasion, and seldom on a carefully-digested plan."[6]

Here is Newman's idea of Christian correspondence, and it is an idea that suffuses his own correspondence, which currently extends to thirty-two volumes, though the dilatory Oxford University Press has yet to supply a comprehensive index. In *John Henry Newman: A Portrait in Letters*, Father Roderick Strange distills Newman's approximately 20,000 extant letters into a rich, revelatory selection, which covers every period of the great convert's long life and gives readers a judicious view of the pastoral counselling, controversies and hard-won accomplishments of the man.

One reason why Father Strange has succeeded in his selection is that he has not sought to produce a "life in letters," knowing that such an epistolary life could never capture the full complexity of his subject. Letters, after all, by their very nature, as Father Strange recognizes, do not lend themselves to a "smooth, rounded, complete narrative."[7] Moreover, if made to do the necessarily multi-faceted work of such a narrative, a selection of letters would inevitably risk being tendentious. Instead, Father Strange has sensibly chosen to make his selection a portrait of Newman, which may not make any claim to definitiveness, but nonetheless gives the reader a

---

2 John Henry Newman, "St. Chrysostom," in *Historical Sketches* (London: Basil Montague Pickering, 1872), II, 222.
3 *Ibid.*
4 *Ibid.*, II, 223.
5 *Ibid.*
6 *Ibid.*
7 *John Henry Newman: A Life in Letters*, ed. Roderick Strange (Oxford: Oxford University Press, 2016), 5.

marvelously evocative, critical sense of the charm, integrity, *caritas*, and genius of his fascinating sitter.

Another laudable aspect of the book is its introduction, especially its acknowledgement of how vital the dogmatic principle was to Newman. Apropos this essential aspect of the man, Father Strange writes with commendable lucidity and point.

> One consequence of the startlingly original intellect with which Newman was blessed was not only the clarity of his thought, but his firm sense of principle. When he had recognized in an issue a matter of principle, his adherence to that principle was unswerving. One such principle was dogma. "From the age of fifteen," he declared in his Apologia, "dogma has been the fundamental principle of my religion." And the outstanding example of such a principled dogmatic conviction was his belief in the visible Church as one, holy, catholic, and apostolic. It shaped his life. He sought for its realization while he was an Anglican, and once he had become a Catholic, he worked for its purification.[8]

Three years before the Second Vatican Council concluded, Evelyn Waugh wrote a famous piece in *The Spectator* entitled "The Same Again, Please" (1962) expressing misgivings about the liturgical changes being proposed for the Church, though he was confident that "There is no possibility of the Church modifying her defined doctrines to attract those to whom they are repugnant."[9] In our own more unsettled age, that confidence has vanished. Newman's recognition of the abiding need to defend doctrinal integrity is, therefore, more appealing than ever.

We should certainly keep Newman's "unswerving" adherence to doctrinal integrity in mind when we read his letters to Renn Dickson Hampden, the Oriel fellow, with whose heterodox Bampton Lectures (1832) he took such spirited exception. "I dare not trust myself to put on paper my feelings about the principles contained in it," Newman wrote Hampden directly of the pamphlet the Socinian don wrote as a follow up to his lectures, "tending as they do in my opinion altogether to make shipwreck of Christian faith."[10] Hampden, a shy, reticent, retiring man, never altogether

---

8 Ibid., 5–6.

9 Evelyn Waugh, "The Same Again, Please," *The Spectator* (23 November 1962), in *A Bitter Trial: Evelyn Waugh and John Cardinal Heenan on the Liturgical Changes*, ed. Dom Alcuin Reid (San Francisco: Ignatius Press, 2011), 28.

10 "While I respect the tone of piety which the pamphlet displays, I dare not trust myself to put on paper my feelings about the principles contained in it, tending as they do in my opinion altogether to make shipwreck of Christian faith. I also lament that by its appearance the first step has been taken towards interrupting that peace and mutual good understanding which has prevailed so long in this place, and which if

recovered from Newman's principled attack, though he did what he could to defend himself. "I charge you with malignity," the indignant don wrote in response to Newman's accusations, "because you have no other ground of your assault on me but a fanatical persecuting spirit," to which Newman replied, in the third-person, with comic formality: "He altogether disallows Dr. Hampden's imputation that he has been guilty of dissimulation, and falsehood, and dark malignity."[11] Later, in an interpolated note, Newman added: "I almost think I should have added two other protests, one against his imputing motives to me—the other against his calling any of the pamphlets [critical of Hampden] *trumpery*, etc. But perhaps this would have been too absurd."[12] To be fair to Hampden, he did have the impeccably Lutheran Prince Consort Albert rally to his side.

Still, the doctrinal issues at stake in the controversy were serious. Hampden's lectures falsified the Trinity and the Incarnation, and Newman was scarcely alone in calling him to account for them—in fact, over eighty Oxford dons across the theological spectrum protested against the Melbourne government appointing him to Oxford's Regius Chair of Divinity. Moreover, when Lord John Russell offered Hampden the bishopric of Hereford, thirteen bishops protested. Even the amiable Dr. Routh of Magdalen found him *outré*, remarking to the president of Balliol: "The infinite art of that unhappy man makes it very difficult to answer [him] in detail. I think it had better be done by fixing upon ... certain positions of which it might be easy to shew the falsehood, the impiety, or the poison. But he is very cunning."[13]

What is most significant about the Hampden controversy is how it reveals the unsparing polemicist in Newman. When it came to principles of doctrine, he never compromised. As he wrote one of his friends with regard to Hampden, "There is no doctrine, however sacred, which he does not scoff at—and in his Moral Philosophy he adopts the lowest and most grovelling utilitarianism as the basis of Morals—he considers it is a sacred duty to live to this world—and that religion by itself injuriously absorbs the mind." For Newman, the other fellows of Oriel might not be irreproachable, but they each had virtues to counterbalance their flaws. Hampden, on the other hand, as far as Newman could see, "*judging by his writings,* [was] the most lucre loving, earthly minded, unlovely person one

---

once seriously disturbed will be succeeded by dissentions the more intractable because justified in the minds of those who resist innovation by a feeling of imperative duty." Newman to Renn Dickson Hampden (28 November 1834), in *LD*, IV, 371.

11 Hampden to Newman (23 June 1835), in *LD*, IV, 83.
12 Newman to Hampden (24 June 1835), in *LD*, IV, 85.
13 Routh, quoted in R. D. Middleton, *Dr. Routh* (Oxford: Oxford University Press, 1938), 142.

ever set eyes on."[14] With an opponent as fierce as this, Hampden could be forgiven for deciding to spend most of his later career in his garden, far away from the brickbats of debate, only emerging briefly to oppose the heretical *Essays and Reviews* in 1860, by which time Newman had long since removed himself from the jousts of Anglicans.

In his later controversies with William Gladstone (who charged that Catholics could not be loyal to their Church without being disloyal to their Queen and Country) and with the Congregationalist Scot, Andrew Martin Fairbairn (who charged that, in accepting the infallible authority of the Church, Newman was somehow guilty of skepticism), Newman eschewed the sort of *ad hominem* distaste to which he had given vent in his responses to Hampden. Indeed, in the case of Gladstone, after parrying the Prime Minister's distortions of the First Vatican Council with his *Letter to the Duke of Norfolk* (1875), he admitted: "I do not think I ever can be sorry for what I have done, but I never can cease to be sorry for the necessity of doing it."[15] Nonetheless, for all of the suave forbearance he showed his opponents, Newman was always careful to defend the inviolability of dogmatic truth, especially in an ethos where, for Protestants, as one controversialist put it, "perjury is a dogmatic principle of popery."[16]

Of course, the most famous proponent of this widely accepted view was Charles Kingsley, whose contention that neither Newman nor his Catholic co-religionists felt bound by the truth inspired Newman to write his great autobiography, *Apologia pro Vita Sua* (1865). Father Strange includes the first letter Newman wrote to Kingsley, which offers a fair specimen of the sense of honor that always animated Newman's controversial conduct. "When I received your letter," Newman wrote, "taking upon yourself the authorship I was amazed."[17] By expressing the amazement he felt in receiving the letter, Newman was doing Kingsley a favor by implying, at the very least, that it was out of character for so respectable an author to write so insulting and so unprovoked an attack on another's man integrity.

Then, again, after the Kingsley controversy, when Newman's contemporaries finally came round to seeing the point of having so principled a

---

14 Newman to Simeon Lloyd Pope (3 March 1836), in *LD*, V, 251.
15 Newman to W. E. Gladstone (16 January 1875), in *LD*, XXVII, 193.
16 "Mr. Puxley, whose purpose was to show 'the comparative purity and virtue of Protestant countries and their practical religion—showing the contrasted iniquities of papal lands,' and 'that perjury is a dogmatic principle of popery.'" in *LD*, XX, 461, n. 1. Henry Lavellin Puxley (1834–1909) of Dunboy Castle, County Cork, was at Eton and Brasenose College, Oxford. He succeeded his brother in 1860. Near the castle ruins stands Puxley Mansion, a nineteenth-century manor house, which was burnt down by the Irish Republican Army in 1920 in reprisal for the destruction of houses harboring IRA terrorists by forces of the Crown.
17 Newman to Charles Kingsley (7 January 1864), in *LD*, XXI, 11.

convert in their midst, it was typical of Newman never to harbor grudges. In a letter to the unscrupulous biographer, Edmund Purcell who made such unfair mincemeat of poor Cardinal Manning, Newman wrote:

> My own feeling about the past is "Let bygones be bygones." The change of sentiment about [me] is so satisfactory that to speak about it is to interfere with it, and is to revive occurrences which are at present in simple oblivion. Of course you cannot help stating the circumstances, which led to the Apologia, but I am pained to find the name of Kingsley recalled, who by his passionate attack on me became one of my best friends, whom I always wished to shake hands with when living, and towards whose memory I have much tenderness.[18]

If Father Strange's selection gives one a good sampling of Newman the controversialist, it also provides fascinating glimpses into the gestation of his writings. In one letter to the Oratorian whom he would make his literary executor, Father William Neville, for instance, Newman wrote from Switzerland:

> The fare is fair here—the bread, butter, honey, cream, good. They won't give us cheese, though it is the pride of the country—the wine and brandy bad. I am very suspicious of the water, as having lime in it. The meat tolerable—dinner, alas, at one; a nice, clean house; about 40 inoffensive inmates, most of them women and children. The Church quite close by, we said Mass there this morning ... I have done some certitude—little enough in quantity—but, (unless my whole theory be a maresnest, of which I am not sure) good in quality. I can do it when lying down, or travelling. It is a work of analysis, not of many words.[19]

Here, in 1866, Newman was referring to work he had begun on his great essay in epistemology, *Grammar of Assent* (1870), the purpose of which was to defend the certainty of religious belief against the naysaying of rationalists. The idea for the book had first occurred to Newman while struggling to convince his wayward brother Charles to return to the Christian fold in the 1820s. Yet, it is fitting that he should have finally set to work on what would prove one of his most arduous undertakings on vacation in Champéry in the Swiss Alps. To James Hope-Scott, the Catholic lawyer and generous patron of Catholic causes whose own faith Newman found so exemplary, he described the writing of the book as "like tunneling through a mountain—I have begun it, and it is almost too much for my strength ... Perhaps the tunnel will break in, when I get

---

18 Newman to Edmund Sheridan Purcell (22 June 1881), in *LD*, XXIX, 388.
19 Newman to William Neville (12 August 1866), in *LD*, XXII, 274.

fairly into my work. When I have done it, if I am to do it ... then I shall say, Nunc dimittis."[20]

Another virtue of Father Strange's selection is that, while never masquerading as a biography, it accomplishes many of the ends of biography by showing how Newman's contemporaries viewed the priest, poet, theologian, educator, philosopher, historian, satirist, and novelist. Although Father Strange does not find space for that wonderful letter of Jemima, in which she says of her beloved brother, "I often think what a wonderful creature you are, and what a singular history yours is,"[21] he does include this gem from John Keble, to whom Newman had sent a draft of his *Apologia* after being estranged from his old Tractarian friend for nearly twenty years.

> My very dear Newman I will not wait any longer before thanking you with all my heart for your loving words *to* me and far too loving *of* me—If I wait till I write as I could wish, I should never write at all—for indeed dear friend the more and the more intently I look at this self drawn photograph (what a cruel strain it must have been to you) the more I love and admire the Artist—Whatever comes of controversial points, I see no end to the good which the whole Church, we may reasonably hope, may derive from such an example of love and candour under most trying circumstances.
>
> You have said things which by the blessing of God will I trust materially help us in our sad weary struggle against Unbelief.[22]

To give his readers an insight into the *caritas* of Newman, Father Strange includes an exchange of letters between Newman and a brave young girl named Emily Fortey, who, in 1882, at the age of sixteen, wrote to the Cardinal to ask him his advice on how she should set about becoming a Catholic, since, as she said, she was "a Catholic at heart." She had read Lilly's anthology of Newman's work and his *Loss and Gain* (1848) and they had had a deep influence on her. Newman's initial response was cautious: "Our Lord tells us to 'count the cost'—the change of religion is a most serious step—and must not be taken without great preparation by meditation and prayer."[23] However, once Miss Fortey made the momentous step of being received into the Faith, with her father's grudging consent, she wrote Newman an ebullient letter, which must have deeply moved him: "And now I am writing to thank you very much for your kindness to me more than two years ago," she wrote. "Perhaps if you had not written to me I might never have become a Catholic."[24]

---

20 Newman to James Hope Scott (7 December 1868), in *LD*, XXIX, 184.
21 Mrs. James Mozley to Newman (3 December 1841), in *LD*, VIII, 363.
22 John Keble to Newman (28 June 1864), in *LD*, XXI, 143.
23 Newman to Emily Fortey (6 July 1882), in *LD*, XXX, 110.
24 Emily Fortey to Newman (2 October 1884), in *LD*, XXX, 404.

Newman's response could have been a response to his own younger, more ardent self, before the lacerations of conversion had opened his eyes to the reality of the Cross. "You must not suppose your present state of peace and joy will always continue," he told his bright young correspondent.

> It is God's mercy to bring us over difficulties. As time goes on, you may be cast down to find that your warmth of feeling does not last as it once was, and instead of it you may have trials of various kinds. Never mind; be brave; make acts of faith, hope, and charity; put yourself into God's hands, and thank Him for all that he sends you, pleasant or painful. The Psalms and Saint Paul's Epistles will be your great and abiding consolation.
>
> "Rejoice with trembling." I say all this, not as dissuading you from enjoying your present joy and peace, but that you may enjoy them religiously.
>
> I repeat, God bless you, keep you, and direct you. Through His grace you have begun life well. May he give you perseverance.[25]

This testament to the power of personal influence—even if imparted through the penny post—would surely have reminded Newman of the decisive influence that the letters of the Irish priest Charles Russell had had on him while he was making the final step of his own conversion. "He had, perhaps, more to do with my conversion than any one else," Newman would later say of Russell, who went on to become the President of Maynooth.[26] After the publication of the *Apologia*, he thanked Russell for the vital support he had given him during the writing of that harrowing book.

> I write you at length a line to thank you for the true encouragement your letters gave me. It has been a great deal of suffering, as well as toil, to get through what I have been at—now it is over, and I am very thankful. Letters, such as yours, came to me, as the stimulant or refreshing applications which are administered to a man who is at some hard bodily toil, and were as acceptable as they were serviceable. It was a great pleasure to find that your name came so naturally into my narrative. Besides the real benefit which you did me in my anxieties 20 years ago, you then evidenced what you have shown now, and what is part of your character, your great sympathy for others.[27]

Then, again, a year later, Newman wrote to Russell of Cardinal Wiseman's funeral in London, to which he was pointedly not invited: "the Newspapers remark that the son of that Lord Campbell, who talked of

---

25 Newman to Emily Fortey (3 October 1884), in *LD*, XXX, 404.
26 *Apologia*, 176.
27 Newman to Charles Russell (24 June 1864), in *LD*, XXI, 130.

trampling on his Cardinals hat 14 years ago, was present at the Requiem Mass."[28] Being a Catholic convert in Victorian England may never have been an easy charge but it would always appeal to Newman's exquisite sense of humor.

The shelf of good books on Newman is small, but Father Roderick Strange's *John Henry Newman: A Portrait in Letters* is a welcome addition to it. Those familiar with Newman and those unfamiliar with him will find it an altogether splendid read.

---

28 Newman to Charles Russell (2 March 1864), in *LD*, XXI, 426.

✛ 11 ✛

Hagiography, History and John Henry Newman

Hagiography, History, and John Henry Newman

In October of 1848, John Henry Newman wrote to Frederick Faber that he had consulted

> the [Oratorian] Fathers who are here on the subject of the Lives of the Saints, and we have come to the (unanimous) conclusion of advising you to suspend the Series at present. It appears there is a strong feeling against it on the part of a portion of the Catholic community in England, on the ground ... that the Lives of foreign saints, however edifying in their respective countries, are unsuited to England, and unacceptable <offensive> to Protestants. To this feeling we consider it a duty for the sake of peace, to defer.

Having given Faber this disappointing news, Newman was quick to add:

> For myself, you know well without my saying it how absolutely I identify myself with you in this matter; but, as you may have to publish this letter, I make it an opportunity, which has not as yet <may not again> been given me, of declaring that I have no sympathy at all with the feelings to which I have alluded.[1]

In 1847 Faber had begun translating lives of Italian, French, and Spanish saints, which he planned to publish in a series under the auspices of the then nascent English Oratory. However, when Faber published a translation of the life of St. Rose of Lima by Jean Baptist Feuillet, a seventeenth-century Dominican friar and Missionary Apostolic in the Antilles, Father Edward Price, a Catholic convert from Presbyterianism and editor of *Dolman's Magazine* took vehement exception to a passage in which Feuillet described the devotion inspired by a statue of the Blessed Virgin in Lima, which I shall quote at length.[2] "For more than a century the people of the town of Lima had honoured a statue of the Blessed Virgin in the church of the

---

[1] Newman to F. W. Faber, 30 October 1848, *LD*, XII, 316.
[2] The copy Faber translated is the third edition, published at Paris in 1671, the year of St. Rose of Lima's canonization by Clement X, who also beatified Pius V, the Spanish mystic John of the Cross (1542–91).

Friar Preachers, under the name of Our Lady of the Rosary, a devotion which these monks had taught to the people at the time that they planted the faith by their instructions in the most celebrated provinces of America," wrote the French Dominican hagiographer.

> But before we speak of the graces which St Rose received by this means, we must go farther back, and show what rendered the people so devout to this image. It was a wooden statue of our Blessed Lady, five feet high, which the first Spanish Christians who passed over into Peru with our forefathers brought from Europe with them, to be the powerful protectress of their project. She holds the Infant Jesus with her left arm, and with the right-hand offers a Rosary. When they had settled in this country, and had built this famous town now called Lima, they raised a superb church for the religious of the Order of Friar Preachers, under the name of the Holy Rosary, which was the first church and the first parish in which baptismal fonts were erected for the regeneration of spiritual children to Jesus Christ in the New World; and they placed in it this image, which was honoured by the people with special veneration, on account of the signal favours received through the protection of the Blessed Virgin of the Holy Rosary. The year 1535 was marked by one of these instances of her patronage. The Indians had assembled near Caxaguana, in the province of Cusco, to the number of two hundred thousand, in order to massacre the Christians; and they felt more assured of the victory as the Spanish army opposed to them consisted only of six hundred men. In this consternation the religious men, having placed themselves at the head of the Christian troops, exhorted them to implore the protection of our Lady of the Holy Rosary. They did so, and, filled with confidence in her assistance, they gave battle to this great multitude of Indians. At the moment in which the engagement began, they perceived in the air the Blessed Virgin, under the same form as she is represented in the Church of the Rosary, holding a rod in her hand, and threatening the Indians with death if they did not withdraw. The infidels were so alarmed at this vision, and so dazzled with the splendour that surrounded the Blessed Virgin, that they begged for quarter, and submitted not only to Spain, but also to the yoke of Jesus Christ by becoming Christians. This memorable victory increased the devotion of the people towards our Lady of the Rosary so much that Philip IV, king of Spain, having placed his kingdom of Peru under the protection of the Blessed Virgin on the 27th May, 1643, and having given notice of his intention to the archbishop, the viceroy, and magistrates of Lima, exhorted them to choose some image of the Blessed Virgin, and address to it their prayers, that they might obtain succour from her in the dangers which threatened the country. When the orders of his Catholic majesty were received, the archbishop, the viceroy,

and the two states ecclesiastical and secular, chose our Lady of the Rosary to be the protectress of the whole kingdom of Peru, and resolved that the people should every year go in procession, on the Monday in Low Week, to the Church of the Friar Preachers, to offer their prayers to her.[3]

For Price, that the Spanish king should have exhorted the people of Lima "to choose some image of the Blessed Virgin and address to it their prayers" was "gross, palpable idolatry" and Faber was culpable for turning a blind eye to "the dangerous tendencies of this species of modern hagiology."[4] In March of 1848, Newman had expressed his contrary view in a sermon called "Our Lady in the Gospel," telling his auditors:

> I do not wish you to take up books containing the praises of the Ever Blessed Virgin, and to use them and imitate them rashly without consideration. But be sure of this, that if you cannot enter into the warmth of foreign books of devotion it is a deficiency in you. To use strong words will not mend the matter; it is a fault which can only gradually be overcome, but it is a deficiency, for this reason, if for no other. Depend upon it, the way to enter into the sufferings of the Son, is to enter into the sufferings of the Mother. Place yourselves at the foot of the Cross, see Mary standing there, looking up and pierced with the sword. Imagine her feelings, make them your own. Let her be your great pattern.[5]

After seeing Price's diatribe, Bishop William Ullathorne was concerned "that the spirit of the 'Lives' as given in these translations is not adapted to the state of this country." He was convinced "That even religious persons and nuns do not find in them a wisdom according to sobriety, and that to the laity in general they are a source of uneasiness." Moreover, "By proposing more than the Church proposes even of the wonders of God in his saints ... we may lay burdens greater than can be born by a weak faith, an act which our Lord avoided doing, and we may deter those who are only seeking after the beginnings of faith altogether."[6]

Newman saw matters differently. "Protestants are converted by high views, not low ones; to hide from them the Lives of the Saints, is to escape

---

[3] *The Lives of St. Rose of Lima, the Blessed Colomba of Rieti, and of St. Juliana Falconieri*, trans. F. W. Faber (London: Thomas Richardson and Son, 1847), 104–6. One wonders what Price would have made of the prayers that were said to Our Lady of Victory before and after the Battle of Lepanto in 1571.

[4] Appendix 6: Extracts from Rev. E. Price's review of *The Lives of St Rose of Lima*, in *LD*, XII, 403–4.

[5] "Our Lady in the Gospel" (1848), in *Faith and Prejudice and Other Unpublished Sermons of Cardinal Newman* (New York: Sheed & Ward, 1956), 95–6.

[6] Bishop Ullathorne to Newman (31 October 1848), in *LD*, XII, 318–19.

indeed offending those who never would be converted, but at the same time to miss those who would; nay, those who might in the event be Saints themselves. We sacrifice the good to the bad."⁷ At the same time, Newman was sensible enough to recognize that any response to Price's fulminations must be prudent. "I am anxious about the Saints' Lives," he wrote Faber on 4 October after he had first read Price's letter and heard through Ambrose St John of the Bishop's concerns. "There is a row blowing up. Now, if we are advocates of doctrines, however true, with no authority to back us, it is the story of the Oxford Tracts over again—we shall be in a false position, and the harm and scandal done to religion, and the mischief to the Oratory, will be incalculable. I never can think this will be right."⁸ Nevertheless, Newman was adamant that "it is *shameful* to recommend us to stop the Lives, BEFORE they have made Price eat his words publicly."⁹ Price did recant, writing what Newman characterized as not "mere kind words ... but a retraction."¹⁰

Ullathorne, after conferring with the English bishops, as Newman had recommended, wrote in a public letter to *The Tablet* that the series "would become more widely acceptable, if various of the works were in some parts abridged ... [and] it would be yet better, if the lives were rewritten by good hands, both for the sake of style, and with a view to the better adapting them to the general reader in a country so ignorant and prejudiced on such subjects as this, with the introduction of remarks and reflections in suitable places to prepare the mind for entering into the spirit of the more wondrous parts of the narrative." Ullathorne was also careful to state that by recommending that the lives be suspended he did not mean that they be stopped altogether. "I sincerely regret that they have ceased. I should have preferred that they might be edited in some things differently as a whole; but I would not have had one authenticated miracle suppressed, for Almighty God worked them for those who should hear of them, as well as for those who witnessed them; nor would I have had one heroic act of virtue kept back."¹¹

Throughout the row, Newman and Ullathorne were at cross-purposes. Newman was upset because Ullathorne did not initially take the Oratorians'

---

7 Newman to Bishop Ullathorne (2 November 1848), in *LD*, XII, 319.
8 Newman to F. W. Faber (4 October 1848), in *LD*, XII, 278–9.
9 Newman to R. A. Coffin (22 October 1848), in *LD*, XII, 304.
10 Newman to J. M. Capes (6 December 1848), in *LD*, XII, 365.
11 Appendix 7, Bishop Ullathorne's letter on *The Lives of the Saints* to the editor of the Tablet (22 November 1848), in *LD*, XII, 405–7. Yet the English had not always been "ignorant" and "prejudiced" when it came to the saints. As Christopher Haigh notes, saints in the pre-Reformation English Church "played their part in the worship of all churches." Christopher Haigh, *English Reformations* (Oxford: Clarendon Press, 1993), 31.

part and simply denounce Price; instead, he suspended the series, first, and then—rather weakly for Newman's taste—took issue with Price's letter. Ullathorne was upset because Newman was "curt, trenchant, and somewhat polemical."[12] Their misunderstanding notwithstanding, Newman managed to come away from the dispute with a memorable apothegm: "just as gentlemen make acquaintance with bowing and civil speeches, so the way to be good friends with him is to begin with a boxing match."[13] Ullathorne's biographer, Judith Champ says that "This was a perceptive assessment" since "there were several instances throughout life when Ullathorne launched a hostile broadside at a new acquaintance, only to find later that they had the basis of a firm friendship. Fierce disagreements were never a barrier to friendship with Ullathorne, in fact, they were almost an expectation."[14] Once Newman learned of the apology that Price sent Faber, he wrote himself to Price to thank him for his "kind and generous letter" and invited him to St. Wilfrid's in Staffordshire so that he and the other Oratorian fathers could show him the "love and respect" they felt for him, only adding: "Once, I believe, in your kind charity, you thought of calling to me at Littlemore, when I was a Protestant; fulfill this long intention now, and accept the hospitality of a Catholic house."[15] On 6 January 1849, Ullathorne approved the recommencement of the series, and it was duly resumed under the editorial auspices of the English Oratory.

This was a tell-tale episode for a number of reasons. It highlighted what would become Newman's abiding recognition of the need in England for Catholic education, not only in the lives of the saints but in all aspects of the Faith. It initiated what became his vital friendship with William Ullathorne, a friendship emblematic of the sort of saintly friendships that Newman would cultivate throughout his life. (Indeed, towards the end of Newman's life, Ullathorne became convinced that "There is a Saint in that man!")[16] And it foreshadowed the opposition to the very notion of sanctity and sainthood with which Newman's legacy continues to be involved. In this chapter, I shall endeavor to show how hagiography is vital to any critical estimate of that legacy by showing how the historical Newman cannot be understood unless one takes into account his views on sanctity, sainthood and the popular faith that gave rise to the cult of the

---

12 Ullathorne, quoted in Judith Champ, *William Bernard Ullathorne: A Different Kind of Monk* (Leominster: Gracewing, 2006), 171.
13 Newman to J. M. Capes (9 November 1848), in *LD*, XII, 337.
14 Champ, *William Bernard Ullathorne*, 171.
15 Newman to Edward Price (3 December 1848), in *LD*, XII, 362. Newman was always keen on reconciling with anyone with whom he found himself in controversy.
16 Bishop Ullathorne, quoted in Cuthbert Butler, *The Life and Times of Bishop Ullathorne 1800–1889* (London: Burns, Oates and Washbourne, 1926), II, 283–4.

saints, all of which necessarily influenced and, in some respects, formed his own sanctity.

In his account of the *fracas* over the "Lives of the Saints," the founding editor of *The Letters and Diaries of John Henry Newman*, Father Stephen Dessain wrote: "Newman's loyalty made him support Faber fully under a wanton attack, and his Catholic docility may have blinded him to defects in these fully authorised *Lives*. Newman later suggested that he had been led on too far by the younger men around him; also that the view which came naturally to him did not differ from that of the old Catholics."[17] To substantiate this reading of the matter, Dessain cited the passage in Newman's *A Letter to the Rev. E. B. Pusey* (1866). "When I returned to England," Newman wrote, "the first expression of theological opinion which came in my way was apropos of the series of translated saints' lives which the late Dr. Faber originated." Then, referring to Ullathorne, he explained how

> That expression proceeded from a wise prelate, who was properly anxious as to the line which might be taken by the Oxford converts, then for the first time coming into work ... If at that time I was betrayed into any acts which were of a more extreme character than I should approve now, the responsibility of course is mine; but the impulse came not from old Catholics or superiors, but from men whom I loved and trusted who were younger than myself. But to whatever extent I might be carried away, and I cannot recollect any tangible instances, my mind in no long time fell back to what seems to me a safer and more practical course.[18]

Of course, this is true, as far as it goes, but it is not the whole truth. It is true that Newman would always take a critical view of devotions to Our Lady that might call the belief of Catholics into legitimate question. Indeed, in his *Apologia pro Vita Sua* (1864), he admitted that "the writings of St. Alfonso ... prejudiced me as much against the Roman Church as anything else, on account of what was called their 'Mariolatry.'" When Dr. Charles Russell of Maynooth, the man whom Newman credited most for helping him to convert, sent him sermons by St. Alfonso, they were heavily bowdlerized, proof that "Italian authors were not acceptable to every part of the Catholic world." For Newman, "Such devotional manifestations in honour of our Lady had been my great *crux* as regards Catholicism; I say frankly, I do not fully enter into them now; I trust I do not love her the less, because I cannot enter into them. They may be fully explained and

---

17 *LD*, XII, 278, n. 2.
18 John Henry Newman, *A Letter to the Rev. E. B. Pusey on his Recent Eirenicon* (London: Longman, 1866), 22–3.

defended; but sentiment and taste do not run with logic: they are suitable for Italy but they are not suitable for England."[19] When Newman took to composing his own hagiographical writings, many of which can be found in the second volume of his *Historical Sketches* (1873), they were considerably more restrained, though what is interesting about them is their oblique autobiographical character. Writing of St. Augustine's conversion, for example, he says:

> in proportion as the view of Christian truth opened on Augustine's mind, so was he drawn on to that higher state of Christian conversation on which our Lord and His Apostle have bestowed special praise. So it was, and not unnaturally in those times, that high and earnest minds, when they had found the truth, were not content to embrace it by halves; they would take all or none, they would go all lengths, they would covet the most excellent gifts, or they would remain as they were. It seemed to them absurd to take so much trouble to find the truth, and to submit to such a revolution in their opinions and motives as its reception involved ; and yet, after all, to content themselves with a second-best profession.[20]

In his *Letter to Pusey* in response to Pusey's first *Eirenicon* (1866), in which the Canon of Christ Church had cited certain extravagant Catholic devotions to Our Lady as one of the main Anglican objections to the Church of Rome, Newman made his view of these exorbitant devotions perfectly plain.[21] "I never can deny my belief that the Blessed Virgin prays efficaciously for the Church," he wrote, "and for individual souls in and out of it. Nor can I deny that to be devout to her is a duty following on this doctrine — but I never will say, even though St Bernardine said it, that no one is saved who is not devout to her."[22] Pusey confused devotion with doctrine. For Newman, "Suarez teaches dogma, and dogma is fixed. St. Bernadine is devotional, and devotion is free."[23]

Yet, at the same time, unlike the Old Catholic gentry, who, as Newman told a friend, "rejoice in their religion themselves, but make it a matter of private concern, and make no effort at converting others," he was not prepared to condemn these devotions out of hand.[24] After all, Pusey had

---

19 *Apologia*, 176–7.
20 John Henry Newman, *The Church of the Fathers* (London: J. G. F. Rivington, 1842), 234–5.
21 For a good critical overview of Newman's response to Pusey's *Eirenicon*, see Mark D. Chapman, *The Fantasy of Reunion: Anglicans, Catholics and Ecumenism, 1833–1882* (Oxford: Oxford University Press, 2014).
22 Newman to John Keble (8 October 1865), in *LD*, XXII, 68.
23 Newman to Edward Pusey (31 October 1865), in *LD*, XXII, 90.
24 Newman to John Hungerford Pollen (6 January 1859), in *LD*, XIX, 10.

couched his criticisms of Catholic devotions to the Blessed Virgin in such a way as to obscure a defining aspect of Our Lady.

> You seem, in one place in your Volume, to object to the Antiphon, in which it is said of her, "All heresies thou hast destroyed alone." Surely the truth of it is verified in this age, as in former times, and especially by the doctrine concerning her, on which I have been dwelling. She is the great exemplar of prayer in a generation, which emphatically denies the power of prayer in toto, which determines that fatal laws govern the universe, that there cannot be any direct communication between earth and heaven, that God cannot visit His earth, and that man cannot influence His providence.[25]

Moreover, the parish priest in Newman could not have failed to recognize that the Marian devotions of the faithful are not dry, theological exercises. "Religion acts on the affections," he reminded his readers.

> And of all passions love is the most unmanageable; nay more, I would not give much for that love which is never extravagant, which always observes the proprieties, and can move about in perfect good taste, under all emergencies. What mother, what husband or wife, what youth or maiden in love, but says a thousand foolish things, in the way of endearment, which the speaker would be sorry for strangers to hear; yet they are not on that account unwelcome to the parties to whom they are addressed ... So it is with devotional feelings ... What is abstractedly extravagant may in particular persons be becoming and beautiful ... When it is formalized into meditations or exercises, it is as repulsive as love letters in a police report. Moreover, even holy minds readily adopt and become familiar with language which they would never have originated themselves, when it proceeds from a writer who has the same objects of devotion as they have ...[26]

No one exemplifies the truth of what Newman is saying here better than Newman himself. In his sermon, "The Second Spring," which he preached in 1852 at St. Mary's Oscott to celebrate the reestablishment of the English Catholic hierarchy, it was only fitting that he should take up the same language of fervent, intercessory prayer that he would later urge his old Tractarian friend to reconsider.

> Arise, Mary, and go forth in thy strength into that north country, which once was thine own, and take possession of a land which knows thee not. Arise, Mother of God, and with thy thrilling voice, speak to those who labour with child, and are in pain, till the babe

---

25 *Letter to Pusey*, 81–2.
26 *Ibid.*, 80–1.

of grace leaps within them! Shine on us, dear Lady, with thy bright countenance, like the sun in his strength, *O stella matutina*, O harbinger of peace, till our year is one perpetual May. From thy sweet eyes, from thy pure smile, from thy majestic brow, let ten thousand influences rain down, not to confound or overwhelm, but to persuade, to win over thine enemies. O Mary, my hope, O Mother undefiled, fulfil to us the promise of this Spring. A second temple rises on the ruins of the old. Canterbury has gone its way, and York is gone, and Durham is gone, and Winchester is gone. It was sore to part with them. We clung to the vision of past greatness, and would not believe it could come to nought; but the Church in England has died, and the Church lives again. Westminster and Nottingham, Beverley and Hexham, Northampton and Shrewsbury, if the world lasts, shall be names as musical to the ear, as stirring to the heart, as the glories we have lost; and Saints shall rise out of them, if God so will, and Doctors once again shall give the law to Israel, and Preachers call to penance and to justice, as at the beginning.[27]

Considering this moving passage, we need to ascertain whether Newman was right in assuming that his own view of foreign hagiography was, in fact, the view held by the Old Catholics. After all, Newman, to put it mildly, was never sympathetic to the Cisalpine party, even though he was equally opposed to the Ultramontanes, or those whom Edward Caswall nicely called "bumptious Romans."[28] When it came to sharing with his contemporaries the popular faith that often underlay the cult of the saints, Newman was not inveterately inclined to take the "safer and more practical course." He may have appreciated that the religion of the ordinary man was not always either logical or dignified, but, for all its incidental corruption, he still saw it as a vital part of the Church. Certainly, he was intent on seeing the religion of ordinary men objectively, insisting that: "what has power to stir holy and refined souls is potent also with the multitude; and the religion of the multitude is ever vulgar and abnormal; it ever will be tinctured with fanaticism and superstition, while men are what they are. A people's religion is ever a corrupt religion, in spite of the provisions of Holy Church. If she is to be Catholic, you must put up with fish of every kind, guests good and bad, vessels of gold, vessels of earth."[29]

Nevertheless, it was characteristic of Newman to recognize that all Christians had shortcomings, and it was with these in mind that he responded in 1866 to Bishop Ullathorne's request for prayers for the beleaguered Pius IX, faced as he was by a situation in his own backyard in which, to use the Bishops words, Italian statesmen "imprison and exile the bishops and

---

27 Newman, *Sermons on Various Occasions*, 177–8.
28 Newman to Ambrose St. John (25 July 1865), in *LD*, XXI, 165.
29 *Letter to Pusey*, 86.

clergy, leave the flocks without shepherds, confiscate the Church's revenues, suppress the monasteries and convents, incorporate ecclesiastics and religious in the army, plunder the churches and monastic libraries, and expose religion herself, stripped and bleeding in every limb, the Catholic Religion in the person of her ministers, her sacraments, her most devoted members, to be objects of profane and blasphemous ridicule."[30] In "The Pope and the Revolution," preached on the feast of the Holy Rosary of the Blessed Virgin Mary, Newman urged his flock "with feelings of solemn expectation" and "joyful confidence" to come before "God and pray Him to have mercy on His chosen Servant, His own Vicar, in this hour of trial." And in a sermon in which Newman demonstrated his shrewd understanding of the pope's true as opposed to his merely temporal power—"the desolateness of Rome is as befitting to a kingdom which is not of this world as it is incompatible with a creation of modern political theories"—he proceeds to show how the shortcomings of the faithful only make their prayers more wholehearted.

> We come to Him, like the prophet Daniel, in humiliation for our own sins and the sins of our kings, our princes, our fathers, and our people in all parts of the Church; and therefore we say the Miserere and the Litany of the Saints, as in a time of fast. And we come before Him in the bright and glad spirit of soldiers who know they are under the leading of an Invincible King, and wait with beating hearts to see what He is about to do; and therefore it is that we adorn our sanctuary, bringing out our hangings and multiplying our lights, as on a day of festival. We know well we are on the winning side, and that the prayers of the poor, the weak, and the despised, can do more, when offered in a true spirit, than all the wisdom and all the resources of the world. This seventh of October is the very anniversary of that day on which the prayers of St. Pius, and the Holy Rosary said by thousands of the faithful at his bidding, broke for ever the domination of the Turks in the great battle of Lepanto. God will give us what we ask, or He will give us something better. In this spirit let us proceed with the holy rites which we have begun,—in the presence of innumerable witnesses, of God the Judge of all, of Jesus the Mediator of the New Covenant, of His Mother Mary our Immaculate Protectress, of all the Angels of Holy Church, of all the blessed. Saints, of Apostles and Evangelists, Martyrs and Confessors, holy preachers, holy recluses, holy virgins, of holy innocents taken away before actual sin, and of all other holy souls who have been purified by suffering, and have already reached their heavenly home.[31]

30 Ullathorne, quoted in John Henry Newman, "The Pope and the Revolution" (1866), in *Sermons Preached on Various Occasions*, 3rd edn (London: Burns, Oates & Co., 1870), 297.
31 *Ibid.*, 298.

Here, Newman could not have given more definite expression to his respect for the faith of ordinary Catholics—Catholics, that is to say, who batten on hagiography: "the prayers of the poor, the weak, and the despised, can do more, when offered in a true spirit, than all the wisdom and all the resources of the world."

At the same time, Newman was appreciative of how the faithful laity could often reaffirm the true Faith when the episcopate went missing. In *On Consulting the Faithful in Matters of Doctrine* (1859), he remarked how: "It is not a little remarkable, that, though, historically speaking, the fourth century is the age of doctors, illustrated, as it was, by the saints Athanasius, Hilary, the two Gregories, Basil, Chrysostom, Ambrose, Jerome, and Augustine, and all of these saints bishops also, except one, nevertheless in that very day the divine tradition committed to the infallible Church was proclaimed and maintained far more by the faithful than by the Episcopate"—a reality that must give our own beleaguered faithful hope.[32]

Hilaire Belloc saw the same dynamic at play in the case of St. Thomas Becket of Canterbury, the great foe of English Erastianism. Once Thomas was murdered in the north transept of Canterbury Cathedral, "Those few moments of tragedy … had done what many years of effort had so far failed to do. The whole movement against the Church was stopped dead. The tide ran rapidly backward—within an hour St. Thomas was a martyr, within a month the champion not only of religion but the common people, who obscurely but firmly knew that the independence of the Church was their safeguard."[33] And this was an independence that all of the faithful laity—from courtiers to commoners—could celebrate in their shared devotion to St. Thomas. As even the skeptical historian John Guy points out in his portrait of the martyr: "The 'Book of Miracles' begun by the first guardian of the shrine, Benedict of Peterborough, and faithfully continued by his successors reports St. Thomas showing special favor to fine courtiers, knights, merchants, and their families … But since a majority of pilgrims were women, priests, and commoners, it also records innumerable cases of safe delivery in childbirth; poor folk cured of blindness, palsy, dropsy, and leprosy; and even instances of babies brought back from the dead."[34]

---

32 John Henry Newman, *On Consulting the Faithful in Matters of Doctrine*, ed. John Coulson (New York: Sheed & Ward, 1962), 75.

33 Hilaire Belloc, "Saint Thomas of Canterbury" (1933), in *Studies in English Sanctity from Bede to Newman*, ed. Maisie Ward (Washington: Cluny Media, 2016), 125–6. Cf. "The people know their Church a tower of strength / A bulwark against Throne and Baronage." Alfred Lord Tennyson, *Becket and Other Plays*, ed. Hallam Tennyson (London: Macmillan, 1920), 25.

34 John Guy, *Thomas Beckett: Warrior, Priest, Rebel* (New York: Random House, 2012), 341.

Moreover, Anne Duggan, the editor of Becket's letters, insists that the popular veneration that led to his canonization was "spontaneous"; it was not "a monk-led movement." Fifteen cures, all of them remote, had been reported within three months of Becket's murder, at a time when Canterbury Cathedral itself was shut.[35] What the ordinary people of England saw and revered in Becket was what the historian David Knowles saw and revered in him: a champion of the embattled Church. "As the struggle wore on," Knowles writes in the superb Raleigh Lecture that he gave on Becket in 1949, "the precise object for which the archbishop fought had changed its appearance in his eyes. At the beginning it had been the forensic rights of the Church and the clerical order; then it had become at Clarendon the freedom of the English Church as a part of the Universal Church in its relations with Rome; finally, it had broadened into a defense of the rights of God as against Caesar."[36]

In light of Newman's recognition of the merits of the faith of the laity — a faith which has always animated hagiography — it is striking to recall Cardinal Manning's characterization of Newman's view of these matters. After reading Newman's *Letter to Pusey*, Monsignor Talbot had written Manning to express his displeasure with the book, most of which he found "detestable." Of course, from Talbot's Ultramontane standpoint, it was insufficiently Roman: "Every Englishman is naturally anti-Roman," he conceded. But "Dr. Newman is more English than the English." And it followed for Talbot that "His spirit must be crushed."[37] To which Manning replied:

> Whether he likes it or not, [Newman] has become the centre of those who hold low views of the Holy See, are anti-Roman, cold and silent, to say no more, about the Temporal Power, national, English, critical of Catholic devotions, and always on the lower side. I see danger of a Cisalpine Club rising again, but I see much danger of an English Catholicism of which Newman is the highest type. It is the old Anglican, patristic, literary, Oxford tone transplanted into the Church. It takes the line of deprecating exaggerations, foreign devotions, Ultramontanism, anti-national sympathies. In one word, it is worldly Catholicism, and it will have the worldly on its side, and will deceive many.[38]

---

35 Anne Duggan, *Thomas Becket* (London: Arnold, 2004), 216–17.

36 David Knowles, *The Historian and Character and Other Essays* (Cambridge: Cambridge University Press, 1963), 121.

37 Talbot to Manning (20 February 1866), Edmund Sheridan Purcell, *Life of Cardinal Manning, Archbishop of Westminster* (London: Macmillan & Co., 1896), II, 322–3.

38 Manning to Monsignor Talbot (25 February 1866), *Life of Cardinal Manning*, II, 322–3.

Hagiography, History, and John Henry Newman

For Manning to see what he characterized as "the old Anglican, patristic, literary, Oxford tone" in Newman's *Letter to Pusey* was odd because, in fact, in that book, Newman not only describes but accepts the very popular religion on which so much of the success of Pope Pius IX's Ultramontane pontificate (1846–78) was based. Eamon Duffy is good on this aspect of that flamboyant pontificate:

> Ultramontanism ... held the Pope in mystical reverence. This devout papalism was just one aspect of a devotional revolution within Catholicism, away from the sober decorum of eighteenth-century religion towards a more emotional and colorful religion of the heart, a new emphasis on ceremonial, on the saints, on the Virgin Mary. The reform Catholicism of the previous century had frowned on and played down such manifestations of popular religious feeling. Nineteenth-century Catholicism welcomed them ... And indeed in the age of cheap popular prints and the emergence of the mass media, the Pope himself became, quite literally, a popular icon. Catholic households from Africa to the Americas were as likely to display a picture of the Pope as a crucifix or statue of the Virgin, and the face of Pio Nono was better known than that of any pope in history ... Even his critics, exasperated by his stubbornness and unimpressed by his modest intellect, admitted that it was impossible to dislike him. He was genial, unpretentious, wreathed in clouds of snuff, always laughing.[39]

Duffy, however, is wrong when he says that Newman "was scathingly critical of the authoritarian papacy of Pope Pius IX ... and he opposed the definition of papal infallibility in 1870 as an unnecessary and inappropriate burden on consciences."[40] After all, Pius IX blessed the foundation of the Oratory and restored the Catholic hierarchy in England. Newman may have been "scathingly critical" of "the insolent, aggressive faction"[41] that was attempting to impose an extreme definition of infallibility on the First Vatican Council but he had no problem accepting the definition of infallibility that the Council eventually adopted, even though, paradoxically, it was drafted by his *bête noire* in Dublin while he was putting together his Oxford on the Liffey, Archbishop Paul Cullen. And if he was opposed to the Ultramontanes, especially in England, who were trying to lead the pope's papacy into untenably immoderate positions, he saw the good points in Pio Nono himself. For Newman:

---

39 Eamon Duffy, *Saints and Sinners: A History of the Popes*, revised edn (New Haven and London: Yale University Press, 2006), 315–18.

40 Eamon Duffy, "A Hero of the Church," *New York Review of Books* (23 December 2010).

41 Newman to Ullathorne (28 January 1870), in *LD*, XXV, 19.

> His misfortunes indeed had something to do with his popularity. The whole world felt that he was shamefully used as regards his temporal possessions; no foreign power had any right to seize upon his palaces, churches, and other possessions; and the injustice shown him created a wide interest in him; but the main cause of his popularity was the magic of his presence, which was such as to dissipate and utterly destroy the fog out of which the image of a Pope looms to the ordinary Englishman. His uncompromising faith, his courage, the graceful intermingling in him of the human and the divine, the humour, the wit, the playfulness with which he tempered his severity, his naturalness, and then his true eloquence, and the resources he had at command for meeting with appropriate words the circumstances of the moment, overcame those who were least likely to be overcome.[42]

Unlike Talbot and Manning and so many other Ultramontanes, however, Newman was clear enough to see that the pope's very popularity, although in some respects welcome, was not without grave dangers. Pio Nono's insouciant boast, *La tradizone son' io* ("*I* am the tradition") was eloquent proof of that. While appreciative of popular religion, Newman saw it with a critical judiciousness of which Talbot and Manning—let alone Pusey—were incapable. "You may beat religion out of men, if you will," he pointed out, "and then their excesses will take a different direction; but if you make use of religion to improve them, they will make use of religion to corrupt it. And then you will have effected that compromise of which our countrymen report so unfavourably from abroad:—a high grand faith and worship which compels their admiration, and puerile absurdities among the people which excite their contempt."[43]

If Newman could be wary of popular religion, for all its vitality, he could also be wary of the logic of the educated, convinced as he was that it often proved an unreliable antidote to popular excesses. "Theology both uses logic and baffles it; and thus logic acts both as a protection and as the perversion of religion," he wrote. "Theology is occupied with supernatural matters, and is ever running into mysteries, which reason can neither explain nor adjust. Its lines of thought come to an abrupt termination, and to pursue them or to complete them is to plunge down the abyss. But logic blunders on, forcing its way, as it can, through thick darkness and ethereal mediums. The Arians went ahead with logic for their directing principle, and so lost the truth."[44] Then, again, in the *Grammar of Assent*, he remarks:

---

42 "Address at the Birmingham Annual Catholic Reunion" (27 January 1880), in *Addresses to Cardinal Newman and his Replies*, ed. W. P. Neville (London: Longman, 1905), 243.

43 *Letter to Pusey*, 86.

44 *Ibid.*, 86–7.

Hagiography, History, and John Henry Newman

> It is natural ... to ask the question, why ratiocination should be an exception to a general law which attached to the intellectual exercise of the mind; why it is held to be commensurate with logical science and why logic is made an instrumental art sufficient for determining every sort of truth, while no one would dream of making any one formula, however generalized, a working rule at once for poetry, the art of medicine, and political warfare?[45]

Here, Newman might have been taking aim at the Noetics of the Oriel Senior Common Room, especially Thomas Arnold, Edward Copleston, Renn Dickson Hampden and Richard Whately, all of whose trust in logic led them to embrace a static, ahistorical, lifeless Christianity, which, in its way, drew on the same private judgment and contempt for the faith of ordinary Catholics that animated the Arian heresy.

It was apt that Newman should remind Pusey of these logical pitfalls because while John Ruskin might have described him as "not in the least a picturesque or tremendous figure, but only a sickly and rather ill put together English clerical gentleman, who never looked one in the face, or appeared aware of the weather," he was nonetheless a consistent and clear-sighted critic of the rationalism that vitiated so much of the religious thinking of his Protestant contemporaries, a rationalism from which the Noetics were never free.[46] Certainly, Pusey was more prophetic than he could have realized when he said apropos the rationalism that had taken root in Germany in the 1820s: "This will all come up us in England, and how utterly unprepared for it we are!"[47]

Another aspect of the Noetic faith that Newman would come to know to his own personal chagrin was its ardent No Popery. Whately gave a good example of this in his *Errors of Romanism* (1845) where he inveighed against: "the spirit of Superstition ... the spirit of Persecution, the spirit of Insincerity, of Fraud, and of Indifference to truth,—in short, all those evil propensities which are fitly characterized in one word as the spirit of Romanism."[48] Whately's view of those who opposed the English Reformation was similarly skewered:

> Those ... who opposed the Reformation were probably most of them neither worldly-minded hypocrites, altogether indifferent about true religion, nor, on the other hand, sincere believers in the justice

---

45 *Grammar of Assent*, 231.
46 John Ruskin, *Praeterita: Outlines of Scenes and Thoughts Perhaps Worthy of Memory in My Past Life* (London: Rupert-Hart Davis, 1949), 191.
47 Pusey, quoted in Henry Parry Liddon, *Life of Edward Bouverie Pusey* (London: Longman, Green & Co., 1897), IV, 3.
48 Richard Whately, *Essays on the Errors of Romanism: Having their Origin in Human Nature* (London: B. Fellowes, 1845), 17.

of all the claims of the Romish See which they supported, and in the truth of all the Romish doctrines which they maintained; but men who were content to submit to some injustice, and to connive at some error, rather than risk, in the attempt to reform abuses, the overthrow of all religion. They preferred an edifice, which, though not faultless, they considered highly serviceable, to the apprehended alternative of a heap of ruins.[49]

For Whately, if one chose to subscribe to a communion founded on pious fraud, a certain amount of equivocation was unavoidable.

Then, again, Edward Hawkins, the Provost of Oriel made no bones of his contempt for the popular devotions of Roman Catholicism. After Newman resigned his Oriel Fellowship on 3 October 1845, he received a letter from the Provost, which was a fair specimen of the reaction he received from many Anglican quarters.

You say nothing of your present position or intentions. Possibly you are thinking of retiring into Lay Community; and against this, if you hold the opinions which I suppose, I could say nothing. But your letter is so strong a confirmation of the rumours I have heard of your intention to join the Roman Church, that I venture to write to you as if it were so. And indeed, in any other case, where I could speak officially or as a friend, I should do what I could to dissuade any member, much more any minister, of the Church of England, from what you know I cannot but regard as very grievous error. It is not from want of regard for you, if I forebear to say anything in your case, but only because I despair of doing any good, when you have been so long studying all questions of this kind; and indeed much more, and more anxiously, no doubt, than I have myself. And yet I cannot forbear expressing the most earnest hope (in all sincerity and feelings of real kindness) that, whatever course you have resolved upon, you may still at least be saved from the worst errors of the Church of Rome, such as praying to human Mediators or falling down before images—because in you, with all the great advantages with which God has blessed and tried you, I must believe such errors to be most deeply sinful.[50]

Apropos Hawkins's comments here, Bishop Ullathorne was clairvoyant when he wrote Newman during the row over Faber's translation: "My dear Mr. Newman ... I know that your lives have been lives of warfare and contest, and that you have had painfully to controvert the authorities under which you were brought up. We have not had that fierce trial."[51] That the

---

49 *Errors of Romanism*, 152.
50 Edward Hawkins to Newman (6 October 1845), in *LD*, X, 782.
51 Bishop Ullathorne to Newman (29 November 1848), in *LD*, XII, 353.

man who had spent so much of his earlier life converting the convicts of New South Wales should have instinctively known how fierce the religious wars of Oxford could be says much for his discernment. For Ullathorne, converting drunkards to the true faith must have seemed infinitely easier than converting dons.

In retrospect, it is striking that Pusey prompted Newman to reveal so much of his views on the popular faith of Catholics because while he was involved in the controversy over Faber's *Lives of the Saints*, he had occasion to correspond with someone who was taking spiritual direction from Pusey, Catherine Ward, who had written Newman to ask his help with her religious difficulties. Having grown uneasy with Pusey's "mimic Catholicism," she was eager to hear what Newman made of the Anglican faith of the shy, untidy Biblical scholar—a faith which, again, was the very reverse of any popular faith.[52] In describing what he considered the consequential differences between Anglicanism and Catholicism, Newman naturally chose to see them in terms of sainthood,

> There is another reason why the Anglican Church cannot take support from the high religious excellence of *individuals* who are found in her. It is that the *direction* of their holy feelings, views, and works is, not *towards* that Church, but *away from* it, and bears testimony consequently, not to it, but against it; whereas the whole company of Catholic Saints, not only are indefinitely higher in sanctity than the best Anglicans, but are the natural fulfilment of the idea, the due exemplification of the teaching, of the Catholic Church. Who will say that fasting, devotion, and the like are in any sense the fruit of the historical, real, tangible Church of England? Is not *the idea* of an Anglican Bishop or clergyman, that of a gentleman, a scholar, a good father of a family, a well conducted, kindhearted, religiously minded man, and little more? The devotion of the living Church of England is not in the *line* of saint-ship. There are bad men in all systems; I put such aside on either hand; take a really true specimen of an Anglican, a *fair* specimen; e.g. (to take public men) the Bishop of London or Dr. Hook; they are not the tenth, the twentieth, the infinitesimal part of a Saint; you could not multiply them up until they became saints; they tend to something different; their perfection is something different. By contrast, take Dr. Pusey; no one would call him a *specimen* of the *Church of England*; he is undeniably foreign, outlandish; whereas everyone would call St Carlo or St Francis de Sales, a *specimen* of the Catholic Church; I mean a specimen of its teaching, its profession, its aim. Is Dr. Pusey more like a Monk or a Dignitary? is he of the Anglican type? How then can such as he be witnesses for the sanctity and divine life of the

52 *Difficulties Felt by Anglicans*, 4.

Anglican Church? As well might you say that the Irish character was cool, self possessed, patient, and unimaginative, because the Duke of Wellington is an Irishman.[53]

At about the same time that Newman drew these witty distinctions, he also wrote what he intended to be a preface for Faber's *Lives of the Saints*, which gives excellent insight into Newman's understanding of the sanctity that goes into the making of a saint. "The Saints are the glad and complete specimens of the new creation which our Lord brought into the moral world, and as 'the heavens declare the glory of God' as Creator, so are the Saints the proper and true evidence of the God of Christianity, and tell out into all lands the power and grace of Him who made them," Newman wrote. But he also recognized that they were a reflection of the faith of ordinary Catholics that so many of Newman's educated contemporaries found *outré*. "What the existence of the Church itself is to the learned and philosophical, such are the Saints to the multitude. They are the popular evidence of Christianity, and the most complete and logical evidence while the most popular." Here, too, Newman made a plug for hagiography, recognizing as he did that "in the life of a Saint, we have a microcosm, or whole work of God, a perfect work from beginning to end, yet one which may be bound between two boards, and mastered by the most unlearned. The exhibition of a person, his thoughts, his words, his acts, his trials, his fortunes, his beginnings, his growth, his end, have a charm to every one, and when he is a Saint they have a divine influence and persuasion, a power of exercising and eliciting the latent elements of divine grace in individual readers, as no other reading can claim." If what Newman says here of the study of saints in general is true, surely it is equally true of the study of his own life and work. "We consider that the Lives of the Saints are one of the main and special instruments, to which, under God, we may look for the conversion of our countrymen at this time."[54]

This last point is important because for Newman, and, indeed, for Faber, the *Lives of the Saints* were to be a means of practical evangelization, not merely an exercise in scholarly hagiography. They meant the *Lives* to convert souls. They were not of the view common in our own addled age that proselytism is "poison."[55] On the contrary, Newman was sensible

---

53 Newman to Catherine Ward (25 September 1848), in *LD*, XII, 273.

54 Appendix 5: Draft of a Preface for Faber's *Lives of the Saints*, probably written in the autumn of 1848, in *LD*, XII, 399–400.

55 "One of the most quoted statements of [Pope] Francis regarding the 'commemoration' of the 500th anniversary of the Reformation illustrates another effect of the excessive zeal for ecumenism: an ever-expanding definition of 'proselytism.' In response to a question from a girl who was interested in bringing her unchurched friends with her to worship, Francis warned her: 'It is not licit that you convince them of your faith;

enough to realize that without proselytism of some sort there could be no propagation of the Faith. To contend otherwise would be disingenuous. In 1868, he made this amusingly plain in a letter to Pusey.

> As to individual proselytism, you must recollect that we only feel and do what you feel and do towards Dissenters. By what right have you converted from Dissent, as you say, 32 out of 40 Bishops of the Anglo-American Church? By the same right we have converted a number of men who are now among our Priests—You write to the Westleyans and try to co-operate with them; but I am sure you would make a Wesleyan, whom you met with, a good Anglican, if you could. I am not aware that Manning and Ward convert individuals, any more than I should, in order to weaken the Anglican Church, but from love to the soul of the individual converted, as *you* would feel love for the Wesleyan.
>
> By the bye, the position of the Wesleyans is remarkable. They are narrow-minded, self-sufficient, and conceited—but they seem to me to be more likely to make a stand against infidelity than any religious body in England.[56]

Manning's charge that Newman's was a "worldly" faith was obviously meant as a slur but, in a profound sense, Newman's faith *was* worldly, if by "worldly" we mean that it was dedicated to the salvation of souls in a fallen world. One could cite many passages to make this point but here is an especially apposite one from *Lectures on Certain Difficulties Felt by Anglicans in Submitting to the Catholic Church* (1850), in which Newman anticipated the famous animadversion that he would present in *The Idea of a University* (1873) on what constitutes the gentleman.[57]

> I may say the Church aims at three special virtues, which reconcile and unite the soul to its Maker;—faith, purity, and charity;—for two of which the world cares little or nothing. The world, on the other hand, puts in the first place, in some states of society, certain heroic qualities; in others, certain virtues of a political or mercantile character. In ruder ages, it is personal courage, strength of purpose, magnanimity; in more civilized, honesty, fairness, honour, truth, and benevolence:—virtues, all of which, of course, the teaching of the Church comprehends, all of which she expects in their degree in all her consistent children, and all of which she exacts in their fulness in her saints: but which, after all, most beautiful as they

---

proselytism is the strongest poison against the ecumenical path.'" Matthew Cullinan Hoffman, "Ecumenism, 'Proselytism,' and the Danger of Doctrinal Ambiguity," *Catholic World Report* (9 December 2016).
56 Newman to Pusey (16 August 1868), in *LD*, XXIV, 125.
57 *The Idea of a University*, 179–81.

> are, are really the fruit of nature as well as of grace; which do not necessarily imply grace at all: which do not reach so far as sanctity, or unite the soul by any supernatural process to the source of supernatural perfection and supernatural blessedness.[58]

Here, it is clear, Newman was contrasting the Church and the world in a way that went well beyond the toy theatre of church politics in which the Archbishop of Westminster expended so much restless energy. Yet, what is always extraordinary about Newman's meditations on the world is their reality. Although he spent most of his days outside the world, he never saw the world in unreal or abstract terms. For Newman, the world might be suffering desperately from spiritual hunger but "it talks of religion being a matter of private concern, too personal, too sacred, for it to have any opinion about." The world "praises public men, if they are useful to itself, but simply ridicules inquiry into their motives, thinks it impertinent in others to attempt it, and out of taste in themselves to invite it." In his King William Street lectures, Newman addressed his auditors like a good Dutch uncle.

> All public men it thinks pretty much the same at bottom; but what matter to it, if they do its work? It offers high pay, and it expects faithful service; but as to its agents, overseers, men of business, operatives, journeymen, figure-servants, and labourers, what they are personally, what their principles and aims, what their creed, what their conversation is, where they live, how they spend their leisure time, whither they are going, how they die,—I am stating a simple matter of fact, I am not here praising or blaming, I am but contrasting,—I say, all questions implying the existence of the soul, are as much beyond the circuit of the world's imagination, as they are intimately and primarily present to the apprehension of the Church.[59]

If the theme of this section of the lecture was on the high stakes implicit in the choice between belief and unbelief, Newman showed the practical cast of his interest in the matter by driving home just how high those stakes were. It is no wonder that such a tough-minded critic as Richard Holt Hutton, the editor of the *Spectator* should never have forgotten the lectures and considered them "marked by all the signs of [Newman's] singular literary genius."[60]

> The Church, then, considers the momentary, fleeting act of the will ... to be capable of guiltiness of the deadliest character, or of the

---

58 *Difficulties Felt by Anglicans*, 204–5.
59 *Ibid.*, 205.
60 Hutton. *Cardinal Newman*, 207.

most efficacious and triumphant merit. She holds that a soul laden with the most enormous offence in deed as well as thought, a savage tyrant, who delighted in cruelty, an habitual adulterer, a murderer, a blasphemer, who has scoffed at religion through a long life, and corrupted every soul which he could bring within his influence, who has loathed the Sacred Name, and cursed his Saviour,—that such a man can, in a moment, by one thought of the heart, by one true act of contrition, reconcile himself to Almighty God, (through His secret grace,) without Sacrament, without Priest, and be as clean, and fair, and lovely, as if he had never sinned. Again, she considers that in a moment also, with eyes shut and arms folded, a man may cut himself off from the Almighty by a deliberate act of the will, and cast himself into perdition.[61]

In Newman's appreciation of the way the Church looked at the souls of men, as opposed to the world, we can see where he acquired his appreciation for the force of popular religion, so much of which, then as now, educated men of the world were inclined to scorn. Of course, in the eighteenth century Hume and Gibbon had argued that the theism of Christianity was nothing more than a vulgar offshoot of the more sophisticated polytheism of the ancients, but it was the nineteenth-century historian Henry Hart Milman who renovated this polemical commonplace by arguing that the "enlightened" Early Church was corrupted by the saints and hagiographers of the "benighted" Middle Ages. Peter Brown, in his groundbreaking *The Cult of the Saints: Its Rise and Function in Latin Christianity* (1981) quoted Milman to give his readers a sense of the influential contempt that animated the skeptical historian's view of centuries of vibrant Catholic faith: "Now had commenced what may be called, neither unreasonably nor unwarrantably, the mythic age of Christianity. As Christianity worked downwards into the lower classes of society, as it received the crude and ignorant barbarians within its pale, the general effect could not but be that the age would drag down the religion to its level, rather than the religion elevate the age to its own lofty standards."[62]

Newman's own response to Milman's *A History of Latin Christianity* (1840) nicely identifies the inherent inadequacy of any account of Church history that refuses to take into account her divine aspect, which, of course, is true of any saint's life as well. Seeing this divine aspect in the life of a saint is, after all, the essence of hagiography.

> The Christian history is "an outward visible sign of an inward spiritual grace:" whether the sign can be satisfactorily treated sep-

---

61 *Difficulties Felt by Anglicans*, 205–6.
62 Henry Hart Milman, *A History of Latin Christianity* (New York, Armstrong, 1903), III, 417. Brown quotes the passage on page 16 of his book referenced in the text.

arate from the thing signified is another matter; but it seems to be Mr. Milman's intention so to treat it, and he must be judged by that intention, not by any other which we choose to impute to him. Christianity has an external aspect and an internal; it is human without, divine within. To attempt to touch the human element without handling also the divine, we may fairly deem unreal, extravagant, and sophistical; we may feel the two to be one integral whole, differing merely in aspect, not in fact: we may consider that a writer has not mastered his own idea who resolves to take liberties with the body, and yet not insult the animating soul.[63]

Dean Church's review in the *Saturday Review* of Milman's *Savonarola, Erasmus and Other Essays* (1871) would make the same point: "Of course a history of religion which inadequately understands and estimates religious belief and doctrine, and the earnestness which desires above all things that it should be complete and true, cannot be a perfect one; an account, however excellent, of what is outward in the fortunes and conduct of a religious body, cannot make up for the neglect or superficial understanding of those inward and spiritual ideas and efforts which are its soul and life."[64] For both Newman and Church, sympathy is a *sine qua non* of good critical history. Refusing to extend sympathy, as Milman did with his subjects, would always result in bad, superficial, *uncritical* history.

In the Preface to the third edition of *The Via Media of the Anglican Church* (1877) Newman refuted Milman's charge that the mediaeval Church was a corruption of the Early Church by invoking the Gospel of St. Mark.[65] As Newman took pains to show, the corruption that the fastidious Milman deplored was hardly unfamiliar to Our Lord.

As neither the local rulers nor the pastors of the Church are impeccable in act nor infallible in judgment, I am not obliged to maintain that all ecclesiastical measures and permissions have ever been praiseworthy and safe precedents. But as to the mere countenancing of superstitions, it must not be forgotten, that our Lord Himself, on one occasion, passed over the superstitious act of a woman who was in great trouble, for the merit of the faith which was the real element in it. She was under the influence of what would be called, were she alive now, a "corrupt" religion, yet she was rewarded by a miracle. She came behind our Lord and touched Him, hoping "virtue would go out of Him" without His knowing it. She paid a sort of fetish reverence to the hem of His garment; she stole, as

---

63 Newman, "Milman's View of Christianity" (1841), in *Essays Critical and Historical*, II, 188.
64 "Dean Milman's Essays," in Richard William Church, *Occasional Papers* (London: Macmillan & Co., 1897), I, 157–8.
65 Gospel of St. Mark 5:34.

she considered, something from Him, and was much disconcerted at being found out. When our Lord asked who had touched Him, "fearing and trembling," says St. Mark, "knowing what was done in her, she came and fell down before Him, and told Him all the truth," as if there were anything to tell to the All-knowing. What was our Lord's judgment on her? "Daughter, thy faith hath made thee whole; go in peace."[66]

After reminding his readers of this account of the Lord's response to what the educated Milman might have styled a "crude and ignorant" woman, Newman asks his readers: "Do not such incidents in the Gospel as this, and the miracle on the swine, the pool of Bethesda, the restoration of the servant's ear, the changing water into wine, the coin in the fish's mouth, and the like, form an aspect of Apostolic Christianity very different from that presented by St. Paul's Pastoral Epistles and the Epistle General of St. John? Need men wait for the Medieval Church in order to make their complaint that the theology of Christianity does not accord with its religious manifestations?"[67] It is in light of these incidents, Newman shows, that the very concept of "idolatry" must be revisited. And in making this point thirty years after he had sent off that letter to Faber telling him to suspend his series of *The Lives of the Saints*, it is almost as though Newman were keeping faith and making belated amends.

> This woman, who is so prominently brought before us by three evangelists, doubtless understood that, if the garment had virtue, this arose from its being Christ's; and so a poor Neapolitan crone, who chatters to the crucifix, refers that crucifix in her deep mental consciousness to an original who once hung upon a cross in flesh and blood; but if, nevertheless she is puzzle-headed enough to assign virtue to it in itself, she does no more than the woman in the Gospel, who preferred to rely for a cure on a bit of cloth, which was our Lord's, to directly and honestly addressing Him. Yet He praised her before the multitude, praised her for what might, not without reason, be called an idolatrous act; for in His new law He was opening the meaning of the word "idolatry" and applying it to various sins, to the adoration paid to rich men, to the thirst after gain, to ambition, and the pride of life, idolatries worse in His judgment than the idolatry of ignorance, but not commonly startling or shocking to educated minds.[68]

With respect to Milman's own passage, although Brown is right to see it as illustrative of an entire society's disdain for the mediaeval Church (how-

---

66 *Via Media*, lxvii.
67 Ibid.
68 Ibid., lxviii.

ever it might revel in the appropriations of mediaevalism in Scott, Coleridge, Keats, Tennyson, Pugin and the Pre-Raphaelites[69]), he wrongly assumes that Newman somehow shared this disdain by claiming that "those who wished to maintain the elevated truths of traditional Christianity had to draw with even greater harshness the boundaries between their own versions of 'true religion' and the habitual misconceptions of these by the vulgar."[70] This might have been true of Milman and other Liberal Anglicans (even though theirs was a skeptical, not a traditional Christianity) but it was most decidedly untrue of Newman. On the contrary, far from disdaining the religion of ordinary Catholics, Newman held it up as something that the English upper classes might profitably emulate.

> Take a mere beggar-woman, lazy, ragged, and filthy, and not over-scrupulous of truth—(I do not say she had arrived at perfection)—but if she is chaste, and sober, and cheerful, and goes to her religious duties (and I am supposing not at all an impossible case), she will, in the eyes of the Church, have a prospect of heaven, which is quite closed and refused to the State's pattern-man, the just, the upright, the generous, the honourable, the conscientious, if he be all this, not from a supernatural power—(I do not determine whether this is likely to be the fact, but I am contrasting views and principles)—not from a supernatural power, but from mere natural virtue. Polished, delicate-minded ladies, with little of temptation around them, and no self-denial to practise, in spite of their refinement and taste, if they be nothing more, are objects of less interest to her, than many a poor outcast who sins, repents, and is with difficulty kept just within the territory of grace.[71]

Of course this was one of the passages that caused Charles Kingsley, the muscular Christian to lash out at Newman. Even so, Kingsley's response was revelatory: "He has taught the whole Celtic Irish population," Kingsley's wrote, "that as long as they are chaste ... and sober ... and 'go to their religious duties' ... they may look down upon the Protestant gentry who send over millions to feed them in famine; who found hospitals and charities to which they are admitted freely; who try to introduce among them capital, industry, civilization, and, above all, that habit of speaking the truth, for want of which they are what they are and are likely to remain such, as long as they have Dr. Newman for their teacher."[72]

---

69 See Michael Alexander, *Medievalism: The Middle Ages in Modern England* (New Haven and London: Yale University Press, 2007).

70 Peter Brown, *The Cult of the Saints: Its Rise and Function in Latin Christianity* (Chicago and London: The University of Chicago Press, 1981), 16.

71 *Difficulties Felt by Anglicans*, 207.

72 Charles Kingsley, "A Reply to a Pamphlet: What, Then, Does Mr. Newman

That anyone, even in the grip of impassioned controversy, should have argued as Kingsley argued here is fairly astounding. To say that the import of Newman's comparison of the faithful poor with "the State's pattern man" and "polished, delicate-minded ladies" was tantamount to encouraging the Irish to be ungrateful for the famine relief they received is too grotesque. "The Population in Ireland in April 1846," Benjamin Disraeli observed in *Lord George Bentinck* (1852) "was eight million and a half: in 1851 it was six million and a half. So great a diminution of population in so short a time is not to be found in the history of any civilized people, and fills the mind of the statesman with almost appalling thoughts."[73] How in the face of such statistics Kingsley could have seen Newman's passage in this light argues something worse than the "intellectual incompetence" that George Eliot saw in his response to Newman.[74] Nevertheless, it was not the presumed friend of the Irish that Kingsley found offensive in Newman: it was the saint, a saint the Broad Churchman in him could scarcely fathom. After Newman published his *Apologia*, Kingsley sent off a defiant letter to Alexander Macmillan, in whose magazine his initial charge against Newman's veracity appeared: "I have determined to take no notice whatever of Dr. Newman's apology," he wrote. "I have nothing to retract, apologize for, explain. Deliberately, after 20 years of thought, I struck as hard as I could. Deliberately I shall strike again ... though not one literary man in England approved. I know too well of what I am talking." As for Newman's *Apologia*, "I cannot trust—I can only smile at—the autobiography of a man who (beginning with Newman's light, learning, and genius,) ends in believing ... in the Infallibility of the Church, and in the Immaculate Conception. If I am to bandy words, it must be with sane persons."[75]

Far from holding any grudges against Kingsley for casting such wild aspersions, Newman would always be grateful to him for being "the instrument in the good Providence of God by whom I had the opportunity given me ... of vindicating my character and conduct in my Apologia."[76] Moreover,

---

Mean?" in *Apologia*, 373–4.

73 Benjamin Disraeli, *Lord George Bentinck: A Political Biography* (London: Colburn & Co., 1852), 397.

74 *Selections from George Eliot's Letters*, ed. Gordon Haight (New Haven and London: Yale University Press, 1985), 296. "I have been reading Newman's *Apologia pro Vita Sua* with such absorbing interest that I have not found it possible to forsake the book until I finished it ... I have been made so indignant by Kingsley's mixture of arrogance, coarse impertinence and unscrupulousness with real intellectual incompetence, that my first interest in Newman's answer arose from a wish to see what I consider thoroughly vicious writing thoroughly castigated. But the Apology now mainly affects me as the revelation of a life."

75 Charles Kingsley to Alexander Macmillan (8 June 1864), n. 1, in *LD*, XII, 120.

76 Newman to Sir William Cope (13 February 1875), in *LD*, XXVII, 220.

one can see the charity that Newman showed Kingsley throughout their controversy in his response to a correspondent who had encountered his old antagonist before his death in 1875: "As you mention Kingsley, it is pleasant to think that he had no feeling of resentment against me, (as you showed me in your letter after meeting him at Chester) as I am sure I had none against him. And lately he has softened in his opinions—especially, to the surprise of his theological friends, he stood up for the Athanasian Creed. I said Mass for his soul on the news of his death."[77] As in the case of Price, and so many others with whom he found himself in controversy, Newman was always keen to reconcile once controversy had run its course.[78]

To understand the essential saint in Newman that Kingsley and, indeed, Manning found so exasperating, we need only go to his own understanding of the Blessed Virgin, which shows not only how much he pondered her in relation to her Son and her Son's Church in the years between Faber's translation in 1847 and his response to Pusey in 1866 but how much he turned this understanding to account in the apostolate that had been given him to accomplish in nineteenth-century England and the communion of saints beyond. "I consider it impossible then," Newman wrote, "for those who believe the Church to be one vast body in heaven and on earth, in which every holy creature of God has his place, and of which prayer is the life, when once they recognize the sanctity and greatness of the Blessed Virgin, not to perceive immediately, that her office above is one of perpetual intercession for the faithful militant, and that our very relation to her must be that of clients to a patron, and that, in the eternal enmity which exists between the woman and the serpent, while the serpent's strength is that of being the Tempter, the weapon of the Second Eve and Mother of God is prayer."[79]

If we are to understand Newman's legacy in any faithful way, we must enter into these realities, for Newman's devotion to the Mother of God is a vital aspect of his sanctity. No one would have understood this better than Newman's patron saint, that discerning, joyous Florentine, Philip Neri, who was convinced that "There is no more excellent way to obtain graces from God than to seek them through Mary, because her Divine Son

---

77 Newman to Geraldine Penrose Fitzgerald (27 January 1875), in *LD*, XXVII, 206–7.

78 Newman's detractors have always been fond of citing Newman's attack on Renn Dickson Hampden (1793–1868) as evidence of his lack of charity in controversy, but even there, for all of the warrantable zest with which he excoriated Hampden's gross Socinianism, he made a point of corresponding with Hampden's daughter, Henrietta, after her father's death, to praise the "considerateness towards opponents" and the "sound judgement" of her *Memorials of Renn Dickson Hampden, Bishop of Hereford* (1871). See Newman to Miss Hampden (26 March 1871), in *LD*, XXV, 306–7.

79 *Letter to Pusey*, 78–9.

cannot refuse her anything."[80] Certainly, the Divine Son gave Newman an incomparable ability to articulate and share with others his love of the Blessed Virgin. In his sermon entitled "The Glories of Mary for the Sake of her Son," which he delivered in the "gloomy gin distillery"[81] in Alcester Street in Birmingham in 1849 and published in his first book as a Roman Catholic, *Discourses Addressed to Mixed Congregations* (1849), we can see that ability in all of its radiance.

> Mary is exalted for the sake of Jesus. It was fitting that she, as being a creature, though the first of creatures, should have an office of ministration. She, as others, came into the world to do a work, she had a mission to fulfil; her grace and her glory are not for her own sake, but for her Maker's; and to her is committed the custody of the Incarnation; this is her appointed office—"A Virgin shall conceive, and bear a Son, and they shall call His Name Emmanuel." As she was once on earth, and was personally the guardian of her Divine Child, as she carried Him in her womb, folded Him in her embrace, and suckled Him at her breast, so now, and to the latest hour of the Church, do her glories and the devotion paid her proclaim and define the right faith concerning Him as God and man. Every church which is dedicated to her, every altar which is raised under her invocation, every image which represents her, every litany in her praise, every Hail Mary for her continual memory, does but remind us that there was One who, though He was all-blessed from all eternity, yet for the sake of sinners, "did not shrink from the Virgin's womb." Thus she is the *Turris Davidica*, as the Church calls her, "the Tower of David;" the high and strong defence of the King of the true Israel; and hence the Church also addresses her in the Antiphon, as having "alone destroyed all heresies in the whole world."[82]

---

80 *The Wisdom of the Saints: An Anthology*, ed. Jill Haak Adels (Oxford: Oxford University Press, 1987), 18.
81 Newman to Henry Wilberforce (9 December 1848), in *LD*, IX, 382.
82 *Discourses to Mixed Congregations*, 348–9.

Epilogue

Epilogue

Times come and go, and man will not believe, that that is to be which is not yet, or that what now is only continues for a season, and is not eternity. The end is the trial; the world passes; it is but a pageant and a scene; the lofty palace crumbles, the busy city is mute, the ships of Tarshish have sped away. On heart and flesh death is coming; the veil is breaking. Departing soul, how hast thou used thy talents, thy opportunities, the light poured around thee, the warnings given thee, the grace inspired into thee? O my Lord and Saviour, support me in that hour in the strong arms of Thy Sacraments, and by the fresh fragrance of Thy consolations. Let the absolving words be said over me, and the holy oil sign and seal me, and Thy own Body be my food, and Thy Blood my sprinkling; and let my sweet Mother Mary breathe on me, and my Angel whisper peace to me, and my glorious Saints, and my own dear Father, Philip, smile on me; that in them all, and through them all, I may receive the gift of perseverance, and die, as I desire to live, in Thy faith, in Thy Church, in Thy service, and in Thy love.

John Henry Newman, "God's Will the End of Life" (1849), in *Discourses Addressed to Mixed Congregations*

Index

Index

Acton, John Emerich Edward Dalberg-
Acton, 1st Baron
on history's reliance on letters 287
on Newman's learning 194
on why Gibbon and Hume did not suffer from their unbelief 68
Achilli, Giovanni Giacinto viii
and Achilli libel case 274–84
Adamus, Edmund, and "the epicenter of the culture of death" 273
Aeschliman, Michael 153
Alaric and the Fall of Rome 41
Albert, Prince Consort to Queen Victoria 106–7
Alembert, Jean-Baptiste le Rond d' 17
Alexander, Michael, *Medievalism: The Middle Ages in Modern England* (2007) 322
Alfonso, St. 304
Allen, John, Evangelical Anglican, friend of Thackeray 147
Allies, Thomas William 30
and conversion with help of Newman 30–1
on Great Exhibition 107
Ambrose, St. 237
Amoris Laetitia 155
Anglicanism vii, 39, 83, 91, 93, 101, 102, 105, 143, 146, 150, 165, 246, 247, 250–1, 252, 282, 315
and Newman's history of in French edition of *Apologia* 166
Anglo-Catholics 93, 246, 253
and aversion to Newman's *Anglican Difficulties* (1850) 224
and Eliot, Thomas Stearns 246

and Europe 226
and Hooker, Richard 246
and lesson drawn from *Tract 90* 223
and Nichols, Father Aidan O.P. 253
and quixotic attempts to portray Tractarianism as an international movement 223–8
and their exotic 'catholicity' 225
Anti-Christ 66–7, 155–6
Antinomians 5, 129, 271
Apostolical Succession 83, 192
and 'Tracts for the Times' 192
Apostasy ix–x, 50, 51
and Burke's prophetic reading of French Revolution 62
and "confederacy of evil" making way for a "general Apostasy" 157
and Donne, John 269
and French Revolution 172
and Hampden, Renn Dickson 186
and Keble's sermon "On National Apostasy" (1833) 101
and White, Blanco 150
Arian heresy 32, 33, 34, 158, 313
Arnold, Matthew
on liberalism 191–2
on Lord Byron 119–20
Arnold, Thomas 313
and contempt for "Newmanites" 192–3
on Newman and the English gentry 194
and Oriel 197, 210
and "Oxford Malignants and Dr. Hampden" (1836) 192–4
Ashton, Rosemary, on James Fitzjames Stephen 142

Athanasius, St. 18, 29, 237
  on Incarnation 18
Atheism 147, 148, 172, 173, 177, 172, 207, 248, 252, 272
  and establishment of Radical societies in England in wake of French Revolution 272
Atonement 44, 56, 178
Augustine, St. viii, 29, 35, 40–1
  and Dawson, Christopher 41
  on heavenly city 2
  on rationalism in the decadent Roman empire 40–1
  and "*securus judicat orbis terrarum*" 83, 171
  Tolle et lege viii
  City of God 2, 41

Barberi, Father Dominic 105, 250
Bacon, Francis, Baron Verulum of Verulum 87
  "On Atheism" 207
Baddesley Clinton, recusant manor house 268
Bagehot, Walter
  on Blanco White 152
  on Gibbon 52
  and Metaphysical Society 90
Balliol College 4, 5
Barbarians 16, 23, 24, 48, 51, 108, 319
Barrow, Isaac, Anglican theologian and chaplain of Charles II 134
Basil the Great, St. 29
Batchelor, John, and John Ruskin 68
Baur, F. C. 21
Bayle, Pierre 29, 102–3
  and Macaulay, Thomas Babington 102–3
Beatitudes 17
Beaumont, Keith
  on Newman's idea of conscience 129
  and Newman's insistence on the principle of *semper eadem* 129
Bebbington, David 123

Beckford, William 10
  and abuse of Gibbon and *Decline and Fall* 10
Bede, Venerable 10
Beethoven, Ludwig von 11
Belloc, Hilaire
  on brilliance of Gibbon's style 37
  on Gibbon's lack of sympathy for Christian subject 37–8
  on Gibbon's reliance on Voltaire and French rationalists 38
  on Oxford Movement 213–14
  on Saint Thomas of Canterbury 309
  A Conversation with an Angel and Other Essays (1928) 37
Benedict XVI, Pope 128, 215
  and Anglican Ordinariate 215
Benedict of Peterborough, Abbot 309
Bentham, Jeremy 95
Benthamism 39
Bergoglio, Jorge Mario 128
Bernadine, St. 305
Bible 11, 13, 15, 55, 113, 121, 156, 169, 178, 194, 195, 196, 260
  and Bible Christianity 68, 102, 106
Birch, Henry, on Great Exhibition 106–7
Blake, Lord Robert 176
Boodle's Club 9
Bolingbroke, Henry St. John, 1st Viscount 176
Boswell, James 9
  on Gibbon, Edward 9
Bowden, John 134
Bowles, Frederick 194
Brinkworth, Guy 244
Broad Church 75, 93, 95, 98, 102, 141, 194, 196, 323
Brontë, Charlotte, and advice to Protestants inclined to convert to the Church of Rome 227
Brougham, Henry, Lord Brougham 14
  on Gibbon's anti-Christian prejudice 14

334

Index

on Gibbon's chapter XV: a monument to the historian's gross injustice 50
on Gibbon's treatment of St. Cyprian 50–1
and Tamworth Reading Room 162
Broughton, Rhoda 153
Brown, Peter 321–2
The Cult of the Saints: Its Rise and Function in Later Christianity (1981) 319
Browning, Oscar 3
on Charles Devas' conversion after reading Gibbon's *Decline and Fall* 4
Memories of Sixty Years at Eton, Cambridge, and Elsewhere (1910) 4
Bulteel, Henry, Fellow of Exeter and founder of Evangelical sect "in the very shadow of St. Aldate's" 165
and "style of apocalyptic evangelicalism" 123
Burgess, Anthony, "Mr. Gibbon and the Huns" (1988) 67
and Gibbon's style 67
Burke, Edmund
and his sense of the significance of the past 38
on "false philosophy" of the *philosophes* 59
and Gibbon's claim that he was "as high an aristocrat as Burke" 59
on great conflict between Christianity and Jacobinism 174
on Jacobins and public opinion 170
and Johnson, Samuel 38
on primacy of religion in social order 59
and problem of apostasy 62
and Womersley's view of Gibbon's response to *Reflections on the French Revolution* (1790) 60–1

Burrow, J. W.
on Christianity as opposed to Roman polytheism 75
A Liberal Descent: Victorians and the English Past (1983) 100
Bury, John Bagnell 9
and Dawson, Christopher 35
on Gibbon, Edward 9
Butterfield, Herbert, *The Whig Idea of History* (1931) 100
Byron, George Gordon, 6th Baron Byron of Rochdale 119

Calvin, John 171
Campbell, Lord John, and Achilli libel case 277–81
Campion, Edmund, English martyr 7
Canning, George 176
Carey, Arthur 208
Carlyle, Thomas x
and Froude, J. A. 101
and impatience with Oxford Movement 28
and Islam 28
Catholic Encyclopedia (1913) and definition of *conversion* 232–3
Catholic Emancipation (1829) 160
Catholic University College (Kensington) 3
Catholics and Catholicism vi, viii, 56, 79, 90, 91, 93, 100, 103, 104, 124, 138, 154, 166, 174, 177, 179, 213, 220, 224, 227, 228, 232, 234, 242, 253, 254, 267, 268, 280, 281, 282, 283, 291, 304, 305, 322
and Newman's appreciation of faith of ordinary Catholics 309, 313, 315, 316
Cecil, Algernon 16
on Gibbon's preference for base motivations for rise of Christianity 51
on why Gibbon lamented decline and fall of Rome 16

Celsus, second-century Greek
philosopher opposed to
Christianity 98
  Newman cites his derogatory accounts
    of Christianity in *Essay on
    Development* 98
Chadwick, Owen
  on *Decline and Fall* as arena for
    English Protestant disputants 55
  on Gibbon's depiction of LeClerc 55
  and Frederick Meyrick 124
Champ, Judith, on Ullathorne's
  asperity before forming firm
  friendships 303
Charles I, King of England 176
Charles II, King of England 166
Charles V, Holy Roman Emperor 101
Charles IX, King of France 234
Chatterton, Henrietta Georgiana Marcia
  Lascelles, Lady Chatterton 267, 268
  and recusant manor house, Baddesley
    Clinton 268
Chavasse, Francis, Master of St. Peter's,
  Oxford and Bishop of Rochester, on
  Wadham, the "Evangelical" college
  of Oxford 164
Chesterfield, Philip Dormer Stanhope,
  Fourth Earl of 13–14
  Letters to his Son (1774) 13–14
Chesterton, Gilbert Keith
  on conversion, stages of 235–6
  on dogma 227
  and "The Falling Value of Words"
    (1927) 136–7
  and Froude, Hurrell 89
  on Giotto 205
  on "man at the crossroads" 262–3
  on Nicene Creed 241–2
  on Newman's logic 272
  on Oxford Movement 227
  on St. Francis 205
  on saints 205
  on theory that Newman went over to
    Rome to find peace vi
  on why Our Lord chose for the
    cornerstone of His Church St.
    Peter 72
  The Everlasting Man (1925) 241
  Heretics (1905) 72
  Saint Thomas Aquinas (1933) 205
  The Victorian Age in Literature vi
Chillingworth, William 8, 102–3, 196
  Chillingworth's Bible Christianity and
    Victorian delight in material
    progress 106
Christianity
  and Gibbon's five causes of rise
    of 24–7
  in contrast to heathen belief 79–80
  secret of its sustained energy 61
  viewed today by its critics in same
    light in which it was viewed by
    critics in 1st century 99
  whether a mere work of man vi
  writing of history vi
Christianity, rise of 5, 15, 21, 24, 25, 26,
  30, 34, 41, 42, 71, 91, 92, 46, 47, 48
  and Dawson, Christopher 48–9
  and its sheer marvel 22
  and God's kind Providence 65
  and martyrdom 43
  and Mosheim, Johann Lorenz 54
  and *sola scriptura* distortion 54
Christendom vii, 232
Chrysostom, John St. 29
Church, Richard William 14, 164, 179,
  184
  on Gibbon's resemblance to the
    Empire he revered 60
  on Gibbon's treatment of
    Byzantium 14–15
  on Milman's superficial understanding
    of history of Christianity 320
  on Newman's prose style 261
  on older Oxford Liberals 190
  and sympathy as the *sine qua non* of
    good critical history 320
  The Gifts of Civilization (1891) 14–15

*The History of the Oxford Movement
1833–45* (1891) 127, 187–8
Church of England 7, 83, 85, 142–3, 140,
 165, 166, 177, 192, 193, 200, 214, 216,
 217, 224, 237, 252, 273, 280, 314
 and Gladstone's appreciation of
  Newman's "immeasurable work"
  for 85
 and Hare, Julius 141
 and Newman's loss of confidence in
  after *Tract 90* 65
 Newman on its character 120–2
 from standpoint of French in 1840s
  when Tractarianism was at its
  height 227
 from standpoint of sainthood 315
 and Stanley's quip that Newman's
  knowing German might have
  changed its fortunes 195
Church of Ireland 101
Church Temporalities Bill (1833) 160
Cicero, Marcus Tullius 263
Clark, Jonathan 173–4
Clement of Alexandria, St. 29
Clive, John, *Not by Fact Alone: Essays on
 the Writing and Reading of History*
 (1989) 100
Clough, Arthur 191
Cobbett, William x, 82, 270
 and Reformation gentry 244
 *A History of the Protestant Reformation
  in England and Ireland* (1827) 82
Cockburn, Alexander James Edmund,
 Twelfth Baronet 277
 and biographical profile 277
Cole, Henry Sir
 and Great Exhibition 107
 and Newman 107
 and Thomas Love Peacock 206
Colenso, John William, Bishop of
 Natal 178
Coleridge, Samuel Taylor
 on Blanco White's sonnet, "To the
  Night" (1828) 152

 and German philosophy 195
 on Gibbon's claim to be a
  philosophical historian 29–30
 on Gibbon's mistaking scepticism for
  Socratic philosophy 30
 on Gibbon's style 29
 and mediaevalism 322
 and his "philosophy of conservatism
  against Benthamism and
  radicalism" 39
Collingwood, Robin George 18
 on Enlightenment and Gibbon 18
 on Voltaire 18
Colonies and India, and obituary on
 Newman 259
Condition of England 157
Condorcet, Marie Jean Antoine Nicolas
 de Caritat, Marquis 17
Congreve, Richard, Founder of London
 Positivist Society 165
Constantine, Emperor 33–4, 51
Conversion viii, 8, 25, 36, 85, 88, 105,
 108, 122, 141, 143, 166, 167, 174, 180,
 186, 187, 213, 215, 23, 227, 269, 294,
 305, 316
 and conversions of Newman and
  Lewis 231–55
 and Newman on conversion of St.
  Augustine 305
Cooper, Sir Alfred Duff, 1st Viscount
 Norwich, on Roman Catholicism
 and the English 143
Copleston, Edward 191, 225, 313
Cossa, Baldassare, Anti-Pope 20
 and Gibbon's delight in exposing
  Catholic debâcles 20
Cotton, Richard, Provost of
 Worcester 164
Craddock, Patricia 8
 on Gibbon's refusal to enter into the
  reality of martyrdom 52–3
Cromwell, Thomas 244, 270
Cullen, Archbishop Paul, and definition
 of papal infallibility 311

Curchod, Susanne 8
Cyprian, St. 48–51
  and Wilken, Robert Louis 49
Cyril of Jerusalem, St. 29

Dalgairns, John
  and Metaphysical Society 90
  and Mark Pattison 194
Darley, Gillian 10–11
Darnell, Nicholas, and evidence compiled for Achilli libel case 275
Darwin, Charles Robert, and Döllinger's reading of Newman's idea of doctrinal development 85
David, King 22
David, Francis H., first postulator of Newman's cause for canonization 113–14
Dawson, Christopher
  on the Roman Catholic Church 66
  on dead religion 244
  on Gibbon 34–5, 36
  on Gibbon and Tillemont 35–6
  on martyrs and the "vast servile state" of imperial Rome 48–9
  on true progress of history 66
  "Edward Gibbon and the Fall of Rome" (1934) 35
  "St. Augustine and his Age" (1933) 35
  "The Kingdom of God and History" (1938) 66
Derby, Edward Geoffrey Smith Stanley, 14th Earl of 276
Descartes, René 17
Deshayes, André-Jean-Jacques 279
Dessain, Stephen Charles 5, 180, 188
  on row between Newman and Ullathorne over *Lives of the Saints* 304
Devas, Charles 4, 5, 6, 72, 79
  on John Henry Newman 5–6
  The Key to the World's Progress (1906) 5
Devil vii

Dickens, Charles 224
  and David Copperfield (1849–50) 224
  and Wilkins Micawber 224
Diderot, Denis 17
Dissent 100, 123, 166, 172, 174, 190, 197 198, 317
Disraeli, Benjamin
  on the Irish potato famine 323
  on liberalism 175–6
  on Newman's secession from the Anglican Church 85–6
Dissolution of Monasteries 270
Dogma 28, 35, 40, 87, 128, 141, 145, 162, 167, 174, 180, 184, 186, 193, 200, 228, 233, 248, 288, 289,291, 305
  and Chesterton 227
  and Lecky 78
  and superstition 87
Döllinger, Joseph Ignaz von
  on Newman's idea of doctrinal development 85
  on Newman's learning 194
  on what he regarded as Newman's "scanty" insights into Church history 85, 97
Dublin Review 83
Duggan, Anne, on St. Thomas of Canterbury 310
Duffy, Eamon 128
  on Turner, Frank 168
  on Pius IX 311
Dunsany, Edward John Moreton Drax Plunkett, 18th Baron, and *Jorkens Remembers Africa* (1933) 218
Dyson, Hugo 238

Eagleton, Terry, on Newman 157–8
Edinburgh Review 101, 192
Egypt 98
Elagabalus, Roman emperor 51
Eliot, George
  and "Key to all the Mythologies" 195
  on Kingsley, Charles 323
  and *Middlemarch* (1872) 195

Index

Ellacombe, Thomas 121–2
Elizabeth I, Queen of England 79, 82
  and cult of Virgin Queen to replace devotion to Blessed Virgin 270–1
Elton, Geoffrey 269
English Reformation and the Law 271
Enlightenment vii, 6, 16, 29, 33, 252
  and contempt for Roman Catholicism 17
  and freedom 17
  and Gay, Peter 17
  and irrationality 18
  and Kant 17
  and Novalis 252
  and rationalist zeal 6
  and tolerance 32–3
Enlightenment, Scottish 17, 87
Epipodius, martyr 43
Erasmus 60
Erastianism 105, 139, 140, 141, 157, 176, 213, 232, 309
Eton College 3
Eusebius 47–8
Evangelicals and Evangelicalism viii, 123, 163–5
  Newman on Evangelicals 167–8
  and propensity of Evangelicals "to smell popery in every Tractarian line" 165

Faber, Frederick 299, 301, 302, 303, 304, 314, 321, 324
  and hagiography and cure of souls 316
  and life of St. Rose of Lima 301
  and *Lives of the Saints* (1848) 315
Fabian Society 218
Facts 31
Fairbairn, Andrew Martin
  and faith and reason 122
  and Newman's alleged agnosticism 124
  on what he saw as Newman's scepticism 94–5, 122

Faith as doorway to reality of history 71
Fall of Rome 41
Fathers of the Church 6, 12, 13, 20, 35, 36, 82, 166, 180, 193, 214, 237, 305
  and Gibbon 55, 57
  and letters of the Fathers 287–8
  and Newman's embrace of the Fathers after disenchantment with Oriel's liberalism 171
Fenlon, Dermot xi
Ferguson, Adam 17
Fichte, Johann Gotlieb, and Liberal Anglicans 195
Fidei depositum 32
Firminger, Walter K. 189
  on the man who wrote the *Apologia* 189–90
  on Newman's detractors 218–19
First Reform Bill (1832) 160
Fisher, Herbert Albert Laurens 107–8
  on superstition and barbarians 108
Fitzgerald, Penelope 239–40
  and *The Blue Flower* (1991) 240
Fock, Heinrich Friedrich 225
Fortey, Emily, and Newman's correspondence 293–4
France 38
  Belloc, H. on French rationalists and Gibbon 38
  Young, G. M. on Gibbon and French rationalism 38
Francis of Assisi, St. 125, 205
French Revolution vii, ix, 8, 28, 39, 60, 68, 139, 158, 169, 172, 173, 174, 175, 228
  and Cult of Reason 173
  and Revolutionary Tribunals of 1793 and 1794 establishing state atheism 173
  and September Massacre (1782) against Catholic priests 173
Froude, Hurrell 39, 101, 177, 179, 207, 208, 235
  Remains of the Late Reverend Richard Hurrell Froude (1838) 89

Froude, James Anthony x, 176–7
  and Charles V and "the superstition of a thousand years" 101–2
  and liberalism 177
  and style 259
Froude, William 207–8
Fursey, St. 10

Galerius, Roman proconsul 49
Garnet, Henry, English Jesuit and martyr 268
Garrigou-Lagrange, Reginald
  on "culminating point of history" 18
  on how embracing or rejecting God's graces constitutes personal history 71
Gash, Norman, on sporting parson 143
Gay, Peter 17–18
  on the Enlightenment 17–18
Gambetta, Léon 176
  and Newman's comparison to Gladstone 176
Geck, Albrecht, and "The Oxford Movement in Germany" 223–4
German philosophy 195
  and Eliot, George 193, 195
  and Hilton, Boyd 195
Gibbon, Edward vii, 1–80, 2, 3
  account of rise of Christianity, Newman's refutation of 6
  and Acton 68
  always eager to make a good impression 9
  and Arian controversy 32, 33
  anti-Catholic masterpiece vii
  and anti-Semitism 53
  and contention that theism stems from superstition 319
  and Beckford, William 10
  biography 6–10
  and Board of Trade 8
  and Boswell, James 9
  and Burke, Edmund 58, 59–61; on Mr. Burke's creed on the revolution in France 60
  and Bury, John Bagnell 9
  and Capitol, ruins of 8; and *Decline and Fall* 8
  and Christianity 15; and Anglican clergy 53–4; and miraculous character 18; and rise of Christianity 15
  and Christian historiography 31–2
  and Church, Roman Catholic, intellectual character of 29
  and Church of Lausanne 8
  and Churchill, Winston 13
  and Coleridge, Samuel Taylor 29–30
  and Collingwood, Robin George 18
  and contempt for Catholicism 20
  and contempt for the faith of ordinary people 71–2, 74
  and contention that the fall of one mythology merely begets another 72
  and contention that martyrs were motivated by human fame 57
  on contrast between theologian and historian vis-à-vis religion 2
  conversion 7; and Robert Persons (1546–1610) 7
  on credulity of Christians 29
  and cults of the primitive Germans 33
  and cupidity 8
  on St. Cyprian 23, 50
  on day he completed *Decline and Fall* 10
  and death 10
  and Deyverdun, Jacques-Georges 8
  and difference between St. Augustine and John Calvin 27–8
  on Elagabalus, Roman Emperor 51
  on "episcopal cause" of Christianity's spread 23
  and fall of Constantinople 9
  and Enlightenment 16; and French and Scottish Enlightenment 17
  and fame 9

Index

and German language 8
and heresy 33
and Holroyd, John Baker, 1st Earl of Sheffield 9–10, 16, 60
and Hopkins, Gerard Manley 261
and hostility to theology 28
and Hume, David 58; and contention that theism stems from superstition 319; and response to *Decline and Fall* 58; and "Superstition and Enthusiasm" (1741) 58
and "hypothesis of faith, hope and charity" 27
and irony 52
and Islam 28, 33
and Jesuits 7
and Julian the Apostate, Roman Emperor 16, 33
and liberalism 18
and Liberty of the Swiss 8
and love of fine clothes 9
and love of reading 7
on martyrs 51
and minutiae of theological argument 33
and miracles 19, 20, 35
and Momigliano, Arnaldo 26, 29
and *philosophes* 17, 50, 60, 61, 62
and Porter, Roy 26
on polytheism, Roman 74
on primitive Church 16
and Protestant indoctrination 7
and "proud fabric of French monarchy" 62
on Providence 67–8
and Radice, Betty 33–4
and religious values, no understanding of 35
and Rome, Antonine 15
and Roman creed 7–8
and Rome, fall of 41
on Roman worship 15
and snobbery 53
and South Hampshire militia 8
and superstition 20
and sympathy with subject of *Decline and Fall*, lack of 27
and Taylor, A. J. P 27
and Temple of Jupiter 8
and tolerance 15, 16, 32–3
and "triumph of barbarism and religion" 16, 18
and views of Magdalen College 7
and Voltaire 16, 18
and will 8
Decline and Fall of the Roman Empire 3, 8, 9; scope of 9; success of 9
Letters of Edward Gibbon 8
Memoirs of Edward Gibbon 7, 8, 9, 53, 67
Gissing, George 206
Gladstone, Mary 287
Gladstone, William Ewart 97, 177
  on Gorham Case 140
  and allegation that Newman was ignorant of 16th-century history 85
Godfrey of Bouillon 137
Golightly, C. P. 164
Gooch, George Peabody 82
  and the "mediaeval ideal of the *respublica christiana*" 239
Gordon, Joseph, and evidence compiled for Achilli libel case 275
Gorham Case 140
Gospel vii, 10, 17, 28, 55, 68, 69, 75–6, 100, 107, 108, 110, 145, 150, 185, 103, 244, 260–1, 269, 301, 320, 321
Goya y Lucientes, Francisco José de 96
  and "The Sleep of Reason Produces Monsters" (1799) 96
Gregory of Nazianzus, St. 29
Gregory of Nyssa, St. 29
Greene, Graham 111–12
Green, Peter, on the "Voltairean revolution" in history 45

Green, Vivian
  on Evangelicals in Oxford 164–5
  and John Le Carré's character George Smiley 164
  and obituary in *Daily Telegraph* 164
Groom, Nick 173
Guy, John, on St. Thomas of Canterbury 309

Hagar 68–9
  and God's particular Providence 68–9
Hagiography 43, 299–325
Haigh, Christopher 269
Hallam, Henry 100, 101
  on "devotion of multitude" 100
  on "exclusive worship of saints" 100
  on mediaeval Church 100–1
Hamilton, J. A., on Sir Frederick Thesiger 276
Hampden, Renn Dickson 40, 192, 313
  and Arnold, Thomas 193
  and Brent, Richard Brent 193
  and Newman 193–4
  and Oriel 197, 210
Hardiman, John, and Achilli libel case 282
Hawkins, Edward
  on liberalism 183–4
  and Oriel 210, 225
  and response to Newman's conversion 314
Hare, Julius Charles
  and Trinity College, Cambridge 196
  on "true wisdom" of Erastianism 141
  on untenability of "antiquarian resuscitations" 93–4
Harrison, Frederic, Fellow of Wadham 165
Heaven 17
Hegel, Georg Wilhelm Friedrich, and German philosophy 195
Hell vii
Henry VIII, King of England xi, 101, 105, 106, 259, 268
  and Henrician Reformation 105–6
Herder, Johann Gottfried 196
  and nationalist Christianity 196
Heywood, Lady Margaret 236, 252
High Church 192
Hill, Geoffrey, on Newman and the *Oxford English Dictionary* 137
Hilton, Boyd 123
  on Frank Turner's "mistaken" claim that Newman opposed Evangelicalism, not liberalism 123
  on Liberal Anglicans and their susceptibility to the modishness of German philosophy 195
Hinds, Samuel, Bishop of Norwich 178
Hoadly, Benjamin, Low Church Anglican Bishop 40
Hobbes, Thomas 94–5
Holland House 101
Holroyd, John Baker 1st Earl of Sheffield 9–10, 16, 60
  Letter from Gibbon showing what a fop the historian was 9
Holy Spirit viii
Honorius III, Pope 5
Hook, Walter Farquhar 197
Hooper, Walter 252
Hope-Scott, James, and *Grammar of Assent* 292–3
Hopkins, Gerard Manley 112
  on Newman's prose style compared to that of Gibbon 261
Howard, Henry Fitzalan-, fifteenth duke of Norfolk 254–5
  and Achilli libel case 278–9
  and the Catholic Union 254
Howard, Thomas 252–3
Huguenots 233, 234
  and Mrs. Jemima Newman 233–4
Hume, David 17, 39, 57, 58, 95
  and response to Decline and Fall 58
  and "Superstition and Enthusiasm" (1741) 58

Index

Hutton, Richard Holt 85, 180, 188, 208
  and Metaphysical Society 90, 149
  on Newman's *Anglican Difficulties*
    (1850) 228, 318
  on Newman's "singular literary
    genius" 318
  on Newman's "solid block of spiritual
    substance" 120
  on Newman and superstition 114–15
  on unity of Newman's work 120, 122
Huxley, Thomas. 149
  and Newman's alleged
    agnosticism 124
  and Metaphysical Society 90

Idolatry 75, 101, 107, 114, 301
  and Newman on idolatry 321–2
  and Victorian idolatry of
    knowledge 163
Ignatius, St. 171
  and *Spiritual Exercises* (1522–4) 268
Incarnation 5, 18, 69
  as "the wisdom and effulgence of the
    Father" 18
Infallibility: for Newman's critics, his
  embrace of Church's infallibility sign
  of his scepticism 145
Infidelity vi
  its work against the Church vi
Innocent III, Pope 5
Irenaeus, St. 29

James, Angell, Nonconformist
  clergyman of Birmingham 232
James, Henry
  on the outbreak of Great War 153
  "The Art of Fiction" 245
Jaki, Stanley 127
Jesuit Mission in Elizabeth England 7
John, St. 15
John Paul the Great, St., on Newman
  and "the mystery of the Lord's
  Cross" 125–6
Johnson, Samuel 9, 244

and definitions for 'conversion' 231–2
and Literary Club 9
and Newman's praise of 11
and yearning for religion 208
Jones, Carleton Parker xi
Jortin, John, Anglican Church
  historian 171
Joshua 22
Jowett, Benjamin 178
  on Newman 87–8
Joyce, James 93
  and fondness for the heretical
    Bruno 78
Julian the Apostate, Roman Emperor 11
  Newman's character of 11–12
  Newman's comparison of Gibbon and
    Julian 11–12
Justin, St. 171
Justinian, Roman Emperor 30

Kant, Immanuel 17
  and Enlightenment 17
  and German philosophy 195
  and "man emerging from his self-
    imposed tutelage" 17
Keats, John, and mediaevalism 322
Keble, John 38–9, 90, 101, 168–9, 179,
  235, 268, 305
  on Newman's *Apologia* 293
  On National Apostasy 101
  and opposition to liberalism 161
  on Newman's "struggle against
    Unbelief" 293
  and *The Christian Year* 38–9
Kent, Christopher A., on Metaphysical
  Society 90
Ker, Ian xi, 180, 188
  on Chesterton's respect for the
    common man 72
  on Newman's "*Ex umbris et imaginibus
    veritatem*" 120
  on Newman's letters 263
  on Newman's opposition to
    liberalism 201–2

on Newman's radical
  conservatism 157–8
and Newman's letter writing 213
on *sola scriptura* view of
  Christianity 54–5
on unity of Newman's work 122
The Genius of John Henry Newman
  (1989) 259–64
G. K. Chesterton: A Biography
  (2011) 72
John Henry Newman: A Life
  (1988) 202
Newman on Vatican II (2014) 157
Kingsley, Charles 86, 158, 177, 196–7,
  291–2
and Irish famine 322–3
Knowles, James
and Metaphysical Society 90
on St. Thomas of Canterbury 310
Knox, Edmund Arbuthnott, Bishop of
  Manchester 178
on Newman's handing Oxford over to
  Liberalism after his secession to
  Rome 178
Knox, Ronald 31, 240
on Gibbon and his sophistries 31
and "hidden spell of heavenly
  seed" 31
and philosophical history 31
and sermon, "The Church and the
  World" (1952) 31
Koran 28

Lacordaire, Jean-Baptiste-Henri 158
Larkin, Philip, on Spenser's *The Faerie
  Queene* 245
Latitudinarianism 177, 180, 246
Laud, William 176
Lawrence, D. H. 244
Lecky, William Edward Hartpole
on demonic possession and
  exorcism 102
on Newman's historical
  attainments 77–9, 87, 97

on Oxford Movement 87
on Oxford's backing wrong horse
  in contest between modern
  civilization and tradition 87
on Rationalism and Dogma 78
and scepticism 77–9
on superstitious character of
  Church between 6th and 13th
  centuries 102
Leo XIII, Pope ix, 5, 153–5
and Feast of Holy Family 153
and liberalism 155
and Newman 128
and Sacred Heart of Jesus 153
and Ward, Wilfrid 154
On Christian Marriage (1880) 5
*On the Evils of the Time and their
  Remedies* (1901) 154
On the Nature of Human Liberty
  (1888) 153–4
Leo the Great, St. 29
Lessing, Gotthold Ephraim, and Liberal
  Anglicans 195
Lewis, Clive Staples viii
and Anglicanism 245–8
and anti-Romanism of Belfast 243–4
on St. Athanasius 240
and Blessed Virgin 246–7, 255, 325
and conversion viii 231–55; vis-à-vis
  Newman 248–9
and "The Decline of Religion"
  (1946) 253–4
delight in the created universe 240
and Eliot, Thomas Stearns 246
and experiences in trenches in Great
  War 240
and faith and reality 241
and Greeves, Arthur 250
and historical sense 245–6
and Hooper, Walter 252
and Howard, Thomas 252–3
and "Is Theism Important?" 243, 249
and longing for Paradise 240
and "mere Christianity" 246

344

and "mere Christian intellectuals" 254
and Hooker, Richard 246
on miracle of Nature 240–1
on Newman 249
and "Priestesses in the Church" (1948) 246–7
on Theism 242
Letters to Malcolm (1964) 249
Mere Christianity (1952) 244, 250
English Literature in the Sixteenth Century (1944) 245
The Pilgrim's Regress (1943) 248
The Screwtape Letters (1941) 246
Surprised by Joy (1955) 250
Liberalism vii, viii, 5, 160
  Newman and the Liberals 133–202
  and education 198–200
  and false liberty 18
  and Gibbon, Edward 6, 57
  and Hilton, Boyd 123
  and Lewis, C. S. 250
  and liberal relativism 212
  and liberal Victorian reviews 90
  and licentious misuse of reason 18
  and Newman as guide to the abiding essence of liberalism 212
  and Oddie, William 128–9
  and Oxford 87–8, 127
  and relativism 212
  and Roman Catholicism and its liberal enemies 210
  and "the whole bar of liberalism" vs "God and dogma" (Robert Pattison) 40
Liddon, Henry Parry 90, 177, 179, 313
  on 'Germanism' 186
  on liberalism 184–6
Lingard, John x, 103–4
  and Newman 103
  and the "pure, rational, unadulterated system of Protestantism" 104
Lobban, Michael, on Sir Alexander Cockburn, Newman's lead counsel in the Achilli libel case 277

Locke, John 87, 95
Lockhart, William 194
London University 162
Louis XVI, King of France 8
Lucian 50
Luther, Martin 51, 171
Lyall, Charles 171

Macaulay, Lord Thomas Babington x, 36, 129
  on Cock Lane Ghost 103
  on Gibbon being "grossly partial to pagan persecutors" 36
  and "savage envy of aspiring dunces" 119
  on superstition 102–3
Macbride, J. D., Principal of Magdalen Hall 164
Macmillan, Alexander 323
McGrath, Alistair 239
Magdalen College and Edward Gibbon 6
Mahomet, Prophet 28
Maitland, Frederic William 147
Malone, Edmond 9
  on Gibbon, Edward 9
Mandler, Peter, on Liberal Anglicans and Herder's notions of nationality and religion 196
Manning, Henry Edward 3, 179
  and Gorham Case 140
  and Jerusalem Bishopric 225
  and London University 162
  on Newman at Solemn Requiem Mass 3
Mantel, Hilary 244
Marcellus, St. 93
'March of Mind' 161–2
Mariolatry 304
Martineau, James 149
Martyrs and martyrdom viii, 13, 20, 23, 25, 27, 43–4, 46, 47, 48, 49, 50, 51, 52, 53, 57, 58, 61, 63, 64, 308
  and St. Chrysostom 288

and Dawson, Christopher 48–9, 66
and Eusebius 47–8
and Gibbon, Edward 53
and Newman's contention that martyrdom was essential cause of rise of Christianity 65
and Origen 48
and "The Second Spring" (1850) 63, 64, 268
and St. Thomas of Canterbury, 309–10
and Wilken, Robert Louis 49
Maurice, F. D. 165, 177, 178, 196–7, 227
Maurice, Peter, Chaplain of New College 164
Mayers, Walter, and Newman's conversion 233
Medici, Catherine de 234
Melbourne, William Lamb, 2nd Viscount 192
Metaphysical Society 90–1
Metcalf, Priscilla 90
Methodism 166
Meyrick, Frederick, Bursar of Trinity College 39, 124, 213, 214
Mill, James 95
Mill, John Stuart 4, 40, 95, 169–70
Milman, Henry Hart 44, 319
and Dean Church's criticism that Milman only covered the externals of Christianity 320
on Newman's *Essay on the Development of Christian Doctrine* (1845) 86, 91
and the "contemptuous heathen in the first centuries" 97
and Oriel 197
A History of Latin Christianity (1840) 319
Milner, Joseph 13–14, 54, 171
History of the Church of Christ (1794–1809) 13
Milton, John 11
Minucius, 3rd-century Christian Apologist 93

Mirow, Matthew C., "Roman Catholicism on Trial in Victorian England: The Libel Case of John Henry Newman and Dr. Achilli" (1996) 274–84
Mitchell, Richard, Principal of Magdalen Hall 164
Mivart, St. George Jackson 149, 273
Modernists 128
Modestinus 93
Möhler, Johann Adam 82
Momigliano, Arnaldo
on Enlightenment's insistence that Christianity brought nothing new into the world 42
on Gibbon's limitations as philosophical historian 42
on relation between Christianity and Europe's political and social development 26
Monsell, Thomas, later Lord Emly 215–16
Montalembert, Charles-Forbes-René 138–40
on religious character of France after the French Revolution 140
Montesquieu, Charles-Louis de Secondat, Baron de La Brède et de 17, 33
More, Hannah, on death of Gibbon 77
Morris, Jeremy, and "French Catholics and the Oxford Movement" 227
Morley, John, and Lord Salisbury, the National Church and the education of schoolchildren 197–8
Mosheim, Johann Lorenz von 54, 55
and sola scriptura view of Christian history 54–5
Mozley, James 179
Murray, James 244
and *OED* definitions of 'conversion' 232

Napier, Sir William Francis x

Necker, Jacques 8
Nero, Roman Emperor 34
Newman, Charles (Newman's older brother), and kernel of *Grammar of Assent* 292
Newman, Francis (Newman's younger brother) 149–50, 272
Newman, Jemima, later Mrs. Mozley (Sister) 250–1, 293
Newman, John (Newman's Father) 272

NEWMAN, JOHN HENRY
  and Achilli trial viii, 274–84
  and Americans 213
  and Arnold, Thomas 192–4
  and *Biglietto* speech ix, 138, 182–3
  and British monarchs vii
  and Campbell, Lord John 277–81
  and Catholic education 198–9, 262, 303
  and Catholic Emancipation 87
  and Catholicism and atheism 256
  and Celsus 98
  and cholera 157–8
  and Chesterton, G. K. 227–8, 262–3, 272
  and Cisalpine party 307
  and Cockburn, Sir Alexander 277
  and communion of saints 324
  and contemporaries' misunderstandings of his work character 6
  and critique of Gibbon, Edward 21–2
  and early Church 89, 91
  and Cromwell, Thomas 270
  and Cullen, Archbishop Paul 311
  and Francisco José de Goya y Lucientes 96
  and Froude, J. A. 259
  and Gladstone, E. W. 291
  and hagiography viii, 299–325
  and Hawkins, Edward 314
  and Heywood, Lady Margaret 236, 252; and Newman's letter regarding the self-sacrifices of conversion 236
  and history viii, 42–3, 245
  and Holmes, Mary 245
  and Hope-Scott, James 292–3
  and Hopkins, G. M. 112
  and Howard, Henry Fitzalan-, fifteenth duke of Norfolk 254–5; and the Catholic Union 254
  and irony 56
  and Isaiah 22
  and Jowett, Benjamin 87
  and Keble and Pusey, shilly-shallying of 213
  and Kenrick, Francis Archbishop of Baltimore 283–4
  and Kingsley, Charles 291–2
  and the Law 267–84
  and Leo XIII ix
  and Lewis, C. S. 231–53
  and liberal critics 145
  and Lilly, W. S. 147
  and Littlemore 237
  and Manning, Cardinal 310, 311, 312, 317
  and martyrs viii
  and Meynell, Charles 88
  and Milman, Henry Hart 91
  and Neville, William 292
  and Newman, Jemima, later Mrs. Mozley (Sister) 250–1, 293
  and Newman, Francis (Brother) 149–50, 272
  and Newman, Mrs. Jemima (Mother) 233–4
  and nominal Christianity 213
  and Oriel colleagues 104–5
  and Oxford Movement 84
  and Pharaoh 23
  and St. Philip Neri 324
  and Purcell, Edmund 292
  and Oratory, Birmingham 5, 125, 130, 147, 148, 216, 219, 220, 278, 279, 299, 302, 303, 311

and Oratory, Brompton 3, 216
and Palgrave, Francis 219–20
and Pattison, Mark 87
and St. Paul 114
and Peel, Sir Robert 87
and "philosophical mind" 22
and popular faith 303
and Protestant Establishment: reliance on coercive power of the law 271
and Providence viii, 6
and receptions to his work 190–31
and recusants 268
and Rogers, Frederick, Lord Blachford 87, 130–1, 176, 237, 238
and rumors alleging him ready to bolt from Catholic Church 121–2, 216–17
and Ruskin, John 259
and Russell, Charles S.J. 294
and St. Mary's Church 51
and sanctity and sainthood 303
and secession to Rome 87
and self-criticism 126–7
and Shakespeare vii, 287
and Stephen, Sir James 182, 183
and style 259–60
and Talbot, George: and Newman's *Letter to Pusey* 310
and Thesiger, Sir Frederick 276, 280
and Tristram, Henry 220
and two ends: educating English Catholics and helping Anglicans resolve their difficulties in submitting to Catholicism 220
and Ullathorne, Bishop William 179, 301, 302, 303, 304, 307, 308, 311, 314, 315
and Ultramontanes 123, 149, 307, 310, 311, 312
and ultra-Protestant principle 122
and unshriven intellect 160
and *via media* 209, 215
and Ward, William George 149

CHARACTERISTICS
articulate about faith 219
attractive to contemporaries 3
and confidence, loss of after *Tract 90* 65–6
controversialist 5–6, 146
conversion viii; and Barberi, Dominic 105, 250; and conversion of C. S. Lewis viii, 229–55; and Russell, Charles S.J. 105
defender of doctrinal integrity 289–91
diarist vii
epistemologist 145
essayist vii
energy, physical and mental vii
fine sense of history ix, 8
founder of English Oratory vii
friends 3
genius ix
good shepherd ix
guilelessness 262
letter writer vii, viii, 263, 268
love of God 219
poet vii
preacher vii, 268
satirist 56, 263
simplicity 218
unity of work 63–4, 120, 262, 263

OPINIONS
on "aboriginal calamity" 112
on Achilli libel case 281–2, 282–3, 284
on St. Alfonso 304
on St. Ambrose 309
on angels vi
and Anglican Church vii, 65–6, 250–1
on Anglicans "kept where they are" 252
on Anti-Christ 66–7
on Antoninus, Emperor 11
on Apollonia, martyr 43
on apostasy 62
on Arians 312

Index

on St. Athanasius 309
on the Atonement 44
on St. Augustine 305, 309
on barbarians 23, 24
on Baronius 54
on St. Basil 309
on Beethoven, Ludwig von 11
on Bible 11
on bishops of Early Church 23–4
on Bull 54
on Catholic Church vi, 66; and her "own ways of praying" 267; and "present state of Roman Catholics" (1844) 267–8; and secret of her strength 131
and Catholic community viii
on cause of Christianity 24; on Gibbon's five causes for rise of Christianity 24–7
on "certainty of future retribution" vi
on charity 149
on Christianity 6, 15, 21–2; on Christian duty 115; and heaven 23, 131; and Gibbon's account of rise of Christianity 6; and heathen belief 79–80; on historical Christianity 15; and Hohenzollern 22; and Orleans family 22; and perceptions of in first and nineteenth centuries 110–11; and "philosophical mind" 22; on rise of Christianity, "sheer marvel of" 21–2; and "sanctity and suffering" 21–2; on secret of its sustained energy 61; on views taken of Christianity by "a civilized age" 148
on St. John Chrysostom 288, 309
on Cistercians 267–8
on "claims of the moral law" vi
on Comte, Auguste 147
on conscience 129; as "voice of God" 145

on contrast between Church of England and English Catholic Church 272–3
on controversy vi, 149
on conversion 25; and Walter Mayers 233; whether Gibbon's five causes account for Rome's conversion 25
on conversion of England 254–5
on Councils, Principal Church 54
and defection from Rome vii
on devils vi, 102
on dichotomy between science and religion, presumed 28–9
on difference between Anglicanism and Catholicism 315
on difference between the objects of Christianity and heathen belief 79–80
on Divine Word 18
on dogma 233
on "due formation" necessary for understanding Christianity and its history 27, 89–90, 148
on early Christians and Christianity 23, 98; "all members of strictly and similarly organized societies" 23
on Elizabeth I, Queen of England 270
and English Catholic community vii
on English Reformation 269–70; on advisability of tying English Sovereign to new Protestant religion 269–70
on Epipodius, martyr 43
on Euclid 11
on Eusebius 47–8
on Evangelical party in Oxford 163
on Evangelicals and Evangelicalism 167–8
on Fabricius 11
on fact vi
on failure, the providential blessing of 66

349

on faith in Christ 27, 70
on faith in progress 152–3
on faith of uneducated, contrasted with Gibbon's contempt for the multitude 72
on fallen world 69
on Fathers of the Church 171; and their letter writing 288; and their saving him from dangers of liberalism 171
on first principles 147, 149
on French Revolution 172–3
on "gauntlet of Protestantism" 282
on Gibbon, Edward 6, 11–12, 21–2, 24–7; and evolution of the meaning of the word "liberal" 136; and five causes of rise of Christianity 24–7; and "hypothesis of faith, hope and charity" 27, 79; and inability to enter into "depth and power" of Christianity 30; and liberalism 56–7; and reference to historian as "one of the masters of a new school of error" 77; and subjectivism 30; and "the tape and measuring-rod" of Gibbon's "merely literary philosophy" 43; and unbelief 57
on Gladstone, W. E. 176
on God's love for Judas 70
on God's particular Providence "almost too good for our faith" 70
on Gospel vii, 10, 17, 28, 68, 69, 75–6, 100, 107, 108, 110, 145, 150, 103, 244, 260–1, 269, 301, 320, 321
on St. Gregory of Nazianzus 309
on St. Gregory of Nyssa 309
on Pope Gregory VII 251, 287–8
on hagiography 316
on Hampden, Renn Dickson 192–4, 324
on the heart vi
on heaven 23, 249
on heresy 155
on St. Hilary 309
on history vi; and "field of history" vi; and Gibbon and Newman's idea of history contrasted 64; and nineteenth-century history ix; and philosophical history 42–3; and Protestantism 245; and his understanding of his place in history viii
on "homage of friends" vi
on hope vi, 64, 206, 217–18
on "the hope of supernatural help" vi
on human society vi
on humility necessary to understand Christian Church 89–90
on "hypothesis of faith, hope and charity" 27
on idolatry 320–1
on Incarnation 69
on infidelity and Rome, a great encounter between 175
on invisible world vi
on St. Jerome 309
on Jubber Affair 273–4
on Keble, John and authority 169
on Kingsley, Charles 323–4
and Lactantius 98
on St. Laurence 43
on Leonidas, father of Origen 43
and law viii, 267–85; and response to Francis Wood's decision to pursue a legal career 273; and youthful readiness to pursue a legal career 272
on liberals and liberalism 18, 134–202; and act of faith regarded by liberals as "dishonest" 143–4; and definitions of liberalism 138, 155, 160, 250; and his "drifting in the direction of Liberalism" at Oriel 159; and knowledge

Index

and liberalism 163; and Lewis, C. S. 250; on "Liberal Knowledge" 198–200; on liberalism within Catholic Church 181–2; and London University 162; and university reform 159–60; on younger liberals ("Dr. Arnold's pupils") 191–2
on liberty 18, 160–1; difference between true and false liberty 18
on "license of opinion" 161
on the light vi; and "light to guide us from this world to the next" vi
on Locke and the "standard of truth" 95
on logic of educated, as opposed to excesses of uneducated 312
on London University 162
on martyrs 43–4, 46, 47, 48, 49, 50, 63–5
on Maurice, F. D. 196–7
on Mayers, Walter and conversion 233
on Middle Ages 260–1
on Middleton, Conyers, English Protestant polemicist and Fellow of Trinity College, Cambridge 54
on Mill, J. S. 144
on Milman, H. H. 44
on Milner, J. 54
on Monophysite heresy 84, 237
on Montalembert 139
on Mosheim, J. L. 54
on nature and grace 317–18
on Old Catholics 305
on Oriel colleagues 104–5
on Origen 43
on paganism 23
on St. Paul 65
on Peacock, Thomas Love 206–7
on Peregrinus 25
on persecution 23
on personal influence 294
on Petavius 54
on St. Peter 65
on philosophy 12
on philosophy of history 30
on Pope Pius IX 311–12
on Pliny 11
on Plutarch 96–8
on Potamiaena, martyr 43
on Pope, Alexander 11
on popular religion 312, 319
on prayer 63
on Prayer Book 11
on "pride of reason" 159
on priests 63–4
on probability and belief 242–3
and progress, faith in 66
on proselytism 316–17
on Protestantism 15
on Protestantism and history 15, 267–84
on Providence; on "God's kind Providence" 65–6; and how it shapes and transforms history 68
on rationalism 38–40
on "realities of our being" 12
on the reality of the Resurrection 45
on "reality of sin" vi
on reason as opposed to rationalism 40
on restoration of English Catholic hierarchy 62–5
on Regulus, Marcus Atilius, 3rd-century Roman consul 11
on religion of ordinary Catholics and English upper classes 322
on religion of the multitude 307
on religion as private luxury x
on "Religion of Reason" 11
on repentance 27
on Revealed Truth 40
on rise of Christianity 21–2, 26–7, 63; and rise of superstition 92–3
on Roman Empire 23, 24

on Rome 22, 23
on rule of Providence 66
on sainthood 315–16
on saints as "popular evidence of Christianity" 316
on science 28
and science and knowledge, promises of 152–3
on scientists, intellectual arrogance of 28–9
and Scott, Sir Walter 278; and mediaevalism 322
on Simon Magus 25
on Sixtus, Bishop of Rome and martyr 43
on slaves 22, 43
on Socinian approach to Christian history 44, 45
on "the sons of God and the children of the wicked one" vi
on souls vi
on Stephen, James Fitzjames 147–8
on Stuarts 273
on style "as a thinking out into language" 260
on success vi
on superstition viii 81, 88–9, 90, 95, 108, 109, 110, 320–1; as means of demonstrating continuity between Early and 19th-century Church 111; on superstition and scepticism 111
on Swift, Jonathan 11
on Symphorian of Autun, martyr 43
on tendency of the educated to be most opposed to early Church 98
on Tillemont 35
on Toryism 158, 161
and Tractarians and Tractarianism vii, 215
on "true spirit of philosophical investigation" 28
on *via media*, pulverization of 171

and Waterland, Daniel, English theologian and Fellow of Magdalen 54
on Wellington, Arthur Wellesley, 1st Duke of 316
on Wesleyans 317
and Whig faith in progress 112
and Wilberforce, Henry 84
on the world as "a rough antagonist to spiritual truth" vi
on the world's religion 75–6
on the world's view of Catholicism 145
on worldly pseudo-religion 260
on "worldly madness" of apostate English 106–7
on "wound of human nature" 61

WORKS
Apologia pro Vita Sua (1864) vii, xiii, 88, 112, 123–4, 127, 134, 138, 143, 147, 155, 166, 168, 180, 187, 192, 233, 237, 250, 262, 304, 305
The Arians of the Fourth Century (1833) 155
Discourses Addressed to Mixed Congregations (1849) xiii, 329
An Essay in Aid of a Grammar of Assent (1870) vii, xiii, 6, 27, 88, 108, 115, 145, 148, 160, 262, 292–3
An Essay on the Development of Christian Doctrine (1845) vii, xiii, 85, 86, 91, 92, 95, 110–10, 215, 226, 233, 245
Essays Critical and Historical (1873) xiii, 40
Fifteen Sermons Preached before the University of Oxford (1843) xiv, 28, 76–7, 89, 108, 109, 160, 207
Historical Sketches (1873) 287, 305
Idea of a University (1873) vi, xiii, 95, 160, 241, 260, 262
Lectures on Certain Difficulties Felt by Anglicans in Submitting to the

Catholic Church (1850) vi, 120–1, 144, 224, 228, 315, 318, 322, 317, 318
Lectures on the Doctrine of Justification (1838) 114
Lectures on the Present Position of Catholics in England (1851) xiii, 91, 103, 152, 269–70
Lectures on the Prophetical Office of the Church (1837) 214–15, 226
A Letter to the Duke of Norfolk (1875) 85, 144
A Letter to Rev. E. B. Pusey (1866) 304, 306, 307, 312, 324
Letters and Diaries of John Henry Newman (1961–2008) xiii
Meditations and Devotions (1907) 2, 217–18
On Consulting the Faithful in Matters of Doctrine (1859) 309
Parochial and Plain Sermons (1824) vi, xiii, 262
Sermons bearing on the Subjects of the Day (1869) xiii
Sermons Preached on Various Occasions (1857) xiii, 212, 283, 307, 308
Tamworth Reading Room (1841) 79, 162
The Via Media of the Anglican Church (rev. edn 1877) xiv, 90, 321

ESSAYS
"The Anglo-American Church" (1839) 263
"Milman's view of Christianity" (1841) 44, 51, 320
"Reformation in the Eleventh Century" (1841) 251

TRACTS FOR THE TIMES
Tract 38: "Via Media I" 82
Tract 73:"On the Introduction of Rationalistic Principles into Revealed Religion" 39–40
Tract 90: "Remarks on Certain Passages in the Thirty-Nine Articles" 83, 123, 223–4

SERMONS
"Christ: A Quickening Spirit" (1831) 46
"Christ upon the Waters" (1850) 105, 283
"The Communion of the Saints" (1837) 42
"Contest between Faith and Sight" (1832) 76–7
"Faith and Reason, Contrasted as Habits of Mind" (1839) 209–10
"The Glories of Mary for the Sake of Her Son" (1849) 323
"Holiness Necessary for Blessedness" (1826) 249
"Illuminating Grace" (1849) vi
"The Individuality of the Soul" (1836) vi
"The Kingdom of the Saints" (1835) 22
"Love, the One Thing Needful" (1839) 73–4
"On Justice, as Principle of Divine Governance" (1832) 108, 109
"Our Lady in the Gospel" (1848) 301
"Our Lord's Last Supper and His First" 189
"The Philosophical Temper: First Enjoined by the Gospel" (1826) 28
"A Particular Providence as Revealed in the Gospel" (1835) 68
"The Patristical Idea of Anti-Christ" (1835) 155–6, 172–3
"The Pope and the Revolution" (1866) 308
"The Religion of the Day" (1832) 75, 88
"Religious Faith Rational" (1829) 88
"The Second Spring" (1852) 62–5, 268, 306
"Unreal Words" (1939) 259

VERSE
"The Age to Come" (1833) 201

Newsome, David 167
Nicene Creed 241
Nichols, Aidan O.P.
  and Lewis, C. S. 253
  and reconversion of England 253–4
  Christendom, Awake (1999) 253
  The Realm (2008) 253
  Lessons in a Rose Garden: Reviving the Doctrinal Rosary (2012) 253
Nietzsche, Friedrich 244
Nockles, Peter 39, 124, 165–6, 187, 213, 223, 224, 225
Noetic School, Oriel College 39, 104–5, 197, 313
Non-Catholic Christianity vii
Nonconformists 38
Norwich, John Julius Lord 15
  on Gibbon's treatment of Byzantium 15
Novalis 239–40, 252
Nuttall, Anthony David, and *Middlemarch* (1872) 195

Oddie, William, on Newman and liberalism 128–9
Old Catholics 304, 305–6
Oldcorne, Edward, English Jesuit and martyr 268
Oliphant, Margaret, on Montalembert 139–40
Oratory, Birmingham 5, 147
Oratory, London 3, 216
Oriel College 83, 104–5
Origen 29, 43, 48
Oxford 4
  Poor religious instruction according to Gibbon 7
Oxford Dictionary of National Biography 5
Oxford Movement 28, 101, 173, 218, 223–8

Paganism 19, 42, 74, 75
Paley, William 171
Palgrave, Francis, on visit with Newman in old age at the Oratory 219–20
Pattison, Mark 87
  and recollections of Tractarian Oxford 87
  and search for brighter intellectual company 194–5
  on Newman's influence 207
  on Newman, Laud and "a unity of all thought" 194–5
Pattison, Robert 40
  on Newman as "the master of those who dissent" 200
  on John Stuart Mill 144–5
Paul, St. 15, 183
Pavillard, Daniel 7
  and Gibbon 7
Peacock, James 10
  and low view of Gibbon, Edward 10
Peel, Sir Robert, and Tamworth Reading Room 162
Persons, Richard 7, 79
Philip IV, King of Spain, and Our Lady of the Rosary 300
Phillimore, J. S. 37
Phillipson, Nicholas, on Hume's influence on Gibbon 58
Philippe, Jacques 17
  on freedom 17
  on holiness 125
  Interior Freedom (2012) 17
  In the School of the Holy Spirit (2007) 66
Philosophes 17, 50, 60, 61, 62, 169
Pitt, William the Younger 176
Pius IX, Pope vii
  and *Syllabus of Errors* (1864) 239
Pius X, Pope 128
Pliny 93, 98
Plutarch 96–8
  and Newman's use of Plutarch's

comparison between the superstitious and atheist man 96–7
and Shakespeare 96
"On Superstition" 96
Pocock, John 13, 18, 31
  on the elements of historical Christianity 31–2
  on the Enlightenment and Christian truth 44–5
  on Gibbon and Christianity 13
  on Gibbon, Hume and Voltaire's preference for Graeco-Roman polytheism 17
  on Mosheim and Gibbon 55
  on Newman and the writing of Christian history 44
  Barbarism and Religion (1999–2015) 13, 31, 44, 54
Pollen, John Hungerford 206, 305
Polytheism 17, 18, 19, 72, 74, 75, 100, 319
Pope, Alexander 11
Porson, Richard
  and Cider Club 52
  on Gibbon's "luxury of speculation" 52
  and Lord John Campbell 52
Porter, Roy 13–14
  on Gibbon and Lord Chesterfield 13–14
  on Gibbon's historical method 26
Praed, Winthrop Mackworth, on London University 162
Pre-Raphaelites and mediaevalism 322
Price, Edward 299, 301, 302, 303, 324
  and "gross palpable idolatry" in Jean Baptist Feuillet's life of St. Rose of Lima 301
Pritchett, Victor Sawdon 28
Protestantism viii
Providence xvi, 1, 2, 30, 31, 79
  Newman's sense of God's kind Providence 65–6
Pusey, Edward Bouverie 83, 90, 177, 179, 226, 235
  and confusion of devotion with doctrine 305
  and first *Eirenicon* (1864) 305
Puxley, Henry Lavallin, Irish Protestant controversialist 291

Radcliffe, Anne, *The Italian* (1797) 173
Radicalism 39, 139
  and Montalembert's comparison between radicalism and liberalism 139
Rationalism vii, 17, 27, 38–9, 40, 313
  and ethos of anti-Catholic rationalism 210–12
  and Newman, J. H. on Rationalism 40
  and Taylor, A. J. P. on Whig rationalism 27
Ratzinger, Joseph 20–1
  and "radical anthropocentricism" 20
  on Comte 21
  on Darwin 21
  on heaven 21
  on Hegel 21
  on man knowable only "at the level of fact" 20
  on Marx 21
  on history 20–1
  Introduction to Christianity (1968) 20–1
Recusants 268
Reform Bill of 1832 101
Reformation, continental 51, 56, 78, 82, 101, 102, 214, 232, 239, 316
Reformation, English 105, 106
  and Reformation gentry 244
Renan, Ernest 93
Restoration of English Catholic Hierarchy 62–5, 105–6
  and confounding of Gibbon's Enlightenment view of history 62–3
  and martyrdom 63–4
Rickards, Samuel 54

355

Roberts, Andrew, and Lord Salisbury 197
Roberts, Charlotte
  on Gibbon's response to Burke and the French Revolution 60
  on Chapters XV and XVI of *Decline and Fall* 34
Robertson, George Croom 149
Robertson, John Mackinnon, on H. H. Milman 86
Robertson, William 17
Rogers, Frederic, Lord Blatchford 176
Rome 8, 15, 16, 19, 22, 23, 24, 29, 34, 35, 36, 41, 42, 53, 58, 74
  Antonine Rome 19
  and Goldsworthy, Adrian 19
  and polytheism 17, 18, 72, 74, 75, 100, 319
  and theology 19
  and tolerance 19
Roncalli, Cardinal Angelo (later Pope John XXIII) 20
  and Cossa, Baldassare 20
Rosary, Our Lady of, and history of devotion 300
Rose, Hugh 171
Rose of Lima, St. 299
  and Life of St. Rose of Lima by Jean Baptist Feuillet 299
Rousseau, Jean-Jacques 17
Routh, Dr. Martin, and Renn Dickson Hampden 290
Rowell, Geoffrey 226
Royal University (Dublin) 3
Ruskin, John 68
  and prose style 259
  on Pusey 313
  Praeterita (1885–9) 313
  The Stones of Venice (1851–3) 259
Russell, Charles S.J. 105
  and Newman's *Apologia* 294
  and sermons of St. Alfonso 304
  and Wiseman's funeral 294–5
Russell, George William Erskine 177–8, 184

on liberalism 178

Saints 20, 22, 24, 36, 42, 47, 51, 56, 63, 64, 65, 66, 71, 80, 100, 105, 143, 205, 220, 268, 270, 271, 288, 299, 301, 302, 303, 304, 307, 308, 309, 311, 315, 316, 317, 319, 321, 322, 324, 325, 329
St. Bartholomew's Day Massacre (24 August 1572) 234
St. John, Ambrose 194
St. Mary's, Oscott 62
Salisbury, Robert Arthur Talbot Gascoyne-Cecil, 3rd Marquess of, on collaboration between Dissenters and Infidels 197–8
Scarisbrick, Prof. John Joseph xi, 268, 269
  Foreword vii–viii
Schelling, Friedrich Wilhelm Joseph von, and Liberal Anglicans 195
Scott, Christina, on how Gibbon inspired her father, Christopher Dawson to become a historian 35
Scott, Thomas 167–8
  The Force of Truth (1815) 167–8
Scott, Sir Walter 11, 119, 278, 322
Secularism vii
  secular education x
Selborne, Roundell Palmer, 1st Earl of 149
Shaftesbury, Anthony Ashley Cooper, 7th Earl of, and evidence of Achilli's sexual misdeeds in Malta 275
Shakespeare, William 9
  and *Antony and Cleopatra* 287
Short, Augustus, Bishop of Adelaide 225
Short, Edward John Joseph Sebastian xv
Short, Sophia Thérèse Mariana xii
Shrimpton, Paul xi
Sidgwick, Henry 4
  and Metaphysical Society 90
Sin vii
  and Gibbon, Edward 12

Index

Skinner, Gerard 253
  Newman the Priest: A Father of Souls (2010) 253
Skinner, Simon 165, 166, 188, 200–1
  and Eamon Duffy's ripostes to "History vs. Hagiography" 168, 200
Slaves 22
Sloane, John, and fondness for Enlightenment authors, including Gibbon 10
Smith, Adam 4
Smith, Sydney 177
Sorensen, David R. 28
South, Robert, Laudian divine 233
Southwell, Robert, poet and martyr 268
Speaight, Robert 37
Staël, Anne Louise Germaine de 8
Staffordshire Gazette and obituary for Cardinal Newman 129–30
Stanley, Arthur Penrhyn, Dean of Westminster 178, 237
  and biography of Arnold, Thomas 192
  on how Newman's knowing German might have changed fortunes of Church of England 195
Stephen, Sir James 182, 183
Stephen, James Fitzjames 124
  and "common rules of evidence" 145
  and Comte, Auguste 145
  and Descartes, René 145
  and "Dr. Newman and Liberalism" (1865) 142
  and Metaphysical Society 90
  and "Newman and the Universities" (1859) 143
  and Newman's alleged agnosticism 124
Stephen, Leslie
  and faith and reason 122
  on Gibbon's five causes for the rise of Christianity 25–6
  on Gibbon's historical method 26
  on Gibbon and martyrdom 57
  and Metaphysical Society 90–1, 149
  and Newman's alleged agnosticism 124
  on need to verify creeds formed in erroneous times 90
  on reluctant controversialist in Newman 146–7
  and anti-Christian sense in which he accounted himself a Darwinist 179
  and what he saw as Newman's scepticism 122
  History of the English Thought in the Eighteenth Century (1876) 25
Stewart, Dugald 87
Stoics 98, 150
Strachey, Lytton
  on Gibbon 37
  Eminent Victorians (1918) 246
Strafford, Thomas Wentworth, 1st Earl of 176
Strange, Roderick, *John Henry Newman: A Portrait in Letters* (2015) 287–95
Stubbs, William x
  and illustration of word *conversion* in *OED* 232
Suetonius 98
Superstition 20, 60, 83–115, 108, 109, 110, 196
Surtees, Robert, on Evangelical character, James Blake 164
Swift, Jonathan 11, 100
Symons, Ben, Warden of Wadham 164
Symphorian of Autun, martyr 43

Tacitus 9, 38, 93, 98
Tasso 137
Thackeray, William Makepeace 10
  and Achilli libel case 280–1
Taylor, A. J. P.
  on "cocksure historians" 43
  on Gibbon 27
  on Whig rationalism 27
Tennyson, Alfred Lord

and mediaevalism 322
on St. Thomas of Canterbury 309
Tertullian 29
Theodosius, Emperor 34
　and founding of the Christian state in
　　380 34
　and love of history 34
　and savagery 34
Theology 28, 29
　Christian theology and Islam 28
　Christian theology and science 28–9
Theological Virtues 27
　and Philippe, Jacques 27
Thesiger, Frederick, first Baron
　　Chelmsford
　and Achilli libel case 275, 276, 280
　and biographical profile 276
Thirlwall, Connop
　and Trinity College, Cambridge 196
　on what he saw as Newman's
　　"bottomless unbelief" 94
Thomas Aquinas, St. 5, 205, 209
Thomas of Canterbury, St. 309
Thomas, Keith, on preoccupation with
　fame on part of unbelievers 57
Thucydides 9
Tillemont, Louis-Sebastian Le Nain de,
　compared to Gibbon 35–6
Tillotson, John 171
Toqueville, Alexis de 174
　on religious aspects of Jacobin
　　revolution 174–5
Tolkien, J. R. R. 238
Tractarianism vii, 14, 28, 83, 87, 101, 123,
　124, 130, 157, 164, 165, 166, 167, 171,
　176, 178, 183, 184, ,186, 187, 188, 191,
　192, 194, 197, 207, 213, 215, 220, 223,
　293
　and Australia, Port Middlebay and
　　Wilkins Micawber 224
　and Froude, James Anthony and
　　Whigs, Tractarians and Catholic
　　converts 177
Trevelyan, George Macaulay 100, 107

Trevor, Meriol 180, 188
Trevor-Roper, Hugh 153
Tristram, Henry 180, 220
Turner, Frank 94, 122, 123, 126, 127, 135,
　163–8, 175, 178–9, 180, 183–8, 191,
　199–02
Tyrell, George 128

Ullathorne, William 179, 301, 302, 303,
　304, 307, 308, 311, 314, 315
Unbelief ix, 39, 48, 57, 82, 94, 111, 142,
　175, 180, 208, 213, 293, 318
　and contrast between belief and
　　unbelief 318

Velleius (Marcus Velleius Paterculus),
　first-century Roman historian 98
Vere, Aubrey de, on Newman's "especial
　vocation" 39
Victoria, Queen of England 122, 191
Victorian idolatry of knowledge 163
Voltaire, François Marie Arouet de 15,
　16, 18, 60
　Gibbon pinched thesis for *Decline and
　　Fall* from Voltaire 16

Ward, Mary Augusta, Mrs. Humphry,
　and *Robert Elsmere* (1888) 218
Ward, Catherine 315
Ward, Wilfrid 180, 188
　on Erastianism and liberalism 140–1
　on Leo XIII's last encyclical, "The Evils
　　of the Time and their Remedies"
　　(1901) 154
　on Newman's view of rationalism vis-
　　à-vis Gibbon 38–9
Ward, William George 237
　and Metaphysical Society 90
Waugh, Evelyn 12–13
　and Churchill, Winston 13
　on Gibbon, Edward and his irresistibly
　　malign style 12–13
　on labarum of the Emperor
　　Constantine 16

on Lactantius 12–13
Helena (1950) 12
"The Same Again, Please" (1962) 289
Wesley, John 166
Westminster School 6
Wilken, Robert Louis, on St. Cyprian 48
William Henry, Duke of Gloucester 9
Williams, Penry, on John Donne and Elizabethan Terror 268–9
Whately, Richard 178, 191, 210, 225
and *Errors of Romanism* (1845) 313–14
and opponents of the Reformation 313–14
Whiggery vii
Whig historians 84, 100, 102, 103, 107, 109, 113
Newman's travestying of one of their favorite ploys 99
and Taylor, A. J. P. on "linotype school of history" 27
and Whig faith in progress and rationalism 112
White, Blanco, and liberalism and apostasy 150–2
Whitfield, George 166
Whitehead, Alfred North, on indispensability of "systematic theology" 180
Wilberforce, Henry 150–1, 238
Williams, Robert 83, 237
Wilson, Daniel, Bishop of Calcutta 164

Wiseman, Nicholas
and Achilli libel case 275
and funeral 294–5
"The Anglican Claim of Apostolic Succession" (1839) 83, 237
Womersley, David
on Gibbon's response to Burke and the French Revolution 60–1
on Gibbon's treatment of St. Cyprian 50
on Mosheim, Johann Lorenz von and Gibbon's anachronistic treatment of Christianity 34
on response of Anglican clergy to *Decline and Fall* 54
Wood, Samuel Francis 152
and Newman's response to his decision to pursue a legal career 273
on *Tract 90* 83
Woolf, Virginia, on Gibbon 52

Young, George Malcolm
on Gibbon 38
on Victorian idolatry of knowledge 163
on Milman's criticism of Newman's *Essay on the Development of Christian Doctrine* (1845) 86, 91
on Newman the historian 84–5, 86, 97

Zanzibar Mission 147
Zoroastrianism 33

www.ingramcontent.com/pod-product-compliance
Lightning Source LLC
Chambersburg PA
CBHW032016230426
43671CB00005B/98